THE CAMBRIDGE COMPANION TO

NATURAL LAW ETHICS

Natural law ethics centres on the idea that ethical norms derive from human nature. The field has seen a remarkable revival since the millennium, with new work in Aristotelian metaphysics complementing innovative applied work in bioethics, economics and political theory. Starting with three chapters on the history of natural law ethics, this volume moves on to various twentieth-century theoretical innovations in the tradition, and then to natural law as embedded in the three Abrahamic faiths. It closes with sections on applied natural law ethics and the challenges and prospects for natural law ethics in the twenty-first century. Uniquely interdisciplinary and written without technical jargon, the book will be of great interest to students and researchers in philosophy, theology, political theory and economics. They will find this the go-to resource for cutting-edge thinking in natural law ethics.

TOM ANGIER is Senior Lecturer in Philosophy at the University of Cape Town. In addition to many journal papers, his recent publications include two edited volumes: *Virtue Ethics* and *The History of Evil*, both published in 2018. He is the author of *Natural Law Theory* in Cambridge's Elements in Ethics series (forthcoming).

OTHER VOLUMES IN THE SERIES OF CAMBRIDGE COMPANIONS

ABELARD *Edited by* JEFFREY E. BROWER *and* KEVIN GUILFOY
ADORNO *Edited by* THOMAS HUHN
ANCIENT ETHICS *Edited by* CHRISTOPHER BOBONICH
ANCIENT SCEPTICISM *Edited by* RICHARD BETT
ANSELM *Edited by* BRIAN DAVIES *and* BRIAN LEFTOW
AQUINAS *Edited by* NORMAN KRETZMANN *and* ELEONORE STUMP
ARABIC PHILOSOPHY *Edited by* PETER ADAMSON *and* RICHARD C. TAYLOR
HANNAH ARENDT *Edited by* DANA VILLA
ARISTOTLE *Edited by* JONATHAN BARNES
ARISTOTLE'S 'POLITICS' *Edited by* MARGUERITE DESLAURIERS *and* PAUL DESTRÉE
ATHEISM *Edited by* MICHAEL MARTIN
AUGUSTINE *2nd edition Edited by* DAVID MECONI *and* ELEONORE STUMP
BACON *Edited by* MARKKU PELTONEN
BERKELEY *Edited by* KENNETH P. WINKLER
BOETHIUS *Edited by* JOHN MARENBON
BRENTANO *Edited by* DALE JACQUETTE
CARNAP *Edited by* MICHAEL FRIEDMAN *and* RICHARD CREATH
THE COMMUNIST MANIFESTO *Edited by* TERRELL CARVER *and* JAMES FARR
CONSTANT *Edited by* HELENA ROSENBLATT
CRITICAL THEORY *Edited by* FRED RUSH
DARWIN *2nd edition Edited by* JONATHAN HODGE *and* GREGORY RADICK
SIMONE DE BEAUVOIR *Edited by* CLAUDIA CARD
DELEUZE *Edited by* DANIEL W. SMITH *and* HENRY SOMERS-HALL
DESCARTES *Edited by* JOHN COTTINGHAM
DESCARTES' 'MEDITATIONS' *Edited by* DAVID CUNNING
DEWEY *Edited by* MOLLY COCHRAN
DUNS SCOTUS *Edited by* THOMAS WILLIAMS
EARLY GREEK PHILOSOPHY *Edited by* A. A. LONG
EARLY MODERN PHILOSOPHY *Edited by* DONALD RUTHERFORD
EPICUREANISM *Edited by* JAMES WARREN
EXISTENTIALISM *Edited by* STEVEN CROWELL
FEMINISM IN PHILOSOPHY *Edited by* MIRANDA FRICKER *and* JENNIFER HORNSBY
FICHTE *Edited by* DAVID JAMES *and* GUENTER ZOELLER
FOUCAULT *2nd edition Edited by* GARY GUTTING

Continued at the back of the book

The Cambridge Companion to

NATURAL LAW ETHICS

Edited by

Tom Angier

University of Cape Town

CAMBRIDGE
UNIVERSITY PRESS

CAMBRIDGE
UNIVERSITY PRESS

University Printing House, Cambridge CB2 8BS, United Kingdom

One Liberty Plaza, 20th Floor, New York, NY 10006, USA

477 Williamstown Road, Port Melbourne, VIC 3207, Australia

314–321, 3rd Floor, Plot 3, Splendor Forum, Jasola District Centre, New Delhi – 110025, India

79 Anson Road, #06–04/06, Singapore 079906

Cambridge University Press is part of the University of Cambridge.

It furthers the University's mission by disseminating knowledge in the pursuit of education, learning, and research at the highest international levels of excellence.

www.cambridge.org
Information on this title: www.cambridge.org/9781108422635
DOI: 10.1017/9781108525077

First published 2019

A catalogue record for this publication is available from the British Library.

Library of Congress Cataloging-in-Publication Data
Names: Angier, Tom P. S., editor.
Title: The Cambridge companion to natural law ethics / edited by Tom Angier, University of Cape Town.
Description: New York : Cambridge University Press, 2019. | Series: Cambridge companions | Includes bibliographical references and index.
Identifiers: LCCN 2019012489 | ISBN 9781108422635 (alk. paper)
Subjects: LCSH: Ethics. | Natural law.
Classification: LCC BJ1012 .C28 2019 | DDC 171/.2–dc23
LC record available at https://lccn.loc.gov/2019012489

ISBN 978-1-108-42263-5 Hardback
ISBN 978-1-108-43561-1 Paperback

Contents

Contributors

Philipp Brüllmann is Assistant Professor of Philosophy at LMU Munich and a faculty member of the Munich School of Ancient Philosophy. He is the author of *Die Theorie des Guten in Aristoteles' 'Nikomachischer Ethik'* (2011) and has published papers on Aristotelian and Stoic ethics.

Sophie Grace Chappell is Professor of Philosophy at the Open University. She is the author of *Ethics and Experience* (2011), *Knowing What to Do* (2014) and *Ethics beyond the Limits: New Essays on Bernard Williams* (2019).

Anver Emon is Professor in the Faculty of Law and Department of History at the University of Toronto. He is the author of *Islamic Natural Law Theories* (2010) and co-author of *The Natural Law: A Christian, Jewish, and Islamic Trialogue* (2014).

Edward Feser is Associate Professor of Philosophy at Pasadena City College in California. His books include *Aquinas* (2009), *Scholastic Metaphysics: A Contemporary Introduction* (2014) and *Aristotle's Revenge: The Metaphysical Foundations of Physical and Biological Science* (2019).

Jennifer A. Frey is Assistant Professor of Philosophy at the University of South Carolina. She is the co-editor of *Self-Transcendence and Virtue: Perspectives from Philosophy, Psychology, and Theology* (2019) and has published many papers on action theory, ethics and the history of ethics.

Samuel Gregg is Research Director at the Acton Institute and a Fellow of the Center for the Study of Law and Religion at Emory University. He is the author of *For God and Profit: How Banking and Finance Serve the Common Good* (2016), *Becoming Europe* (2013), *Wilhelm Röpke's*

Political Economy (2010), *The Modern Papacy* (2009) and *The Commercial Society* (2007).

Jennifer Herdt is Gilbert Stark Professor of Christian Ethics at Yale University Divinity School. Her most recent book is *Forming Humanity: Redeeming the German Bildung Tradition* (2019).

Steven J. Jensen is Professor of Philosophy at the Center for Thomistic Studies at the University of St Thomas (Houston). He is the author of *The Human Person: A Beginner's Thomistic Psychology* (2018), *Sin: A Thomistic Psychology* (2018), *Knowing the Natural Law: From Precepts and Inclinations to Deriving Oughts* (2015) and *Good and Evil Actions: A Journey through Saint Thomas Aquinas* (2010).

Jacqueline Laing has taught Jurisprudence, Criminal Law and Moral Philosophy at the Universities of Cambridge, Oxford and London. She is the co-editor of *Human Lives: Critical Essays on Consequentialist Bioethics* (1997) and *The Natural Law Reader* (2013) and has published articles in many academic journals.

Patrick Lee is John N. and Jamie D. McAleer Professor of Bioethics and Director of the Center for Bioethics, Franciscan University of Steubenville. He is the author of *Body-Self Dualism in Contemporary Ethics and Politics* (2008, with Robert P. George), *Abortion and Unborn Human Life* (2010) and *Conjugal Union: What Marriage Is and Why It Matters* (2014, with Robert P. George).

Johan Olsthoorn is Assistant Professor in Political Theory at the University of Amsterdam and Postdoctoral Fellow at the Katholieke Universiteit Leuven (2015–21). His research on early modern natural law theory has appeared in the *Journal of the History of Philosophy*, the *British Journal for the History of Philosophy* and *History of Philosophy Quarterly*, among other journals.

Tracey Rowland holds the St John Paul II Chair of Theology at the University of Notre Dame (Australia). Her most recent books are *Catholic Theology* (2017) and *The Culture of the Incarnation: Essays on Catholic Theology* (2017).

Tamar Rudavsky is Professor of Philosophy at Ohio State University. She is the author of *Jewish Philosophy in the Middle Ages: Science, Rationalism and Religion* (2018) and *Maimonides* (2010) and is co-editor of *The Cambridge History of Medieval Philosophy: From Antiquity to the Seventeenth Century* (Cambridge University Press, 2009).

Christopher Wolfe is Distinguished Affiliate Professor of Politics at the University of Dallas and Emeritus Professor, Marquette University. He is the author of *Natural Law Liberalism* (2006).

Introduction

Tom Angier

Natural law ethics is a normative theory, which, as its name implies, centres on two key notions: nature and law. It is animated by the idea that nature, and human nature in particular, is the source and ground of the moral laws (or, more widely, moral norms) which govern our nature. Historically, the 'nature' component was first theorised in Ancient Greece and Rome, where philosophers argued that human beings are intrinsically directed to and fulfilled by certain ends – the claim of natural teleology. The 'law' component found its most pronounced embodiment far earlier, in the scriptures of Ancient Israel, which proclaim a binding set of moral commandments that issue from a transcendent deity. The history of natural law ethics is, put broadly, a mediation between these two cultural inheritances – and is therefore the site of several recurrent controversies. How, exactly, are moral norms embedded in nature? If God is the ultimate source of morality, is the role of nature normatively redundant? Can nature generate its own moral norms independently of God? Is the entire notion of a natural moral law incoherent or misconceived? These perennial questions have, as we shall see, elicited markedly different and conflicting responses from both philosophers and theologians. What binds the tradition of natural law ethics together is the questions themselves.

With the Greek and Roman Stoics (Part I, Chapter 1), we encounter the first explicit references to and theorisation of natural moral law. As Philipp Brüllmann maintains, these ancient philosophers affirm a rational, providential law governing the whole of the natural world or 'cosmos'. Theirs is not, however, the law of a transcendent God; it is a law embodied wholly in nature, a nature that is, contra the God of Israel, itself divine. The moral universe of the Stoics is thus firmly legal in form – Cicero refers extensively to a *lex naturalis*, or 'law of nature'. For them, the central points of contention are: does the natural moral law consist in exceptionless rules? or rules of thumb? or merely the particular judgements of the Stoic 'sage'? As Brüllmann details, the Stoics tackle these questions by distinguishing moral 'precepts' from 'principles', and the so-called progressor from the full-blown moral 'sage'.

Our second historical port of call, Thomas Aquinas (Chapter 2), is widely acknowledged as giving definitive shape to natural law ethics. In the *Summa Theologiae*, he draws on the Stoics, but also on the biblical notion of a transcendent, commanding God. For Aquinas, then, the need to reconcile a moral law immanent within nature and one originating in a transcendent deity is acutely felt. According to Steven Jensen, he achieves this by invoking what he calls natural (yet essentially non-conscious) 'inclinations', which are directed at various objective goods, themselves either protected or promoted by divine law. In short, it is in our nature to obey this law, because it is the guarantor of our and others' well-being. As Jensen argues, furthermore, it is the pivotal notion of natural inclination that saves Aquinas' ethics from the pitfalls of modern ethical theories: subjectivism, error theory, consequentialism and Kantian non-naturalism.

While Aquinas makes a valiant and arguably successful attempt at marrying nature with law, by the time of Grotius and Pufendorf (Chapter 3), the marriage is under severe strain. For in an increasingly secular Europe, the idea that God is necessary to underwrite the moral law is thought by many to be both false and unnecessarily divisive. As Johan Olsthoorn shows, the tendency is hence to affirm that the moral law is binding 'even if', as Grotius puts it, 'we grant [*etiamsi daremus*] ... that there is no God'. In this context, the rearguard action is fought by Pufendorf. Whereas Grotius holds that the natural law is self-standing in both content and force, Pufendorf maintains that 'all law supposes a Superior Power'. Indeed, 'all acts of themselves were indifferent', Pufendorf asserts, 'before the announcement of a law'. Olsthoorn summarises this intricate and wide-ranging argument as follows: 'Grotius was a naturalist about both morality and obligation; Pufendorf a [divine] voluntarist in respect of both'.

Part II documents the revival of natural law ethics in the twentieth century, and opens with Patrick Lee on the 'new natural law theory' (Chapter 4). What is immediately apparent is how far we have travelled from Aquinas, and even from Grotius and Pufendorf. For first, God or God's law is no longer foundational, either as specifying the content of natural law, or as guaranteeing the force of its norms. And secondly, New Natural Law is determined to avoid any (purportedly) fallacious inference from natural teleology to moral norms. Instead, new natural lawyers like John Finnis posit a range of 'basic goods' they claim are practically self-evident. For traditional Thomists, this direct appeal to the practical order, in abstraction from the natural order, constitutes a betrayal of Aquinas' integration between nature and moral law. But as Lee contends, New Natural Law has mustered a battery of arguments against natural teleology, i.e. the notion that nature, as such, has various goods dynamically 'inscribed within it'.

If New Natural Law represents a move away from any transcendent, theistic grounding for natural law, Neo-Aristotelian ethical naturalism completes it (Chapter 5). As Jennifer A. Frey holds, this form of naturalism rejects 'ethical supernaturalism' in favour of a thoroughly this-worldly grounding for normativity. This consists in what Michael Thompson calls the 'Aristotelian categorical', which registers what flourishing for any particular species – human or non-human – amounts to. When we claim, for instance, that 'yellow finches breed in spring', or 'humans have the practice of promise-keeping', we are making judgements about how particular life forms flourish or avoid defect. This Neo-Aristotelian ethical naturalism faces two clear challenges, however: first, that it contravenes post-Darwinian natural science, and second, that its atheism evacuates the idea of natural *law* of coherent content. Frey tackles these challenges head-on, reaching conclusions that are both nuanced and tightly argued.

Part III returns us to authors for whom and sources for which the 'God question' is a live, indeed, a pressing one. This is because the God in question is the God first encountered in Ancient Israel, whose authority wholly transcends nature. Why, then, should such a God be concerned with nature at all? When it comes to Judaism (Chapter 6), this question is, as Tamar Rudavsky maintains, peculiarly difficult to escape. For with one exception, no mediaeval Jewish philosopher makes use of the term 'natural law'. The presumption is that divine command is the foundation of ethics, with no need for appeal to anything beyond it. It is only in the seventeenth century, indeed, that natural law theorising first makes a significant impact within Jewish tradition. But it finds widespread resistance among Jewish philosophers even now, notably by Aharon Lichtenstein and Marvin Fox, the latter contending that 'there is no natural moral law, only the law of God'.

While Catholic Christianity (Chapter 7) clearly has inextricable roots in and manifold debts to Judaism, its openness to natural law ethics has been generally greater. We have seen this, already, in the seminal case of Aquinas. But as Tracey Rowland demonstrates, natural law debate within the Catholic tradition is not confined to Thomism.

A more capacious approach, receptive to both scriptural and patristic sources, finds its full flowering in the period of the Second Vatican Council (1962–5). At that time, moral theologians like Servais Pinckaers OP argued that we need both grace and revelation to grasp the natural law in its fullness. And this is taken up, later, by Pope Benedict XVI, who maintains that nature should be understood 'not in terms of biology or rational metaphysics, but rather in terms of the concrete history that has taken and is taking place between God and man'. To its detractors, however, this 'theonomous' approach misconceives natural law ethics, confusing its content with the content of divine revelation.

When it comes to Protestant Christianity (Chapter 8), there is a common perception that it embodies a return to Judaism's relative suspicion of natural law ethics. But as Jennifer Herdt argues, this is, in the main, a misperception. Luther construes natural law as Jeremiah's (and later St Paul's) 'law written on the heart', and his close relation, Melanchthon, gives Greek ethics pedagogical pride of place. Richard Hooker, for his part, criticises the Puritan view of the Bible as 'a divinely authorised guide to all aspects of life', reasserting the traditional, Catholic view that human reason retains significant autonomous authority. Where Protestant thinkers depart, nevertheless, from their Catholic counterparts, is in emphasising human nature as 'fallen', and in their antipathy to natural law as a purely rationalistic or biologistic artefact.

The final religious tradition considered in Part III is Islam (Chapter 9). Anver Emon argues that any disjunction between religion and law is deeply inimical to an understanding of Islamic ethical thought. In Islam, as in Judaism, the two are inextricable. This leaves undecided, of course, the role, if any, of *natural* law in Islam. Yet according to Emon, one finds its functional equivalent at work in *fiqh* (legal doctrine) and *khilaf* (legal disputes), which contain at least implicit natural law reasoning. Another site of natural law–type debate in Islam is the legal dialectic between *huquq Allah* (literally 'the claims of God', i.e. the claims of public welfare) and *huquq al-'ibad* (the claims of individuals). Here, as elsewhere in Islamic tradition, Emon claims, we find little consensus over universal, natural moral norms and more a general agonism, wherein 'the challenge is to create maximal space for claims about what the universal might be'.

Part IV shifts ground to various applications of natural law ethics. Jacqueline Laing opens with the crucial area of natural law bioethics

(Chapter 10). For Laing, natural law bioethics adheres firmly to Cicero's view that the human good is objective, eternal and unchanging, resting, as it does, on a teleological philosophical anthropology. The human good cannot be defended, Laing maintains, without respecting the principle of double effect, which safeguards all innocent life by precluding any intentional attack on it. This principle classes as impermissible the deliberate targeting of innocent civilians in war and by terrorist organisations. It rules out, furthermore, the deliberate killing of the unborn, as innocent human persons, along with the euthanising of the elderly and terminally ill. By extension, this mode of reasoning stands against all punitive excess, such as death for apostasy or blasphemy, and the harvesting of organs from bodies without prior consent.

Perhaps least hospitable to natural law reasoning is the relatively young social 'science' of economics (Chapter 11). As Samuel Gregg holds, this is because it aspires, unlike bioethics, to be a 'value-free' discipline. What natural law ethics can usefully effect, nonetheless, is a demarcation of issues that are properly part of the value-free 'economic technique', from those that have a direct and significant impact on social justice. Germain Grisez, for example, distinguishes between the commensuration and weighing of non-moral goods and that of moral goods, the latter threatening to bring the whole moral domain within the destructive remit of cost–benefit analysis. If this occurs, Gregg argues, economics descends into economism, and what was a genuine discipline, meant to protect and promote moral goods, becomes instead a self-serving, profoundly anti-social pseudo-discipline.

The final applied topic is political theory (Chapter 12). After summarising Aquinas' natural law ethics, Christopher Wolfe outlines the main contours of a natural law politics. The central theme here is the political or common good as superior to the individual good, and as irreducible to a mere aggregate of individual goods. Yet because human persons are subsistent beings, in whom the political good is realised, that good cannot be achieved without treating such beings with 'equal concern and respect'. As to positive law, it is governed by natural law, though the determinations of the latter are, in general, less certain than those of speculative reason. Safe to say, natural law does not command all virtue, or suppress all vice – on pain of counterproductive results. According to natural law political theory, the common good is mediated by different, sub-state groups, and owing to the principle of subsidiarity, the family is afforded strong rights of its own.

Part IV examines the challenges and prospects for natural law ethics, and begins with Sophie Grace Chappell on the former (Chapter 13). At the heart of Chappell's critique is the claim that an organism's flourishing can, and often does, come apart from its natural *telos* or end. An example is the miserable life of the average wild rabbit. Granted, one can infer natural *telē*, instead, from what it is for organisms to flourish, but this both isolates them from their wider, ecological role and affirms behaviours that seem bad (e.g. lions' tendency to kill lion cubs). It follows that we should submit 'traditional teleological beliefs' to severe scrutiny, including the 'tests of science'. Chappell is convinced, indeed, that a more fruitful source of normative reflection lies – at least in the human case – in the deliverances of phenomenology and conscience, and finishes by making the case for a 'not-just-naturalism' along exactly these lines.

Diametrically opposed to Chappell is Edward Feser, who provides a magisterial overview of the revival of Aristotelian metaphysics (Chapter 14). The revival of Aristotelian essentialism and teleology is owing to recent work by Anglophone analytic philosophers. A key application of their work is to ethics, where goodness can now be understood – as it always was by natural lawyers like Aquinas – as the goodness of a substance, realising its own, intrinsic finality or end. True, the 'mechanical world picture' ushered in by the scientific revolution claims to eviscerate final causation and substantial forms, replacing them with mathematically expressed laws governing aggregates of particles. But, as Feser holds, this was never a scientific finding itself, so much as a tendentious interpretation of such findings. After elaborating an Aristotelian ontology in the chemical and physical domains, Feser criticises evolutionary theory, which (contra Aristotle) reduces natural functions to ones favoured by evolutionary history.

In the final chapter, I assess the prospects for natural law ethics in the twenty-first century (Chapter 15). I begin by outlining three propitious philosophical developments as we approach the first quarter of the new millennium. First, the concerted critique of the fact–value dichotomy; second, the revival of Aristotelian metaphysics; and third, the development of Neo-Aristotelian ethical naturalism. I go on to consider four forms of the latter, namely the naturalisms of John McDowell, Rosalind Hursthouse, Michael Thompson and John Finnis. As I argue, their grounding of norms in nature demonstrates an unacknowledged and troubling dissociation between nature and normativity. Not that the dissociation here, in the four forms I outline, is irreparable – it will just take work to overcome. And given the propitious developments with which I began, there is every chance of this being achieved.

With Neo-Aristotelian ethical naturalism, we have a species of normative theory in which law is fundamentally side-lined, while nature is to the fore. In this way, the dialectic between nature and law now firmly favours the former, with the latter on the defensive. At the very least, law is no longer thematised – as it is by most monotheists, including the majority of Jewish philosophers, Aquinas and even the Stoics – as promulgated or as requiring a lawgiver. And this raises the question of whether a natural *law* ethics is fully present in mainstream, contemporary Anglophone philosophy. This highlights nicely an issue that has confronted us from the start: is nature mere 'material' into which moral norms must be introduced, as it were, from the outside, or does it constitute an arena of norms from the start? I hope that this volume settles this question, if not definitively, at least further than it was before.

PART I The History of Natural Law Ethics

1 The Stoics

Philipp Brüllmann

INTRODUCTION

Any attempt to offer an account of natural law in Stoicism is confronted with the notorious problem of evidence. Not a single work of the 'early' Stoics (Zeno of Citium, Cleanthes and Chrysippus, all working in the third century BCE) has fully survived from antiquity. Reconstructions of their views depend on reports by authors who wrote much later and are in many cases anything but unbiased. The information that these authors provide usually leaves a rather wide scope for different interpretations. And the decision between these interpretations is often a matter of the general assumptions which guide our approach to the Stoics: whether we tend to think, for instance, that the early Stoics stood on common ground with their predecessors and contemporaries or whether we assume that they tried to distinguish themselves from other philosophers. As we shall see, this alternative is particularly relevant in the case of the natural law.

The best, yet still problematic, entry point for an account of the natural law ethics of the Stoics is Cicero (first century BCE). Cicero offers the first 'theory' of natural law that has come down to us, and this theory both draws on and thus transmits Stoic ideas.[1] The concept of natural law (*lex naturalis*) is an important element of Cicero's political philosophy, as developed mainly in his *De Re Publica* (*Rep.*) and *De Legibus* (*Leg.*).[2] Cicero introduces this concept with at least two aims. For one thing, he wishes to establish the natural law as a basis for legislation in the ideal state. In this role, the natural law is both the 'source' and the 'norm' of civil laws (*Leg.* I.17; II.8–14). For another, Cicero refers to the natural law in order to reject a conventionalist account of justice (*Rep.* III; *Leg.* I.42). Justice is not an agreement among people who have understood that not harming each other is to their mutual benefit. It is something that exists by nature and is thus objective in a much stronger sense.

As regards the content of the natural law (what exactly it prescribes or forbids), Cicero is not very informative.[3] But we can draw from his testimony a number of features that characterise the natural law and are pertinent to the aims just mentioned (*Rep.* III.33; *Leg.* I.18–33, 42–7): (1) the natural law is a *law*, i.e. it issues commands and prohibitions concerning what must be done and what must not be done; (2) the natural law differs from the diverse and ever-changing laws of existing communities by being *constant, eternal* and *universal*; (3) it is a *natural* law, i.e. a law that regulates nature in general; (4) as a natural law, it is ordained by those who rule the cosmos, i.e. God or the gods; (5) the natural law is a manifestation of the perfect rationality of nature and can thus be identified with 'right reason' (*recta ratio*); (6) accordingly, it is qua rational that human beings are able to grasp the law of nature; (7) since being rational is what defines us as human beings, disobedience to the natural law is against our nature; and finally, (8) the natural law invites us to take a *cosmopolitical perspective*, according to which the whole cosmos is a 'state' of gods and humans, who have reason, law and justice in common.

The picture emerging from these features definitely has a Stoic ring to it: it matches information we possess about the philosophy of the early Stoics. For instance, law (*nomos*) is a basic concept in the Stoic philosophy of nature.[4] According to the Stoics, the cosmos is a cohesive unity guided by an all-pervasive 'active principle' that is identified with Zeus. Since this active principle is perfectly rational and beneficent, it governs the cosmos in the best possible way. Every single state of affairs and every single event is determined in accordance with a perfect plan; and if we had perfect knowledge, we could see how everything that happens is part of that plan. The notion of a law seems to denote precisely this idea of a rational plan determining the natural course of events. The Stoics can thus say that the cosmos is guided in accordance with a law, and they typically identify law, right reason (*orthos logos*) and God.[5]

Furthermore, we possess a number of programmatic remarks by the early Stoics, indicating that the 'common law' (*koinos nomos*) plays a foundational role for ethics. Most prominent is a fragment from Chrysippus' *On Law*, transmitted by Marcian:

> (T 1) Law is king of all things human and divine. Law must preside over what is honourable and base, as ruler and as guide, and thus be the standard of right and wrong, prescribing to animals whose nature is political what they should do, and prohibiting them from what they should not do. (Long and Sedley 1987 [LS]: 67 R)

Most probably, Chrysippus is referring here to the law of nature that guides the cosmos. For in a fragment from his *Physical Postulates*, he says,

> (T 2) There is no other or more appropriate way of approaching the theory of good and bad things or the virtues or happiness than from universal nature and from the administration of the world. (LS 60 A)

The similarities between these programmatic remarks and Cicero's view of the natural law are striking.

Finally, there is the cosmopolitical perspective. It is the political philosophy of the Stoics that introduces this perspective and notoriously invites us to conceive of the cosmos as a city of sages and gods, claiming that what makes them citizens is that they participate in reason and law.[6]

Given these similarities, it comes as no surprise that Stoic ideas are usually taken to be the most important influence on Cicero's conception of the natural law, although Cicero does not reveal his sources.[7] To bring out this influence, it is not uncommon to draw a contrast with Aristotle, whose role in the development of natural law theory is much less obvious. Aristotle knows, of course, the distinction between what is just by nature (*phusis*) and what is just by convention (*nomos*). He uses this distinction as a tool against positivistic conceptions of justice (*Nicomachean Ethics* [*NE*] V.7).[8] The observations just sketched, however, seem to mark a difference between Aristotle and the Stoics.[9] Aristotle works with a concept of nature which focuses not on the cosmos as a whole but on natural substances and their properties.[10] According to Aristotle, the standard of ethics is not a law but the *spoudaios*, i.e. the excellent person (*NE* III.4). And since Aristotle is sceptical about the use of rules in ethics (e.g. *NE* II.2, 1103b34–1104a11), there is good reason to assume that he would not characterise virtue as obedience to a law. Finally, Aristotle's political philosophy centres on the city-state or *polis*; the cosmopolitical perspective is virtually absent in his work.

This agreement on the influence of Stoicism on the theory of natural law stands in striking contrast to a fundamental disagreement over how to describe the natural law ethics of the early Stoics (in fact, over how deep a difference there exists between Aristotle and the Stoics in this respect). In recent decades, the debate on this topic has become extremely complex.[11] Although it is common to distinguish between two basic approaches, their demarcation is difficult; often, it is hard to tell what exactly interpreters disagree on.

The aim of this chapter is to identify the roots of this disagreement. I will explain what is so difficult about spelling out the programmatic remarks in T 1 and T 2 and thus about defining the role of the natural law in early Stoic ethical theory. And I will outline what I think are the major interpretative alternatives. To do that, it is first necessary to look at the tenets of Stoic ethics and the ideal of a life 'in agreement with nature'.

LIVING IN AGREEMENT WITH NATURE

The ethical theory of the early Stoics can be characterised by four core claims that help situate the Stoics within the landscape of ancient ethical debates.[12]

1 *Virtue Is Sufficient for Happiness*

The basic idea behind this first claim is that, for the quality of someone's life, it doesn't matter whether that person is rich or poor, healthy or sick. The only relevant question is whether she possesses virtue. If she does, she will lead the best possible life, no matter what the circumstances; if not, her life is a failure. This claim distinguishes the Stoics from positions which assume that happiness (*eudaimonia*) requires a number of goods, of which virtue is only the most important. The sufficiency of virtue for happiness is reflected in Stoic axiology, according to which virtue is the only 'good' (*agathon*) and vice the only 'bad' (*kakon*) thing. Everything else, which includes health, wealth etc., is 'indifferent' (*adiaphoron*) – indifferent, that is, with respect to happiness.

2 *Virtue Is a Perfection of Reason*

Like Socrates, the Stoics advocate an intellectualist conception of virtue that implies that virtue is a kind of 'wisdom' and the virtuous person a 'sage'.[13] The basis of this conception is the Stoic view of the human soul. According to the Stoics, the human soul does not consist of different 'parts', representing a plurality of motivational forces, but is a single rational faculty, called the *hēgēmonikon* ('commanding centre'). In adult human beings, mental events are essentially judgements or, as the Stoics put it, 'assents' (*sunkatathēseis*) to 'impressions' (*phantasiai*) with propositional content. This has important consequences for moral psychology. For whatever might go wrong in someone's actions or reactions must be due to a cognitive failure. It cannot be explained in terms of, say, irrational desires winning out over reason; it has to be explained as some kind of rational error or delusion. With respect to the perfection of reason, two points are noteworthy. First, rationality is not a formal concept. Of course, the perfection of reason requires skills in rational argument (logic and dialectic). But it also requires knowledge. Although a Stoic sage is probably not omniscient,[14] we can safely assume that she will know, for instance, the principles of ethics (see below). Second, perfection of reason means consistency (*homologia*). It means that a sage possesses a set of perfectly consistent beliefs and that every judgement she makes (every assent to an impression) is consistent with that set. In other words, there is no assent that a sage will ever have to revise. This explains why virtue is extremely rare and appears like an all-or-nothing affair in Stoicism. Either someone is in a state of perfect consistency, or she is not.

3 *Being Virtuous Includes Doing What Is Right in a Given Situation*

The Stoics subscribe to the familiar idea that someone who is virtuous behaves correctly in different kinds of situation. There is, as it is often called, a 'what' of virtuous action, meaning that virtue is related to what someone is doing. The Stoics have a technical way of spelling out this familiar idea. Within their conceptual framework, doing what is right means performing an 'appropriate act' (*kathēkon*), which in turn means choosing correctly among the aforementioned 'indifferent things' (choosing health and what promotes it, for instance). An appropriate act is defined by the Stoics as an act that, when done, admits of a 'reasonable defence' (*eulogos apologismos*; DL VII.107). We will return to the notion of a defence below. For now, we should notice that if an act is appropriate, there is always a rational account of why it is appropriate (e.g. why it is appropriate to choose health). Again, this idea is reflected in Stoic axiology. Although health, disease, wealth, poverty etc. are indifferent with respect to happiness, they are not indifferent with respect to choice and avoidance. The Stoics thus draw a distinction between 'preferred' (*proēgmena*) and 'dispreferred' or 'rejected' indifferents (*apoproēgmena*), asserting that the former (e.g. health and wealth) possess 'value' (*axia*) and the latter (e.g. disease and poverty) 'disvalue' (*apaxia*).

4 *Doing What Is Right in a Given Situation Is Not Sufficient for Virtue*

This claim represents the idea that there is not only a 'what' but also a 'how' of virtuous action. Virtue requires that we do the right thing from the right disposition. The Stoic term for an action that meets this condition is *katorthōma* (often rendered 'right action'). Again, the general idea is not unfamiliar. Aristotle, for instance, also claims that in order to count as virtuous, an action must be done from a certain disposition: the agent must act knowingly, she must choose the action for its own sake and she must act from a character that is 'firm and unshakable' (*bebaiōs kai ametakinētōs; NE* II.4, 1105a30–33). This firmness and unshakability plays a crucial role in the Stoic account of the 'how' side of virtue, as well. Unlike Aristotle, however, who would trace it back to the habituation of our desires, the Stoics have to put this firmness in intellectualist terms. Here the notion of consistency seems to be pertinent. The sage acts from a firm disposition in the sense that she makes no judgements that she might have to revise later. This seems to imply that the 'what' and the 'how' of virtue cannot be separated as easily as in the case of Aristotle.[15] On the one hand, the content of appropriate acts and right actions (the what) seems to be the same. In some passages, the Stoics explicitly point out that, in principle, one could do what is right in every given situation and yet not be virtuous.[16] On the other hand, it seems that unless one *is* virtuous, and thus perfectly consistent, one is not able reliably to do what is right in every given situation. There is always the possibility of a judgement that will turn out to be wrong in hindsight. As we shall see, this aspect is highly relevant for our understanding of the role of the natural law in Stoicism.

Now there is a fifth claim that we should add to this outline of Stoic ethics.

5 *The Goal Is to 'Live in Agreement with Nature' (*homologoumenōs tēi phusei zēn*)*

This claim is spelled out in a famous passage from Book VII of the *Lives of Eminent Philosophers* by Diogenes Laertius:

(T 3) Thus Zeno first, in his book *On Human Nature*, said that the goal was to live in agreement with nature, which is to live according to virtue. For nature leads us to virtue. And similarly Cleanthes in *On Pleasure* and Posidonius and Hecaton in their books *On the Goal*. Again, 'to live according to virtue' is equivalent to (*ison*) living according to the experience of events which occur by nature, as Chrysippus says in book 1 of his *On Goals*. For our natures are parts of the nature of the universe. Therefore, the goal becomes 'to live consistently with nature', i.e., according to one's own nature and that of the universe, doing nothing which is forbidden by the common law, which is right reason, penetrating all things, being the same as Zeus, who is the leader of the administration of things. And this itself is the virtue of the happy man and a smooth flow of life, whenever all things are done according to the harmony of the *daimōn* in each of us with the will of the administrator of the universe. (DL VII.87–8, translation by Inwood and Gerson 2008 [IG])

This passage brings out that the consistency which is central to the Stoic conception of virtue is not only an 'internal' consistency, concerning our beliefs and judgements, but also a consistency with (human and cosmic) *nature*. The actions of a Stoic sage are perfectly adapted to the natural course of events. They reflect the rational plan of the cosmos. This adaptation obviously requires some kind of knowledge of nature. It requires, as the text says, that we have an 'experience' of the events which occur by nature and that we live in accordance with that experience.[17] But how does this work?

The Stoics assume that the adaptation of one's actions to nature is the result of a process that begins with our first natural impulses and ideally ends in virtue; 'nature leads us to virtue', as T 3 puts it. Here is a sketch.[18] Right after birth, human behaviour is not different from the behaviour of animals, according to the Stoics. It is structured by an instinctive impulse to reach out for things that help us to survive and to avoid things that threaten us. This mechanism of impulses, which is grounded in an innate love for our natural constitution, is part of the rational management of nature; it is how the cosmos takes care of living beings (DL VII.85). And it allows the following distinction: there are things that fit the nature of the animal and are thus 'in accordance' with that nature (*kata phusin*), and there are things that do not fit the nature of the animal and are thus 'against' it (*para phusin*). With respect to sustaining its natural state, it is appropriate (*kathēkon*) for the animal to pursue the former and avoid the latter.

Now human beings are not animals. At a certain age, they have acquired reason (*logos*), which brings with it two changes. First, the impulses of adult human beings are not instinctive drives. They are, as already mentioned, assents to impressions with propositional content.[19] Second, qua rational, human beings are able to understand the mechanism just outlined. They are able to understand that some things are in accordance with their nature, and thus to be preferred, while other things are against their nature, and thus to be avoided. And they are able to understand that there is a general pattern underlying this distinction. By making this understanding the basis of their practice of giving or withholding assent, human beings perform appropriate acts: acts that are in accordance with their nature. This is, in rough outline, how adaptation to nature is possible.

The Stoics emphasise, however, that obtaining agreement with nature is no simple task. It is a matter of a slow and gradual 'progress' (*prokopē*), in which an increasing understanding of nature results in the increasing stability of one's actions. As human beings mature, there are more and different things that fit their rational nature, things related to the different roles and social contexts they find themselves in.[20] If someone reaches virtue (which is rare), her understanding of the workings of nature is so perfected that she will act in perfect consistency with it. Furthermore, her system of value will have undergone a radical change. She has realised that this consistency is more important than the things that are to be taken or avoided. These things according to nature are still the material of her (virtuous) actions, but she will have gained a completely different attitude to them.

T 3 also says that, according to Chrysippus, someone who lives consistently with nature does nothing 'which is forbidden by the common law', i.e. the law that regulates the cosmos and is identical with Zeus. This claim clearly reminds us both of the two programmatic passages T 1 and T 2 (also by Chrysippus) and of our sketch of Stoic cosmology. Yet T 3 does not tell us, unfortunately, what it means exactly – in fact, no text does. And this raises the question: how are consistency with, and adaptation to, the natural course of events, as just outlined, a matter of obedience to the natural law? Against the background sketched in this section, I will now canvas a variety of answers to this question.

THE LAW AS A STANDARD

The first answer starts from the notion of a standard (*kanōn*) mentioned in T 1: we adapt our actions to nature by using the natural law as a standard for our decisions, our practice of giving or withholding assent. The discussion of this answer usually begins with a reference to a simple and straightforward view (which most interpreters then claim to be false). The core idea of this simple view is that laws are *rules*: they prescribe or forbid *types* of action (e.g. 'Do not steal!', 'Honour your parents!') Acting in accordance with the law of nature would thus mean following a rule. And this, in turn, would mean that using the natural law as a standard comes down to applying a rule to particular cases. According to the simple view, deliberation is a matter of identifying an action as being of a certain type (a case of stealing or of honouring one's parents, for example).

One type of evidence in our sources on Stoic ethics seems to support this view. As a matter of fact, the aim of providing rules, or of giving some kind of advice, seems to be a core aspect of the Stoic ethical project. We meet this aspect in different places.

To begin with, one of the most conspicuous features of our texts is the tendency to offer 'lists', for instance of preferred and dispreferred indifferents. Here is an example:

> (T 4) Preferred things are those which also have value; for example, among things of the soul, natural ability, skill, [moral] progress, and similar things; among bodily things life, health, strength, good condition, soundness, beauty, and the like; among external things wealth, reputation, noble birth, and similar things. Rejected are, among things of the soul, natural inability, lack of skill, and similar things; among bodily things death, disease, weakness, bad condition, being maimed, ugliness, and similar things; among external things poverty, lack of reputation, low birth, and the like. (DL VII.106; trans. IG)

The message of T 4 and similar passages seems to be this. If we exclude virtue and vice (as good and bad), on the one hand, and utterly indifferent things (like 'having an odd or even number of hairs on one's head': DL VII.104), on the other, then everything there is can be identified as either a preferred or a dispreferred indifferent. This means, as we have seen, that it either fits or doesn't fit our human nature. The reference to human nature thus generates a map of value and disvalue, which offers a kind of orientation in life.

We noticed that the concept of human nature also provides a point of reference for appropriate acts, defined as acts that admit of a reasonable defence. And we mentioned that, in the case of human beings, the question of what is appropriate becomes more and more complex as they mature. Now we know that works entitled *On Appropriate Acts* (*Peri Kathēkontōn*) were an integral part of the philosophical output of the Stoics. None of these works has come down to us. What we do possess, however, is Cicero's *On Duties* (*De Officiis* [*Off.*]), which is based on a work of that type by the middle Stoic Panaetius ('*officium*' being the Latin translation of '*kathēkon*').[21] Roughly put, Cicero's *De Officiis* is a discussion of, and guideline for, correct behaviour in all kinds of situation, down to the question how we should behave in conversation or what kind of house we should buy. This discussion reflects the complexity just mentioned. It reveals not only that there are different duties related to the different virtues, but also that each of these comes with specific problems and challenges. If we wish to determine what is appropriate, a multiplicity of factors needs to be taken into account, according to Cicero – for example, the different roles we play in life.[22] Furthermore, we might have to decide between conflicting obligations, which is in fact a core topic of *De Officiis*.

Finally, the Stoics aimed to offer ethical 'precepts' or 'instructions' (*praecepta*). The most important source for this 'prescriptive' aspect of Stoicism is Seneca's *Letters* [*Ep.*] 94 and 95. According to Seneca, precepts are derived from the general principles (*decreta*) of philosophy,[23] and just like *officia*, they are grounded in that which is natural (i.e. preferred indifferents).[24] Again, it is remarkable how Stoic ethical advice seems to cover all areas of human life. As Seneca points out, there are precepts 'for each social role, such as advising a husband on how he should behave to his wife, a father on how to raise his children, or a master on how to regulate his slaves' (94.1). Precepts concern the questions of how to treat a friend, a fellow citizen, or an ally (94.11), of how to speak or walk or behave in public or private (94.17). They tell us that we should fight for our country (95.37), or that we should lend a hand to the shipwrecked, show the way to the wanderer, and share our bread with the starving (95.51).

This type of evidence, combined with the premise that a law is a rule, has led some interpreters to the conclusion that the natural law of the early Stoics is basically a body of rules.[25] This body of rules consists of the general principles of a life in agreement with nature (such as 'Preserve your natural constitution!'), along with an enormous number of general rules that are deduced from these principles, down to the very specific precepts mentioned by Seneca. These rules are the content of the natural law. They determine what is appropriate in a given situation and thus provide a guideline for deliberation.

Other scholars, however, have been quick to point out difficulties for this interpretation. The most important of these difficulties is that our sources also provide another kind of evidence, which indicates that the deliberation of the Stoic sage does not take the form of an application of exceptionless rules.[26] On the contrary, some passages explicitly claim that, in some situations, a sage will do something *exceptional*.[27] For instance, we have seen in T 4 that life belongs to the category of preferred indifferents. Yet the Stoics famously argue that under certain circumstances a sage will commit suicide (Cicero, *Fin.* III.60–61).[28] We have also seen that health belongs to the same category; being healthy is obviously in accordance with our nature. However, there are situations in which the sage will choose disease:

> (T 5) if it were necessary for healthy men to serve a tyrant and for this reason to be executed, whereas sick men were released from service and so also freed from destruction, the wise man would choose sickness over health on such an occasion. (Sextus Empiricus, *Adversus Mathematicos* [SE *M*] 11.66, trans. IG)

In a similar vein, the Stoics draw a distinction among appropriate acts, claiming that some (e.g. looking out for one's health) are appropriate 'without regard to special circumstances', while others (e.g. maiming oneself) are 'conditioned by the circumstances' (DL VII.109). In the latter type of case, a 'reasonable defence' would not describe the act as one that falls under a rule but rather as one in which circumstances require that a rule be *broken*. A crucial aspect of wisdom would be to know when breaking a particular rule is appropriate.

A number of writers have been inclined to draw from this second kind of evidence the following lesson. Whatever rules our sources on Stoic ethics might provide – be it in the form of lists of preferred and dispreferred indifferents, of a treatise on appropriate acts, or of specific precepts – these rules will always be defeasible. For it is always possible that the right thing to do in a given situation is to act against the rule or rules in question.[29] Appropriate acts are always subject to special circumstances. Since it is the sage who has the authority to break the rules, it requires wisdom to know what to do in a given situation.[30]

It seems but a small step from this lesson to the suspicion that rules are of no use at all when it comes to the question of what we should do. Aristo of Chios, a student of Zeno and Stoic of the first generation, is famous for having taken this step.[31] According to our reports, Aristo suggested restricting Stoic axiology to the distinction between good, bad and indifferent, and abandoning the further distinction between preferred and dispreferred indifferents. The reason he gives draws on precisely the aspect just mentioned (T 5 is in fact by Aristo): what we should do in a given situation is always a matter of the circumstances; nothing is preferred unconditionally (SE *M* 11.64–7 = LS 58 F). Seneca reports that Aristo also claimed that precepts are useless (*Ep.* 94.5–17). For the task of giving precepts for each situation would be 'endless' (94.14–15); and someone who has 'understood and learned the structure of the ultimate good [can] prescribe to himself what should be done in each situation' (94.2).

Aristo, however, is a renegade. We can safely assume that mainstream Stoicism stuck to the distinction between preferred and dispreferred indifferents, as well as to the project of giving advice. We need to take seriously the evidence that supports the straightforward view of the natural law as a body of rules. This allows us, then, to offer a more precise formulation of the problem at stake. The problem is to ascribe a role to the lists of preferred indifferents, the discussion of appropriate acts, and the concern to offer precepts, while taking into account the importance of exceptions, the relevance of circumstances and the authority of the sage.

In order to understand how this problem might be solved, we should begin with the distinction between the progressor and the sage (see above). A progressor is someone whose beliefs and actions are not yet perfectly consistent, but who finds herself approaching such consistency. As her understanding of the overall pattern of nature increases, she becomes better and better at adapting her actions to the natural course of events. It is uncontested that rules in the above-mentioned sense play a role in this process. Seneca, in particular, makes clear that precepts can help the progressor 'to learn what to do and how to do it' (94.50). Against Aristo, he claims that knowing the principles of philosophy does not, by itself, tell us how to act. Even if we acquire a correct view about good and bad, we might still need guidance to see what is required by the situation at hand. The value and use of precepts seem to lie in this guidance.

Letter 94 gives a number of hints on how this works.[32] These hints add up to the picture of a 'training' in deliberation. This training does not seem to consist in just telling the progressor which rule fits a certain case. The aim is rather to help her recognise the relevant aspects of a given situation. Seneca introduces this idea by pointing out what might go wrong, or how we might fail to recognise those aspects. Among other things, we might have forgotten something (94.22). We might know something but not apply this knowledge (94.25). We might be confused by the complexity of the situation (94.21). The relevant considerations might be 'scattered' over the mind's different compartments (94.29). And we might be influenced by the opinions of the many or be under the sway of emotions (94.31). In all these cases, precepts can help. They call our attention, they arouse us, they focus our memory and prevent it from waning. They force us to take notice and support our struggle against corrupting influences.

On the other hand, precepts are not sufficient for acquiring virtue. They need to be combined with principles (*decreta*) as a point of reference (95.44–5); otherwise we will go wrong. In *Letter* 95, Seneca outlines this idea and tells us what those principles are.[33] But although he is unambiguous in his claim that principles and precepts need to go hand in hand, he is not very clear on the question of how this collaboration is supposed to work. How, for instance, is our religious practice, which is taught by precepts, modified, once we have grasped the true nature of God? The hints given by Seneca indicate that the difference must lie in the 'how' of virtuous action. But as already mentioned, there are two ways to conceive of this aspect, and these two ways seem to be present in Seneca as well. In some places, Seneca seems to assume that we might be able to do what is right on the basis of precepts. But without principles, we will not do it in the right way. For instance, we might act for the wrong motives, as when we visit a sick friend for the sake of inheritance (95.43). In other places, his view is rather that on the basis of precepts we can do what is right in many situations. But in order to always and consistently do what is right, an interplay between precepts and principles is necessary. Unless we refer the situation at hand to the holistic perspective, our actions will not fulfil all the relevant measures, 'so as to know when, how much, with whom, and why a certain action is appropriate' (95.5).

This problem notwithstanding, it cannot be denied that rules of some kind play a role for the progressor. The true question is hence whether they also play a role for the sage or ideal deliberator, given that doing the right thing in a particular situation requires a high degree of flexibility and context sensitivity. Although the debate on this question is complex, it seems possible to distinguish between two basic approaches.

The first approach assumes a crucial discontinuity between the progressor and the sage. According to this approach, the perfection of reason implies that we leave behind the rules which guide the process of progression: actual wisdom needs no admonition about how to conduct oneself (*Ep.* 94.50). The result is a quasi-Aristotelian picture of ideal deliberation, verging on a kind of moral particularism.[34] If rules play a role, on this approach, then this is only under non-ideal circumstances, which concerns the progressor but also anyone who lacks relevant knowledge about the situation at hand. As a famous passage in Epictetus puts it:[35]

> (T 6) Chrysippus did well to say, 'As long as the consequences remain unclear to me, I always hold to what is better fitted to secure such things as are in accordance with nature (*kata phusin*); for God himself created me with the faculty of choosing those things. But if I in fact knew that illness had been decreed for me at this moment by destiny, I would welcome even that; for the foot, too, if it had understanding, would be eager to get spattered with mud'. (*Dissertationes* 2.6.9–10, trans. Hard, modified)

What T 6 suggests is that we should think of the list of things in accordance with nature as providing rules of thumb. There is no guarantee that my recovery right now is part of Zeus' overall plan. But given that health is among the things that fit human nature in general, it is rational, under the circumstances, to pursue health rather than disease. The corresponding account of this choice is in fact a *defence*: it justifies the application of a rule of thumb by referring to the suboptimal epistemic situation of the deliberator, who is still perfectly aware that her choice might turn out to be wrong. Since suboptimal epistemic conditions might be quite common (not even the sage knows all consequences), rules of thumb might play an important role. There is perhaps good reason for the Stoics to entrench those rules, while holding fast to the claim that, under ideal circumstances, they would be superfluous.[36]

The second approach, by contrast, assumes a relevant continuity between the progressor and the sage, between non-ideal and ideal circumstances of deliberation. On this approach, Seneca describes (in

Letters 94 and 95) a training for the kind of deliberation the sage herself will apply, though in a perfected way. These letters, and Cicero's *De Officiis*, tell us something about how the use of generalisations is compatible with context sensitivity. This again can be spelled out in different ways.

One option is to think of context sensitivity as guaranteed by the system of rules itself. One might argue that this system is of such complexity that it will always provide a rule to decide controversial cases.[37] This option can draw on Cicero's remarks on how to solve conflicts between different duties (duties referring to different roles, to different communities or to an apparent conflict between the honourable and the beneficial). For Cicero's general assumption seems to be that it is always possible to establish a ranking of those duties by referring to a higher principle.[38] Another option is to find context sensitivity in the interplay between precepts and principles that was sketched above.[39] As one interpreter has put it, this interplay does not reveal a grid-like system.[40] It rather shows how precepts can play a role in the application of general principles without being merely deduced from them, and how principles can constrain our deliberation without being simply the most generic precepts. Flexibility is guaranteed here not by the body of rules itself, but by how someone makes use of it. Different though these options may be, they both insist that rules play a role in ideal deliberation.[41]

ORDERS AND PROHIBITIONS

In the previous section, we took a look at one type of answer to the question of how living in agreement with nature can be a matter of following the natural law. According to this answer, the natural law is a standard (*kanōn*) that determines the content of virtuous action. It tells us *what* to do. There is, however, another way of interpreting what it is to follow the law of nature. Consider Cicero, *Rep.* III.33:

> (T 7) True law is right reason, consonant with nature, spread through all people. It is constant and eternal; it summons to duty by its orders, it deters from crime by its prohibitions. Its orders and prohibitions to good people are never given in vain; but it does not move the wicked by these orders and prohibitions ... and the person who does not obey it will be in exile from himself. Insofar as he scorns his nature as a human being, by this very fact he will pay the greatest

> penalty, even if he escapes all the other things that are generally recognised as punishments. (trans. Zetzel)

The focus of this passage is not on the law as determining the 'what' of virtuous action but on the law as something which we obey (if we are 'good people') or disobey (if we are not). Following the natural law here means to think of it as a law that *binds* us. It is a matter, not of the content, but of the psychology (and thus the 'how') of virtuous action.

This focus on moral psychology matches the aim of Book III of Cicero's *Republic*. As already mentioned, Cicero introduces the concept of natural law to rebut a conventionalist account of justice, propounded in the 'Speech of Philus'. This conventionalist account is connected with the psychology of rational egoism: human beings pursue their own interests in whatever they do. If the convention of justice has any value, this value must be derived from those interests; and if acting unjustly should be to our benefit, we have no reason to abstain from it.[42] Cicero takes this challenge very seriously. He thinks that if it succeeds, then justice, and with it the ideal of a *res publica*, are virtually destroyed (*Rep.* II.70; cf. *Leg.* I.40–49).

Introducing the concept of natural law in the 'Speech of Laelius' thus serves two purposes. It offers an alternative to both conventionalism as a theory of justice and egoism as a theory of human psychology.[43] The alternative to egoism lies in the idea of obedience to the natural law, where obedience means precisely that we not pursue our egoistic interests, but take ourselves to belong to a community which is, in a sense, more important than its parts.

Although this strategy seems sufficiently clear, its details are difficult to understand on the basis of Cicero's text. What he obviously assumes is that the Stoic perspective on human beings and the cosmos offers an attractive foundation for this kind of argument: qua rational, human beings can come to understand that they are part of a rational order, and this understanding can have an effect on their motivational set-up.[44] If this is the correct view of the role of natural law in early Stoicism, then early Stoicism seems to introduce a strikingly modern, 'proto-Kantian' approach to ethics, connecting the natural law with the idea of an imperative that trumps our selfish desires.[45]

Scholarship on early Stoicism has raised serious doubts about this view.[46] One of these doubts relies on the observation that, like all other ancient philosophers, the Stoics are 'eudaimonists'. They conceive of happiness as the goal of human life and the highest end of our actions.

Everything we do is referred to our happiness. According to a common understanding, called 'rational eudaimonism', this also means that the rationality of our actions depends on their contribution to our happiness. But this seems incompatible with the idea that some of our actions are rational by being in accordance with the law of nature (that we have reason to obey this law just because it is a law). A good way to illustrate the difference is to consider how a eudaimonist approach would answer the egoistic attack on justice.[47] Instead of showing that, in the case of a conflict between justice and self-interest, the former always wins, it would rather show that any such conflict is merely apparent, and that being just conditions our happiness.

One of the most fundamental disagreements in scholarship on Stoic ethics is marked by the question whether the reference to living in agreement with cosmic nature indicates a departure from the eudaimonist framework that is familiar from Plato and Aristotle. This question cannot be answered here. But we should note, at least, that it is with their emphasis on the law of nature that the Stoics offer a conceptual tool for such a departure.

CONCLUSION

The aim of this chapter was to explain how there can be wide agreement on the influence of Stoic ideas on the history of natural law and at the same time deep disagreement over the natural law ethics of the Stoics. As it has turned out, it is precisely the notion of a law that makes things difficult. Despite the unambiguous praise of law in T 1 and T 3 (perhaps the most important pieces of evidence), it is no trivial task to define what role that law is playing in the ethical theory of the early Stoics. The reason is that our evidence points in different directions. While some arguments suggest a straightforward understanding of the natural law as a rule which we must obey, others speak against such a view.

Two lessons can be drawn. First, the disagreement among scholars on the natural law in early Stoicism reflects deeper disagreement on a number of core issues, such as the Stoic concept of deliberation and their moral psychology, the relation between the sage and the progressor, and the relation between appropriate acts and virtuous actions. Second, the most fundamental contrast in the debate on Stoic natural law seems to be this. On one side, there are interpreters who tend to read Stoic ethics as standing in a tradition that was formed in important ways by Aristotle. These interpreters are inclined to understand references to the law in a less straightforward way. On the other side, there are interpreters who insist on taking those references seriously. These interpreters are more open to thinking of the Stoics as departing from the ancient tradition and as foreshadowing, in important respects, modern moral theories. Our picture of the natural law in Stoicism cannot be separated from how we conceive of the overall character of Stoic ethics – and vice versa.

NOTES

1. E.g. Watson 1971; Crowe 1977: 28–51; Hammer 2014: 36–8. For a more nuanced view of Cicero's sources, see Horn 2017.
2. Cicero 1999.
3. A core idea of his account is that of a fundamental similarity between all human beings. This idea grounds the claims that it is natural for human beings to act for the sake of others and that the community is more important than the individual (*De Finibus* [*Fin.*] III.64–6; Cicero 2001). Far from clear, however, is whether Cicero takes the code of laws he outlines in *Leg.* II and III as representing the precepts of a natural law; see Asmis 2008.
4. The most relevant fragments on Stoic natural philosophy are collected in Long and Sedley 1987 [LS]: 43–55.
5. For impressive testimony to this view, see Cleanthes' *Hymn to Zeus* (Thom 2005). It should be noted that the *identification* of law, right reason and Zeus marks a difference from Cicero; see Klein 2012: 69–75.
6. On Stoic cosmopolitanism, see Schofield 1999; Vogt 2008.
7. See e.g. Asmis 2008. There is a striking similarity between the theory of natural law in *De Re Publica* and *De Legibus*, on the one hand, and Cicero's account of Stoic ethics in *Fin.* III (esp. III.62–8) and Stoic theology in *De Natura Deorum* II (Cicero 2008), on the other.
8. Aristotle 2000.
9. Cf. Striker 1987.
10. But see Sedley 2007: chapter 6.
11. For an overview with extensive bibliography, see Vogt 2008: chapter 4; Jedan 2009: chapter 11.
12. The most important sources are the three 'full accounts' of Stoic ethics in Diogenes Laertius, *Lives of Eminent Philosophers* [DL] VII.84–131 (Inwood and Gerson 2008: 113–24), Stobaeus, *Anthology* [*Ecl.*] 2.5–12 (Inwood and Gerson 2008: 124–51) and Cicero, *Fin.* III. For an introduction, see Inwood and Donini 1999 and Brennan 2005.
13. See Brouwer 2014.

14. Brouwer 2014: 33–4; Vogt 2008: 128n28.
15. See Kidd 1978.
16. Stobaeus, *Ecl.* 4.39.22; for discussion, see Jedan 2009: chapter 11.
17. For a discussion, see Menn 1995 on 'physics as a virtue'.
18. For the following, see in particular Cicero, *Fin* III.16–21; Kidd 1971; Inwood and Donini 1999: 724–36.
19. There is a deplorable lack of information on the precise content of this proposition. But roughly, the impulse to drink this glass of water is an assent to the impression that I should now drink this glass of water (or to some other normative judgement about my drinking it). See Brennan 2005: part II.
20. See Seneca, *Epistulae Morales* [*Ep.*] 121 (Seneca 2015)
21. Cicero 1991. I put aside here the question of whether there is a difference in the treatment of indifferents between early and 'middle' Stoicism. See Kidd 1971; Mitsis 1994.
22. See Gill 1988 on Cicero's theory of the four *personae* (*Off.* I.107–119).
23. On those principles, see *Ep.* 95.10; Inwood 1999: 117–20.
24. On the relationship between duties and precepts, see *Ep.* 94.33–4: duties are organised by precepts; precepts guide the performance of our duties.
25. For a view of this kind, see Striker 1987, 1991; Jedan 2009.
26. Furthermore, it is not a trivial matter whether we understand precepts as rules or as deduced from principles. See Vogt 2008: 189–98, for the first kind of problem, Kidd 1978 for the second.
27. See Mitsis 1994: 4835–6; Inwood 1999; Vogt 2008: 206–13.
28. Interpreters also refer in this context to the notorious examples of cannibalism, mutilation and incest from Zeno's *Republic*. For a discussion of these examples, see Vogt 2008: chapter 1.
29. On the question of whether there are any clear examples of non-vacuous and exceptionless rules in our sources on Stoic ethics, see Mitsis 1994: 4837; Inwood 1999: 103.
30. See Inwood 1999: 100n17 for the relevant evidence.
31. On Aristo, see e.g. LS 58 F-G, with commentary; Striker 1991: 231–9.
32. On this letter, see Kidd 1978; Mitsis 1993.
33. The nature of God is the point of reference for religious practices (95.47–50). The notion of a community of all human beings is the point of reference for our treatment of others (95.51–3). The treatment of 'things' must be based on a proper assessment of what they really are (namely indifferent) (95.54). And virtuous action must be based on a proper understanding of how the virtues are interconnected and how they are related to life as a whole (95.55–7).
34. Inwood 1999. This approach calls for a different understanding of the claim that a sage acts in accordance with the law. One prominent suggestion is to refer this

claim to the perfect rationality and consistency of the sage: whatever her reason prescribes has the status of law. See Vander Waerdt 1994.

35. Epictetus 2014.
36. For this suggestion, see again Inwood 1999. Inwood refers in his article to the work of the philosopher of law Frederick Schauer. But the general idea has much in common with contemporary reflections on the role of rules in act utilitarianism; see e.g. Smart 1956.
37. Jedan 2009.
38. This does not exclude the possibility of a disagreement among the Stoics about that ranking; for an example, see *Off.* III.90; Jedan 2009: 350–51.
39. See Mitsis 1993, 1994.
40. Mitsis 1993: 294–6.
41. A third option, roughly corresponding to what today would be called a system of '*prima facie* duties', is suggested by Katja Vogt (2008: chapter 4). On her account, flexibility is guaranteed by the fact that, when deciding what to do in a given situation, the deliberator has to weigh the preferred indifferents against each other.
42. One source of this kind of argument is 'Glaucon's challenge' at the beginning of Book II of Plato's *Republic* (358e–62b) (Plato 2004).
43. On this connection, see Brüllmann (forthcoming).
44. In his accounts of Stoic appropriation (*oikeiōsis*), Cicero lays great stress on precisely this change: *Fin.* III.21–5, 62–6.
45. See Klein 2012: 58.
46. See Klein 2012 for this kind of argument and the relevant evidence.
47. I.e. how Socrates answers Glaucon's challenge.

2 Aquinas

Steven J. Jensen

The account of the natural law given by Thomas Aquinas has two claims to the title 'natural'. First, the basic precepts of the natural law are naturally known, that is, they are accessible to us by the nature of our human minds.[1] Second, the human good depends upon our nature.[2] Philosophical inquiry, for instance, is part of the human good because of the nature of our minds. If we had the minds of squirrels, then philosophical inquiry would be alien to the human good.

For Aquinas, these two aspects of the natural law are intimately linked by way of natural inclinations. To possess a true nature – and not merely some abstract mathematical 'nature' – is to move towards certain ends. This natural movement or impetus Aquinas calls a 'natural inclination', not to be confused with an inborn desire.[3] Aquinas' inclinations need not be desires in any literal sense. They are simply movements to an end inherent in a species. A tree has natural inclinations as much as a human being. The natural inclination to philosophical inquiry, for instance, is not some conscious longing to know the truth. Rather, it is the natural bent of the human mind to discover the truth. Whether or not individuals are born with some conscious desire to discover the truth, they are all born with minds that tend towards the truth.

Our natural good is nothing other than the completion or fulfilment of our natural inclinations. Just as a doctor is complete and good insofar as he realises his purpose of healing, so the eye and the power of sight are good insofar as they realise their natural tendency to the act of seeing. Our natural inclinations might be described as functions built into our very nature. Just as a pen has the function of writing and so is good insofar as it writes well, so also the power of reproduction has the function of bringing about new life, and the fulfilment of this function is a human good. While the pen is an artefact that does not have a function or impetus in itself, the power of reproduction is part of a natural being with an inherent movement towards various forms of fulfilment.

The good of a pen is different from the good of a knife because the 'nature' of the pen differs from the 'nature' of a knife. Likewise, because we have a human nature, rather than the nature of a grasshopper, we have certain goods that fulfil the inclinations that compose this nature. Consequently, our human good is indeed founded in our nature.

It is not difficult to see how these natural inclinations also underlie our natural knowledge. We need no argumentation to perceive that a good pen writes well and that a good eye sees well. When we understand the purpose of the pen, we also understand its first or primary good. Similarly, if we had no idea of the purpose or function of an eye, we would also have little idea of what a good eye is. By understanding its function, we immediately grasp its good.

We wish to show how Aquinas uses natural inclinations to resolve three difficulties that have plagued modern ethical theory. First, modern moral philosophy has had difficulty identifying the good. This difficulty is most evident in twentieth-century philosophy, beginning with G. E. Moore's claim that the good is a non-natural quality.[4] Various subjectivist accounts of the good followed Moore, such as emotivism and prescriptivism.[5] Finally, error theory has construed the good simply as an erroneous social construct.[6]

Second, modern moral philosophy has been unable to account for justice. On the one hand, consequentialism has adopted an aggregate good that is adverse to justice, since it subordinates the individual to a good that is not his own. On the other hand, in order to inoculate against the aggregate good, deontology has promoted the right thing to do, as opposed to the good thing to seek. As we will see, the true notion of justice relies not upon an aggregate good but upon shared goods, which derive from natural inclinations.

Third, modern ethical theory has failed to understand moral obligation. Common hypothetical 'ought-statements' begin with a conscious desire and command the means to attain it. If Clare wants to lose weight, for example, then she commands the hypothetical ought-statement, 'I ought to go on a diet'. These imperatives seem inadequate to capture moral obligation, since the agent can simply opt out of the command by changing her desires. Consequently, modern ethical theory has often sought moral obligation outside the domain of hypothetical imperatives. It has placed moral obligation in the domain of logic – reflected in Immanuel Kant's categorical imperative, and the consistency demands of prescriptivism – as if logical consistency demanded certain imperatives.[7]

Aquinas resolves all three of these difficulties by way of natural inclinations. We will consider each of these resolutions in turn. First, however, we must better understand what Aquinas means by natural inclinations.

INCLINATIONS

Aquinas himself says little concerning the role of natural inclinations within the natural law. Following Cicero, he provides three broad categories of inclination.[8] First, some inclinations are shared with all creatures, such as the inclination to preserve one's own being. Second, some inclinations are shared with animals, such as the inclination to sexual activity and the inclination to nurture offspring. Third, some inclinations are peculiar to human beings, such as the inclination to know the truth about God. Throughout Aquinas' corpus, we find scattered references to other natural inclinations, such as the natural inclination to set aside time for rest, or the natural inclination to offer sacrifice to some higher being.

Aquinas describes two different kinds of natural inclination: those that are conscious and those that are non-conscious.[9] In English, we are more apt to bestow the designation 'inclination' upon conscious inclinations (whether natural or otherwise), which are desires either of the emotions or of the will. When Kim desires pizza, for instance, she has a conscious inclination for pizza. We are apt to designate non-conscious inclinations by other names, such as 'tendencies' or 'aptitudes': a tree has a non-conscious inclination – a tendency or aptitude – to grow roots.

Human beings have both conscious and non-conscious inclinations. The conscious inclinations are obvious; the non-conscious inclinations less so. The tendency to heal wounds, for instance, is not a conscious inclination. Rather, it is a tendency that operates apart from any conscious desire of the person. Non-conscious inclinations should not be confused with Freudian 'unconscious' desires. Thomas is not Sigmund. Unconscious desires seem to be some sort of buried conscious desires. In contrast, non-conscious inclinations are found in trees, rocks, dogs and human beings.

Conscious inclinations are not themselves a kind of cognition. Rather, they are a movement or impetus to some end point. Nevertheless, they depend upon cognition.[10] Prior to conscious desire, we must first have some awareness that an object is good or bad. Before Kim can desire pizza, for instance, she must have some idea that pizza is good.

All three classes of natural inclination mentioned by Aquinas (those shared with all beings, those shared with animals and those peculiar to human beings) can include non-conscious inclinations. We might suppose that the natural inclination to know about God is a conscious inclination. In fact, Aquinas explicitly identifies it as a non-conscious inclination. Within the context of his discussion of the ultimate end, he says that the inclination to know God belongs to the intellect, not to the will:

> Therefore, if the human intellect knows the essence of some created effect but knows of God only that he exists, then the completion of that intellect does not yet attain simply to the first cause, but there remains in it a natural desire to seek this cause.[11]

This natural desire, says Thomas, remains *in the intellect*. Thomas is saying that the intellect itself – not the will or the emotions, where we find our conscious inclinations – moves out to a certain completion. In short, our minds, by their nature, have a tendency to knowledge, a tendency that is fully realised only with the knowledge of God. Upon this non-conscious inclination of the intellect follows a conscious inclination in the will to know the truth concerning God. First of all, however, our minds have moved out to this end by their very nature.

Likewise, Thomas says that the natural inclination to continue the species, as found in animals, is ultimately non-conscious:

> Those that do not have the power to maintain their individual existence forever, but only the power to preserve perpetually their existence according to the species, also naturally desire this perpetuation ... but they do so without knowledge, for the power of generation, which is ordered to this end, is prior to knowledge and not subject to it.[12]

Through the power of generation, then, animals are inclined to procreate and to bring their offspring to maturity. Any conscious emotional desire for sexual activity or for nurturing the young is derivative from this original non-conscious desire.

For Aquinas' natural law, non-conscious inclinations will prove to be more important than conscious inclinations, which will turn out to be derivative, always depending upon non-conscious inclinations.[13] The conscious inclinations of the will and of the emotions always depend upon some prior awareness of the good. Before Kim can consciously desire pizza, she must first be aware that pizza is in some manner good. Every conscious desire of the will, then, presupposes an initial awareness of the human good.

But from where does this awareness arise? Ultimately, it cannot arise from some conscious inclination. Before there can be a conscious inclination, there must first be some awareness of the good. But before there can be an awareness of the good, there must first be an awareness of an inclination, which is fulfilled by the good. Clearly, then, the initial inclination by which we know the good cannot itself be conscious. If Kenny is to desire health consciously, for instance, he must first recognise that health is good, that it fulfils some inclination. Certainly, health does fulfil his conscious desire for health, but the recognition of this desire could not possibly have given rise to the conscious desire in the first place.

We recognise the good of a pen (to write well) insofar as we perceive the pen as directed to some end. Absent this direction, the good itself ceases to be. Likewise, only insofar as we perceive human beings as moving to some end can we perceive a human good. This movement to an end, however, cannot be itself a conscious movement, at least not initially, because our conscious movements to an end presuppose that we have already perceived some human good. Underlying the human good, then, is the idea that human beings have non-conscious inclinations; human beings are moving towards some end point by their very nature.

Because modern philosophy has rejected non-conscious inclinations, it has been faced with the three difficulties mentioned above: the identity of the good has remained elusive, justice has proven an enigma, and moral obligation has become a puzzling special case. Aquinas' natural law account is not plagued by these difficulties precisely because he recognises the central role of non-conscious inclinations. Let us begin, then, by examining the role that non-conscious inclinations play in the identity of the good and our knowledge of it.

THE IDENTITY OF THE GOOD

As mentioned above, we recognise the good as the completion of some purpose or function.[14] We perceive that the good of an eye is to see well, for instance, because we recognise that an eye has the purpose of seeing. In the modern age, however, purpose is often relegated to conscious human desires. On this view, Clare may have the purpose of losing weight, but our eyes do not really have the purpose of seeing, for nature has no purposes.

We reject this conception of human beings as functional realities at no small price. When the natural end is lost, so will the human good be lost. Human beings will become like triangles. A triangle, since it is not a functional concept, has no good. Likewise, a human being that is mere stuff tossed about by the forces of nature, with no inherent movement to any end point, has no good.

If we cannot discover the good, we will create a good of our own. The possibilities for this fabricated good are limited. First, we might suppose that the good is a non-functional concept, a positive attribute applying to certain realities, somewhat as the colour green belongs to leaves. It may not be exactly like green, since 'good' (once divorced from its functional moorings) is a bit odd; perhaps it might be described as a 'non-natural' property. Second, we might suppose that the good is simply the correlate of conscious desires. The word 'good' is a way of expressing our liking for an object, or perhaps a way of recommending it to someone else. Finally, having despaired of the first two approaches, we might conclude that the 'good' is simply a fabrication of human society.

The first approach has been adopted by intuitionists of various sorts, and even by some who claim to be advancing an account of natural law.[15] The second approach has been adopted by emotivists, prescriptivists and the like.[16] The third approach is advanced by Friedrich Nietzsche and by error theory.[17] All three views reject a functional conception of the good. The first approach tries, but fails, to provide a substitute objective good.[18] The last two approaches concede that the good is relative to our conscious desires: we do not desire something because it is good; rather, something is good – or at least called 'good' – because we desire it.

Thomas never enters the debate between these three views because he recognises that the good is a functional concept. Furthermore, he recognises that human beings are indeed functional beings. Unlike triangles and squares, but like trees and worms, they have non-conscious tendencies to achieve certain ends. The good is an objective reality. Furthermore, our discovery of the good precedes our conscious desire for it. We are not aware of the good because we consciously desire it; rather, we desire an object because we are aware that it is good.

JUSTICE

Non-conscious natural inclinations have a second feature of great importance for the natural law: they concern a common or shared good.[19] This feature leads immediately to the precepts of the natural law that Aquinas considers most fundamental: we should love God above all else and we should love our neighbour as ourselves.[20] We might suppose that these two precepts arise from those natural inclinations peculiar to human beings, such as the inclinations to live in society and to know the truth about God.

While initially plausible, these correlations must be rejected. Lawrence Dewan has shown that the natural inclination to love God above all else is not peculiar to human beings.[21] It belongs to those inclinations common to all creatures. Similarly, not just human beings have an inclination to love those within their own species; all creatures do.

Throughout his career, Aquinas argues that the love of God above all else is natural to all creatures, even rocks and trees.[22] The love of God is a particular instance of a tendency towards the common or shared good. The hand naturally exposes itself for the sake of the whole body in order to deflect a blow to the head. This tendency reveals that, by nature, things seek not only their own private good; they seek a shared good beyond themselves. Since God is the highest shared good of all creation, Thomas concludes that all things must have a natural tendency towards God above all else:

> The universal good is God himself, and under this good is contained the good of angels, of human beings, and of every creature, since every creature, according to its essence, naturally belongs to God. Consequently, angels and human beings love God, with a natural love, more than they love themselves.[23]

A similar conclusion applies to the love of the members within the species. Even fire, Thomas says, 'loves' the good of fire in general, which is why fire tends to spread itself.[24] Likewise, one angel has a natural love for another angel and one human being has a natural love for another human being. Like the love of God, this love seems to be a particular instance of loving some shared good:

> Everything that is one with another, in genus or in species, is one by way of nature. Consequently, everything loves, with a natural love, that which is one with it according to species, insofar as it loves its very species. This natural love appears even in those things that lack knowledge, for fire has a natural inclination to spread to others its form, which is its good.[25]

According to Thomas, we love those that are similar to us.[26] Even fire 'loves' other fire based upon similarity. The importance of similarity, however, ultimately depends upon a union in some good:

> Union relates to love in three ways. One union is the cause of love ... For the love of others, it is a union of likeness. A second union is essentially the love itself, which is the union according to the bond of affection ... A third union is the effect of love, and this is the real union, which the lover seeks from the one loved.[27]

The good of the cellist within a symphony, for instance, is attained only together with others. In other cases, our good is realised more completely in union with others. Someone who is interested in studying horses, for instance, can do so on his own, but he can also do it with a friend, through the united activity of discussing horses, which completes the two together. We seek the good of others, then, insofar as we seek a united good. When others have a good similar to our own, we seek to share it with them.

We should not restrict this love for a shared human good to some particular natural inclinations, such as the inclination to nurture offspring and the inclination to live in society with others. These inclinations, no doubt, are immediately directed to some shared good. Other inclinations, such as the inclination to preserve one's own existence, immediately concern some individual good, but they ultimately refer to a shared good.[28] After all, our own good – including our own existence – is not solitary. It is good as shared with others. It is part of the good of the species. Similarly, the inclination of the intellect to know the truth is not an inclination to know the truth as a solitary individual; it is an inclination to know the truth together with others.

We must avoid a misunderstanding of the shared good. For a truly shared good, the good of an individual is found (at least in part) outside himself, that is, in others. It is not merely a shared means, useful for producing isolated individual goods. A band of thieves has a shared means. Like the members of the orchestra, they unite in an activity, such as robbing a bank, which they cannot realise individually. The good they seek, however, is not this united activity; rather, they seek a product of it, namely the money they will each get. The good sought, then, is ultimately private. Only the means of attaining it is shared.

For a true shared good, the good itself is possessed together. The good of playing symphonic music is not possessed by the cellist alone. It is possessed through an activity that belongs not only to herself but also to the other members of the orchestra. The completion of the cellist, then, is realised beyond herself. The goal of the union is not simply her own completion; it is 'our' completion.

Thomas is aware that we sometimes unite with others only for our personal gain and not for a truly shared good.[29] We can seek the good of society, for instance, simply so that we might have it for ourselves. A true love of society, however, seeks to preserve and increase the good for society itself.[30]

When we seek a good as shared, we seek it not simply insofar as it is possessed by ourselves; we seek it as possessed together with others. We desire that others have the good, as well as ourselves. At the heart of a shared good, then, is a love for those with whom we share the good. In short, the fundamental precept of the natural law, that we must love our neighbour as ourselves, follows upon the nature of the shared good.

In its turn, justice follows upon this fundamental precept. Thomas says, for instance, that the Golden Rule is a way of expressing the rule to love one's neighbour.[31] And Thomas cites the Golden Rule in order to justify the fundamental norm of justice, that we should give to others what is their due.[32]

The connection between love and justice is not difficult to see.[33] Often, of course, love goes beyond justice; nevertheless, justice is itself a kind of minimal requirement for love. When we love others, we seek their good. What is due to someone – that at which justice aims – is one particular good for that person. When we love others, then, we will be just towards them:

> Insofar as it is a special virtue, justice concerns the good under the formality of what is owed to one's neighbour. In this respect, it belongs to special justice to do good to one's neighbour under the formality of what is owed. Indeed, it belongs to general justice to do the good that is owed as ordered to the community or to God and to deny the opposite evil.[34]

Justice, then, is founded upon the love of others. Furthermore, as we have seen, the love of others is founded upon a shared good, to which we are directed by way of non-conscious inclinations. Absent such inclinations, then, justice – at least as Aquinas conceives it – must disappear.

The disappearance of justice is most evident in the modern ethical theory of consequentialism. On the face of it, consequentialism is directed to some kind of shared good, since it concerns the good of many. Consequentialism, however, has a distorted notion of the good of the group. Rather than a shared good, it seeks an aggregate good; it seeks the sum total of each individual's private good. Such a good is not shared. If Anna has $5000, Louis has $3000 and Clare has $1000, then who has the sum total of $9000? Not any one of the individuals. Nor again does the whole group possess the $9000, for there is no united possession. Ultimately, the sum total belongs to no one.[35] In contrast, the members of the orchestra play symphonic music precisely as united; the united playing belongs to everyone within the orchestra.

Because consequentialism aims at a sum total rather than a shared good, it has little concern for justice. If the sum total can be increased by directly harming one individual, then so be it. We can, then, kill, torture, rob, lie or otherwise harm others, as long as we thereby increase the aggregate good that belongs to no one. The justice that Aquinas conceives, in which we do good to others and avoid their evil, has entirely disappeared. So has love, which seeks to share the good with others. In contrast, consequentialism aims at the good of no one.

In an attempt to reject consequentialism and restore justice, deontological approaches to ethics have supposed that justice arises from a defence of individual goods – or perhaps 'rights' rather than goods – in opposition to the good of the group. By contrast, for Aquinas justice can be found in the good of the individual precisely as belonging to the group; the shared good is sought insofar as it is possessed by each member. Aquinas has no need – as does deontology – to promote the right thing to do as in some manner opposed to the good; he has no need to promote the good of individuals in opposition to the good of the whole.

Within consequentialism, the individual plays the moral role of a 'producer', that is, he must produce the good. In contrast, for the shared good, the individual plays the role of a possessing part. The faithful consequentialist must direct himself to a product distinct from himself. In contrast, a member of the shared good must direct himself, and his own good, to a union with others, who possess the good with him. No doubt, he will sometimes be producing goods, but that is not his primary role. His primary role is to possess the good with others. His fundamental order to the good, then, is not production; rather, it is relation, chiefly a relation of union. He does not wish to produce a good that is not his own; rather, he wishes his good to belong to others, and he wishes their good to belong to him.

As indicated above, this notion of the love for others, and justice within love, rests upon non-conscious natural inclinations to a shared good. The human good is shared precisely because individuals – by their nature – are moving beyond themselves to a good possessed together with others. In the modern era, with the denial of non-conscious inclinations, justice has lost its foundations. Absent non-conscious inclinations, the shared good quickly dissolves and the order of justice with it.

As we have seen, when the functional character of the good is denied, the objective character of the good can be affirmed only at a price. The very nature of the good itself changes. It becomes some positive quality of things. The upshot, almost invariably, is that the good is perceived as good – however dimly – simply insofar as it exists. No longer is the good a relational concept, involving one thing completing another. Rather, the good is an absolute concept, belonging to things simply as they exist. Consequentialism follows naturally. Since the good is good simply by existing, all that matters is bringing more good into existence. Any notion of a shared good disappears, to be replaced with the consequentialist aggregate of goods. Deontological attempts to restore justice presume the same notion of the good: precisely because the good tends to be an aggregate, it is perceived as opposed to the individual; justice, then, demands something to counteract the aggregating tendency of the good.

On the other hand, the subjective approach to the good, which claims that the term 'good' is used simply to express a person's attitude, tends towards egoism. If one begins with conscious desires, then one will conclude with the satisfaction of desires, which is a personal fulfilment, not a shared good. Of course, human beings do have conscious desires for the good of others. According to Aquinas, however, these desires are rooted in non-conscious natural inclinations. The subjective approach, however, consistently eschews non-conscious inclinations. Consequently, it is left with only the satisfaction of personal desires entirely disconnected from a shared good.

When non-conscious natural inclinations to a shared good are denied, then few options remain. First, the good might be absolute, in which case the shared good is replaced with the aggregate good, which good gives rise, if accepted, to consequentialism or, if rejected, to deontology. Second, the good might be perceived as relative to our desires, in which case – by all rights – we have a Nietzschean will to power.[36] We do not desire things because they are good; rather, they are good, or at least called good, because we desire them. As such, the shared good atrophies; my desire and my satisfaction become paramount.

Aquinas avoids these options through the primacy of non-conscious inclinations. The good is not some natural or non-natural attribute of things, to be desired just for its existence. Rather, the good is what completes an individual. Nothing restricts this completion to the individual himself. Non-conscious inclinations are movements to a certain end, but the end need not be simply the end of the individual. It might be the end of a union of individuals. The demands of justice are not so mysterious once we realise that our good belongs to others, that our own good is realised in the good of others.

The move from natural inclinations to the fundamental precepts of the natural law, then, is not a black box.[37] We should love God and we should love others. From these precepts flow the norms of justice. These primary precepts are themselves, however, founded upon non-conscious natural inclinations. There is not some special inclination to love God and another special inclination to love others. Rather, each and every inclination moves to a shared good, shared both with God and with other human beings.

The move from non-conscious natural inclinations to the love of others is mysterious only because we have rejected the functional nature of human beings. As such, modern ethical theories have conceived a distorted notion of the good of the group. This distorted good is not the completion of the individual; rather, it is an independently existing good that belongs to no one.

OBLIGATION

Natural inclinations resolve, for Aquinas, another difficulty that has plagued modern ethical theory, namely the problem of obligation.[38] The problem, as laid out by Immanuel Kant, concerns two different kinds of 'imperatives', or ought-statements. First, hypothetical imperatives begin with some end desired and then command the means to attain the end. If Clare desires the end of losing weight, for instance, she might then command herself to the means of going on a diet. These imperatives, however, appear inadequate as a grounding for morality, since their force derives from the desire for the end. The person can opt out of the imperative simply by changing her desires. If Clare finds the diet unpleasant, then she can release herself from the imperative simply by abandoning her desire to lose weight. In contrast, the force of morality seems absolute. A person cannot simply opt out of morality by changing her desires.

Consequently, Kant devised a second kind of imperative, the categorical imperative, which derives its force simply from the law and not from some end desired. Since the law applies to everyone, the most essential feature of the categorical imperative is its universality. An agent must will that his rule of behaviour apply to everyone.

Aquinas knew nothing of categorical imperatives. Indeed, he clearly indicates that the obligatory force of the law derives from necessity in relation to some end:

> A precept of the law, since it is obligatory, concerns that which ought to be done. That something ought to be done, however, arises from the necessity of some end. Clearly, then, it belongs to the very notion of a precept that it implies an order to an end, insofar as that which is commanded is necessary or expedient for the end.[39]

Should we conclude that Aquinas thought the natural law derives its force from a hypothetical imperative? This conclusion would be unwarranted. Once again, Aquinas' doctrine of natural inclinations allows him to avoid a false dichotomy. The two imperatives proposed by Kant do not exhaust the possibilities, at least if there are non-conscious natural inclinations. These inclinations provide an end from which the command for some means might be derived. Given the end of discovering the truth, for instance, we might conclude (given individual limitations) that human beings ought to work together for this goal.

Such an imperative, one might conclude, fits under Kant's 'hypothetical' imperative, since it derives its force from an end. This conclusion, however, would be hasty. Kant's 'hypothetical' imperatives derive their force from an end that is consciously desired. The natural ends that Aquinas discusses are not consciously desired, at least not initially. Rather, by his nature, without any awareness, the person is tending towards these ends. It might be better, then, to describe all commands based upon some end as 'conditional', and then divide conditional imperatives into 'Kantian hypothetical imperatives' and 'nature-based conditional imperatives'. The former are based upon a conscious desire for some end. The latter are based upon an end that applies to some nature, even apart from conscious desire.

Nature-based imperatives share one feature with hypothetical imperatives and one feature with the categorical imperative. Like hypothetical imperatives, they derive their force from some end. Like the categorical imperative, an individual cannot opt out of them by changing his desires. A nature-based imperative has its force from the end of some non-conscious inclination. Changing one's conscious desires, then, does not remove the force of the non-conscious inclination.

As we have seen, non-conscious natural inclinations are directed to a shared good. This feature provides a further source of obligation for nature-based imperatives. An end that belongs simply to an individual seems to have less force than an end that involves other people. A person who needs to get a job to provide for his own well-being, with no concern for anyone else, has less reason to seek a job than someone who needs to provide for his family. Their good – and not simply his own personal good – makes demands upon him.

This sense of obligation is increased when the determination of the means is made by the community or by those in charge of the shared good. Consider a simple matter such as driving on the right or left side of the road. Given the end of safe driving, everyone must drive on the same side of the road. Whether that side be the left or the right is largely indifferent, but that everybody should follow one rule is paramount. Consequently, those in charge of the shared good determine one side or the other. Once they determine that everyone must drive on the left side, then everyone is bound to follow this rule. This case provides a stronger sense of obligation for two reasons. First, the end involved is a shared good (safety in driving). Second, each individual must submit to a determination of the means made by others. Still, the obligation is conditional. If the individual does not have the end of safe driving, then the means does not apply to him.

Aquinas discusses the case of sexual relations outside of marriage. The end of the sexual act is the generation and education of offspring, which is usually obtained best of all within the context of marriage. Nevertheless, this end can be achieved, in some cases, outside the context of marriage. Nevertheless, the individual does not have the authority to make this determination, just as the individual cannot decide for himself on which side of the road he should drive:

> The act of generation is ordered to the good of the species, which is a common good. While the private good is subject to the directive of each person, the common good must be ordered by law ... Therefore, to determine in what way the act of generation is to be performed does not pertain to just anyone, but to the legislator, whose care it is to direct the begetting of children. Although in some cases of fornication it might happen that the intention of nature with respect to the generation and education of children is salvaged, nevertheless the act is of itself disordered and a mortal sin, for the law does not consider what might happen in some cases but what happens usually.[40]

If the shared good is a good of nature, then it might happen that nature itself makes the determination. According to nature, for instance, the power of reproduction must be used between male and female. Even if (given modern technology) an individual thinks that he can accomplish the end apart from the union of male and female, he is nevertheless bound by the determination made by nature.

Kant might protest that these nature-based imperatives have no leverage upon an individual's will. The person, for instance, has a non-conscious natural inclination to seek the truth; the shared end of this inclination (we have argued above) conditionally commands working together. Such reasoning, Kant might suggest, is pointless. The resulting imperative is addressed to a non-conscious inclination. It is not addressed to any desire of the will. Consequently, the person might choose to desire this shared good or he might choose otherwise. If he chooses to desire it, then the imperative has force for his will. If he does not desire the shared end, then the imperative concerns his nature alone and has no effect upon his conscious desires and choices. These nature-based imperatives, then, do not command human actions, or at least they need not. As such, they have nothing to do with morality.

In response to this objection, Aquinas might begin by distinguishing between those of good will, who desire the shared good of nature, and those of ill will, who desire some personal good in preference to the shared good of nature. For members of the first group, the conditional imperative of nature does have force for their wills. Those of good will desire the end of nature, and hence they conditionally desire whatever means are needed for this end. Are those with good will *obliged* to follow nature-based imperatives? Not in a strict sense of obligation. Rather, they *voluntarily* desire to follow this imperative. Their wills do take the nature-based imperative as a standard of action, and in that sense their wills are subject to it. They are not subject to it, however, by a kind of external force; rather, they desire the standard of nature-based imperatives.

In contrast, those of ill will are subject to nature-based imperatives by way of force. They are led to follow the imperative against their will:

> Someone can be said to be subject to the law as the one coerced is to the one who coerces. In this manner, virtuous and just men are not subject to the law but only evil men, for what is coerced and violent is contrary to the will. The will of those who are good, however, is in agreement with the law, while the will of those who are evil is in

> opposition to it. In this manner, good men are not subject to the law but only those who are evil.[41]

Nevertheless, even for those of ill will, the force of this imperative is conditional. Indeed, it is conditional on the removal of the shared good to which the non-conscious inclinations direct, for those who exclude themselves from the order to the shared good will lose this shared good, as is only fitting.

In what way, then, does the imperative exert force upon an evil will? After all, the person who rejects the order to the shared good does so precisely because he no longer cares to attain the shared good. The thief, for example, steals not because he thinks he has discovered a better way to attain the shared good; rather, he steals because he prefers his private good to the shared good. It would seem, then, that the threat to remove the shared good will carry no weight with him.

When a robber wishes to exert force upon the will of his victim, he threatens to remove a good desired by the victim. He threatens, for example, to kill the victim unless he hands over the money. The conditional, 'Hand over your money, if you want to live', carries force only for the person who wants to live.

Likewise, the moral law – indeed, all law – imposes a conditional necessity through an act of command: 'Conditional necessity is imposed upon the will through an action. The action by which the will is moved, however, is the command of a ruler or governor'.[42] Thomas explains that conditional necessity is, 'from the supposition of an end, as when the necessity is imposed upon someone such that if he does not act in a certain way then he will not get his reward', which 'can be imposed upon the will, such that it is necessary to choose something if it is required to attain a certain good or to avoid a certain evil'.[43]

The law imposes necessity, then, by threatening to remove the shared good from those who would oppose its order. Those who oppose its order, however, are precisely those who no longer desire the shared good. The conditional, 'If you disobey the law, then you will lose the shared good', seems to carry no force. Those of good will willingly follow the law, so they need no threat to bind them to it. Those of ill will, however, find the threat irrelevant, given their desires.

Nevertheless, the removal of the shared good still carries force for those of ill will. Typically, the person of ill will desires what in fact is the shared good; he just desires it as a private good. Possessions and the use of possessions are shared goods for society. The thief desires these goods, but he does not desire them for others, as he should; rather, he desires them solely for himself. The removal of the shared goods, then, is also the removal of what the thief desires as a private good. Similarly, our freedom is a shared good, but the thief desires it not for others but only for himself. The removal of this good – through a prison sentence – is also the removal of what the thief desires as a private good.

The threat of the law, then, has binding force upon those of ill will. It provides a hypothetical imperative: 'Follow the order of the law, if you want the shared good'. This imperative has force for those of ill will because they do indeed desire the shared good, although they desire it not as shared.

Often, of course, the law has binding force upon those of imperfect good will. These people do desire to follow the law because they desire the shared good. When presented with an opportunity to steal \$100, they find the idea repugnant because they have a true desire for the good of the owner of the money. Their desire, however, is imperfect. They also desire possessions simply for themselves. As they struggle between these conflicting desires, the conditional imperative of the law – 'If you want your freedom, then you should not steal' – may restrain their selfish impulses. The law weakens the selfish impulse by way of another selfish impulse, thereby strengthening the good desire.

When the modern era abandoned the idea of non-conscious inclinations, it was forced to construct a new notion of obligation. Absent non-conscious inclinations, every end must be the end of some conscious inclination. Every conditional ought-statement, then, must concern some conscious desire; each must take the form of a Kantian hypothetical imperative: 'if you desire this end, then you must pursue this means'. These ought-statements, however, appear to have leverage over the person only so long as he desires the end.

Having abandoned non-conscious inclinations, then, the modern era might try to found the obligatory force of morality in two ways. First, it may claim that some conscious desires are always present, so that an individual cannot escape the ought-statements derived from them. Perhaps, for instance, each person has a natural benevolence, by which he desires the greater good of the multitude. This supposition, however, is dubious. Few individuals, if any, seem to desire an accumulation of goods. A miser desires to accumulate money for himself; he does not desire the mere existence of an accumulation of money.

When this first approach is found wanting, then some special moral obligation must be created. It cannot be hypothetical, since all hypothetical ought-statements are based upon an individual's arbitrary desires. Furthermore, it cannot rely upon the shared good, since the shared good has been lost with the abandonment of non-conscious inclinations. The result, it seems, must be some form of obligation that is separated from the good. The law – as opposed to the good – must carry obligatory force.

Modern notions of moral obligation follow upon the denial of non-conscious inclinations. When these inclinations are granted, they supply ends – ultimately, human fulfilment – from which conditional ought-statements may be derived. Furthermore, since these non-conscious inclinations concern shared goods, the community can remove the shared good from those who refuse to abide by these ought-statements. This removal of the shared good is tied inevitably to the removal of some consciously desired private good, so that the force of the non-conscious inclinations carries over to a person's conscious desires.

Absent non-conscious desires, every conditional ought-statement must be based upon fickle conscious desires. Without nature-based ought-statements, a new sort of ought-statement must take their place, which must take its force from the lawgiver, independently of the good. And if the idea of an external lawgiver is rejected, then the individual must give the law to himself by a kind of Kantian autonomy.

CONCLUSION

Non-conscious inclinations play a central role in Aquinas' account of natural law. They also spare him several difficulties faced by modern moral philosophy. He avoids the oddity of a good that is a 'non-natural' attribute, yet he maintains an objective account of the human good. He is not forced to swing between, on the one hand, a consequentialist aggregate good that destroys justice and, on the other hand, a deontological emphasis upon individual rights. Rather, he can rely upon a human shared good, which naturally gives birth to justice. Finally, Aquinas can have conditional ought-statements that derive their force not simply from the personal desire of the individual; rather, they derive their force from the nature of the objective good, which is not an aggregate good but a good to be possessed and shared with others.

The whole idea of non-conscious inclinations is, of course, none other than natural teleology. Aquinas' natural law, then, is founded firmly upon Aristotelian natural teleology. The modern age has largely abandoned any notion of teleology in nature. The impact of this shift in thought bears immediately upon ethics and political thought. Aquinas' unique account of natural law fits within no modern categories, precisely because modern ethical theory views human beings as devoid of an inherent directedness to some completion.

NOTES

1. Aquinas 1882: I-II, 94, 2.
2. Aquinas 1882: I-II, 71, 1.
3. Aquinas 1970: 22, 1.
4. Most notably Moore 2005.
5. For example, Ayer 2014; Stevenson 1979; Hare 2013.
6. For example, Mackie 1990.
7. See, for instance, Hare 2013.
8. Aquinas 1882: I-II, 94, 2.
9. See Aquinas 1882: I, 59, 1; I, 80, 1; and I-II, 26, 1.
10. Aquinas 1882: I-II, 26, 1; I-II, 27, 2.
11. Aquinas 1882: I-II, 3, 8. See also Aquinas 1918: III, 25, 7.
12. Aquinas 1918: II, cap. 55, n. 13, v. 13, 395.
13. Unfortunately, the role of non-conscious inclinations within Aquinas' natural law account has not always been recognised by contemporary commentators. Often, only conscious inclinations are considered, such as inclinations of the emotions. See, for instance, Ashmore 1975: 77–8; Harris 1983: 117–19; Finnis 1980: 64–9; Rhonheimer 2008: 115; Grisez 1965: 180; Matava 2011: 323; Lee 1997: 572; Lombardo 2011: 114–17; Hayden 1990: 133–5.
14. For a more complete treatment of the good and its relation to function, see Jensen 2015: 61–84.
15. For consequentialists, see Sidgwick 2012 and Moore 2005. So-called new natural law theorists eschew the label 'intuitionism', but they do present a knowledge of the good that seems to be built into practical reason. See, for instance, Grisez 1965, 1987; Finnis 1980, 1983.
16. See Ayer 2014; Hare 2013.
17. See Mackie 1990.
18. For an account of the failure, see Geach 1956; MacIntyre 1984: 6–22; Mackie 1990; Almotahari and Hosein 2015.
19. For an insightful discussion of the shared good, see de Koninck 1943.
20. Aquinas 1882: I-II, 100, 3, ad 1. For a good discussion, see Smith 2011.
21. Dewan 1986: 115–17; see also Dewan 2007: 238.
22. See Aquinas 1929: II, d. 3, q. 4, a. 1; III, d. 29, q. 1, a. 3; Aquinas 1882: I, 60, 5; I-II, 109, 3; II-II, 26, article 3; Aquinas 1996: I, q. 4, a. 3. The extensive literature on the

natural love of God includes the following: Rousselot 1908; Gagnebet 1948; Stevens 1953; Gallagher 1999; Osborne 2005: 69–112; Sullivan 2014.

23. Aquinas 1882: I, q. 60, a. 5.
24. Aquinas 1882: I, 60, 4.
25. Aquinas 1882: I, 60, 4.
26. Aquinas 1882: I-II, 27, 3.
27. Aquinas 1882: I-II, q. 28, a. 1, ad 2.
28. See Dewan 1986: 115–17; Dewan 2007: 238.
29. See de Koninck 1943: 17–18.
30. Aquinas 1925: *De Caritate*, a. 2.
31. Aquinas 1882: I-II, 99, 1, ad 3.
32. Aquinas 1996: v, q. 9, a. 1.
33. See, for instance, Smith 2011; McInerny 1992.
34. Aquinas 1882: II-II, 79, 1.
35. Korsgaard 2011.
36. Nietzsche would claim that even the desire for self-destruction is the assertion of a will upon the rest of the world. Perhaps it shows one's superiority or contempt for the world. As I read Nietzsche, all desires instantiate a will to power, even the desires embodied in so-called 'slave morality'.
37. A black box is a device, system or object which can be viewed in terms of its inputs and outputs (or transfer characteristics), without any knowledge of its internal workings.
38. For a more complete treatment of Aquinas' account of obligation, see Jensen 2015: 126–74.
39. Aquinas 1882: I-II, 99, 1.
40. Aquinas 1982: 15, 2, ad 12, 276, 320–37.
41. Aquinas 1882: I-II, 96, 5.
42. Aquinas 1970: 58–70.
43. Aquinas 1970: 47–57.

3 Grotius and Pufendorf

Johan Olsthoorn*

During the seventeenth century, natural law theory became institutionalised as the leading approach to moral philosophy in Protestant Europe.[1] Hugo Grotius (1583–1645) and Samuel Pufendorf (1632–94) were undoubtedly the most influential natural law theorists of the period. Their books went through hundreds of editions and were translated into most European languages. Grotius was widely praised for having been 'the first to have systematised a science that, prior to him, was nothing but confusion ... and impenetrable darkness'.[2] His systematisation of natural law – the science in question – did not consist in deducing moral rules from uncontested definitions and indisputable axioms. His published writings on natural law took no such 'geometric' approach. Rather, in a move mirroring Hans Kelsen's *Reine Rechtslehre*, Grotius purportedly pioneered a 'pure' science of natural law by sharply distinguishing it from divine positive law (i.e. revelation), civil (i.e. Roman) law, and the voluntary law of nations. Grotius, in other words, was said to have turned natural law into ethics proper.[3]

This chapter will reconstruct the structure and philosophical presuppositions of the natural law ethics of Grotius and Pufendorf. Readers interested in the legal and political theories which the two erected upon the back of their natural law doctrines, or in other early modern natural lawyers, are advised to look elsewhere. The natural law theories of Grotius and Pufendorf are often discussed in tandem; indeed, Pufendorf is frequently portrayed as further developing and amending Grotius' basic ideas. The two thinkers indeed strikingly employed the same juridical language in their moral and political philosophy. Moreover, they shared key methodological assumptions, including concerning the importance of divorcing natural law from revealed theology. Both held that natural law is based on human nature and that its precepts require sociality above all: humans ought to perform those acts conducive to a peaceful society and omit those that undermine one. As Pufendorf wrote, natural law 'is so exactly fitted to suit with the Rational and Social Nature of Man, that Human Kind cannot maintain an honest and a peaceful Fellowship without it'.[4] Notwithstanding these many commonalities, this chapter unearths some fundamental philosophical disagreements between the two thinkers, especially concerning meta-ethics.[5] By highlighting and analysing these disagreements, I hope to give some impression of the richness and diversity of ethical thinking in the early modern natural law tradition. This chapter discusses how Grotius and Pufendorf conceived of the interrelations of natural law with, in turn, theology; human nature; natural morality; and rights and justice.

NATURAL LAW AND NATURAL THEOLOGY

It has been suggested that Grotius and Pufendorf developed a minimalist natural law theory in response to the confessional strife plaguing Europe. The problem the two purportedly faced would have been akin to that troubling the later John Rawls: how to arrive at a shared moral framework that allows settlement of disputes over rights between opposing parties of different creeds and convictions. Rather than a free-standing overlapping consensus, Grotius and Pufendorf would have opted for a minimalist morality, grounded in values no one could reasonably reject: self-preservation and peace.[6] If this was indeed their project, then it was not wholly successful. Pufendorf himself criticised Grotius for adding to ethics 'so much that deviates from our true religion'.[7] The Lutheran, we will see, took offence at both the contents of Grotius' natural law doctrine and its meta-ethical presuppositions. Despite avowing to 'abolish in natural law all theological controversies, and adapt it to the understanding of the whole of mankind, who disagreed in many different ways over religion',[8] Pufendorf was likewise constantly embroiled in theological disputes.

To be sure, the notion that Grotius and Pufendorf 'secularised' natural law ethics by disentangling it from theology is liable to be misunderstood. While revelation was jettisoned from natural law, natural theology most certainly was not.[9] Theological principles purportedly knowable by natural reason continued to be fundamental to their natural law ethics. Both Grotius and Pufendorf insisted, for a start, that the existence and providence of God is rationally demonstrable.[10] Pufendorf's textbook on natural law (*De Officio*) contained an entire chapter on natural religion and natural law duties owed to God.[11] These duties included both speculative truths concerning the nature and attributes of God as discoverable by reason, and practical prescriptions concerning the proper ways of worshipping him. Pufendorf controversially confined the domain of natural law theory to 'within the orbit of this life', the immortality of the soul and the existence of otherworldly bliss and punishment being knowable by revelation alone.[12] Leibniz severely chastised Pufendorf for this, insisting that the immortality of the soul and the reality of divine judgement are demonstrable by natural reason.[13] Leibniz's criticisms, it is worth noting, accepted Pufendorf's categorical demarcation of natural law from revealed truth and were thus internal to his project of restricting ethics to what can be known by unaided reason. As the bounds of natural theology were hotly disputed in the period, accusations of impiety continued unabated.

A divine lawgiver was pivotal within Pufendorf's ethics – yet not within those of Grotius. The material content of natural law, both held, can be discovered by reflecting on the human predicament – especially our inclination to self-preservation, quarrelsomeness and mutual dependency. But natural law would have no more force than doctor's orders, Pufendorf insisted, were we to stop there.[14] For the natural dictates of reason to have 'the Force and Authority of Laws, there is a necessity of supposing that there is a God … in as much as all Law supposes a Superior Power'.[15] Grotius had earlier emphasised that law is a matter of strict obligation. 'I say, obliging: for Counsels, and such other Precepts, which, however honest and reasonable they be, lay us under no Obligation, come not under this Notion of Law'.[16] Yet the Dutchman employed a rather different conception of moral obligation, and hence of law, than his Saxon successor. Under the purview of natural law come only those actions which are 'in themselves, or in their own Nature, Obligatory and Unlawful'.[17] This is what differentiates natural law from positive law, whose issuer renders morally optional actions mandatory or forbidden by sheer force of will. Divine commands are hence not required to render natural law obligatory. Grotius' naturalistic conception of moral obligation thus renders 'God in effect … dispensable' to natural law.[18] Hence the significance of the well-known *etiamsi daremus*.

Pufendorf firmly condemned this last 'impious' contention of Grotius, that natural law would have a degree of validity 'even if we grant [*etiamsi daremus*], what without the greatest Wickedness cannot be granted, that there is no God, or that he takes no Care of human Affairs'.[19] Grotius would have failed to grasp that law essentially involves binding obligations imposed by a superior authority. 'Law is a decree by which a superior obliges one who is subject to him to conform his actions to the superior's prescript'.[20] Law is not a matter of agreements or useful conventions; for this reason, the voluntary law of nations is an oxymoron.[21] Pufendorf's doctrine that 'law' presupposes a lawgiver has no parallel in Grotius. It is, however, found in Hobbes. The English philosopher had claimed that the dictates of right reason are properly called laws 'in so far as [they] have been legislated by God in the holy scriptures'.[22] Pufendorf strenuously denied that last clause:

> The Laws of Nature would have a full and perfect Power of binding Men, altho' GOD ALMIGHTY had never proposed them in his Reveal'd Word. For Man was under Obligation to obey his Creator, by what means soever he was pleas'd to convey to him, the Knowledge of his Will. Nor was there any absolute necessity of a particular Revelation to make a Rational Creature sensible of his Subjection to the supreme Author and Governour of things.[23]

The existence of natural law and its divine authorship can be proven by natural reason.[24] Natural theology is thus essential, on Pufendorf's account, for natural law formally to be 'law'.

Their foundational disagreement over the meaning of 'law' in turn informs their diverging views on the content of natural law. Grotius' and Pufendorf's natural law doctrines are often equated with the principle of sociality. For Grotius, the laws of nature are those norms consequent to human rational and sociable nature: 'the Law of Nature ... is the Dictate of a reasonable and sociable Nature, considered as such'.[25] It requires performance only of those intrinsically good actions strictly necessary for the maintenance of orderly society, and omission of those intrinsically evil ones incompatible with it. Grotius' magnum opus, *De Jure Belli ac Pacis* (hereinafter *DJBP*), contains a brief discussion of deviations from the 'true religion' that warrant punishment by humans. It does so without mentioning that such impieties transgress natural law (except perhaps indirectly, by endangering human society – laws would presumably not be kept without fear of a deity).[26] For Pufendorf, by contrast, natural law concerns *all* duties imposed by God and knowable by natural reason. It includes duties to the deity and to oneself; and these spring from other principles than sociality – gratitude and a mixture of religion and sociality, respectively.[27]

Grotius and Pufendorf held conflicting views on the content of natural law even insofar as it concerns what maintains and promotes human society. For Grotius, the principle of sociality directly determines what is by nature morally good and evil, mandatory and illicit. Pufendorf's theory includes the additional step of finding 'signs' of God's legislative will in the present world, since for him natural law obligations derive from divine commands; these obligations are more than simply indications of what is necessary for upholding orderly society. Assuming that God is benevolent and we are needy and prone to conflict, what actions can we reasonably infer He commands us to perform? Not merely those actions, as we will see, without which human society is undermined.

NATURAL LAW AND HUMAN NATURE

In his juvenile works, Grotius equated natural law with the divine plan discovered in nature. According to *Mare Liberum*, the wide ocean and shifting winds, rendering the earth 'navigable on every side round about', and the uneven scattering of resources among nations together attest that rights of trade and free passage belong to natural law.[28] Geographical and meteorological facts no longer evince what natural law requires in Grotius' mature works. *DJBP* explicitly grounds natural law in principles of human nature alone.[29]

This raises two questions. The most salient one concerns the underlying anthropology at issue. What views of human nature did Grotius and Pufendorf hold and what consequences did this have for the content of their natural law doctrines? Much has been written on their respective conceptions of human sociability, generally in contradistinction to Hobbes.[30] Less attention is given to the question of how anthropological data can establish moral facts. That humans have such and such a nature does not entail that they ought therefore to act thus-and-so. Moreover, that certain things are naturally good for humans (given our make-up) does not make them morally good.

In the *Prolegomena* to *DJBP*, Grotius has a moral sceptic proclaim: 'Nature prompts all Men, and in general all Animals, to seek their own particular advantage'. Had this been true, then natural law would have been either non-existent or extreme folly 'because it engages us to procure the Good of others, to our own Prejudice'.[31] The sceptical challenge presupposes a traditional conception of moral goodness as somehow including the common good. In response, Grotius accused the sceptic of having a faulty view of human nature. Transcending a narrow, beastly clinging to self-interest, the human being has a 'Desire of Society, that is, a certain Inclination to live with those of his own Kind . . . peaceably, and in a Community regulated according to the best of his Understanding'.[32] The unique human capacities to follow general rules, required for grasping obligations, and of speech attest to our sociable nature. Natural law is grounded in 'Sociability . . . or this Care of maintaining Society in a Manner conformable to the Light of human Understanding'.[33]

Grotius did not even consider the thought that private advantage can be constitutive of moral goodness (*honestas*). Closely following Cicero's analysis of *oikeiosis* in *De Finibus* III.16–23, Grotius declared that humans by nature love themselves and seek to preserve themselves. Right reason, tracking moral goodness and virtue, is normatively prior to such self-love, albeit ontologically secondary. (Humans are animals first and reasonable creatures second.) 'Right Reason should still be dearer to us than that natural Instinct'.[34] Like the ancient Stoics, Grotius stipulated that right reason manifests what is truly good and evil for the kind of creatures we are – rational and sociable: 'Now such is the Evil of some Actions, compared with a Nature guided by right Reason'.[35]

After Hobbes' scathing attack on the 'superficial view' that 'Man is an animal born fit for Society', Pufendorf could not simply restate Grotius' position.[36] While not entirely unsympathetic to Hobbes' anthropology, Pufendorf firmly dismissed the Englishman's normative conclusions. Humans are indeed naturally inclined to love themselves predominantly, and to put their own advantage first; and natural law, as the law of human nature, takes this fact into account. Yet Hobbes was wrong to deduce the laws of nature 'from the Principle of Self-preservation', if only because a liberty-right cannot conceivably ground moral duties in the same agent.[37] Elaborate qualifications of the various senses of human sociability and the conditions obtaining in real and hypothetical states of nature notwithstanding, Pufendorf endorsed the basic imperative of sociality much like Grotius. Unlike that of Grotius and Hobbes, however, Pufendorf's analysis of human nature was embedded within natural theology – even if his focus was explicitly on fallen man.[38] His objective, in other words, was less to establish directly what is right and good for us, than to search for clues of a divine legislative will.

While Hobbes had argued that the human propensity to cause trouble mandates instituting a civil lawgiver, forcing rabble-rousers to fall in line, Pufendorf regarded the same quarrelsome nature as evidence of the existence of natural laws, explicating the conditions of harmonious living. As weak and dependent creatures, humans rely on society and mutual aid to flourish. As peaceful society cannot exist without laws constraining pride and greed, a benevolent God must have ordained such laws.[39] The unique human capacities of rational reflection, speech and conscience, given to us by God, would moreover be pointless had we stuck to 'a Lawless, a Brutal and an Unsociable Life'.[40] Pufendorf agreed with Grotius and the Stoics that self-love is the first principle of nature in a developmental sense only: 'Man is by Nature sooner sensible of the Love he bears towards himself, than of that which he bears towards others'.[41] Not self-love but sociability should be the rule of our actions. Sociability is not at odds, however, with self-love properly understood: we need the help of others to thrive and survive, and their support is best procured by constant benevolence.[42]

From such empirical observations and premises of divine direction to and concern about human well-being, Pufendorf deduced the following Fundamental Law of Nature:

> Now that such a Creature may be preserv'd and supported, and may enjoy the Good things attending his Condition of Life, it is necessary that he be *Social*, that is, that he unite himself to those of his own Species, and in such a Manner regulate his Behaviour towards them, as that they may have no fair reason to do him harm, but rather incline to promote his Interests, and to secure his Rights and Concerns. This then will appear a Fundamental Law of Nature, *Every Man ought, as far as in him lies, to promote and preserve a peaceful Sociableness with others, agreeable to the main End and Disposition of [the] Human Race in General.*[43]

The demands of natural law focus on conduct rather than cultivation of character; virtues and vices play a minor role in Grotius' and Pufendorf's ethics.[44] For Grotius, natural law merely requires those actions necessary for upholding orderly society. Pufendorf's law of nature is more extensive and demanding: 'all Actions which necessarily conduce to this mutual Sociableness are commanded by the Law of Nature, and all those on the contrary which tend to its Disturbance or Dissolution, are forbidden'.[45] Besides prohibiting harming anyone in their goods or person, natural law mandates 'the real Practice of mutual Good' inasmuch as we can.[46] Benevolence requires both discrete acts of charity and generally contributing productively to society. Monks, 'who in a lubberly Laziness, consume the Fruits of other Mens honest Labour', contravene this last requirement.[47] Rights of innocent use and free passage, which for Grotius are conventional restrictions on private property, are correlates of natural law duties in Pufendorf.[48] As the next section reveals, Pufendorf's law of nature is so extensive because he rejects a natural morality, independent of natural law.

NATURAL LAW AND NATURAL MORALITY

Scholars frequently study early modern natural law ethics through the prism of two rival scholastic positions on moral ontology.[49] Naturalists such as Gregory of Rimini avowed the existence of a measure of moral good and evil independent of God's will. Murder would have been wrong even if God had not issued his *Thou shalt not kill*. Voluntarists like Ockham disliked this view for undermining divine omnipotence. They insisted that natural law consists entirely in divine commands and prohibitions. By the time of Grotius, this straightforward meta-ethical binary had been overturned by Francisco Suárez's momentous interventions. The Spanish Jesuit (1548–1617) developed a self-proclaimed 'middle course' between extreme voluntarism and radical naturalism, based on two philosophical refinements.[50] He distinguished, first, between God as creator and God as lawgiver; and, second, between natural morality and natural law. Crudely put, Suárez combined voluntarism about law with naturalism about morality.[51]

According to Suárez, natural law is truly, not metaphorically, called 'law'. As 'that sort of authority which can impose a binding obligation', natural law presupposes a lawgiver.[52] Binding obligations can be imposed only by a superior. God qua legislator 'decrees that men shall be bound to obey that which right reason dictates'.[53] While the obligation imposed by natural law derives from God's commands and prohibitions, divine legislation does not create moral good and evil. 'On the contrary, it necessarily presupposes the existence of a certain righteousness or turpitude in these actions and attaches to them a special obligation derived from divine law'.[54] Natural law regulates actions that are intrinsically right and wrong, in virtue of their harmony or disaccord with rational nature. For this reason, moral good and evil ultimately derive from God qua creator, who made humans rational creatures.

Grotius followed Suárez in distinguishing the intrinsic moral quality of an action from logically subsequent divine commands and prohibitions:

> NATURAL LAW is the Rule and Dictate of Right Reason, shewing the Moral Deformity or Moral Necessity there is in any Act, according to

> its Suitableness or Unsuitableness to a reasonable Nature and consequently, that such an Act is either forbid or commanded by GOD, the Author of Nature.[55]

Yet he departed from Suárez by omitting his central point: that God's command is needed to create a 'real prohibition or preceptive obligation ... since such an effect cannot be conceived apart from volition'.[56] For the Dutch philosopher, natural law concerns actions that 'are in themselves either Obligatory or Unlawful, and must, consequently, be understood to be either commanded or forbid by God himself'.[57] Like Suárez, Grotius maintained that God cannot *not* command morally necessary actions and prohibit evil ones.[58] But crucially, divine legislation is not needed to render the action obligatory to begin with. Suárez's and Grotius' contrasting explications of the difference between natural and positive law corroborates this reading. Suárez cashed out the distinction in terms of moral value. Positive law renders evil what it forbids, while natural law assumes the depravity of what it proscribes. Grotius, by contrast, explained it in terms of obligation. Positive law renders obligatory what before was morally optional, whereas natural law governs intrinsically obligatory actions.[59] Divine positive law (revealed in scripture) thus deals with actions that are of themselves morally optional and that become mandatory only 'because GOD *wills* it'.[60]

Natural law and natural morality are both conceptually and practically distinct for Grotius. Natural morality captures what is intrinsically morally good or evil; natural law concerns what is intrinsically morally obligatory or forbidden. The two frequently come apart. Grotius was adamant that 'those Things which our Reason declares to be honest, or comparatively good, tho' they are not enjoined us' are beyond natural law.[61] As a voluntarist about law and obligation, Suárez held that spotting the intrinsic moral goodness of an action involves a recognition that God commands us to pursue the same: both indications together make up natural law.[62] The Spanish theologian could therefore not easily admit the thought that some intrinsically morally good or evil actions are first rendered obligatory or unlawful by (divine) positive law. This view is open to Grotius due to his refusal to differentiate natural and positive law in terms of moral value. Positive laws frequently prescribe actions that before were either merely morally commendable or morally blameworthy but not forbidden. (Prescribing the last may be justified as a lesser evil.) Once positive law prohibits some action φ, it becomes morally wrong to φ. Yet the wrong is in that case not an intrinsic one (pertaining to features of the act itself), but rather extrinsic (imposed by law). While natural law and natural morality are co-extensive for Suárez, they are not for Grotius. His naturalistic conception of moral obligation permits a more restrictive conception of natural law, as not capturing the whole of natural morality.

Grotius thereby opened up space for supererogation – morally good actions beyond the call of duty:

> *Honestum*, according to the Nature of the Things upon which it turns, sometimes consists (as I may say) in an indivisible Point; so that the least Deviation from it is a Vice: And sometimes it has a large Extent; so that if one follows it, he does something commendable, and yet, without being guilty of any moral wrong, he may not follow it, or may even act quite otherwise.[63]

Supererogation is pivotal to Grotius' just war theory. *DJBP* teems with examples of morally commendable 'Acts of Humanity' which belligerents are nonetheless not bound to perform 'in Rigour'.[64] Sometimes combatants are bound to perform morally supererogatory conduct by non-moral standards, such as the Gospel or the voluntary law of nations. Christ prescribed more demanding acts of love than natural reason requires. 'The Christian Religion commands, that we should lay down our Lives one for another; but who will pretend to say, that we are obliged to this by the Law of Nature?'[65] Interestingly, Grotius maintained that in certain circumstances, otherwise supererogatory actions can become obligatory as a matter of natural law. 'Circumstances too may sometimes fall out so, that it may not only be laudable, but an Obligation in us to forbear claiming our Right, on account of that Charity which we owe to all Men, even tho' our Enemies; whether this Charity be considered in itself, or as it is what the sacred Rule of the Gospel requires at our Hands'.[66] For Grotius, suitability to a rational and social nature is a criterion for both moral value and moral obligation. But being conducive to human society does not by itself suffice to render an action mandatory: its omission must in addition be a positive moral wrong. Put differently, its omission must be incompatible with human society (whether by its nature or due to present circumstances).

Suárez had combined voluntarism about law with naturalism about morality; Grotius was a naturalist about both morality and obligation; Pufendorf a voluntarist in respect of both.[67] Suárez had argued that natural morality was instituted by God qua creator and natural law by

God qua legislator. Grotius wrote, vaguely, that natural law can 'be justly ascribed to God' because we are rational and sociable by dint of his free creation.[68] According to Pufendorf, natural law exists by 'hypothetical necessity' – the act of freely creating rational beings necessarily involves lawgiving: 'by decreeing to create Man, that is, to create an Animal whose Actions should not be all indifferent, God immediately constituted a Law for his Nature'.[69] The law of nature remains firm and immutable as long as human nature is so.[70]

The German philosopher had little sympathy for Grotius' naturalistic conception of obligation: 'it would remain a most perplexing Doubt what those Acts are which we thus suppose in themselves Unlawful, and by what distinguishing Token they may be clearly known from others'.[71] Not only moral obligations, but also moral good and evil were first introduced by natural law: 'all acts of themselves were indifferent before the announcement of a law'.[72] Indeed, he defined moral goodness (*honestas*) as the voluntary accordance of actions with law.[73] It follows that actions are called 'Naturally Honest or Dishonest' only because natural law 'strictly enjoins' their performance or omission. Natural morality and natural law are thus co-extensive on Pufendorf's account, foreclosing the possibility of supererogation.[74]

Grotius had endorsed the Stoic view that certain actions, discoverable by right reason, are intrinsically right and wrong. Citing the English natural lawyer Richard Cumberland (1631–1718), Pufendorf accused the Dutchman of conflating natural and moral goodness in the second edition of *De Jure Naturae et Gentium*.[75] Natural goodness is a matter of happiness and expediency; moral goodness of conformity to natural law. This legislative conception of moral goodness propelled Pufendorf to insist, contra Suárez, that both natural law and morality presuppose divine lawgiving. That very move forced him to determine the content of natural law further (through the principle of sociality); a law ordering agents to pursue *honestas* and to avoid evil would have been vacuous for him.[76]

These semantic shifts receive justification from Pufendorf's celebrated, albeit hard-to-grasp, idea of moral entities. Moral entities are non-natural properties superimposed upon physical beings, things, and motions by an intelligent power (human or divine) in order to regulate the behaviour of rational agents.[77] The condition of being a person is a moral entity: it generates specific rights, duties and responsibilities. Ditto for being at peace, being elderly, a spouse, a soldier etc. Property is a moral entity superimposed on things. Authority, right and obligation are moral qualities attached to persons; price and esteem are moral quantities. Moral entities do not exhaust the realm of morality. The law of nature, for instance, is not a moral entity. Rather, it is a means by which God imposes moral entities such as obligations on rational beings. Abstaining from wantonly harming others is naturally good for both human and non-human animals insofar as it conduces to self-preservation. Yet only in humans can such conduct also be morally good, in virtue of conforming to a natural law prohibiting unprovoked harming.[78] While natural goodness is a non-imposed, inherent feature of actions, all moral properties – including moral right and wrong – are superimposed by some intelligent agent. The idea of superimposed moral entities thus underpins Pufendorf's voluntarism about natural law and natural morality.

NATURAL LAW, RIGHTS AND JUSTICE

Scholarly research in the intellectual history of rights has long dwelled on the question of when a subjective sense of *ius* as moral qualities attached to persons ('rights') first arose, as distinguished from its objective sense as 'what is right'. A related research agenda, inspired by Leo Strauss, explores when 'subjective' natural rights first gained normative primacy over 'objective' natural law, reflecting the moral individualism allegedly distinctive of modernity. The varying ways in which subjective rights have been conceptualised has been given less scrutiny. *Ius*, we will see, is among a range of basic moral notions which Grotius and Pufendorf understood and classified in divergent ways.

What are we talking about when we talk about natural rights? Sometimes the term denotes a basic moral permission, as in Hobbes: '*Jus Naturale*, is the Liberty each man hath, to use his own power, as he will himselfe, for the preservation of his own Nature'.[79] Sometimes commentators use the phrase loosely to refer to those things which individuals own by nature. 'A Man's Life is his own by Nature ... and so is his Body, his Limbs, his Reputation, his Honour, and his Actions'.[80] For Pufendorf, our natural *suum* includes 'our Life, our Bodies, our Members, our Chastity, our Reputation and our Liberty'.[81] Strictly speaking, however, 'right' signifies not the things we own, but a moral power over what we own. Early modern natural lawyers generally conceived of individual rights as moralised personal and property rights. Since humans were assumed to be equals by nature, personal rights over others (presupposing relations of authority and subordination) were treated as conventional in character. All natural rights were therefore property rights: rights *in* our life, liberty, chastity, reputation etc.

Grotius and Pufendorf contrasted two kinds of individual rights. Perfect rights are enforceable, in court and on the battlefield. Imperfect (i.e. incomplete) rights are unenforceable.[82] They denote that the 'right-holder' is worthy to receive a perfect right: 'an Aptitude or Merit, which doth not contain in it a Right strictly so called, but gives Occasion to it'.[83] Suppose that Hugo has an imperfect right to amnesty. This imperfect right expresses the fact that it is morally fitting to give him reprieve; he deserves it. While Hugo cannot claim amnesty as his due, the world would be morally better for him receiving it. 'Thus then, he who renders to another any thing due by *Imperfect* Right, doth properly *attribute*, give or add to him somewhat which he could not before call *his own*'.[84] Failure to properly respect imperfect rights does not warrant punishment,[85] and damage done thereby does not call for compensation.[86] Since imperfect rights are not actionable, Pufendorf subsumed them under 'passive moral qualities' (allowing us to lawfully suffer, receive or admit something).[87] The distinction between enforceable and non-enforceable rights was crucial to Grotius' just war theory, as it determined which wrongs constitute a *casus belli*.

Grotius recognised three kinds of perfect rights, or 'faculties' (moral powers). *Potestas* includes both rights over ourselves (i.e. liberty) and rights over others. *Dominium* includes all sorts of property titles in things (*ius in rem*), including those that do not involve full ownership, such as tenancies and servitudes. *Creditum* is 'the Faculty of demanding what is due'.[88] 'For he to whom any Thing is due, hath a Right against him from whom it is due'.[89] Pufendorf revamped Grotius' classification by introducing a distinction between moral power (*potestas*) and right (*ius*). *Potestas* (power) covers those moral qualities '*by which a Man is enabled to do a thing lawfully and with moral effect*'.[90] The latter clause is added to signal disagreement with Hobbes, for whom natural right places no moral constraints on others.[91] Personal liberty, property (*dominium*) and authority over others are all types of *potestas*. Notwithstanding its inherent normative effects, the term 'power' does not itself connote that the moral quality in question is obtained and possessed fairly. Rights (*iura*) are just normative bases for *potestas*: they are moral qualities by which we justly obtain or claim moral powers from others. Imperfect rights allow us lawfully to receive property and authority over persons; perfect rights allow us justly to claim the same.[92] Rejecting Grotius' identification of *ius* with subjective moral qualities generally, Pufendorf narrowed the meaning of 'right' considerably. A significant upshot of his reconceptualisation is that for him, rights always entail corresponding obligations ('a Moral Necessity to perform, or admit, or undergo any thing') in some other party.[93] This holds true for both perfect *and* imperfect rights.

Indeed, Pufendorf's dismissal of supererogation led him to revise the status of that last distinction. Both thinkers maintained that respecting perfect rights is essential for peaceful society, while realising imperfect rights merely contributes to the well-being of society.[94] On Grotius' account, the latter is always morally commendable but not normally required by natural law. Showing mercy to a deserving enemy, for instance, is often supererogatory (namely whenever the maintenance of society is furthered by pardoning, without necessitating this).[95] Imperfect rights therefore do not always correlate to obligations in others. Pufendorf dissented on this point, insisting that sociality does generally oblige agents to realise imperfect rights.[96] Dispensing benefits, gratitude and other duties of kindness and humanity are obligatory by natural law. The obligation in question is an imperfect one, however, meaning that no force or compulsion is permitted against derelict obligees.[97] Natural law does not countenance enforcing imperfect obligations, as this would be 'a Remedy more grievous than the Disease'.[98] Unenforceable obligations are still obligations, however: imperfect obligations are incomplete, not in normative force, but in lacking corresponding perfect rights in others.

Contrary to what is often maintained, natural law requires fulfilment of non-enforceable obligations for both thinkers, albeit to differing degrees. This point is best grasped by considering their views on justice – the moral norm regulating rights and desert. Grotius used his pioneering distinction between perfect and imperfect rights to revise the received Aristotelian classification of justice. On the latter view, commutative justice demands that equality is observed in exchanges, while distributive justice calls for allocating common goods in proportion to prospective recipients' merit. The two norms were deemed to differ with respect both to the kinds of equality (arithmetic vs geometric) and to the social relations they concern (private vs communal).[99] Grotius rejected the traditional account, averring instead that commutative justice governs perfect rights, and distributive justice imperfect ones.[100] Since imperfect rights are not enforceable, neither is distributive justice.

Confusingly, distributive justice is not, for Grotius, the only moral norm ordering respect for imperfect rights. Other-regarding virtues such as liberality and mercy do so too.[101] For this reason, Pufendorf accused Grotius of conflating distributive justice with universal justice – the whole of other-regarding morality.[102] The classification of justice advocated by the German natural lawyer was more traditional. Both commutative and distributive justice concern perfect rights. Commutative justice calls for numerical equality in private exchanges; distributive justice demands that partners receive a 'just Share' of the profits made in a corporate society.[103] Partners have a perfect, actionable right to a fair share. Imperfect rights lie beyond particular justice: 'When then, we exhibit to another either Actions or Things due to him only by *Imperfect* Right ... [then] we are said to have observ'd *General* or *Universal Justice*'.[104] For Pufendorf, natural law requires observance of duties of humanity that fall under universal justice. This allowed him to claim that to every imperfect right corresponds an imperfect duty; a claim that is false on Grotius' ethics of natural law and supererogation.

The view that Grotius reduced natural law to commutative justice is widespread in the literature. 'Through his distinction between rights and imperfect moral qualities', Stephen Buckle maintains, 'Grotius thus limits the law of nature to the protection of the *suum* of each individual member of society, restraining it from requiring any positive acts of private benevolence'.[105] In fact, Grotius was adamant that 'there are many Duties, not of strict Justice but of Charity, which are not only very commendable ... but which cannot be dispensed with without a Crime'.[106] Not all moral duties are accompanied by perfect rights of others: 'Duties of Charity and Gratitude ... lay ourselves under an Obligation, and at the same Time give no Right to any other over us'.[107] Natural law hence requires more than merely abstaining from injury: '*natural Right*, considered as a *Law*, does not only respect what we call *expletive* [i.e. commutative] Justice, but comprehends the Acts of other Virtues, as of *Temperance, Fortitude*, and *Prudence*; so that in certain Circumstances they are not only *honest*, but of an *indispensable Obligation*'.[108] Only violations of perfect rights justify resort to court or arms.[109] Observance of distributive justice, liberality, charity etc. is nonetheless in some circumstances necessary for the maintenance of an orderly society and hence required by natural law – even if such duties remain beyond compulsion.

CONCLUSION

This chapter has highlighted some interconnected ethical disagreements between Grotius and Pufendorf. The latter rejected his predecessor's naturalistic conception of morality and moral obligation as impious and conceptually unsound. His own divine command theory rendered natural morality and natural law co-extensive, as moral goodness consists in the voluntary accordance of actions with natural law. By contrast, Grotius practically disentangled natural law from natural morality, thus creating space for supererogation. My analysis has hinted at how the two thinkers strived to incorporate the language of rights and justice within their natural law framework. Theoretical differences with contemporary natural law thinkers not discussed in detail in this chapter – including Hobbes, Locke and Leibniz – are arguably even greater. Notwithstanding their shared belief that morality is rationally demonstrable, seventeenth-century natural law ethicists disagreed deeply about the nature of morality, about what it requires and about the meaning of basic moral terms – providing a wealth of ideas for moral philosophers to ponder today.

NOTES

* For splendid feedback on an earlier version of this chapter, I would like to thank Aaron Garrett, Heikki Haara and Kari Saastamoinen.

1. For an excellent overview of thinking on natural law and natural rights over the past 2,500 years, see Haakonssen and Seidler 2016.
2. Barbeyrac 2003: 272. Also e.g. Smith 1982 [1759]: VII.4.37.
3. The ensuing analysis of Grotius' ethics draws on Olsthoorn 2018 (outlining his just war theory) and Olsthoorn 2019 (outlining his natural law theory).
4. Pufendorf 1729: I.6.18.
5. I will refrain from offering catchy characterisations of their positions ('Was Grotius a late scholastic or a proto-Hobbist?'), as such shorthand depictions are inevitably imprecise and misleading. For the same reason, I will bracket the much-contested question of what, if anything, was distinctly 'modern' about the Grotian approach to natural law. For two contrasting recent assessments of the innovativeness of Grotius' ethics, see Irwin 2008: 88–99 and Darwall 2012a.
6. Schneewind 1998: 70–73 (Grotius); Schneewind 2010: 170–75 (Pufendorf). Also e.g. Tuck 1987.
7. Pufendorf 2014: 81, also 55–7. Pufendorf also lambasted Grotius for credulously copying ideas 'from the scholastic writers'.
8. Quoted in Saunders 2002: 2180.
9. Schneewind 1987: 134.
10. Grotius 2005: II.20.45–8 and, more generally, Grotius 2012: I.2–12. The arguments the latter text musters in support of the truth of Christianity are not restricted to those demonstrable by unaided reason. Also e.g. Pufendorf 1729: I.6.13.

11. Pufendorf 1991: I.4.
12. Pufendorf 1991: preface, I.4.8. Pufendorf 1729: II.3.19 explains that the immortality of the soul is 'abstracted from', rather than denied by, his natural law doctrine.
13. Leibniz 1972: 66–7.
14. Pufendorf 1991: I.3.10.
15. Pufendorf 1729: II.3.19.
16. Grotius 2005: I.1.9, also II.14.6.1.
17. Grotius 2005: I.1.10.2.
18. Haakonssen 2002: 34.
19. Grotius 2005: prol. 12. Cf. Pufendorf 1729: II.3.19.
20. Pufendorf 1991: I.2.2, also 1729: I.6.4, II.3.6.
21. Pufendorf 1729: II.3.23.
22. Hobbes 1998: 3.33. Cf. Hobbes 2012: 15.41.
23. Pufendorf 1729: II.3.20, also I.6.4.
24. Pufendorf 1729: I.6.13.
25. Grotius 2005: II.20.5.1, also I.2.1.3.
26. Grotius 2005: II.20.45–8.
27. Pufendorf 2002: § 24; Pufendorf 1991: I.3.13, I.4.6.
28. Grotius 2004: 11.
29. Grotius 2005: prol. 12.
30. E.g. Tuck 1987; Hont 2005: 159–84; Palladini 2008; Darwall 2012b: 200–202; Haara 2018.
31. Grotius 2005: prol. 5.
32. Grotius 2005: prol. 6.
33. Grotius 2005: prol. 8.
34. Grotius 2005: I.2.1.2; also II.20.5.1. For helpful discussion, see Saastamoinen 1995: 114–16; Brooke 2012: 37–58; Straumann 2015: 88–119.
35. Grotius 2005: I.1.10.5.
36. Hobbes 1998: 1.2. Cf. Pufendorf 1729: II.2.4.
37. Pufendorf 1729: II.3.16. Hobbes had defined natural law as 'the Dictate of right reason about what should be done or not done for the longest possible preservation of life and limb' (in 1998: 2.1). The incorrect view that Pufendorf, too, derived natural law from the principle of self-preservation is widespread (e.g. Tuck 1987: 105; Hont 2005: 175; Palladini 2008: 30n) and the result of mistaking an empirical principle of human behaviour for a normative one. Saastamoinen 1995: 65–77, 83–94 offers a helpful corrective.
38. Pufendorf 1991: preface.
39. Pufendorf 1729: II.1.8.
40. Pufendorf 1729: II.1.5. On the moral psychology underpinning Pufendorf's natural law ethics, see Haara 2016: 425–38.

41. Pufendorf 1729: II.3.14.
42. Pufendorf 1729: II.3.16.
43. Pufendorf 1729: II.3.15.
44. Schneewind 2010: 181–5.
45. Pufendorf 1729: II.3.15.
46. Pufendorf 1729: III.3.1.
47. Pufendorf 1729: III.3.2.
48. Grotius 2005: II.2.11–7; Pufendorf 1729: III.3.5–10.
49. E.g. Simmonds 2002: 218–20; Haakonssen 2004.
50. Suárez 2015: II.6.5.
51. Insightful analyses of Súarez's ethics are found in Haakonssen 1996: 16–24; Irwin 2008: 1–69; Irwin 2012.
52. Suárez 2015: II.6.6.
53. Suárez 2015: II.6.10.
54. Suárez 2015: II.6.11, also e.g. II.7.1, II.9.4.
55. Grotius 2005: I.1.10.1.
56. Suárez 2015: II.6.13.
57. Grotius 2005: I.1.10.2. This naturalistic conception of moral obligation – actions can be morally obligatory of themselves, independent of human or divine legislative will – is new to *DJBP*. In the earlier *Jurisprudence* (written 1619–20; first published 1631), Grotius still endorsed the Suárezian thesis that any obligation to do what is naturally right is superimposed by God: 'Natural law in man is an intuitive judgement, making known what things from their own nature are honourable or dishonourable, involving an obligation to follow the same imposed by God'. Grotius 1926: I.2.5. Cf. Suárez 2015: II.6.13.
58. Suárez 2015: II.6.20–24.
59. Suárez 2015: II.7.1, 6; Grotius 2005: I.1.10.2.
60. Grotius 2005: I.1.15.
61. Grotius 2005: I.1.10.3.
62. Suárez 2015: II.6.8.
63. Grotius 2005: I.2.1.3. The metaphor recurs in I.2.8.4 and II.1.5.1.
64. Grotius 2005: III.15.1.
65. Grotius 2005: I.2.6.2; also II.1.10.1, II.20.10.
66. Grotius 2005: II.24.2.3; also e.g. II.1.9.1, III.20.50.1.
67. Irwin 2008: 284–307.
68. Grotius 2005: prol. 12.
69. Pufendorf 1729: II.3.4.
70. Pufendorf 1729: II.3.5.
71. Pufendorf 1729: II.3.4.
72. Pufendorf 1729: II.3.4, also I.2.6, II.3.19. Cf. Hobbes 2012: 13.10.

73. Pufendorf 1729: I.7.3.
74. Pufendorf 1729: I.2.6. Protestants generally disliked the idea of super-meritorious actions because Catholic thinkers had invoked it to support the sale of indulgences and masses. For the same reason, Protestants insisted on justification by faith alone. Pufendorf dismissed supererogation on anti-Catholic grounds in 1991: I.5.3.
75. Pufendorf 1729: I.2.6, II.3.4; Cumberland 2005: 5.9. Schneewind 1998: 123–5 argues that Pufendorf, innovatively, makes moral goodness entirely independent of natural goodness.
76. Hence his accusation that Grotius' natural law is circular. Pufendorf 1729: II.3.4. See Irwin 2008: 292.
77. Pufendorf 1729: I.1.3.
78. Pufendorf 1729: I.2.6.
79. Hobbes 2012: 14.1. Also Spinoza 2016: 16.2–3.
80. Grotius 2005: II.17.2.1, also I.2.1.3.
81. Pufendorf 1729: III.1.1, also Pufendorf 1991: I.6.3. Incidentally, for Hobbes nothing is exclusively our own by nature because his right of nature permits agents to seize anything which may prove beneficial for their preservation, even 'one anothers body'. Hobbes 2012: 14.4.
82. Grotius 2005: II.22.16; Pufendorf 1729: I.1.19, I.7.7; Pufendorf 1991: I.9.4.
83. Grotius 2005: II.2.20.2.
84. Pufendorf 1729: I.7.11.
85. Grotius 2005: II.2.20.1.
86. Grotius 2005: II.17.3.1, II.17.9, II.17.13; Pufendorf 1729: III.1.3.
87. Pufendorf 1729: I.1.20.
88. Grotius 2005: I.1.5.
89. Grotius 2005: II.2.20.2.
90. Pufendorf 1729: I.1.19.
91. Pufendorf 1729: III.5.3.
92. Pufendorf 1729: I.1.20, III.5.1, VIII.3.5. On moral powers, see Saastamoinen 2006: 230–31; Darwall 2012b.
93. Pufendorf 1729: I.1.21, III.5.1. Cf. Mautner 1999.
94. Grotius 2005: prol. 8–10; Pufendorf 1729: I.7.7.
95. Grotius 2005: III.11.7; cf. II.10.11, III.14.6.4.
96. Pufendorf 1729: I.1.20, I.7.15, III.3.17.
97. Pufendorf 1729: III.3.9.
98. Pufendorf 1729: I.7.7.
99. Aristotle 2000: 5.2–5; Aquinas, *Summa Theologiae* 2a.2ae.61.1.
100. Grotius 2005: I.1.8, II.20.2.
101. Grotius 2005: I.1.8.1; cf. Pufendorf 1729: I.7.11.

102. Pufendorf 1729: I.7.9, 11. Also Smith 1982 [1759]: VII.2.1.10. Cf. Aristotle 2000: 5.1 (1129a20). Pace Pufendorf, Grotius distinguished distributive justice from universal justice in 1926: I.1.9–10.
103. Pufendorf 1729: I.7.9, also VIII.3.5.
104. Pufendorf 1729: I.7.8.
105. Buckle 1991: 31–2; also e.g. Straumann 2015: 126. Olivecrona 2010 argues that the natural law theories of Grotius and Pufendorf can, paradoxically, do without the idea of natural law. Virtually all the normative content in their ethical thinking could be captured, he claims, by rights, obligations, wronging and justice – ideas which neither presuppose laws nor lawgiving. Olivecrona's argument rests on an untenably narrow conception of natural law, as requiring nothing other than keeping promises and avoiding injury (2010: 209). Cf. Haakonssen 1996: 39–41.
106. Grotius 2005: II.25.3.3, also e.g. II.22.10.1, II.24.2.3, II.25.3.4, III.1.4.2, III.18.4.
107. Grotius 2005: II.11.3, cf. II.14.6.1.
108. Grotius 2005: II.1.9.1, also I.1.9.
109. Grotius 2005: II.1.2.1; Pufendorf 1729: I.7.7.

PART II The Revival of Natural Law Ethics

4 The New Natural Law Theory

Patrick Lee

The New Natural Law (NNL) theory[1] is the name given to a particular revival and development of Thomistic natural law theory, first proposed in the 1960s by Germain Grisez in an interpretative article on St Thomas Aquinas, in which Grisez challenged the then-dominant interpretation of Aquinas on natural law. In subsequent decades Grisez, John Finnis, Joseph Boyle and others richly developed the theory and applied it to other issues (free choice, moral absolutes, abortion, euthanasia, marriage and others).

According to the interpretation of Aquinas' natural law theory standard in the 1960s, the basic moral criterion is human nature itself. Actions are morally permissible if they conform to the teleologies inscribed within human nature, morally wrong if not. Since the standard for what is morally right is what fulfils human nature, one must first determine by a theoretical procedure what end or ends fulfil human nature. The standard account was that human nature is orientated to union with God as its ultimate end, and to other goods as means or subordinate ends. Thus ethics depends on philosophical anthropology or the philosophy of nature.

In his ground-breaking 1965 article, Grisez argued that Aquinas' theory of practical reason and moral principles was quite different from the one just indicated.[2] According to Grisez, knowledge of the natural law does not, for Aquinas, begin with theoretical knowledge of human nature; rather, practical reason begins with its own, self-evident practical principles. Moreover, these principles direct one to *several* basic human goods (life, marriage, friendship and society, and others), and each of these is inherently and irreducibly good in itself. On Grisez's interpretation of Aquinas, the basic moral criterion of the natural law is that we should choose in line with an openness to and respect for all of these basic human goods, both in ourselves and in others.

Since the NNL theory originated with a new interpretation of Aquinas, I will try to clarify the relations between it, Aquinas and the more usual or conventional natural law theory. After that, I will consider in more detail two of the distinctive areas where the NNL theory has developed beyond Aquinas' theory.

THE NEW NATURAL LAW THEORY'S INTERPRETATION OF AQUINAS

The central text in Aquinas on the first principles of the natural law is *Summa Theologiae* Part I-II, question 94, article 2. Grisez's 1965 article was a commentary on this article. In this article, Aquinas sets out his view of how reason discovers its first practical principles, which he also identifies as the precepts of the natural law.

The article makes five main points. Aquinas' first point is that the precepts of the natural law are related to practical reasoning (reasoning about what is to be done) as the first principles of demonstration are to speculative reasoning (reasoning about what is). In both cases, he says, the first principles are self-evident (*per se nota*), that is, known without proof, through direct insight.[3]

NNL theorists read this as indicating that, according to Aquinas, reason becomes practical by beginning that way (rather than, as the conventional interpretation claims, beginning with speculative propositions proved in metaphysics or philosophy of human nature). It is precisely because practical reason does not derive its starting points from speculative knowledge that practical reason needs its own first principles. Because reason is practical by performing a different type of function – not attempting to conform one's mind to what is (as in speculative reasoning) but ordering acts of will – the criterion of truth in this type of thinking is not what is the case, but an end or ends.[4] So the presupposition and beginning of practical reasoning is an apprehension that certain activities or conditions are goods worth pursuing – in Aquinas' terminology, goods-to-be-done-or-pursued. NNL holds that Aquinas' use of the gerundive mood – for example, *prosequendum*, 'is to be pursued' – instead of the indicative, is significant. It indicates, say NNL theorists, that a different type of thinking – thinking aimed at shaping acts of will rather than conforming to what is – is the focus of this article.

In the second part of this article, Aquinas explains how each of these first practical principles is known through itself. A proposition, he says, is known through itself (is self-evident – *per se notum*), if its predicate is contained in the intelligibility of the subject. He gives the example of the proposition *A whole is greater than its parts.* The predicate belongs to the intelligibility of the *thing* or *reality* designated by the subject term (not to the meaning of the word). And if one does understand the reality picked out by that subject term, then one understands that the predicate belongs to that thing, is true of it. For example, if one does understand what a whole is, one thereby understands – that is, *per se* – that the predicate, *greater than its parts,* belongs to it. Knowing something *per se,* then, is the opposite of knowing it *per aliud* – knowing it through a middle term, as in an argument or syllogism. According to Aquinas, all of the principles he discusses in this article are *per se nota*.

Third, Aquinas says that there is a first principle of practical reason analogous to the principle of non-contradiction, viz. the first principle of all demonstration. That principle (a thing cannot both be and not be in the same respect) is founded on the notion of being. Analogously, '[T]he first principle of practical reason is one founded on the notion of good ... This first general practical principle is: "*Good is to be done and pursued, and evil is to be avoided*"'. It is self-evident in that the predicate (*is to be done and pursued*) is immediately apprehended in the intelligibility of the subject, *Good.* The other self-evident principles of practical reason will be specifications of this general directive.

How is this proposition to be understood? Conventional natural law theorists interpret it as itself the basic moral principle, and as prescribing that one pursue the ultimate end of human life or the complete good for the human being. NNL theorists interpret it as directing that one pursue some human good or other, and that one avoid pointless activity. According to NNL, in this principle one sees in a general way that what is fulfilling, what is perfective, is to be done or pursued. What more specifically is fulfilling is grasped in other self-evident practical principles.

According to NNL, this first practical principle does not itself function as a premise in arguments; it is not a proposition that is typically enunciated separately. Like the principle of non-contradiction, its influence is formal. Specific objects are grasped as worth pursuing – as to-be-done – inasmuch as they are good or fulfilling.

According to NNL, this principle is not yet a moral principle. It is practical, it is an apprehension that the good, or the perfective, is to be pursued. But since both moral agents and immoral agents act in accord with this principle – that is, both moral and immoral agents are pursuing some good or other – though in different ways – this principle does not distinguish morally good acts from morally bad ones.[5] It does not exclude immoral actions, but irrational ones: it prescribes that there must be a point to one's acting, a good. For this reason, NNL theorists speak of this as the first principle of *practical* reason, and claim that the first *moral* principle is a distinct proposition.

In the fourth step of his account of the principles of practical reason, Aquinas says that there are several more specific practical principles, which are also self-evident: 'Since, however, good has the nature of an end, and evil, the nature of a contrary, hence it is that all those things to which the human being has a natural inclination, are naturally apprehended by reason as goods, and therefore to be pursued by action, and their contraries as bad and to be avoided'. He then lists several human goods corresponding to various natural inclinations. Aquinas mentions as basic goods the preservation of being (life), the union of man and woman and the education of offspring (marriage and family), the knowledge of the truth about God, and life in society. He does not say that this is a complete list.

NNL theorists read this as saying that the corresponding basic self-evident principles of practical reason would be: *Life is a good to be pursued, marriage and family is a good to be pursued, knowledge* (presumably not just about God) *is a good to be pursued, life in society is a good to be pursued,* and so on. These practical propositions do function as premises in practical syllogisms. NNL theorists read these as truly underived (and Aquinas asserts this in the text). These propositions express our apprehensions of ultimate reasons for action. One begins to reason practically by apprehending that certain activities or conditions are goods worth pursuing.

Developing these points in Aquinas, NNL theorists explain that when one deliberates about what to do, one considers different options or possible actions. These possible actions are appealing insofar as one understands that they are ways of realising, promoting or protecting – either directly or indirectly – a type of good such as life or health, understanding or another basic human good. A good that an action can help realise is a reason for selecting it, a reason for acting versus not acting, and for that specific action. Basic goods – such as those enumerated by Aquinas as grasped in the first principles of practical reason – provide ultimate reasons for action: that is, reasons for acting that do not require any further reason. Each of these actions is appealing ultimately insofar as each offers a way of promoting or protecting a basic human good – health, understanding and so on. Thus, in the first principles of practical reason one arrives at several ultimate reasons for action, expressions of several irreducible goods.[6]

NNL theorists explain that these basic practical judgements are not just *intuitions* – intellectual acts without data. One first knows that life, knowledge or friendship is a good to be pursued, by direct insight into experiences of participating in and enjoying these goods, and perhaps also by contrast with deprivations of them. One comes to understand, for example, what it is to find answers to questions and achieve understanding, and one understands that arriving at such knowledge is possible. But by a practical insight one sees that doing so is both a possibility and an opportunity, a good worth pursuing. Or one experiences the difference between being healthy and being sick and one sees it is possible to pursue health, and that it is a good worth pursuing. These are practical insights by which one intellectually grasps more than what is, will be, or is possible, and one grasps those conditions – such as knowledge or health – as goods worth pursuing. What has been achieved is a practical insight, a rational apprehension that knowledge or health is an aspect of human flourishing, worthy of pursuit and protection. In a similar way, one comes to understand that play or skilful performance is a good to be pursued, harmony with other people is a good to be pursued, and so on.

Since human beings are complex, there are many basic human goods. NNL theorists have proposed the following as a complete list: life and health, knowledge of truth, aesthetic experience, play or skilful performance, self-integration (the harmony among the different aspects of the self), practical reasonableness (harmony among moral truth, judgements of conscience and choices; that is, moral goodness),[7] harmony with other human beings (friendship of various kinds, social unity or communion), harmony with the more-than-human source(s) of meaning and value in the universe (the human good of *religion*), and marriage.[8] Other goods are reducible to these: for example, happiness or beatitude (as natural rather than supernatural) is a composition of these, patriotism is a specific form of community, and so on.

Fifth, Aquinas ends this article on the precepts of the natural law without saying precisely how these several principles actually provide a moral standard. NNL theorists interpret Aquinas as holding that these principles as a whole set, or in their totality constitute, the moral standard.[9] In other words, these are the principles of practical reason, and reason operates correctly – that is, one has *right* reason – which of course Aquinas repeatedly says is the standard in morals – when one reasons fully in accord with all these practical principles. Morally false propositions are those that, while in accord with some of the practical principles, are not fully in accord with all of them: in some way or other, one fails to act in a way that reason, informed by all of these principles, would recommend.

Since the practical principles direct one to love and respect the various basic goods – as instantiated either in oneself or in others – the moral principle is equivalent to the proposition that one ought morally to choose in line with love and respect for all the basic goods.

THE IS–OUGHT ISSUE

The most controversial position of NNL theorists is their view on the is–ought problem. They hold that what is often called the is–ought fallacy is indeed a fallacy, and so they hold that the first principles of practical reason are self-evident, underived propositions, which they also hold was Aquinas' position.

Conventional natural lawyers have strongly objected to this position. They argue that practical reason derives its fundamental moral directives from a speculative knowledge of human nature. One can and must, they claim, infer the morally obligatory end from one's knowledge of human nature. And they claim this was Aquinas' position.[10]

Hence on the conventional natural law view, deriving a moral ought proposition from premises all of which are is-propositions – the so-called is–ought fallacy referred to by David Hume – is not a fallacy at all, but part and parcel of any real natural law theory. True, the conclusion of any sound argument cannot state more than what is implicit in the premises, but, they say, human nature is dynamically orientated to its genuine perfection and so has value – namely the good to which it is orientated – inscribed within it.[11] Thus, metaphysics or philosophy of nature discovers the proper goal or goals for human living.

NNL theorists reject this argument, which can be expressed as follows:

> Every act that fulfils human nature is *good*.
> X is an act that fulfils human nature.
> Therefore X is *good*.[12]

The problem is that the term 'good' in the premise has a speculative or theoretical meaning: *what realises the inherent tendencies or potentialities of a being*. However, for the argument to establish a normative conclusion, the term must have a *practical* sense, namely: something fulfilling *that is to be done or pursued*.[13] For if the meaning of the conclusion were merely: *X realises the inherent tendencies or potentialities of a human being*, then an additional proposition would be required to reach the properly practical or normative proposition. That is, one would need the properly practical proposition: *That which realises the inherent tendencies or potentialities of a human being is to be done or pursued.*[14] Propositions describing the orientation of a nature to its actualisation do not by themselves imply that one morally ought to pursue that actualisation.

The problem just stated can also be seen as follows. The kind of inference pointed to by conventional natural lawyers establishes only a hypothetical proposition: *If* one desires a certain goal, then one ought to perform certain actions that lead to it. But such an ought is characteristic of technical oughts – directives of external actions to pre-selected external goals – rather than moral oughts. Moral oughts are not hypothetical: morality is not something one can opt out of. Moral knowledge is directive of acts of will, rather than external acts directly, and provides categorical directives, precisely by beginning with the knowledge of what ends are to be pursued. The first act of practical knowledge that grounds moral propositions must be a knowledge of which ends are worthwhile.

Furthermore, NNL theorists contend that a person apprehends that there are *several* basic goods and so has several reasons for acting. Each of these basic goods is, according to NNL, directly apprehended as an opportunity, as in itself perfective and worth pursuing, and each provides a reason for acting. And so, when one deliberates about what to do, the question is: how ought I respond to those several reasons for acting, not all of which can be acted upon presently? The specific moral question is: how should I respond to these various options for choice which answer to several different reasons for action? Speculative knowledge of human nature will not provide an answer to *that* question. For the issue is how one's choice or act of will ought to be related to the several basic goods.

Finally, NNL theorists argue that the conventional natural law view is reductionist: it reduces the moral dimension of being to the natural dimension. NNL theorists follow and develop Aquinas' distinction between four orders of being, based on how reason is differently related to what it knows:[15] first, the order of beings that reason considers but does not produce – the order of nature; second, the order that reason introduces into its own acts – the order of meaning and logic; third, the order that reason introduces into acts of will – the moral order, understood by ethics; and fourth, the order that reason introduces into external matter – the order of technique. According to NNL theorists, the attempt to identify the moral criterion with human nature itself is a reduction of the distinct moral order to the natural order. The fulfilment of the whole human person cannot be identified with the actualisation only of the natural dimension. The fulfilment of the whole human person must include fulfilment in that dimension, but must also include fulfilment in the logical, technical (or cultural) and of course moral dimensions. Moreover, the identification of the standard for morality as a goal within the natural order leads to missing or denying what is unique to the moral order.

Thus the difference between the conventional natural law view and NNL is more than a difference in how to explain or defend a common moral standard. They differ on what the moral standard is, even though they usually agree on specific moral conclusions.[16] Of course, in both approaches, the moral standard involves human flourishing or human goods. But conventional natural lawyers seem to view the human good as a target that morally good acts aim at, while morally bad acts do not, the latter aiming rather at merely apparent goods (such as inordinate pleasure or status). According to NNL, *some* morally bad choices aim at merely apparent goods,[17] but many immoral choices aim at real goods. For example, killing as a means to support one's family, and stealing a library book, may be motivated by genuine goods rather than, as conventional natural lawyers conceptualise morally bad acts, aiming at merely apparent goods. So according to NNL, many immoral actions aim at a genuine good but do so in an unreasonable way, namely in a way that is not respectful or open to other basic goods.

Thus, on the NNL view, and on Aquinas' view as well (if NNL theorists' interpretation is correct), the human good does not function as an end providing a criterion for distinguishing between morally good and morally bad actions in the same way that ends function in natural or technical matters. It is not that morally good actions aim at a certain goal while bad actions aim at the wrong goal. Rather, morally good actions are choices in line with a love and respect for all of the basic goods realisable in oneself and in others, while morally bad actions are choices that involve a diminishing of love and respect for some human good in oneself or in others. The moral badness is a privation of love – of openness or respect – in relation to the integral human good.

These points are closely connected to the difference between the conventional and New Natural Law theories regarding the general first principle of practical reason. According to the conventional view, the first principle of practical reason is itself the basic moral principle. On this view, the principle, *Good is to be done and pursued,* means: one ought morally to pursue the complete good, or the real good (as opposed to the apparent good) of the human being.[18] Thus, Ralph McInerny objected to the NNL position that the general first principle of practical reason, as well as the more specific first principles (e.g. *Life is a good to be pursued*), are 'pre-moral'. Speaking of Germain Grisez's position that the first general principle is practical but not moral, McInerny objects: 'But if the first practical principle is not a moral principle, how can the precepts of the natural law be determinations of it?'[19] Conventional natural law theorists reject this two-tiered approach.

NNL theorists reply that for Aquinas, the first practical principle must be operative in the reasoning of someone acting immorally as well as in someone acting morally – that it is needed as a presupposition of any practical reasoning at all.[20] The first practical principle must be operative in the reasoning of someone who, for example, immorally concludes that lying about one's rival is to be done. Such a person reasons that a good – something in some way fulfilling – is to be pursued, and that since lying about his rival might promote that good, lying is the thing to be done. The liar may be pursuing a real good, and thus acting in accord with – at least to some extent – the first general practical principle, and in accord with some specific first practical principles. However, while he acts in accord with some practical principles, or partly in accord with some practical principles, he is not responding to the *integral or full* directiveness of those principles. He is not acting *fully in accord with* the practical principles, which direct him to love and respect *all* the basic goods, as realisable not only in himself and in those dear to him, but also in others, including his rival. Thus the first general practical principle is not by itself a moral principle. Still, it is the integral directiveness of that principle (along with the more specific practical principles) that provides ethical direction. And so one might call it *incipiently* or *virtually* a moral principle.[21]

Moral knowledge thus involves a two-tiered process: one first apprehends basic practical principles or ultimate reasons for acting, and then the specifically moral knowledge is realised when one discerns how one ought to act in relation to those first-level reasons. The basic moral principle directs the will to an openness to the basic goods of all persons – that is, it prescribes that we should not limit the full directiveness of our practical reason, for example by partiality or through emotion (desire, fear, hostility). The moral principle directs that we should choose to pursue some good, but in a way that does not slight or negate other goods not chosen or other persons not benefited by one's choice. Thus Grisez, Boyle and Finnis at one point write:

> Moral truth as a kind of practical truth is not differentiated from moral falsity by the addition of any intelligibility other than the intelligibility proper to practical knowledge as such. Rather, moral truth is differentiated by the integrity with which it directs to possible human fulfillment insofar as that can be realised by carrying out choices. Thus moral falsities – for example, 'That so-and-so should be wiped out' and 'One must look out for number one' – are specified by the incompleteness due to which they lack adequacy to possible human fulfillment insofar as that can be realised by carrying out choices.[22]

Grisez and Finnis have developed the theory by articulating various intermediary moral norms – more specific norms implied by the general first moral principle but not so specific as a judgement of conscience bearing on a specific kind of human act. The first principle directs one to choose or will in line with a love and openness to every aspect of the intrinsic good of persons. But there are various ways of falling short of that full-hearted openness to the basic goods of all persons, and so one can conclude that one ought not to restrict one's openness to human good in a specific way, for example, through partiality or hostility. One can thus be deterred from choosing in line with a love of integral human good by desires for pleasure or comfort not integrated with respect for genuine goods, or by fear not grounded in a will to prevent destruction of genuine good. Or in an unfair choice, one is moved to exclude from one's care a person's genuine good, on the basis of an emotional preference for other persons or by an emotional aversion to that person, hence unnecessarily restricting one's love or appreciation. The intermediary norms – what Grisez calls 'modes of responsibility' – exclude various ways of falling short of love of the human goods prescribed by the first principle of morality. Grisez, Boyle and Finnis have thus developed a helpful methodology for moving from the very general moral principles to the more specific ones directly applicable to deliberation.

INCOMMENSURABILITY OF BASIC GOODS AND OF OPTIONS FOR CHOICE

NNL theorists hold that the basic human goods are, just as such, incommensurable. They also hold that in situations where one has a significant choice – a free choice – the concrete goods and bads brought about by the different live options for choice are incommensurable. These are distinct types of incommensurability: the first refers to different categories of good, the second refers to concrete options for choice. These two different incommensurabilities play different roles in their theory.

According to the first, the basic categories of human good – life and health, speculative knowledge and so on – are incommensurable. No one of these goods is higher or more excellent than the others. So when choosing among life plans, for example, one cannot rightly settle one's choice by concluding that one of these basic goods is in itself more excellent than the others.[23]

This view is contested by conventional natural law theorists, who claim that one detects in human nature itself a structure that implies a superiority of some basic goods to others, of religion in relation to all the others, or of knowledge in relation to bodily goods. This ontological hierarchy is, on their view, essential to rightly ordering one's life. So the NNL's denial of an objective hierarchy among basic goods prior to moral norms (and so as a source of ethical direction) seems to some conventional natural lawyers a move towards subjectivism or, as one put it, towards 'autonomous reason in contradistinction to genuine natural law'.[24]

According to NNL theorists, precisely because the basic goods *are* basic and thus irreducible to a more common ground of value, each of them provides a distinct, ultimate reason for acting, and each grounds a first principle of practical reason. What makes each desirable is not its utility in relation to some other good but what it is itself. While each basic good *can* be pursued as a means in relation to others, the latter, as such, are no more excellent than the former.

None of this is to deny that these basic goods can be measured against one another in other respects. For example, life is more fundamental than the others in that it is the condition of enjoying the others. Practical understanding is more regulative than most of the others, and so on. But NNL theorists argue that they cannot be commensurated precisely with respect to what makes them intelligibly appealing; they are incommensurable precisely with respect to rational desirability. For one good could be better than another with respect to rational desirability only if (1) their rational desirability consisted entirely in their being means to some further good (and so one could be judged to be more effective than others in helping to realise that further good) or (2) they had some common measure, some property with respect to which one excelled the other, and which entirely grounded or exhausted their rational value. But since each of the basic goods is in itself good and not merely instrumentally good, one cannot be simply better than the others on the basis that one is more effective in helping to realise a further end – against (1). And one cannot excel another because it has more of some property than that other – against (2). For if that were the case, that common property – the one that provided the common measure – would be the basic good and ultimate reason for acting, rather than any of the distinctive goods themselves, such as life, knowledge, friendship and so on. As Joseph Boyle expressed this last point, if two goods did have a common measure and one did excel the other in respect of that measure, then it would 'not be precisely the intellectual, social, or biological benefit respectively of knowing, having friends, or being alive and healthy that makes each of these rationally desirable, but some further intelligibility of good which they share more or less fully or perfectly'.[25]

Some conventional natural lawyers argue that the basic goods do form a hierarchy. McInerny, for example, writes approvingly of what he takes to be Aquinas' position: 'Thomas himself, as Aristotle had before him, insists on the inequality of the basic values and recognises a hierarchy among them. That a good might be end-like yet not an ultimate end, but, subordinable to a further end, does not make it merely instrumental. Both Thomas and Aristotle take that perfection of rational activity which they call contemplation to be objectively the highest'.[26]

While Aquinas in various places seems to say that goods of the soul are higher than goods of the body, NNL theorists argue that the positions he sets out in his treatise on natural law logically lead to a denial of an objective hierarchy. In the first place, none of the basic goods is purely material: the good of life and health, for example, is the life and health of a human person and a human being's biological life is not separate from her spiritual soul and spiritual powers. Second, if the NNL theory's argument to show that basic goods are incommensurable is sound, then a basic good that can provide a reason for acting can't be both objectively less excellent than another and yet irreducibly and distinctly good. For if it is the latter then it can't be commensurated with other goods that provide reasons for acting. This point applies to the basic human goods of understanding and religion, as well as to others. According to NNL, one should not view participation or dedication to goods such as life, health, aesthetic experience or skilful performance (including play) as merely second class.[27]

At the same time, according to NNL, some basic goods are more organisational – that is, organise more levels of choice for the pursuit of other goods – and thus properly have a more architectonic role in one's life than other goods. The basic good of religion, considered even in its dimension as a natural good, should have a central and prior *organisational* role. The basic goods of integrity (practical reasonableness) and religion by their nature involve regulating the pursuit of the other goods. When one becomes aware and reflects on the fact that the basic moral norms have God as their source – that God is the creator and so the source both of the natural inclinations directing one to the basic human goods, and of one's intelligence, by which one apprehends those directives – then one understands that one's choosing fully in line with the basic practical principles is a way of cooperating with God, and that failing to do so is disobeying God (in that one substitutes one's subjective preferences for God's wisdom). Thus, the basic good of religion has an organisational priority to the other basic goods, given that the good of religion is at stake in all of one's actions (something not true of the other basic goods). All that one does should be a way of cooperating with, rather than setting aside, the wisdom of God the Creator (I suppose here a monotheistic view). Still, as a human good, religion is not of itself more excellent than the other basic goods.[28]

In addition to holding that the categories of basic good are incommensurable with each other, NNL theorists also hold that in those situations where one has a morally significant choice – that is, where it would be possible for one to choose between two or more possible actions – the options for choice are incommensurable. That is, NNL theorists hold that in such situations it is not possible to measure the two (or more) options against each other with respect to the sheer amount of good to be produced or the sheer amount of bad to be avoided. In such situations, one cannot say that one option offers all of the goodness that the other option does plus more; one cannot say that one option offers more good, simply speaking, than the other. The goods and bads in the options for morally significant choices cannot be measured against one another. For if one *could* measure the goodness of the options, such that one of the options offered all of the good offered by the other, plus more, then one would have no reason for choosing the lesser option. And so it would not be a situation of significant choice; but there are morally significant situations of choice.

This position provides NNL theorists with a strong argument against consequentialism. The consequentialist holds that one must perform that action which will produce the best consequences in the long run, or, put otherwise, one should always perform the action which will maximise the good. But if the options for choice in morally significant situations are incommensurable, then there is no 'greater good', simply speaking. Each option will offer some distinctive type of good or type of concrete benefit – if not, then it would not be a live option, it could not be chosen.[29]

NNL theorists also refer to this type of incommensurability when they defend moral absolutes, that is, certain specific exceptionless moral norms, such as those excluding intentional killing, torture and lying. They argue that one ought never choose to destroy, damage or impede one instance of a basic good in order to promote or protect another instance (or instances) of a basic good. Doing so is always contrary to reason, violating the first moral principle, that one ought always to choose in line with love and respect for integral human fulfilment. For the fact that an option would be an intentional damaging or impeding of an instance of a basic good provides a reason against that option. And the only way that reason could be overridden is if the damage or impeding of that instance of a good were outweighed by the good or avoidance of bad that this option produced compared with the alternatives. But since the concrete goods and bads in the options for these choices are incommensurable, that overriding is not possible. Grisez articulates the rationale for the moral norm prohibiting intentionally harming one instance of a basic good for the sake of another instance (or instances) as follows: 'Practical reason provides the same sort of grounds for respecting the good one proposes to injure as for pursuing the good one proposes to pursue. Still, one is moved by the desire which is stronger at the emotional level, that is, the desire which draws one to this rather than that imagined outcome'.[30]

THE ULTIMATE END OF HUMAN LIFE

NNL's insistence that each basic human good can rightly be an ultimate reason for acting is a significant shift in emphasis compared to the conventional natural law views. Against this shift, some conventional natural law critics object that instead of union with God as the natural ultimate end[31] – which is the true view and that of Aquinas, they say – NNL theorists have eight disparate ultimate ends, with no guidance on how to order them.

To these criticisms NNL theorists make several replies. In the first place, NNL theorists argue that Aquinas' views on the ultimate end are not as otherworldly as is often portrayed, nor does he identify the natural ultimate end with a definite activity – and thus instrumentalise the other basic goods – as is often claimed. While Aquinas does say that the 'essence' of beatitude consists in the intellectual contemplation of the divine essence, he is speaking there not precisely about natural human perfection, but the condition that will set to rest all of the desires that in fact arise in us.[32] And this condition turns out to be partly supernatural and partly natural.

Moreover, for Aquinas beatitude in its fullest sense – what he calls the '*bene esse*' [full-being] of beatitude – will include more than the essence of beatitude. It will include a supernatural vision of God as He is in himself, but also fulfilment with respect to all the other aspects of human nature, including health, friendship and so on.[33] Thus for Aquinas neither the natural ultimate end, nor the full state of affairs that is the ultimate end to which God has freely invited human beings, can be identified with a single activity over and above and distinct from the basic human goods, reducing them to an inferior status.

Second, NNL theorists who are Christians do hold, on the basis of faith, that human beings are called to union with God.[34] But they hold that this offer and invitation is a free and gratuitous gift on God's part, not an end to which our *nature* orientates us. They hold that direct union with God is a *super*natural end. For natures differ according to their ends. Seeing the divine essence is the infinite perfection proportionate to the *divine* nature. So human nature, which is finite, must be orientated to a distinct end, one proportionate to a creature. Thus human beings are not *naturally* orientated to the beatific vision.[35]

Third, NNL theorists who are Christians hold that the supernatural end to which human beings are called does not negate, or substitute for, the fulfilment to which human beings are orientated by their nature. They believe that the goal of the Christian life is the Kingdom of God. And that will be a community of divine and created persons richly sharing in supernatural good and created, natural goods.

Lastly, NNL theorists also hold that the fulfilment to which our human nature inclines – that is, the ultimate natural end – is not a single, definite act, but is participation in a manifold of goods, befitting a complex, body-soul person. The natural perfection of the human being cannot be located in the actualisation of only one part of the human being, the intellect. The actualisations of the capacities of free self-determination, bodily health, work and play, as well as the actualisation of the intellect, are irreplaceable constituents of the fulfilment of a human being. Every aspect of human nature is an aspect of a human person and so is never 'merely animal' or sub-personal as it exists concretely in a human being. Hence the natural fulfilment of human nature includes participation in all the basic human goods, the bodily as well as the spiritual perfections, and this natural fulfilment is part of the total fulfilment to which human persons are freely called by God.[36]

Thus the NNL theory offers a distinctive natural law approach to the fundamental ethical questions. It can be called a *new* natural law theory in that it is different from the view traditionally attributed to Aquinas. But it claims to have a more accurate interpretation of Aquinas, and with respect to basic moral principles it claims to present a view closer to Aquinas' than does the conventional natural law view. According to NNL, the moral good is grounded in the human good and yet human nature itself is not the standard. Rather, the basic moral standard is to choose in line with love and openness to all the intrinsic goods of human persons. There is thus both a respect for all the intrinsic goods of human persons and an emphasis on the uniqueness or irreducibility of the moral domain.

NOTES

1. As I hope to show, this name is not entirely appropriate. NNL theorists hold that their interpretation of Aquinas' view is more accurate. Their own view on the basic principles of the natural law is essentially Aquinas', though they develop it and do not agree with Aquinas on all specific points.
2. Grisez 1965.
3. On the difference between practical and speculative reasoning in Aquinas, see *Summa Theologiae* Part I, question 79, article 12.
4. See Grisez 1965: 168–80.
5. According to another interpretation, this principle affirms that one ought to do what is *morally* good and avoid doing what is morally evil. One then discovers what is morally good by consulting one's speculative knowledge of human nature, so that what is morally good is what is in accord with human nature. For this view and references, see Grisez 1965: 177–80.
6. Finnis 2011a: chapters 3 and 4. Note that the first edition of this book was published in 1980; Grisez 1983: chapter 5; Finnis et al. 1987b, especially 102–8; Finnis 2011b, especially 38–40.
7. John Finnis holds that moral goodness, or what he terms practical reasonableness, is a distinct basic good. Grisez and Boyle, however, think that it is not a distinct

good but that it should be viewed as a form of inner harmony or self-integration. See Grisez 2013: 443–58, at 443–6.

8. In early works Grisez, Boyle and others believed marriage was not a distinct basic good but a form of friendship. But partly because friendship seems to be only a component of marriage and marriage fulfils human beings precisely as man and woman, Grisez concluded in 1993 that it is a distinct basic good. See Grisez 1993: 567–73.
9. See also St. Thomas, *ST*, I-II, q. 100, a. 3, where Aquinas seems to identify the first moral principle with the love command: *Love God and love one's neighbour.* To love is to will good to someone, so to love God and love one's neighbour is to will the fulfilment of God's plan and to will to one's neighbour her genuine good. Thus the love command is the same in content as the first moral principle articulated by Grisez et al.
10. E.g. McInerny 1980, 1982, 1992: 184–92; Jensen 2015: chapter 7.
11. E.g. Lisska 1996: chapter 8; Feser 2009: 175.
12. See also MacIntyre 2000: 107. According to this approach, just as from the theoretical knowledge that, say, gathering acorns is good for a squirrel one can infer squirrels ought to gather acorns, so it is from theoretical knowledge of what human nature is that one will infer what a human ought to do. See Feser 2008: 137.
13. Also, to have a practical meaning, the term will have to be part of a practical *proposition*.
14. Commenting on the conventional Thomistic interpretation decades ago, Kai Nielsen made a similar point, in Nielsen 1959: 64.
15. Aquinas 1934, *In Decem Libros Ethicorum Aristotelis ad Nicomachum* (*Commentary on Aristotle's Nicomachean Ethics*, Bk. I, Lecture 1).
16. Not always: most NNL theorists hold that capital punishment is intrinsically immoral – a point on which, of course, they also disagree with Aquinas. See e.g. Grisez 1993: 891–4; Brugger 2014; Tollefsen 2018a.
17. But even in those cases, the apparent goods are either instrumental goods falsely viewed as ultimate or fragments of basic goods treated as good by themselves.
18. According to another interpretation, this principle affirms that one ought to do what is *morally* good and avoid doing what is morally evil. Then, according to this interpretation, one discovers what is morally good by consulting one's speculative knowledge of human nature so that what is morally good is what is in accord with human nature. Germain Grisez criticises such a view in Grisez 1965: 168–78.
19. McInerny 2000: 66; also see Jensen 2015: chapter 9.
20. NNL theorists also point out that Aquinas compares this principle to the principle of non-contradiction, which suggests that it is a formal principle rather than a directive to a specific good such as the ultimate end. It also suggests that as the

principle of non-contradiction does not by itself exclude false conclusions or unreasonable arguments, so the first general practical principle does not by itself exclude all immoral actions. As the principle of non-contradiction excludes only incoherence, so the first practical principle excludes only irrationality in the form of pointlessness – but not all practical unreasonableness.

21. John Finnis describes the *ought* of the first practical principles in this way. See Finnis 1998: 87.
22. Finnis et al. 1987b: 125–6. They continue: 'In the moral domain truth is the whole, and falsity a part, abstracted from the whole and thereby made to rationally guide action in a misguided way, just as if the part were itself the whole'.
23. This seems to be at odds with Aristotle's view, for example.
24. Long 2004.
25. Boyle 2002: 127. See also Finnis et al. 1987a: chapter 8; Grisez 1999; Finnis 1997; George 1999.
26. McInerny 1980: 339.
27. It is well to remember that the good of religion – harmony with God – is not *identical* with God, the infinite Good. Religion itself is a created reality and so is a finite instance of a good, and none of the bodily goods such as life and health are *merely* bodily.
28. Boyle 1998.
29. Boyle 2002.
30. Grisez 1983: 217.
31. By 'natural' here is meant an end to which human nature orientates one, and that one can know by reason unaided by faith.
32. *Summa Theologiae* I-II, q. 3.
33. *Summa Theologiae* I-II, q. 4, aa. 4–8.
34. NNL theory is a *philosophical* project and not all NNL theorists are Christians. Nevertheless, those who are Christian reflect on the logical relations of their natural law positions to matters of faith. While Germain Grisez began as a philosopher and wrote many philosophical works, from the 1980s on his main work was in moral theology (though of course his theological works contain many philosophical arguments and reflections).
35. One might object that a human being must have a natural inclination to the direct vision of the divine essence since, as intelligent beings, human beings do have a natural desire to know what God is. This is so, however, only in the sense that once human beings know that something exists, they naturally desire to know what it is, as a consequence of their basic natural inclination to knowledge and understanding in general. This particular natural desire is a concrete effect of the basic inclination towards knowledge in general and so does not show that the

object to which human nature (or the human intellect) is orientated is the direct vision of the divine essence.

36. See Vatican Council II, *Apostolicam Actuositatem*, #7. NNL theorists argue that if the ultimate end were only the spiritual union with God, then it would be difficult to see how non-religious actions in this world could have an intelligible, intrinsic link to such a future and purely spiritual end. Given that view of the ultimate end, the actions and goods in this world would lack intrinsic significance, and would be important only as a test or occasion for the human soul's spiritual activities aimed beyond them. By contrast, Christian NNL theorists emphasise that there is an intrinsic link between the actions and goods in this world, on the one hand, and the completed Kingdom, the total good to which God calls human beings, on the other hand, because the Kingdom will *include* both supernatural union and human fulfilment.

5 Neo-Aristotelian Ethical Naturalism*

Jennifer A. Frey

I

In her famous critique of various 'modern' presuppositions in moral philosophy, Elizabeth Anscombe suggests that philosophers ought to give up on the idea that there is a sense of 'ought' or 'obligation' that is specifically *moral*. This concept, she argues, originally derived its sense from a notion of an authoritative divine law against which human actions could be measured; the presumed existence of such a law made it possible to render absolute verdicts on human acts as licit or illicit.[1] In the absence of recourse to such a law, the terms 'moral obligation', 'moral ought' and 'morally wrong' are empty and best abandoned. It would be better if we look for the ground of normative claims regarding human life and action in our knowledge of our own 'species', where this is understood, 'from the *point of view of the activity of thought and choice in regard to the various departments of life*'.[2] To do this would be to turn away from 'a law conception of ethics' as understood in the Jewish, Christian and Stoic traditions, and towards something supposedly quite different – viz. Aristotelian naturalism. Or so Anscombe famously argues.

Anscombe's suggestion that we look for the grounds of ethical judgements in the concept of the human species, rather than continuing to make use of the concepts central to a law conception of ethics, has been taken up by an increasingly diverse group of theorists often referred to as the 'Neo-Aristotelians'.[3] Neo-Aristotelians (broadly construed) attempt to ground their accounts of the goodness of the virtues in some idea of 'human flourishing' or 'living well' as a human person. This chapter gives an overview of Neo-Aristotelian ethical naturalism, with a particular focus on the theory developed by Philippa Foot, in order to address the question of whether Anscombe was right to oppose it to the natural law tradition.

All Neo-Aristotelians more or less agree that the concept of a virtue is that of a stable disposition of action and feeling that makes this 'living well' possible. As Philippa Foot puts it, 'it is in the concept of a virtue that in so far as someone possesses it, his actions are good; which is to say that he acts [lives] well'.[4]

All Neo-Aristotelians also more or less agree that human beings generally, given the kind of thing they are, *need* and therefore *ought* to develop these virtues. As Peter Geach writes, 'men need the virtues as bees need stings'.[5] Finally, on these accounts, what one 'ought' to do, quite generally, is what the virtuous person would do in similar circumstances, because the virtuous person is disposed to act well and exemplifies a good human life in his actions.

Under this general umbrella of 'Neo-Aristotelians', further divisions can be made. Some, like Peter Geach (1977), argue that the ultimate ground of practical norms must be supernatural, and that many virtues central to living well point us to an ultimate, supernatural end. Let us call them ethical supernaturalists. Ethical naturalists, by contrast, think of the end or goal of human life as something immanent to our nature and our natural condition in this life, and the virtues as dispositions articulated wholly within this immanent frame.

Amongst this group, we can make a further division between first nature and second nature naturalists.[6] According to second nature ethical naturalists, such as John McDowell, we possess practical knowledge of human nature only once we come to possess a well-formed 'second nature' through the cultivation of moral virtue and practical wisdom. On this version of ethical naturalism, there are no foundational facts about human nature to which the virtuous and non-virtuous alike have equal epistemic access as a matter of common sense; rather, the knowledge of human nature that is characteristic of practical reason only comes by way of a well-formed 'second nature'.[7]

By contrast, first nature ethical naturalists, such as Philippa Foot (2001), Rosalind Hursthouse (1999) and Alasdair MacIntyre (1999) want to make direct comparisons between judgements of how human beings ought to live with judgements about living things more generally. First nature naturalists argue that natural facts, such as that human beings are social and political animals who can flourish together only in cooperation within a society ruled by common norms, serve as the ultimate ground of our practical judgements, and that such facts are available to us just in virtue of having the capacity to observe and reflect upon our own common humanity. Just as a good oak tree is one that has strong, deep roots, which are the kind of roots necessary for an excellent or flourishing oak life, so also a virtuous person is one with good dispositions of thought, will and feeling, which are the dispositions necessary for an excellent or flourishing human life. Here the sense of necessity is taken from Aristotle (via Anscombe), and means that 'without which good cannot be or come to be'.[8] Statements of such necessities determine what it is for members of a particular species to be as they should be and to do that which they should do. Virtues, on this view, are what enable us to make the sort of choices that typically secure our natural good – a good it belongs to the human person to possess, just in virtue of being a human person. Finally, such common-sense knowledge of what is naturally good or bad for human beings is in principle available to the virtuous and non-virtuous alike, although only the virtuous person will be able to attain the fullness of this natural good through her actions.

One of the most compelling accounts of first nature naturalism is found in Philippa Foot's *Natural Goodness* (Foot 2001). Foot's master thought is that judgements of practical or ethical normativity – about what it is good for us to be, do and have in general – share a logical grammar with judgements of natural normativity.[9] On this account, ethical virtue is an instance of natural goodness, while ethical vice is an instance of natural defect – specifically, defect of will and practical reasoning. Since moral judgements are judgements of good and bad action, they are judgements of whether natural (vital) human powers are operating well or badly. Foot claims, therefore, that 'there is no change in the meaning of "good" between the word as it appears in "good roots" and as it appears in "good dispositions of the human will"'.[10]

II

The easiest way into the ethical naturalist's semantics of natural goodness comes by reflecting on the reality of defect, lack, failure, harm and disability in the realm of the living. We all know from everyday experience that many living things fail to be good exemplars of their kind: we see crops that are brown and disease-ridden, animals that have missing limbs, poor eyesight or the lack of some capacity necessary to their survival and flourishing. Yet it is impossible to identify these traits or characteristics as defect, disability or harm in individuals except as measured against some general conception of the species.[11] One must have some conception of an *exemplar* of the species in order to judge that any individual has failed to measure up in some respect. And that is because what it is for any individual living thing to be defective, qua instance of that kind of living thing, is for it to be unable or unwilling to get for itself what it *needs* in order to be what it is in the fullest sense. This lack or absence of something that *ought* or *needs* to be present for the individual to flourish is the basis of the judgement of natural defect.

In order to be able to recognise an individual *F* as a living thing of a specific kind with specific needs, one must already have some general conception of *F*s. More specifically, one must have some kind of general knowledge of the tendencies and activities that are characteristic of the species to which it belongs. This is emphatically not the knowledge of a highly trained specialist; rather, it is the sort of knowledge any human being will come to possess quite a bit of just in virtue of growing up in and coming to have a basic understanding of a world that is full of living things. It is these ordinary, pre-theoretical judgements of human life that interests the ethical naturalist, because it is part of that theory that our moral judgements, such as that a man should keep his promises, are just as ordinary and pre-theoretical as the judgement that the cherry tree should blossom in spring.

Furthermore, seeing that we manifestly do live and come to acquire language in such a world, all human communities come to know that the living things around them have *needs*, and moreover, that if they lack whatever is necessary to fulfil these needs, these living things will be straightforwardly harmed. The fine-grained details of this story – what the living thing needs, how much and when – are worked out at the level of the individual species. But such details are very often unnecessary for making the sort of judgements of goodness and defect that interest us here.

Because this general knowledge of life forms is so central to an account of natural normativity, it will benefit the discussion to briefly (though incompletely) characterise what a life form is and what sort of judgements we make about them.[12]

To identify something – that green stuff on a rock, perhaps – as a living thing – some sheet moss – is to see in the particular something general, what Michael Thompson calls 'the life form'.[13]

A life form is something general, knowledge of which is always implicit in the representation of an individual of a kind. A life form is a kind of substance sortal concept, susceptible to classification, such as:

This *a* is an S.

A substance sortal is characterised by what David Wiggins calls 'some particular way of behaving, coming to be, being, being qualified, or passing away'.[14] So we can use it in kind-characterising generic sentences such as:

S's are (have, do) F.
The S is (has, does) F.
An S is (has, does) F.

Michael Thompson calls these 'natural historical judgements', since they register facts about the life form that falls under the subject term. Such judgements yield informative sentences that Thompson calls 'Aristotelian categoricals'. Some examples are:

Beavers build dams.
The beaver builds dams.
A beaver builds dams.

Now, when such generic statements are 'essence-expressing generics', as Julius Moravcsik calls them,[15] they do not have the form of Fregean universal generalisations. For example, take the proposition, 'Horses have four legs': its truth is not vitiated by an encounter (or even many encounters) with a three-legged horse. Nor do these generic propositions take the form of statistical generalisations about a population. For instance, one might read that 'Mayflies breed shortly before dying'. This is true, despite the fact that, statistically speaking, the vast majority of mayflies die well before they manage to breed. Therefore, we cannot get to the truth of the form of proposition in question from an empirical survey of what happens to be going on with certain populations of Mayflies at any point in time. These considerations prove that these judgements must have a unique logical form.

Though not empirical or statistical generalisations, neither do these judgements purport to describe things in some form of an idealised subjunctive that would express how things would be for members of a species in specifiable 'ideal conditions'. And that is because the specification of 'ideal' conditions, as anyone who studies contemporary physics knows, does not necessarily have any existential import, whereas what is specified by a natural historical judgement does. There must exist, or have at some point in history have existed, something actually corresponding to the subject term of the judgements in question; a natural historical judgement does not concern a mere abstraction or idealisation, but something that is in some sense – either past or present – a real, material substance in the world.[16]

Relatedly, these judgements are typically made in some form of a timeless present tense, and refer to something that can, in principle, be instantiated at various times and places. Though these judgements can be ordered in relations of before or after, they do not concern a specific occasion. Thus, we can say that our judgements reference what 'beavers' do in the course of a typical year of beaver life, but not what particular ones did over the course of this past year in Vermont.

Finally, these judgements are not equivalent to hypotheses about the past, especially not to empirical hypotheses regarding what accounts historically for the tendency of S's to have or do F. The ethical naturalist's category of species or life form is most emphatically *not* the same as that employed by the evolutionary biologist, nor does it somehow stand in competition with it. The biological concept of species is a theory-laden concept that we need not (and of course, typically do not) deploy in order to make the kind of layperson's judgements now under discussion.[17] A representation of something as alive is both logically and phenomenologically more primitive than the empirical concept of a biological species; after all, the evolutionary biologist would fail to have a topic of inquiry if she could not first merely represent something *as* a particular living being or life form. One does not need any such theory to experience certain things as animate, in contrast to others as inanimate. What interests the ethical naturalist is the pre-theoretical representation of life, the perspective of the ordinary human person.[18]

The biological notion of species is further differentiated from the category of life form in that it is an empirical concept, one that we come to possess through observation and inference. The notion of a life form, by contrast, is not a concept at all; therefore it would be a category mistake to ask whether it is 'innate' or 'acquired'.[19] Rather, much like Frege's concept/object distinction, it signifies an a priori form of description or predication, one that we employ whenever it is possible to represent something as *alive* in our judgement or thought.[20] The philosopher is able to articulate this form of description through rational reflection upon our deployment of it in our true judgements about the living. When we reflect on our thought about the living in general, we come to see that for us to represent something in the world as alive – as engaged in any *life* process whatsoever – the material given to us through the senses must be bound up within a certain a priori nexus of interrelated forms of judgement. Making that framework of judgement and inference explicit is not the work of any special science but of philosophy proper.

It follows that no empirical concept of species could play any role in a sound doctrine of natural normativity; thus we cannot and need not look to biology, ethology, zoology, botany or any other special science in order to apprehend the *principles* of 'living well' in the ethical naturalist's sense. Ethical naturalism is non-reductive in the strong sense that it holds we cannot move from the 'is' of empirical science to the 'ought' of moral theory.[21]

Of course, not all 'essence-expressing generics' demand explanation by a form of predication, but what is supposed to be special about what can fall under the subject term of a natural historical judgement is that it does. But the reason for this is not explained by anything said about them so far. What is predicated of the subject in a natural historical judgement is always such that it can be an element in a 'natural history story', because these judgements articulate the relations of dependence among the various parts, aspects and phases of the activity of a given kind of life taken as a whole. Thus they can appear in teleological combinations, as in:

S's (have, do) F in order that S's (have, do) G.

1 Beavers have powerful jaws in order that beavers chop down trees.
2 Beavers chop down trees in order that beavers build dams.
3 Beavers build dams in order that beavers build a lodge in deep and calmer waters.

Such combinations form a system of inter-related judgements. 'Why?' and 'What's next?' are questions that, when applied to the activity of any particular living thing, have answers that will take the form of natural facts about that living thing's general kind. A life form is what is suited to be the subject of this sort of teleological nexus.[22]

The preceding materials give us all the conceptual resources we need to define an abstract, logical schema of natural goodness and defect, by employing the following form of inference among the 'facts' that natural historical propositions pick out:

S's have F & This S has F.
S's have F & This S does *not* have F.
E.g. Beavers have powerful jaws and this beaver has a powerful jaw.
E.g. Beavers have powerful jaws and this beaver does not.

We can infer a normative judgement of natural goodness or defect from this:

> This S is good in that it has F.
> This S is defective, bad or lacking in that it does *not* have F.
> E.g. This beaver is good in that it has a powerful jaw.
> E.g. This beaver is defective in that it does *not* have a powerful jaw.

That there are these two kinds of judgements of 'facts' in relation to one another – natural historical judgements, which relate *general* statements of facts about the life form as such, and judgements about the facts of what is happening with a *particular* individual member of the species, here and now – is what makes judgements of natural goodness and defect possible. It is because we can say that 'A beaver has powerful jaws in order to chop down trees for its dams' that we can say of *this* beaver that it is gnawing on that tree *because* it is building a dam, or that *this* beaver is defective in that it fails in this task on account of having a loose jaw.

That we do make such inferences from natural facts to normative judgements suggests that our description of what a life form is also provides a standard against which we judge whether it is doing well or badly. This standard of goodness or badness is immanent to the life form itself: to do well just is to most completely or most fully exemplify the potential inherent in one's life form. Since this ethical standard is objective, ethical naturalism is a species of moral realism. But since the standard is internal to the thing that bears it, such realism cannot be construed in any sort of quasi-Platonic fashion.

III

The fact that there are natural norms in human beings and living things more generally does not entail that ethical or rational norms are a species of natural norms; the burden is clearly on the ethical naturalist to establish that rational norms are natural norms. In Foot's case, the argument to this effect begins from certain commitments about the semantics of goodness in general.

Following Peter Geach,[23] Foot wants to exploit the fact that the adjective 'good', like 'big' or 'small' and unlike 'yellow' or 'straight', is logically attributive rather than predicative. An attributive adjective is one whose meaning is specified by the nature of that to which the substantive noun it modifies refers. On Geach's account, there is nothing that it is to be 'good' in general, as there is something that it is to be 'yellow' in general; good is not a separably definable predicate.

Geach concludes that we can truly speak about there being goodness only when we are speaking about a good such and such – a good knife, house, lawyer or human being.[24] On this account, what is good for an F depends on what we substitute in for F, where F must be a 'descriptive noun'. Good has no independent, 'objective' meaning; rather, good has 'descriptive force', which depends essentially on the descriptive noun it is modifying in whatever context it is being attributed.

Though what is good for an F depends on what F is, not just any noun can be substituted in for F on Geach's account. There is no such thing as a good state of affairs, for instance, or a good event, or a good possible world. These terms are far too general to have the necessary 'descriptive force'. Likewise, one cannot speak meaningfully of a good smudge, stick or dot, as these things are not what Judith Jarvis Thomson calls 'goodness fixing kinds'.[25] Something is a goodness fixing kind if being an F sets a substantive standard that any particular F has to meet if it is to be good qua F. This account of the grammar of goodness depends on the idea of an internal or immanent measure.

What is especially noteworthy about this view is that it brings to light scores of cases in which the so-called fact–value dichotomy collapses. It allows us to say that something is good or bad by reference to what it *is*.[26] As important as I take Geach's point to be, however, we should not be tempted to think that we can construct out of these materials a general theory of normativity into which 'natural norms' will easily be subsumed. Judith Jarvis Thomson, for instance, writes as if being a toaster, umbrella, tennis player, liar, beefsteak tomato, tiger or human being all equally fit her general category of 'goodness fixing kind', which serves as the conceptual foundation of her general theory of normativity. She does not seem impressed by the thought that there are any philosophically salient differences between the account we would give of the goodness of an artefact, such as a toaster, and the account we would give of the goodness of a living thing.[27]

Though a life form is certainly a 'goodness fixing kind', we must not think that we can take for granted a general notion of 'goodness fixing kind' and then simply add something to it in order to get to natural goodness. For we've already seen that the sort of goodness or badness that pertains to living things is categorially unique. Therefore our account of the goodness or badness of life forms must go beyond a merely attributive account of goodness. A life form is a sui generis category and needs its own account.

IV

The ethical naturalist wants to say that a human action or disposition is good if it is a particular instantiation or exemplification of living well for a human, and bad insofar as it fails to be this. Facts about what constitutes a good life are facts about human form. For instance, Foot argues that 'a moral evaluation does not stand over against the statement of matter of fact', and that 'the evaluation of the human will should be determined by facts about the nature of human beings and the life of our own species'.[28] Just as there are facts about what constitutes good eyesight, hearing and memory for a human being, so too there are facts about what constitutes good dispositions of human choice.

Foot's paradigm case of an ethically salient natural historical fact about human beings is that we are 'social animals'.[29] She argues that, like other social animals, we need to live co-operatively and consider the needs of others in order to live well together. Consequently, we need to perform actions that contribute to the well-functioning of the communities in which we live. This means, inter alia, that our habits of practical reasoning must be fundamentally other-regarding, such that the good of others is always taken into account. If we were not social animals these general claims about how we ought to think and live would not be true.

Relatedly, she argues that we need to depend upon our ability to bind one another's wills through contracts and promises. If human beings had the power to bind one another's wills automatically, then promising would not matter to us, nor would the virtue of fidelity be of any fundamental importance in human life. It is not conceptually impossible to imagine such creatures, but we must admit that their rules of good conduct would be quite different from our own, precisely because what constitutes their natural goodness would be different from ours.

So Foot takes natural historical facts about the species to place quite definite constraints on (1) what we can take excellence of practical reasoning to be (it cannot be egoistic), (2) what we can take the proper goods and ends of human life to be (one of these ends must be the good of the community as a whole) and (3) what the virtues are (justice must be one of them). Because natural historical facts play this role in determining what human goodness is via the concept of human life form, and because judgements about human goodness are moral judgements, it follows that moral judgements are instances of natural normativity. On this account, although there is a change in the meaning of 'good' from 'good' knife to 'good' roots, there is no change of meaning of the word 'good' when we move from 'good' roots in some plant, to 'good' dispositions of the will in a human person.[30] Goodness is still identified with the mature stage or full exemplification of the life form (although now we speak of practical maturity). Therefore, we deploy the same general notion of living well, but now in a logically more determinate way that recognises the shift to rational life – i.e. to a creature with the capacity for practical reason and will. For such a thing, 'living well' is understood in terms of the kind of deep fulfilment that Aristotle calls *eudaimonia*.

Now, Foot is further committed to the claim that acts of will are good or bad insofar as they follow correct judgements of practical reason. A person of good will acts for the right reasons, where the account of what a right reason is involves an essential appeal to facts about human form.

Foot follows Warren Quinn's attempt to provide a 'Neo-Aristotelian version of objectivism' about practical reason.[31] Like Quinn, Foot argues that practical thought and reason is distinguished from theoretical thought and reason in virtue of its distinctive subject matter: it is thought and reasoning *about* human goods, human life and human action. Quinn, in an article that Foot cites as a positive influence, argues that

> practical rationality is not as different from theoretical rationality as the subjectivist supposes. Practical thought, like any other thought, requires a subject matter. And for human beings the subject matter that distinguishes thought as practical is, in the first instance, human ends and action insofar as they are good or bad in themselves ... practical thought deploys a master set of non-instrumental evaluative notions: that of a good or bad human act, a good or bad human life, a good or bad human agent, and a good or bad human action. Practical reason is, on this view, the faculty that applies these fundamental evaluative concepts.[32]

According to Quinn, what provides us with reasons for acting is the cognitive content of our evaluative judgements about human goodness, rather than the content of our subjective desires. The primary work of practical reason, on this view, is the 'correct evaluation of ends'[33] or 'correctness of thought about human good and evil'.[34] This kind of thought, which Quinn calls 'ethical' as opposed to 'calculative', is concerned with what actions or good make up the best kind of life. There is no difference, on this account, between recognising a practical reason and having a goal, because practical reason is a capacity to be motivated by the recognition of what is truly good.[35] Ethical thought is related to calculative thought, on this view, in that the latter is the application of the former; for once one judges that something is good, one thereby gives oneself a reason to pursue it, and once one judges that something is bad, one thereby gives oneself a reason to avoid it.[36] Foot accepts this account, on the whole, and simply adds that the truth makers of these judgements of good and bad are determined by facts about human life and human needs – what she calls 'Aristotelian categoricals'.[37]

When we put this characterisation of what it is to have a reason for action together with the sort of facts about human nature that are relevant to Foot's account, we arrive at the following picture of moral or practical judgement within the schema of natural goodness and normativity. The virtuous person is one who makes true judgements about what is choice worthy (the one who perceives what is truly good), and these judgements are grounded in her recognition of the facts about human needs and goods; the practically wise person is able to see what flourishing for a human being is in any given situation.[38] Let us call Foot's theory of practical reason 'recognitional naturalism', as it weds recognitional realism about practical reasons with a naturalistic account of the human good. According to it, practical reason is a recognitional capacity whose proper exercise makes correct, intrinsically motivating judgements regarding the goods constitutive of human life.[39]

V

Having sketched what Neo-Aristotelian ethical naturalism claims, I want to return to Anscombe's opposition between Aristotelian naturalism and natural law. In short, I want to raise the question whether we can place the ethical naturalists within the natural law tradition, even if only in an attenuated sense.

To answer this question I want to begin with Anscombe's own description of the natural law. In 'The Justice of the Present War Examined', she writes that 'the natural law is the law of man's own nature, showing how he must choose to act in matters where his will is free, if his nature is to be properly fulfilled'.[40] She further argues that if man does not live 'according to his proper nature' he will not attain his end of 'living well'. All of this will sound very much in keeping with ethical naturalism. We might call this a *material* definition of the natural law, since it provides a way to see how the natural gets its specific content.

However, in the same article, Anscombe goes on to note that it is the eternal law of God that is reflected in human nature, such that the law of nature *binds* us to act in accordance with it 'because it is the law of his [God's] nature'. Let us call this the *formal* definition of law as 'the participation in the eternal law of the rational creature'.[41] For Anscombe, as for Aquinas, human nature is normative as a *law* because its source lies in a divine lawgiver who has care over creation. This is a meta-ethical commitment about the ultimate ground of the authority of practical principles, as well as a claim about the nature of the normative demands of practical reason (i.e. we must live in accordance with the norms of right practical reason not only in order to live well, but also because 'living well' is to participate in God's providential plan for his creation, and thus to obey his commands; if we fail to follow the norms, we not only fail to live well, we further incur the guilt of sin).

Whether or not we can speak of human nature as a law obviously depends on one's definition of the essence of law. Aquinas defines law as 'an ordinance of reason directed towards the common good from *him* who has care of the community and *promulgated*'.[42] It should strike us that Neo-Aristotelians such as Foot can endorse every characteristic of law except one: an external lawgiver. Certainly, they make use of some concept of 'ordinances of reason' – practical judgements about human goodness and badness that give us practical reasons to act in specified ways – which are directed towards the common good.[43] We can even say that these ordinances of reason are 'promulgated', since anyone raised in a reasonably well-functioning community can come to know them; and moreover, because the virtuous person is the exemplar of the law – the 'rule and measure' – against which we can assess whether our own actions and lives are good or bad. For Foot, then, nature gives us principles and norms but not laws in Aquinas' sense, because there is no external lawgiver in his sense. Whether or not Aquinas is correct to think that law requires a lawgiver beyond nature is not a question I will attempt to settle here.

Whatever we say about the status of human nature as law, it seems clear that ethical naturalism is not opposed to the natural law tradition, and can even be taken as a development within it insofar as it locates the ground of ethical judgements in human *nature*; in so doing, it supplies precisely that which is often lacking in contemporary natural law theories: viz. a clear enough and thick enough conception of 'nature' that can serve as the ground of normative ethical judgements.

It is true that Foot does not inquire about the ultimate source of the authority of the natural norms she defends. Perhaps she would argue that the question of the source of these norms is irrelevant to ethical thought, since what matters is that we need to operate under them in order to live well. Perhaps she thinks we must say, with Wittgenstein: 'If I have exhausted the justifications I have reached bedrock, and my spade is turned. Then I am inclined to say: "This is simply what I do"'.[44]

If we stick to the bedrock of human nature, and thereby stop short of calling human nature a law that exercises binding force upon our wills, then I think we can say that the ethical naturalist has a merely material conception of natural law; that is, she has a conceptual framework that can generate content about what to do, but that falls short of making substantive meta-ethical claims about the obligatory character of practical norms.

However, if one thinks that human nature poses a question about its own legitimate authority it cannot itself answer, and that we manifestly need an ultimate ground for talk of natural normativity, one will find the merely material conception of natural law offered by the first nature ethical naturalists wanting. For such a person, the question remains why *mere* nature should suffice to provide the measure of human life, especially since the human person always seems to seek something that transcends its limitations.

NOTES

* I am grateful to Tom Angier, Daniel De Haan, Veronica Rodriguez-Blanco, Dominic Farrell, Steven Long and Herlinde Pauer-Studer for helpful feedback.

1. Anscombe 2005a: 169ff.
2. Anscombe 2005a: 188, emphasis added.
3. I will construe 'Neo-Aristotelians' broadly to include those moral philosophers convinced that ethics is, to some extent, grounded in claims about human nature, where human nature is understood in a broadly Aristotelian vein. Notable philosophers in this group include: Peter Geach 1977, David Braine 1992, Warren Quinn

1994, Alasdair MacIntyre 1999, Rosalind Hursthouse 1999, Philippa Foot 2001, Julia Annas 2005, Gavin Lawrence, 2005, 2017, Judith Jarvis Thomson 2008, Michael Thompson 2008, Talbot Brewer 2009, Candace Vogler 2013, John Hacker-Wright 2009a, 2013.

4. Foot 2001: 12. Of course, there is an ambiguity in our use of 'living well', since modern ears are likely to hear this phrase in a curiously a-moral register. While I cannot defend Foot's usage now, I will simply note that for Foot (as for Anscombe 2005b), any properly human act is either 'living well' *sans phrase* (*eudaimonia*) or it isn't. So when Foot uses *moral*, she simply means something that is good in the 'living well' sense.
5. Geach 1977: 22.
6. McDowell 1998b.
7. For a full development of the concept of 'second nature', see McDowell 1994 and 1995. For a more recent example of this second nature naturalism, see Lott 2012. For a critique of second nature naturalism, see Frey 2018.
8. *Metaphysics* 1015a20–27. See also Anscombe 1981c: 15. The idea is that the virtues are necessary for human goodness to be or come to be, just as strong deep roots are necessary for oak goodness to be or come to be.
9. Philippa Foot puts it this way: 'Moral judgement of human actions and dispositions is one example of a genre of evaluation itself actually characterized by the fact that its objects are living things' (Foot 2001: 4).
10. Foot 2001: 39.
11. This knowledge can be vague and inarticulate (and most often is). We needn't be expert gardeners or botanists to judge that a flower is faring well or poorly. However, if we came across a seeding grass or forbs or legumes for the first time, we might think their drying up and their seeds disseminating through the wind is harmful, when it is actually flourishing, which shows that some knowledge of form is requisite to these judgements.
12. My goal in this discussion is to say just enough about this category to be able to comprehend it. For a robust defence, see Thompson 2004, 2008.
13. Thompson 2008.
14. Wiggins 1997: 417.
15. Moravcsik 1994.
16. The operative word here is 'mere', since there is clearly some idealisation at work in these judgements, as they can be said to describe what 'typifies' or is 'paradigmatic' of the species, and this is always in some sense to make reference to an ideal. The main point to stress is that such idealisation is based on the existence of a concrete material substance. As Moravscik writes, 'A species is not just a property. It is a class of actual and derivatively possible entities, causally connected, and with a common causal origin' (Moravcsik 1994: 232).

17. In fact, one could plausibly formulate the claim in even stronger terms: what I am calling a 'life form' is necessary in order for the evolutionary biologist so much as to have a topic for study. For reasons of space, I will not here defend such a claim, though I think it is true. Many readers of Foot have failed to appreciate this point about the theory. See Fitzpatrick 2000, Murphy 2003, Millgram 2009 and Lewens 2010. For an especially emphatic refutation of the idea that this knowledge could be based on 'observational' evidence (let alone evidence that comes from the application of sound evolutionary biological principles), see Thompson 2004.
18. We might say, with Sellars 1962, that the theory is within the 'manifest' rather than the 'scientific' image. Whether we wish to reduce, eliminate or throw a fictional operator around claims within this image is a separate question I will not address here. All that I wish to point to is the fact that the ethical naturalist is interested in our common experience of things, which is the practical point of view of choice and action. Because the ethical naturalist makes claims within the manifest image, objections from evolutionary theory, such as those made by Fitzpatrick 2000 and Street 2006, fail to make contact with her view.
19. Rödl 2007 would call it a formal concept. I have found, however, that once the word concept is used, most philosophers will only ask whether it is innate or acquired. I find the term unhelpful for that reason, and do my best to avoid it.
20. For further discussion of such logical or grammatical categories in Frege, see Frey and Frey 2017.
21. Ethical naturalists are not always as careful about this point as they need to be. Hursthouse, to take one example, goes so far as to say that her claims are 'objective', precisely because 'scientific' (1999, 202). She does not seem to appreciate that (1) this is a contentious and radically un-Aristotelian account of objectivity, and (2) even if true, would render her own theory basically useless. Julia Annas follows Hursthouse. In her article on virtue and naturalism we read that 'the way we should live and act' should be informed by what we can find out from the sciences about nature, 'including aspects of ourselves that form part of that nature' (Annas 2005, 11). Of course, we do learn things about human nature from the empirical sciences, and some of it is practically quite important – nothing I say here denies this. At the same time, however, no sociological study or psychological or neuroscientific experiment will ever tell us whether or not justice is a virtue.
22. Foot tries to capture this thought by talking about how some feature must serve a 'function' in the life cycle of S (Foot 2001: 30–32). I think this talk of function is a mistake for three reasons. First, because we are at present unable to disentangle the practical (and thus psychological) from the non-practical sense of the

term. Second, even if we can hear this word in a non-psychological register, we are apt to confuse it with an account that ultimately reduces final causal explanation to efficient causal explanation or probabilistic explanation, if that is supposed to be something different. And third, this way of speaking makes 'the life cycle' sound like some end over and above the activities in question, which it is not.

23. Geach 1956.
24. It is an important question whether this is the correct account of the logic of evaluation in general or whether Geach has picked out just one kind of evaluation, the account of which fits alongside others (such as mere recommendation or subjective endorsement, which might depend on a predicative account in limited cases). After all, there are other 'attributive' adjectives: 'big', 'tall', 'slow' and 'heavy', to name a few. Though I cannot adequately argue the case here, I think the right way to understand Geach's theory is to say that the attributive use of good is primitive or primary, in that any other account ultimately presupposes the truth of what he is saying. On this reading, while there may be cases where 'good' functions predicatively, ultimately the account of why that is so will fall back on an attributive case, and that ultimately what is subjectively endorsed must be understood in terms of human projects and needs. We might say, following G. E. L. Owen (1960), that this is its 'focal meaning'. Until this sort of case can be argued, R. M. Hare's (1957) prescriptivist objections against Geach will remain legitimate.
25. Thomson 2008: 21ff.
26. Neither Geach nor Thomson has shown that this account defines all legitimate uses of good. On this point, see Hare 1957, and more recently, Smith 2010.
27. Thomson 2008: 74. The only difference she mentions in this regard is that artefacts have 'functions' because they are 'manufactured', whereas living things are not manufactured, and thus it makes no sense to ascribe a specific function to them. But since Foot is happy to talk about 'function' with respect to activities and characteristics of living things, this does not seem to get at the fundamental difference between the two. Hursthouse also speaks in the same terms: see Hursthouse 1999: 195.
28. Foot 2001: 24.
29. Foot 2001: 16.
30. Foot 2001: 39, 47. Again, this is a major difference from Thomson, who does not allow for a fundamental shift in the sense of good that applies to living things. She writes: 'The adjective "good" is not ambiguous. It means the same in "good government" as it does in "good umbrella" (Just as the word "big" means the same in "big camel" and "big mouse")' (Thomson 2008: 37).
31. Quinn 1994: 229.
32. Quinn 1994: 233.

33. Quinn 1994: 234.
34. Quinn 1994: 253.
35. Foot 2001: 23.
36. Quinn also argues that we need an account of the will which would make it clear that it is 'the part of human reason whose function it is to choose for the best', though he leaves this 'part' of reason basically un-theorised. He seems to think it will naturally fall out of an account of practical reason. See Quinn 1994: 240.
37. Foot 2002: 173.
38. Foot 2001: 18.
39. For a critique of this account of practical reason, see Frey 2018.
40. Anscombe 1981b: 72
41. Aquinas, *Summa Theologiae* I-II 91.3.3.
42. Aquinas, *Summa Theologiae* I-II 90.4
43. While MacIntyre 1999, 2016 explicitly thematises the common good in his work, I think that, given her emphasis on justice and its relation to the fact that we are social, political animals, we can naturally extend Foot's theory of virtue to emphasise the common good.
44. Wittgenstein 1958 85.

PART III Natural Law Ethics and Religion

6 Natural Law in Judaism

Tamar Rudavsky

The question of whether Judaism recognises a natural law independent of Jewish law (*halakhah*) is contentious, and pertains to the role played by revelation in the promulgation of law. While some scholars have argued that the very notion of natural law precludes the doctrine of revelation and its complex set of divinely revealed laws, others have tried to reconcile the essential components of natural law theory with a theory of divine revelation. In part, this question reflects, once more, the age-old tension between reason and revelation: whether the basic tenets of Judaism are rational, or are founded in revelation alone. In other words, can we somehow accommodate both reason and revelation within the fabric of Jewish law?

In this chapter, I explore the attempts of major Jewish philosophers, both classical and contemporary, to grapple with these issues. In the mediaeval period, I shall focus primarily upon the status of law in the works of Moses Maimonides (1135/8–1204 CE), Maimonides' predecessor Saadiah Gaon (882–942 CE), as well as his successor Joseph Albo (1380–1444 CE), all three of whom were committed to the project of articulating a rational underpinning to the divine commandments. Part of this discussion centres on the 'Noahide laws', which will be discussed in the penultimate section. I shall argue that while a fully fledged natural law theory in the modern sense is absent in the mediaeval Jewish tradition, nevertheless we can point to evidence of (what I shall term) 'natural law sentiments' in this tradition.

The early modern philosophers Baruch Spinoza (1632–77) and Moses Mendelssohn (1729–86) further elaborate the distinctions found in mediaeval texts. We shall see that Mendelssohn's overarching acceptance of a natural law separate from *halakhah*, coupled with Spinoza's rejection of *halakhah* altogether, marked the start of modernity in Jewish thought. We will end our study with contemporary attempts to make sense of natural law in light of the constraints embedded in *halakhah*. Before turning to these discussions, however, we must first unpack the issues at stake in this study, and address the broader question of why the relation between Jewish thought and natural law theory matters at all.

IS THERE A NATURAL LAW TRADITION WITHIN JEWISH THOUGHT?

How does the Jewish incorporation of natural law theory present itself? The very question is complicated by the fact that, prior to Joseph Albo (to whom we return below), no Jewish philosophers use the term 'natural law'. Albo's *Book of Principles* (*Sefer ha-'Ikkarim*) is the only mediaeval Jewish work devoted (at least in part) to an investigation of the foundations or 'roots' (*'Ikkarim*) of law.[1] While he was one of the very few, if not the only, Jewish philosopher to make use of the term 'natural law', Albo's discussion, drawn primarily from Aquinas, is confused at best.

Compounding our difficulty is the fact that the term 'natural law' took on many different meanings in secular (non-Jewish) circles, ranging from Cicero's emphasis on universality to Suárez's characterisation of it as the infusion of divine light into the human mind. Catherine Wilson notes that the notion of a law of nature appears only rarely in ancient writings, in part because of the distinction between *physis* and *nomos*, the realm of the natural and the realm of the normative, respectively; *nomoi* were viewed not as universal, but rather as local and conventional.[2] Furthermore, numerous writers have pointed out that the term 'nature' does not figure prominently in Jewish legal and philosophical texts. Marvin Fox notes that the Hebrew word for 'nature' (*teva'*) is not mentioned in the Hebrew Bible or the Mishnah, viz. the first written recording of the Oral Torah.[3] The word *teva'* did not come to mean 'nature' in Hebrew until the famous translator Judah ibn Tibbon (1120–90) used it systematically as a translation for the Arabic words *tabi'ah* and *tab'*.[4]

This does not mean, however, that 'nature' as a concept is absent before Jewish exposure to the Arabic language. Rather, the doctrine of natural law is embedded in a number of related issues, including the nature of nature; the nature of reason itself; the relation between reason and revelation; the function of law; and the relation between law and human nature. In this context, natural law refers to a theory of morality according to which there are certain basic moral goods grounded in (human) nature that can be known to all humans by reason alone, and that obligate us.[5] On this picture, natural law is discovered, not invented, and obligates humans in a mode similar to divine law. In those cases where natural law is in conflict with divine law, philosophers must resolve the tension between the particularism of revealed law and the universalism of natural law.[6]

Our concern in this chapter, therefore, is whether any of our Jewish authors recognises the existence of a universal moral law that is natural and/or rational. More specifically, it is whether there exists a realm of morality independent of *halakhah* (Jewish law, both written and oral). Given the ubiquity of *halakhah* in Jewish life, rabbis both ancient and modern have argued over whether *halakhah* is all-inclusive, or whether there exists an independent moral standard to which even *halakhah* (and the giver of *halakhah*, namely God) is subject. For if *halakhah* is the only system governing ethical behaviour, what sense can we make of any natural law theory which locates the foundation of *nomos* in something other than God? While there may be room for natural law in a theology not ultimately dependent upon divine command, this seems inapplicable to Judaism.

A final aspect of this issue pertains to the 'Noahide laws'. The seven Noahide laws, discussed in rabbinic works such as *Sanhedrin* (56–60) and *Melakhim* (8:10, 10:12), represent the minimal moral duties enjoined by the Bible on all human beings, namely prohibitions of idolatry, blasphemy, bloodshed, sexual sins, theft and eating from a live animal, as well as the injunction to establish a legal system. These laws are derived ultimately from the divine commands addressed to Adam (*Genesis* 2:16) and Noah (*Genesis Rabbah* 34; *Sanhedrin* 59b), and are generally regarded by the rabbis as applying universally. Do the Noahide laws constitute a kind of natural law? In *Yoma* 67b, we have the suggestion that these laws 'would have been made mandatory even had they not been revealed', thus suggesting a universally applicable, naturalistic interpretation. Furthermore, the fact that six of the laws were revealed to Adam suggests a universalistic interpretation.[7] If these laws do demonstrate an admission on the part of the rabbis that a moral law exists independently of revelation, is this sufficient evidence of an underlying rationality to the divine commandments? In the next two sections, we turn to these three dimensions of natural law in Jewish thought, then we examine the implications with respect to the Noahide laws.

NATURAL LAW AND THE RATIONALITY OF THE COMMANDMENTS: THE MEDIAEVAL TRADITION

While Joseph Albo is the only Jewish philosopher to talk explicitly about 'natural law', others did discuss the universality of the commandments in the context of investigating the reasons for the commandments. The exercise of providing reasons for the commandments (*ta'amei ha-mitzvot*) dates back to rabbinic times, and continued throughout the mediaeval (and into the modern) period. Two passages are often quoted to support the underlying rationality of the law. The rabbinic Tractate *Eruvin* 100b states that 'If Torah had not been given, we could have learned modesty from the cat, aversion to robbery from the ant, chastity from the dove and sexual mores from the rooster'. Clearly the rabbis were suggesting that some commandments (in fact the very ones reflected in the Noahide laws, more on which below) are 'inherently' or 'intuitively' grounded, and not totally dependent upon divine command. Secondly, Tractate *Yoma* 67b points to the distinction between 'ordinances' and 'statutes' in *Leviticus* 18:5, and states: 'this [viz. statutes] refers to those commands which had they not been written should properly have been written. These include the prohibition of idolatry, adultery, bloodshed, and blasphemy'.[8] The suggestion in both these texts is that at least some of the commandments have a rational component.

THE RATIONAL COMMANDMENTS: SAADIAH GAON

This sense of an independent grounding for some of the commandments is articulated in a more systematic manner by the tenth-century Jewish philosopher, Saadiah Gaon. In *The Book of Beliefs and Opinions* (*Kitab al-Amanat wa-al-I'tiqadat* in Arabic, *Sefer ha-Emunot ve-ha De'ot* in Hebrew) – a work much influenced by Islamic Kalam epistemology and cosmology – Saadiah points to the underlying rationality of the 'rational commandments'.[9] He distinguishes between rational commandments, which in theory are discoverable by reason, and traditional laws, which comprise rituals and ceremonial laws (such as dietary laws) that are not grounded in reason. Saadiah is the first Jewish philosopher, in fact, to discuss ethical precepts in the context of rational apprehension.

In the Introduction to his work, Saadiah distinguishes four sources of reliable knowledge: sensation, reason or *nous*, logical inference and reliable tradition. Sense knowledge depends on empirical contingents and is the indubitable foundation of all other forms of knowledge. Reason is the faculty of immediate, intuitive knowledge, by which we apprehend the self-evident axioms of reason. Reason, Saadiah tells us, derives ultimately from God, yielding an innatist theory according to which ideas are 'implanted' in the mind – the word 'implanted' connotes a source of knowledge that lies outside human consciousness. In chapter II.13, for example, Saadiah asks how it is possible to acquire the concept of

God if we have never seen God, and responds that 'it is done in the same manner ... as the approbation of the truth and the disapproval of lying, although these matters are not subject to the perception of any of our senses'.[10] Similarly, we are able to 'recognise' a violation of the law of non-contradiction, even though the latter is not founded on the senses.

In contradistinction to reason, reliable tradition is not universal, but is common to 'the community of monotheists'. If reason, however, with the help of this external source, enables humans to determine both the self-evident axioms and the necessary principles of thought, what becomes of tradition? Saadiah ascribes two roles to tradition: first, tradition determines the particulars needed to observe the more general rational precepts; and second, it expedites the tedious process of discovering these rational principles. Thus while reason affords one a limited degree of epistemic authority, tradition, with the aid of revelation, enables us to achieve salvation. As Raphael Jospe points out, what is known in revelation is rational, and in principle is identical to the truth arrived at by rational investigation. But revelation allows us to access truth we could arrive at rationally only after a long process.[11]

Based on these epistemological distinctions, the foundations of moral obligation are delineated primarily in Book III, while the details of how to achieve the good life are explored in Book X. The classification of ethical precepts as either rational or revealed is straightforward: rational commandments are those whose 'approval' has been implanted in our minds.[12] In other words, humans have an intuitive grasp of the content of these commandments, insofar as they determine right action. Saadiah further argues that the rational commandments are intrinsically related to the dictates of reason, and that they represent logical inferences from these.[13] Revealed commandments, which constitute the second general division of law, are imposed by God without regard to their inherent rationality. Thus the approbation of these laws implies no more than simple submission to God. As we shall see, however, Saadiah sees a social utility to nearly all these laws. Thus he will argue that, though these laws are not grounded in reason, they too may be justified by rational argument. Saadiah offers many examples (sanctifying certain times rather than others, the dietary laws etc.) to explicate the social utility of such traditional laws.

In short, Saadiah argues that the approval of certain acts is implanted in our mind/reason, and – at the same time – he draws on utilitarian arguments to uphold such acts. While I agree with critics who highlight the tensions in Saadiah's discussion, it is important to emphasise the overall spirit of his distinction between the rational and revealed commandments: the former have their own intrinsic rationality, which, he believes, any rational person can recognise.[14] Seen in this light, his system incorporates a theory of rational obligation into the rubric of revealed commandments, thus affecting a kind of synthesis between reason and revelation. Although I would not describe this as a strict 'natural law theory', we can nevertheless acknowledge Saadiah's sustained attempt at arguing that some of the commandments are based on human nature and hence accessible to human reason.

MAIMONIDES ON THE REASONABLENESS OF THE COMMANDMENTS

Maimonides' analysis of the commandments reflects Saadiah's distinction between rational and revealed commandments, but in contrast to Saadiah, Maimonides claims that *all* the commandments are rational: both the laws and the statutes have beneficial ends, the only difference being that the former are recognisable by all, whereas the latter have ends that are manifest only to the wise. The laws correspond to Saadiah's rational commandments, while the statutes correspond (in general) to Saadiah's ceremonial and ritual laws. For Maimonides, however, both laws and statutes have a basis in reason.

Appeals to the underlying reasonableness of the laws can be found throughout Maimonides' work. Maimonides is clear that 'governance of the Law is absolute and universal'.[15] In the *Guide* 3.25, Maimonides offers several proofs, based on philosophical reasoning, for the rationality of law. He argues that to attribute to God non-purposive and non-rational actions – namely laws that are the arbitrary result of God's will – would be blasphemous, for frivolous actions are the most demeaning. Furthermore, he argues that in order to command the respect of the nations of the world, Jewish law must be rational. In an interesting aside, Maimonides claims that were the law not rational, the peoples of the world would not look up to the Jews, and they would lose their standing among the peoples.

Turning specifically to the utility of commandments, Maimonides distinguishes between the generalities and the particularities of a commandment. While the generalities of the commandments were given for utilitarian reasons, their particular details may lack utility. While the overall purpose of such details is to purify the people,[16] Maimonides castigates those who try to find reasons for every particular detail in the laws. Such individuals are stricken with 'madness' and 'are as far from truth as those who imagine that the generalities of a commandment are not designed with a view to some real utility'.[17] In fact, Maimonides goes to great lengths to warn his readers that, for some particulars, no reason can be found. Why, for example, did the law prescribe the sacrifice of a ram rather than a lamb? No reason can be given – yet one or other particular had to be chosen.

Maimonides argues, furthermore, that the commandments serve to support social and political beliefs. In an extended passage, he offers a historical deconstruction of the law.[18] In order to explain the importance of sacrifices, he traces the laws back to Moses' attempts to combat Sabianism. The Sabians were a polytheistic tribe, steeped in magic and myth. In the context of refuting the idolatry of the Sabians, who 'explicitly asserted that the stars are the deity and that the sun is the greatest deity',[19] Maimonides tells us that the first intention of the law as a whole is to put an end to idolatry: 'it is explicitly stated in the text of the Torah that everything that was regarded by them as worship of their gods and as a way of coming near to them, is hateful and odious to God'.[20] According to his deconstructive analysis, Moses knew that weaning the Israelites away from idolatry would be an arduous task, so in order to accomplish this gradually, the commandments regarding sacrifice were relaxed so as to require sacrifices only to God. The idea was that, eventually, sacrifices would be abandoned altogether.

NATURAL LAW THEORY IN JOSEPH ALBO

Maimonides maintains that humans have an intuitive sense of what is right and wrong; this intuitive sense is reflected in the commandments and supported by generally accepted opinions. Furthermore, by a careful reasoning process, we can often uncover the inherent rationality of the laws. Part of Maimonides' understanding of moral conventions has to do with understanding our nature as human beings. This understanding incorporates both moral and intellectual perfection, and it is reflective of our nature qua both corporeal and spiritual beings. We turn now to Joseph Albo, one of the only Jewish philosophers explicitly to acknowledge and discuss natural law theory. Albo's discussion is much indebted to the work of Thomas Aquinas.

Albo adapts portions of Aquinas' discussion and in the fifth chapter of the first part of the *Book of Principles*, Albo turns to the topic of natural law. He starts this chapter by noting that humans are political by nature, and that it is (almost) necessary for them to be part of a city;[21] but in order to preserve justice and eliminate wrongdoing, humans need what he terms a 'natural law'. This law is natural, in the sense that it is something that humans need as part of their nature. Humans living in a group need a certain modicum of order, allowing them to maintain justice: 'this order the wise men call natural law, meaning by natural that which is necessary for man by his nature, whether the order emanates from a wise man or a prophet'.[22] Albo notes in II.31 that natural law is not sufficient for political society and must therefore be supplemented by a *nomos* or conventional law that enables political life to take place. The prescriptions of natural law are indispensable for achieving the preservation of the species. Thus by the end of chapter 5, the reader realises that natural law must be supplemented by conventional law, and chapter 6 explains that divine law rules all other laws.

In *Principles* I.7, this notion of natural law is amplified. Albo asserts that there are three kinds of law – natural, conventional and divine – and distinguishes them on the basis of both their establishment and intention. There are, he maintains, 'three kinds of law, natural, positive or conventional, and divine. Natural law is the same among all peoples, at all times, and in all places. Positive or conventional is a law ordered by a wise man or men to suit the place and the time and the nature of the persons who are to be controlled by it ... Divine law is one that is ordered by God through a prophet, like Adam or Noah, or like the custom or law which Abraham taught men ... or one that is ordered by God through a messenger whom He sends and through whom He gives a law, like the law of Moses'.[23] Albo suggests that natural law is universal, in that it applies equally to all humans, times and places; the conventional law takes account of contingencies of place and time, and the divine law is ordered by God through a prophet or messenger (e.g. Adam, Noah, Moses or Abraham). Albo's conventional law is thus analogous to Aquinas' 'human law'. The reader is left with the impression that natural law serves as the foundation of the other kinds of law, each of which supplements and completes the natural law. But it is not clear from Albo's work what the content of natural law is.

NATURAL LAW IN MODERNITY: SPINOZA AND MENDELSSOHN

In the early modern period, natural law theory gains increasing prominence, in part because of the rise of natural science. A recent volume, edited by Lorraine Daston and Michael Stolleis,[24] explores natural law as an essential conceptual element in modern science, philosophy and jurisprudence. Why did natural law concepts come to fruition in the seventeenth century? In the area of philosophical theology, scholars have pointed to the prominence of voluntarist theology, and the emphasis on God as lawgiver. But how do we account for the conjunction in jurisprudence and natural philosophy? Is it simply a coincidence, they ask, that the voluntarist theology first advanced in the fourteenth century by Duns Scotus and William of Ockham should be revived in natural philosophy at the same time Protestant jurists were eager to undermine the divine justification for natural law? Not at all.[25] The Condemnations of 1277[26] had already recognised as a threat the 'immanentism' associated with Avicenna and Averroes, namely the notion that the universe might possess an inherent, independent intelligibility. 'Immanentism', it was feared, would permit eternal ideas that coexisted with the creator. This immanentist notion threatened modern Jewish philosophers as well, who struggled with the thought that even intimating the existence of a natural law tradition threatened to undermine the divine authority of *halakhah*.

The Jewish apostate and heretic Uriel da Costa (b. Oporto 1583/4, d. Amsterdam 1640) states this threat explicitly. In his polemical autobiographical work *Example of a Human Life*, written in Latin and published in 1687, da Costa railed against what he took to be Jewish antagonism to natural law. A convert who contemplated a return to Judaism, da Costa was particularly drawn to Neo-Stoic philosophy and its emphasis on human dignity as expressed through natural law. Describing what he takes to be the virtues of natural law theory, da Costa castigates the Jews for not recognising the force of natural law, and for denying that even a Jew may be denied salvation through the seven Noahide laws, which he identifies as a Jewish version of natural law. Explaining the natural law, he points out that 'Whatever is excellent in the law of Moses or any other institution, it is perfectly contained in the law of nature . . . Now there is nothing in these [laws of Moses] which is not dictated by the laws of nature, and does not entirely agree with that rule of right reason'.[27] Da Costa was clearly repulsed by what he took to be the narrow parochialism of Jewish law. Matt Goldish notes that da Costa's treatment of natural law represents a 'brilliant study of an idea originating in pagan antiquity, Christianised during the Middle Ages, gingerly humanised in the Renaissance, and returned to its pagan origins at the hands of a seventeenth-century *converso* rationalist'.[28] The early modern Jewish philosophers, Spinoza and Mendelssohn, approached da Costa's challenge in different ways.

SPINOZA'S POLEMIC AND NATURAL LAW

Writing in the early seventeenth century, Spinoza is influenced by the larger scientific and mathematical world-view in which the new Copernican astronomy was embedded. Focused on the importance of science, even in the interpretation of scripture, Spinoza advocates a methodological programme of natural science that, rooted in a mathematical view of nature, is then applied to scripture. In the *Theological-Political Treatise*, which was published anonymously in 1670 but probably begun much earlier, Spinoza locates the issue of biblical hermeneutics against the backdrop of a theory of demonstrative certainty attained by the New Science. Writing amidst revolutionary changes in natural philosophy, methodology and science, Spinoza claims that religion and science occupy different domains: religion is concerned primarily with the moral sphere, while science pertains to the domain of theoretical truth.

How, then, do we approach the truths of religion, which are independent of scientific method? According to Spinoza, the source of the conflict between science and religion lies here. He recognises the difficulties inherent in understanding religious statements and dogmas. The certainty of prophecy is based on the imaginative and not the rational faculty, he argues, and so does not embody the certainty of metaphysics and ontology: 'the certainty afforded by prophecy was not a mathematical certainty, but only a moral certainty'.[29] The methods of science, which aspire towards the certitude of mathematical geometry, are thus pitted against the constraints of biblical interpretation, and inspired the antagonism of Spinoza's audience.

In order to achieve his aims, Spinoza sees his task as the development of a biblical hermeneutic that can allow for a new understanding of scripture that does not enslave philosophy or would-be philosophers. In his Preface, he rails against those who 'do not even glimpse the divine nature of Scripture, and the more enthusiastic their admiration of these mysteries, the more clearly they reveal that their attitude to Scripture is one of abject servility rather than belief'.[30] Because of their anti-intellectual attitude towards scripture, nothing is left of the old religion but 'the outward form'.[31] Spinoza therefore resolves to 'examine

Scripture afresh, conscientiously and freely, and to admit nothing as its teaching which I did not most clearly derive from it'.[32]

For Spinoza, factual truths are grounded in the laws of philosophy and science. Just as we use the laws of nature to study and understand nature itself, so too we use the history of scripture to understand the meaning of scriptural passages. Based on this methodology, Spinoza proceeds to argue that many statements in scripture are false. By removing theology from the domain of inerrancy, he paves the way for the independence of philosophical (and scientific) truth on the one hand from religious doctrine on the other. Note that this paves the way to denying truth in the religious sphere altogether. The only truths to be found in scripture are moral verities, which should be distinguished from objective, scientific truths.[33] Spinoza's point is simply that scripture does not embody objective truth, not that there *is* no objective truth. Truth is associated with reason, with philosophical reflection, and does not pertain to what we find in scripture, which (as noted above) is associated with the imaginative sphere.

How, then, does Spinoza approach the process of reading scripture? His method is rooted in the New Science. If, as noted above, the Bible has no canonical status, then God has provided us with two sources of knowledge: the book of the law and the book of nature. In order to ascertain the meaning of scripture, the biblical scholar must approach the text much like a scientist approaches nature. Just as the natural scientist collects and orders data, so too must the Bible scholar collect and order the data contained in scripture and interpret them in light of their historical, social, cultural and linguistic context. Spinoza claims that scripture must be read literally and not allegorised, claiming that there must be a clear understanding of the nature and properties of the language in which the text was written and in which the authors spoke.[34] In other words, he reiterates that both nature and scripture should be amenable to a similar methodology: just as we apply the laws of nature to deduce an understanding of nature, so too we must deduce the meaning of scripture from its laws and history. By 'nature', Spinoza means the causal nexus of the universe (a view that is amplified in his *Ethics*), and which leaves no room for supernatural causation.

MENDELSSOHN'S UNIVERSALIST ACCEPTANCE OF NATURAL LAW

The pre-eminent early modern Jewish philosopher, Moses Mendelssohn, wrote *Jerusalem or On Religious Power and Judaism* in 1783. He was responding to the criticisms of the theologian, Christian Wilhelm von Dohm, who (among others) claimed that Jews could never become a part of modern, Enlightenment society. His is one of the first modern Jewish philosophical works written on behalf of a rational conception of Judaism, and in it, Mendelssohn provides an extended argument that Judaism is compatible with the Enlightenment.[35]

The entire first chapter of *Jerusalem* is couched in terms of universal laws of nature, laws that apply in many ethical situations. After describing many 'natural duties', such as the natural duty of parents to provide an education for their children, Mendelssohn argues for the separation of church and state: the state's obligation is to deal with outward behaviour, whereas that of religion is to deal primarily with inward conviction. The state is a 'moral person' that has the power to dispose of the rights embodied in natural law. Whereas the state can achieve its aims by outward compulsion, the church does not have this power. Unlike the relationship between the state and the individual, the relationship between God and individuals, reflected in religious institutions, does not impose duties and obligations that contravene reason.[36] Religious obligations are thus rooted in natural laws. Furthermore, Mendelssohn will argue, the church cannot enter into contractual relations with its constituents: 'The church does not remunerate; religion buys nothing, pays nothing, and allots no wages', he famously proclaims.[37] Religion is incompatible with coercion, and religious institutions should have no civil authority. So, too, the state should have no interest in legislating an individual's religious beliefs, and membership in a religious organisation should be of no consequence to the state.

But if religion cannot coerce, what sense can we make of the *halakhah*, which clearly contains commandments regarded as binding upon Jews? In Part Two of *Jerusalem*, Mendelssohn attempts to respond to his (anonymous) critics who had accused him of rejecting the foundations of Judaism. Mendelssohn's response draws on the distinction between universal rational truths and what he calls 'divine legislation'. The former are self-evident principles of reason, whereas the latter is revealed supernaturally.[38] For Mendelssohn, Judaism comprises three elements: universal, eternal truths of natural religion (including God's existence); historical records concerning the Jewish people; and divine command as represented by *halakhah*. Universal, eternal truths are truths taught (by God) through 'creation itself and its internal relations, which are legible and comprehensible to all men'.[39] Although they are revealed supernaturally, the laws based on these truths are nonetheless accessible to all humans, and so all humans have a claim to salvation. Judaism has no exclusive claim to be the path to salvation.[40]

Although the universal religion of humankind is accessible to all, and was not revealed at Sinai, Mendelssohn does claim that the laws of Moses contain rational truths. In direct contrast to Spinoza, he states that 'all laws refer to, or are based upon, eternal verities, or remind us of them, and rouse us to ponder them'.[41] What, then, is the purpose of the divine laws that form the bulk of *halakhah*? Like his predecessors Saadiah Gaon and Maimonides, Mendelssohn distinguishes between two levels of commandments: those pertaining to behaviour and those pertaining to beliefs. The ritualistic commandments apply to external behaviours alone, and not to beliefs. In fact, Mendelssohn argues that the content of Jewish belief is compatible with what he calls 'the natural religion of right reason'. According to him, the purpose of the commandments is rooted in *Bildung*: educating and moralising human beings. They function as a 'living script' that trains individuals to function in a moral way.[42] Mendelssohn claims that each ceremony and rite has its special meaning and significance, reminding us of the eternal verities: they 'guide the seeking mind to divine truths . . . on which the religion of this people was based'.[43] Like Maimonides, he claims that the commandments have a moral purpose; and like Spinoza, he argues that the revealed law does not teach speculative truths. But unlike Spinoza, he argues that the ceremonial law has authority and requires observance: 'no sophistry of ours can free us from the strict obedience we owe to the law'.[44]

THE NOAHIDE COMMANDMENTS: UNIVERSALIST OR PARTICULARIST?

Christine Hayes distinguishes two conceptions of divine law: the idea found in much of Greek thought, that divine law is divine precisely because it expresses the structure found in a permanent natural order; and the biblical tradition, according to which the law is divine precisely because it emanates from the deity, and embodies the divine will. We have here, in embryo, the so-called *Euthyphro* problem, distilled to its essence. Hayes will want to argue that the struggle to 'resolve the cognitive dissonance between biblical discourses of divine law and the very different discourses of their [the Jews'] Greek (and later, Roman and then Christian) neighbours' continues to inform our thinking about these issues.[45]

One way that this struggle manifests itself has to do with the status of Noahide laws, those laws (discussed above) that supposedly pertain to all human beings, regardless of revelation. Do the Noahide laws commit Jewish thinkers to the existence of a standard of value external to the Torah? If so, do they subscribe to a version of natural law 'according to which there are moral goods embedded in nature, rationally accessible and universally obligating?'[46]

As we shall see, David Novak, among others, has argued that the concept of Noahide laws encapsulates a Jewish natural law theory binding upon all human beings. Hayes disagrees, and claims that these laws do not invoke a rational or universal standard independent of divine law. In contradistinction to Novak, Hayes points out that following Cicero's definition of natural law as both invariable and universal, natural law does not satisfy either criterion. 'Pre-Sinai norms', she holds, 'including the Noahide laws, are not represented in rabbinic literature as invariable laws of universal application embedded in nature and discoverable by human reason, or as objectively valid moral goods that obligate us'.[47] Hayes further questions the universality of obligations pertaining to theft, murder and captive women, and states that 'the blatantly inequitable application of these basic ethical laws is the single most compelling evidence that the seven Noahide laws featured in Talmudic texts are not understood to be invariable and of universal application, and did not originate as a rabbinic version of natural law'.[48]

Maimonides' position is ambiguous with respect to these laws. In Kings 8:11, Maimonides claims that Noahides must not only accept these seven laws, but also accept them as divinely revealed:

> A heathen who accepts the seven commandments and observes them scrupulously is a 'righteous heathen' and will have a portion in the world to come, provided that he accepts them and performs them because the Holy One, blessed be He, commanded them in the Law and made known through Moses, our teacher, that the observance thereof had been enjoined upon the descendants of Noah even before the Law was given. But if his observance thereof is based upon a reasoned conclusion he is not deemed a resident alien, or one of the pious of the gentiles, but one of their wise men.[49]

In this text, Maimonides appears to distinguish between those (gentile) individuals who accept and perform righteous actions because God commanded them, and those who perform those commandments on the basis of 'a reasoned conclusion'. But Maimonides' text on this point is ambiguous, and subsequent editions have incorporated different variations (differing in one letter only) of the last sentence: did Maimonides say 'but one (*ela*) of their wise men', or did he say 'nor (*ve-lo*) one of their wise men'?

On the former, more inclusive reading, a person who does not recognise the divine authority of the Noahide commandments is still considered a wise man, while on the latter, more restrictive reading, it is not enough simply to recognise and abide by these seven Noahide commandments. A truly righteous gentile must obey them out of acknowledgement that they were divinely revealed. The second interpretation of this passage is less supportive of a natural law reading, suggesting that ethical norms are not natural, but must be embedded in a theological framework.[50] In other words, even one who does recognise the wisdom of Torah is not (*ve-lo*) necessarily wise.

We turn now to Spinoza and Mendelssohn, both of whom were critical of Maimonides' views. We have already noted that one of Spinoza's primary goals in the *Treatise* is to offer a reinterpretation of the idea of divine law, according to which it is understood not as the literal command of a sovereign being, but as a law taught by the natural light of reason and 'inferred from the consideration of human nature alone'.[51] For this reason, Spinoza insists, the laws propounded in the Hebrew Bible cannot be understood as universal dictates, binding on all human beings. They are laws revealed and prescribed only to the Jews: 'for as God chose them only for the establishment of a special kind of society and state, they must also have had laws of a special kind'.[52]

Spinoza applies this critical method to the subject of the Noahide laws. We noted above the ambiguity of Maimonides' comments on II Kings: the text can be read as 'but one (*ela*) of their wise men', or as 'nor (*ve-lo*) one of their wise men'. The latter is a more restrictive reading and rules out as righteous any gentile who does not accept divine command, while the former is more inclusive. Spinoza reads this passage in the restrictive sense, accusing Maimonides of being narrow and particularist. He understands Maimonides to have said that one who follows the seven Noahide laws as a result of divine command is counted with the pious among the nations, but that 'if he follows them through the guidance of reason, he is not a dweller among the pious, nor among the wise of the nations'.[53] In other words, Spinoza interprets Maimonides as saying that only gentiles who recognised divine command warranted a share in the world to come. By emphasising the literal reading of Maimonides' text, Spinoza criticises the Jews for having the most particularistic religion of all. Furthermore, in his rejection of Jewish law in the *Theological-Political Treatise*, he capitalises on what he considered the excessive legalism of the ceremonial laws represented in scripture, arguing that these laws precluded both rational and moral content.

Other philosophers, however, including Mendelssohn, have tried to interpret Maimonides in a way that is more inclusive.[54] We have seen that, according to Mendelssohn, any individual can achieve salvation independently of Judaism by practising the tenets of universal ethics, tenets grounded in universal, eternal truths. These eternal verities are identified with the Noahide laws. As Michah Gottlieb points out, whereas Spinoza casts Christianity as the universal religion of reason, for Mendelssohn it is Judaism that recognises the force of the Noahide Laws to lead to salvation.[55] In a letter (1769) to the Protestant theologian Johann Caspar Lavater, Mendelssohn upheld the view that non-Jews were charged to abide by the seven Noahide laws: 'Those who regulate their conduct in accordance with the laws of this religion of nature and reason are called virtuous men of other nations, and they are children of eternal bliss'.[56]

In this early letter to Lavater, Mendelssohn glossed over Maimonides' suggestion that righteous gentiles must acknowledge the divine basis of the Noahide laws. But Mendelssohn was clearly troubled by Maimonides' stance, and in 1793, he wrote a letter to Rabbi Jacob Emden in which he expressed dismay at Maimonides' position. Maimonides' words, he wrote, 'are harder to me than flint ... are then all dwellers on earth ... except for us, doomed to perdition if they fail to believe in the Torah?'[57] Mendelssohn rejected Maimonides' position, and by implication that of Spinoza, arguing that ethical laws are rational, universal laws that follow from our nature.[58] In *Jerusalem*, he recognises that non-Jews are obligated by Noahide law to acknowledge one and only one deity as creator of the universe, but does not rule out ancillary heavenly rulers. This means that gentiles can earn an afterlife without any recourse to revelation, even if they revere or worship idols. Thus in both *Jerusalem* and his letter to Emden, Mendelssohn emphasised the universalistic humanism of Jewish law by referring to the dictum that assigns to the righteous among the nations a share in the world to come.

NATURAL LAW IN CONTEMPORARY JEWISH THOUGHT

I have been presenting a picture according to which, despite the fact that ancient conceptions of natural law totally divorced from a providential, divine lawgiver do not appear in Jewish texts, this does not mean that natural law theorising is totally absent from those texts. Another way of making this point is to return to the *Euthyphro* conundrum, and ask whether any aspects of *halakhah* are discoverable by reason alone, or whether they are completely dependent upon God's will.

Joseph David has provided a useful way of distinguishing two camps in contemporary Jewish thought: the incommensurabilist position, represented by Marvin Fox, who denies the rationality of Divine law, and the compatibilists, such as David Novak, who emphasise the naturalistic components in Maimonides' legal theory, 'which they see as an initial step towards an implied acceptance of Natural law doctrine'.[59]

The incompatibilist strain has found contemporary currency in the words of noted (and controversial) Israeli philosopher Aharon Lichtenstein, who claims famously that there is no such thing as Jewish ethics, there is no natural law, and no room for any *nomos* beyond divine command. Lichtenstein's claims have obvious implications with respect to the status of natural law in Judaism. For if Lichtenstein is right, and *halakhah* is the only framework governing and expounding ethical behaviour, then what sense can we make of a natural law theory that views the foundation of *nomos* as something other than God? On such a view, there may be room for natural law in a theology not ultimately dependent upon divine command – but such a theology is alien to Judaism.

In similar vein, Marvin Fox has argued that the vast majority of laws in the Written and Oral Torah are directed at the Israelites alone, and moreover, that these laws were posited at a particular point in time in history and as such they are not applicable to all of humanity. Fox argues, furthermore, that according to Maimonides, the paramount importance of revelation precludes these laws from being known independently of God's revealed will.[60] Fox makes a case against natural law, in large part by contrasting Maimonides with Aquinas. He argues that 'there is no natural moral law, only the law of God'.[61] His main contention is that Maimonides argues against moral rules being demonstrable: they are not deductive consequences from necessarily true premises. More recently, Jonathan Jacobs and Steven Nadler have reiterated the claim that, in rabbinic Judaism, there is generally no distinction between law and morality. Nadler suggests that Spinoza is the first to depart from Jewish tradition on this issue. Because there is no code of moral behaviour distinct from divine law, Jacobs suggests that 'Jewish moral thought is best interpreted as not including natural law'.[62]

In contrast to Fox and Jacobs, other scholars have offered evidence of, at the very least, a natural morality reflected in both *halakhah* itself, as well as in Jewish texts. Lichtenstein himself makes use of the classic rabbinic passage discussed above from Tractate *Eruvin* 100b, to suggest that a cluster of logically ante-halakhic virtues exists and can be inferred from natural phenomena.[63] He carefully distinguishes between natural law *(lex naturalis)* and natural morality, and mentions numerous biblical passages supporting the thesis that the bulk of revealed Torah could have been naturally and logically discovered. Arguing that, at most, the rabbis rejected natural law, not natural morality, he goes on to maintain that 'the traditional acceptance of some form of natural morality seems to me beyond doubt'.[64] According to Lichtenstein, the notion of *lifnim mishurat hadin* (going beyond the letter/sense of the law) represents in Jewish law the sphere of contextual morality. Thus while divine law imposes fixed objective standards, *lifnim mishurat hadin* depends upon individual circumstances and 'may vary with the agent'.[65]

Perhaps the strongest champion of natural morality is David Novak, who has offered a number of arguments in support of natural law theory in Judaism in general, and in Maimonides in particular. His contention is based primarily on a re-evaluation of Noahide law, and the role played by the Noahide commandments in Jewish thought from rabbinic texts onward. Novak argues that the dichotomy between natural law and *halakhah* is apparent rather than real, and that there is an intelligible basis in reason for moral requirements, which is what we call natural law. But what about the foundational status of *halakhah*? Novak reminds us that the bulk of *halakhah* comes from human reason, and not from divine revelation. According to Novak, then, *halakhah* involves natural law at its very inception.

More specifically, natural law emerges from the Jewish attempt to discover the 'reasons for the commandments'.[66] The task for Jewish thinkers, according to Novak, is hence to 'recover the doctrine of natural law from within the Jewish tradition itself'.[67] The Noahide laws, he argues, could have been discovered without revelation. Consider 'the most unambiguous example of a natural law–type position in Scripture', as exemplified by Abraham's relation with God.[68] According to Novak, Abraham's exchange with God over justice for Sodom and Gomorrah is indicative of Abraham's holding God accountable to an antecedent grasp of justice.[69] In short, he claims there are rational presuppositions of Jewish moral thought that are so basic and so universal that they count as natural law. They provide an intelligible basis in reason for moral requirements, and that is what we call natural law.

CONCLUSION

We have, then, many ways of construing the role of law in Jewish thought, ranging from an explicit denial of any law independent of *halakhah*, to the implicit postulation of natural law theory in Maimonides and other authors. Navigating these waters requires providing a nuanced articulation of what we mean by natural law. Part of the question has to do with the relation between natural law theory and theism.

Mark Murphy's characterisation of natural law emphasises two criteria: first, that natural law represents one aspect of God's divine providence, thus recognising God's role in natural law; and second, that natural law constitutes the principles of practical rationality by which human action is judged as reasonable or unreasonable.[70] Note that, according to this characterisation, natural law is intertwined with divine law; note furthermore that natural law is universally binding and knowable by human beings. Following Murphy, I have argued that we can locate in our authors a fledgling, or qualified, notion of natural law that is universally binding, reflective of human nature and accessible to human reason. I am not suggesting, pace Novak, that our thinkers employed a notion of natural law theory that was totally independent of divine will, but rather, that they were working towards articulating an autonomous sphere of morality that was independent of God's command.

With these criteria, let us return to Uriel da Costa, whose castigation of the rabbis we noted above. It turns out that da Costa was wrong-headed in his assessment of what he took to be the narrow parochialism of the rabbis; in fact, their adherence to a morality infused with natural law principles contradicts that assessment. Maimonides, along with his mediaeval forebears, recognised a law of nature, one that agreed with the 'rule of right reason'. Thus, on the reading I have presented, mediaeval Jewish philosophers, drawing upon ingredients found already in rabbinic sources, were moving towards a natural law theory according to which moral truths are universally binding, reflective of human nature and accessible to human reason. This movement has come to fruition in the works of modern and contemporary philosophers.

NOTES

1. See Sefer Ha-'Ikkarim (Book of Principles) (Albo 1929).
2. See Wilson 2008: 13–28.
3. Fox 1990a: 126. The word *teva'* appears in the Talmud with reference to a coin. Its meaning is similar to the biblical word for 'ring' (*taba'at*) of the same root. See, for example, *Megillah* 14b. The Talmud is the earliest attestation of the Hebrew word *teva'*.
4. For further discussion of the notion of 'nature' in Jewish thought, see Efron 2002: 29–49.
5. See Hayes 2015: 328.
6. See also Jacobs 2010.
7. *Genesis Rabba* 16:6; 24:5. The works referenced in this paragraph are part of the rabbinic corpus.
8. See Newman 1998: 127.
9. See Saadiah Gaon, *The Book of Beliefs and Opinions* (Saadiah Gaon 1948).
10. Saadiah Gaon 1948: 131 (II.13).
11. Jospe 2009: 59.
12. Saadiah Gaon 1948: 14 (III.2).
13. Saadiah Gaon 1948: 106 (II.5), 139 (III.1).
14. For contemporary discussion of Saadiah's theory, see Rudavsky 2018; cf. also Rynhold 2009: 140.
15. Maimonides, *Guide of the Perplexed* [hereafter *Guide*] (Maimonides 1963): 534 (III.34).
16. Maimonides 1963: 508 (III.26).
17. Maimonides 1963: 509 (III.26).
18. See Maimonides 1963: 514–22 (III.29), 525–31 (III.32), 540–50 (III.37), 575–92 (III.45–6).
19. Maimonides 1963: 514 (II.29).
20. Maimonides 1963: 517 (III.29).
21. Albo, *Book of Principles* (Albo 1929) vol. 1: 72.
22. Albo 1929 vol. 1: 27.
23. Albo 1929 vol. 1: 78.
24. See Daston and Stolleis 2008.
25. Daston and Stolleis 2008: 3.
26. In 1277, Bishop Tempier of Paris condemned 219 philosophical theses and arguments considered heretical and threatening to Church doctrine; these theses were associated primarily with the works of Aristotle and Averroes.
27. Da Costa, *A Specimen of Human Life* (da Costa 1967: 32).
28. Goldish 2010–11: 1–23.

29. Baruch Spinoza, *Theological-Political Treatise* (Spinoza 2001): 22 (II).
30. Spinoza 2001: 1, 5 (preface).
31. Spinoza 2001: 5 (preface).
32. Spinoza 2001: 5 (preface).
33. Spinoza 2001: 153–7 (XIII).
34. Spinoza 2001: 87 (VII).
35. Gottlieb 2011: 43.
36. Mendelssohn 1983: 59.
37. Mendelssohn 1983: 61.
38. Mendelssohn 1983: 90ff.
39. Mendelssohn 1983: 93.
40. Mendelssohn 1983: 94 – 'All the inhabitants of the earth are destined to felicity'.
41. Mendelssohn 1983: 99.
42. Mendelssohn 1983: 128. The laws, both written and unwritten, 'are also, in large part, to be regarded as a kind of script'.
43. Mendelssohn 1983: 99.
44. Mendelssohn 1983: 133.
45. Hayes 2015: 3.
46. Hayes 2015: 6.
47. Hayes 2015: 370.
48. Hayes 2015: 359; see also Van Zile 2017: 1–32.
49. Maimonides, 'Kings and Wars' (Maimonides 1972: 221).
50. For further discussion, see Kellner 2006: 247–64.
51. See Rutherford 2010: 143–67.
52. Spinoza 2001: 39 (III).
53. Spinoza 2001: 69 (V).
54. This text is discussed at great length by Menachem Kellner in *Maimonides' Confrontation* (Kellner 2006). Kellner has a universalist reading of Maimonides.
55. Gottlieb 2011: 46.
56. Gottlieb 2011: 9.
57. This portion of the letter is quoted in Gottlieb 2011: 209. See also the complete letter in Gottlieb 2011: 32–5.
58. See Gottlieb 2011: 32–5.
59. David 2010: 3.
60. See Fox 1990a: 199–228.
61. Fox 1990b: 146, 150.
62. See Nadler 2007: 14–34. See also Jacobs 2010: 186.
63. Lichtenstein 1975: 62.
64. Lichtenstein 1975: 64.
65. Lichtenstein 1975: 79.

66. Novak 1998: 125.
67. Novak 1998: 182.
68. Novak 1998: 39.
69. Novak 1998: 41.
70. See Murphy 2008.

7 Natural Law in Catholic Christianity

Tracey Rowland

Since at least the time of St Clement of Alexandria (150–215), natural law has been a fundamental concept in Catholic accounts of private and public morality. But what is natural about this law (an ontological question) and how we understand it (the epistemological question) has been far from stable. In the twentieth century, a number of competing theories became fashionable, and disagreements among their proponents fuelled an academic growth industry. Underpinning every account of natural law is a presupposition about how faith and reason are related, and a presupposition about how nature and grace are related. Depending on how one construes these primary relationships, one can come up with different accounts of natural law all purporting to be Catholic. There are commonly three different ways of reading the relationship between the couplets 'nature and grace' and 'faith and reason'. These are often described in academic short-hand as Neo-Thomist, Transcendental Thomist and Neo-Augustinian or Augustinian-Thomist.[1]

In addition to this foundational issue of how a given scholar chooses to relate nature to grace and faith to reason, there is also the issue of what Russell Hittinger calls the 'three foci of the natural law'. By this he means that natural law can be regarded as (1) a matter of propositions or precepts that are first in the order of practical cognition, or (2) a property of human nature or (3) the ordinance of a divine lawgiver.[2] The first approach views the subject of natural law through an epistemological lens, the second through a broader ontological lens and the third primarily through a theological lens. Some scholars will use only one lens, some two and some all three. For those who use more than one lens, a further issue arises of the relationship between the lenses. How are the epistemological, ontological and theological dimensions to be integrated? Looking into these lenses, Eberhard Schockenhoff has found a further three neuralgic points: the first is whether the fundamental, self-evident insight of practical reason applies only to the highest basic principle that good should be done and evil avoided, or whether it extends to other principles such as those found in the Ten Commandments; the second is how to relate practical reason to natural inclinations; and the third is the relationship between the general principles and the specific judgements.[3]

Given that there are at least three different ways of construing the nature-grace and faith-reason relationships, and given that there are three possible foci and three common neuralgic points within the foci, it should not be surprising to find that there are numerous species of Catholic natural law scholars. The first sorting principle is to distinguish those accounts which claim to require a theological grounding (the third of the foci) and those which purport to be free-standing, without any need for divine support (usually accounts which rely solely on references to practical reason and thus the first of the possible foci). For much of the twentieth century, the free-standing accounts were the most popular. Their alleged virtue was that they could be deployed in public debates with non-Christians. The cultural shift from modernity to post-modernity, with the corresponding collapse of belief in such concepts as 'pure reason' and a common human nature, along with extensive criticisms of the Neo-Thomist manner of construing the faith-reason and nature-grace relationships, has seen the free-standing versions drop in popularity, though they remain in currency, especially in the Anglophone world. Magisterial interventions on the subject during the papacy of St John Paul II (1978–2005) favoured an account of natural law with strong theological foundations and attention to all three possible foci.

THE PATRISTIC AND MEDIAEVAL ERAS

References to the natural law can be found scattered throughout the works of the Early Church Fathers and among the publications of the canonists and scholastic theologians of the mediaeval period. St Justin Martyr (100–165) in his *Dialogue with Trypho* includes an analysis of the relationship between the Mosaic Law and the New Law of Christ, and in this context he refers to a law which is 'universally, naturally, and eternally good'. St Irenaeus of Lyon (130–202) treats the natural law at length in his *Adversus Haereses*. St Clement of Alexandria discusses the relationship between the Mosaic law and natural law in his *Stromata*. In his *Contra Julianum*, St Cyril of Alexandra (378–444) argues that the natural law can be found in the works of the pagans, but also finds expression in the Mosaic law. St Gregory of Nyssa (335–94) in *The*

Life of Moses speaks of 'the intention of the law', which lay embedded in human nature to turn people towards the divine and away from evil. St Isidore of Seville (c. 560–636) in his *Etymologies* defines natural law as:

> That which is common to all peoples, and what is observed everywhere by the instinct of nature rather than by any ordinance, as the marriage of man and woman, the begetting and rearing of children, the common possession of all things, the one freedom of all, and the acquisition of those things that are taken in the air, or on land, or on sea. Likewise the restoring of property entrusted or lent, and the repelling of violence by force.[4]

In his *Homilies XII and XIII on the Statutes* and in his *Homily on St Paul's Epistle to the Romans*, St John Chrysostom (c. 347–405) speaks extensively about the natural law, and ties it to the work of the human conscience. St Jerome (347–420) also links the subjects of natural law and conscience. In his *Commentary on Ezechiel*, St Jerome introduces the concept of *synderesis* – usually construed as the habitual knowledge of the universal practical principles of moral action. Contemporary scholars have put forward the thesis that *synderesis* was an erroneous transcription and that more likely St Jerome meant *syneidesis*, a term used by St Paul referring to that part of the conscience concerned with evaluating past actions. Whatever the case is here, the great trio of mediaeval Church Doctors (Albert, Aquinas and Bonaventure) adopted the concept of *synderesis* from their versions of St Jerome's *Commentary* and set about explaining its relationship to the concepts of conscience and natural law.[5] Of all the patristic authorities, however, by far the most influential was St Augustine (354–430), who moulded a theory of natural law from a synthesis of Christian revelation and elements of Platonic and Stoic thought. For St Augustine, the natural law is tied to the eternal law (*lex aeterna*). Anton-Hermann Chroust summarises the Augustinian account in the following paragraph:

> The *lex aeterna,* which as the universal order also constitutes the *ratio aeterna* of all that is created, resides in every creature in a germinating manner. In other words, the *ratio aeterna* exists in every creature in the form of a *ratio seminaria* or *ratio seminalis.* This *ratio aeterna* becomes manifest in all created things, and does so in the form of 'laws' which, in the final analysis, constitute the 'inner nature' of

> these things. The *ratio aeterna*, or *lex aeterna*, reveals itself in every creature in the form of the *lex naturalis*.[6]

In the early mediaeval period, the topic is taken up by the jurist Gratian, the author of a collection of ecclesiastical laws called the *Decretum*. In this document, he asserts that there are two types of law: natural law and customary law. According to Gratian, the law of nature is a divine law found in the Mosaic law and in the Gospels. A trio of theologians – Alain de Lille (c. 1128–1202), William of Auxerre (1145–1231) and John of Rupella (c. 1200–1245) – then take up the topic of the relationship between the natural law and virtue. The general orientation of their thinking is towards holding that virtue consists in submission to the natural law.[7]

St Albert the Great OP (1200–1280), known as the Universal Doctor, treats the topic in two of his works: first in *De Bono* (composed between 1240 and 1244) and second in his commentary on Aristotle's *Nicomachean Ethics* (composed between 1248 and 1252). Albert is said to have reversed the early mediaeval approach to natural law from something primarily juridical to something primarily ontological and intellect-centric. Stanley B. Cunningham explains this transition in the following passage:

> In an age where natural law was commonly treated in terms of dictates, prohibitions, restriction, and obligation, and where as a result it came to be conceived as if it too were positive law, Albert has effected a noticeable change. The division of his treatise into a question on *ius* followed by another on *lex* both reflects and clarifies this move. The quintessence of natural law for Albert is not obligation and prohibition, but the innate wisdom of practical reason ... Albert reverses the traditional procedure of viewing natural law through the medium of positive law.[8]

Cunningham concludes that, for St Albert, the natural law 'is not an exterior norm to which man *must* conform, but an interior perfection of reason guiding and linking man to the just life from within'.[9] Albert's student, St Thomas Aquinas OP (1225–74), the Angelic Doctor, follows in this trajectory. St Thomas treats the subject of natural law in Book I, Part II, questions 91–5 of his *Summa Theologiae*, especially question 94. In question 91, he describes the natural law as the participation in the eternal law by a rational creature. He also addresses aspects of the subject in his *Commentary on the Sentences of Peter Lombard, Commentary on the Nicomachean Ethics* of Aristotle and *Commentary on the Epistle to the Romans* of St Paul, as well as in his *De Veritate*.[10]

References to natural law also appear in both the literary and political works of Dante Alighieri (1265–1321), including his *De Monarchia*.

NATURAL LAW AS A FOIL TO THE IDEOLOGIES OF THE TWENTIETH CENTURY

The first half of the twentieth century witnessed an explosion of Catholic natural law scholarship. In part, this was fuelled by Pope Leo XIII's enthusiasm for Thomism, which was seen to be the antidote to all manner of modern intellectual errors. It was also a response to the First World War and the rise of tyrannies in Europe. In the 1930s, a number of European scholars fled to the United States to escape persecution. Over the next two decades, their research offered natural law theory as an alternative to the ideologies which claimed millions of lives in violent conflagrations. The leading names in these circles were Jacques Maritain (1882–1973), Yves Simon (1903–61), Heinrich Rommen (1897–1967) and Waldemar Gurian (1902–54). The University of Notre Dame and Georgetown University became centres of natural law research. In post–World War II France, the Catholic jurist Michel Villey (1914–88) would also champion the concept of natural law, though he did so in a more classical key, basing much of his analysis on Aristotle's *Nicomachean Ethics* rather than on a Thomist treatment of the subject. In the same period, the Italian philosopher Alessandro Passerin d'Entrèves (1902–85), author of *Natural Law: An Introduction to Legal Philosophy*, promoted natural law theory from his Chairs at the Universities of Oxford and Turin.

Of all these scholars, the most influential was Jacques Maritain. He was a friend of Pope Paul VI and a French delegate on the drafting committee of the *Universal Declaration of Human Rights* (1948). Maritain's most important works include: *Religion and Culture* (1930), *The Dream of Descartes* (1932), *Integral Humanism* (1936), *The Rights of Man and the Natural Law* (1942), *Christianity and Democracy* (1943), *The Person and the Common Good* (1947) and *Man and the State* (1951). In *Man and the State*, he wrote that 'any kind of thing existing in nature, a plant, a dog, a horse, has its own natural law, that is, the normalcy of its functioning, the proper way in which, by reason of its specific structure and specific ends, it "should" achieve fullness of being either in its growth or in its behaviour'.[11] He also distinguished between what the natural law is (the ontological question) and a person's knowledge of what it is (what he called the gnoseological question). He claimed that 'the only practical knowledge all men have naturally and infallibly in common as a self-evident principle, intellectually perceived by virtue of the concepts involved, is that we must do good and avoid evil. This is the preamble and the principle of natural law; it is not the law itself'.[12] He went on to say that 'natural law is the ensemble of things to do and not to do which follows therefrom in *necessary* fashion and *from the simple fact that man is man*, nothing else being taken into account'.[13] In some eras, Maritain believed that it was easier for people to evaluate this ensemble of things than others. For a variety of reasons, the moral capital of one generation can be quite different from the moral capital of the next.

Maritain was a popular intellectual because he offered principles for a Catholic *rapprochement* with the Liberal tradition. He offered American and French Catholics a way of reconciling themselves to the revolutions of 1776 and 1789. His treatment of natural law was directed more to issues of public than private morality. In particular, he fostered the process of reconciling the Catholic natural law tradition with the Liberal natural right tradition. His most important books were all published before the cultural revolution of the 1960s, so he was not writing about natural law with a view to sexual morality or Liberalism in a Rawlsian key.

Today, Maritain remains an important reference point for students of political theory, but scholars of the twenty-first century tend to regard his *rapprochement* project as a failure, since the Political Liberalism of the last half-century completely rejects the idea of natural law. John Rawls (1921–2002), the leading proponent of Political Liberalism, described the ideas of St Thomas as 'dangerous' and those of St Ignatius of Loyola as 'mad'.[14] As James V. Schall noted, 'Maritain does not anticipate that those with whom he is to discourse on natural rights would come to deny, in their effort not to admit any binding reason to natural law, the very validity of reason itself'.[15]

Yves Simon was a friend of Maritain, who joined the University of Notre Dame after the outbreak of World War II. In his *The Tradition of Natural Law: A Philosopher's Reflections*, Simon observed that historical situations may work either for a theory of natural law or against it; and, furthermore, that the very meaning of 'natural law' is modified by historical and doctrinal contexts. Diverse meanings of the concept are thus found in the works of a vast array of scholars from Cicero, the Patristics and mediaevals, through to eighteenth-century atheists and deists and twentieth-century Thomists. With specific reference to the eighteenth century, Simon noted that when natural law is associated with individualistic attitudes and economic preoccupations, we can expect the words to mean something different from the 'naturally just' (or adequate) of Aristotle, or the *jus naturale* of Aquinas. Much of the remainder of the work is taken up with an intellectual history of the various mutations in meaning taken on by the concept through the centuries. Many of Simon's fundamental insights anticipate the later ideas of Alasdair MacIntyre, who also found an academic home at the University of Notre Dame and defends the Catholic natural law tradition, though MacIntyre's own treatment of natural law occurs in the context of its relationship to virtue ethics.[16] Simon's focus on understanding the historical context for various expressions of natural law doctrine is proto-MacIntyrean. Simon also emphasises that the understanding of natural law will be impaired if there is no reference to nature. In Hittinger's parlance, this is like saying that a theory of natural law will be defective if it omits consideration of the second possible focus.

With reference to the issue of the relationship between natural law and theology, Simon acknowledged that 'one may wonder whether the study of moral nature and of natural law is a way to the knowledge of God or whether the knowledge of God must be had before the proposition that there exists a natural law of the moral world is established'.[17] He concluded that acquaintance with natural law, being a way to God, would be logically antecedent to the knowledge of God's existence, however from this logical priority in the order of discovery it does not follow that the understanding of natural law can be logically preserved in case of failure to recognise in God the ultimate foundation of all laws. Thus, 'if the way to God is blocked, no matter what the obstacle, the intelligence of natural law is itself impaired'.[18] This he thought was the case in the atheistic forms of existentialism.

Like Simon, Heinrich Rommen arrived in the United States to escape Fascism. From 1953 to 1967, he was based at the University of Georgetown. His *magnum opus, The Natural Law: A Study in Legal and Social History and Philosophy,* was primarily a reflection on the jurisprudential foundations of government. In it, Rommen argues that the natural law tradition bifurcated in the Middle Ages into an account based on reason and an account based on will. He called these two alternative treatments the *lex-ratio* tradition, which he associated with

St Thomas, and the *lex-voluntas* tradition, which he associated with Franciscan nominalism and later theorists like John Locke (1632–1704). What is most interesting about Rommen's narrative is that he regards the so-called Enlightenment philosophers, as well as the Nazi legal apologists, as heirs to the Franciscan *lex-voluntas* tradition.

Waldemar Gurian's major contribution was to found the journal *Review of Politics*. It remains in publication today and continues to carry articles on natural law and the relationship between theology and political theory.

NEW NATURAL LAW OR NEW (CLASSICAL) NATURAL LAW

With the 1960s comes a transition from a focus on the value of natural law for public morality to its prominence in debates about private morality. The encyclical *Humanae Vitae*, promulgated by Paul VI in 1968, expressly forbade the practice of artificial contraception on the grounds that it was contrary to the natural law. This gave rise to both defenders of the natural law tradition, foremost of whom was Karol Wojtyła (St John Paul II), and opponents of it, who offered new theories of morality such as situation ethics, consequentialism and proportionalism. After a decade of these 'new morality' publications, John Finnis published his seminal work *Natural Law and Natural Rights* (in 1980). It became the flagship for what is now called 'New Natural Law' or 'New Classical Natural Law' (the latter term is preferred by Finnis but is less used). Other key texts of this genre include: Germain Grisez, *The Way of the Lord Jesus* in three volumes (1983–97) and Robert P. George, *Natural Law Theory* (1992), *In Defense of Natural Law* (1999), *Natural Law, Liberalism and Morality: Contemporary Essays* (1996) and John Keown and Robert P. George (eds.), *Reason, Morality and Law: The Philosophy of John Finnis* (2013).[19]

These authors were united in their effort to defend the idea of moral absolutes against the relativising tendencies of the new moral theories. They also wanted their theories to appeal to Catholics and non-Catholics alike. Their account of natural law was new because it focused on only one of the three possible foci (practical reason), it eschewed any engagement with ontological issues (apart from practical reason) on the grounds of David Hume's principle that 'no ought can be derived from is', and it purported to be a free-standing theory without recourse to theological foundations – though one could, they claimed, supplement it with a theological superstructure. Though these authors treat religion as a 'good of human flourishing', it does not matter which religion this is, and in any case religion is only one of seven incommensurable goods. Finnis lists the other six as life, knowledge, friendship, play, aesthetic experience and practical reasonableness. Grisez offers self-integration, practical reasonableness, authenticity, justice and friendship, life and health, knowledge of truth, appreciation of beauty and playful activities as well as religion.

Finnis was a student of the legal positivist jurist H. L. A. Hart, who commissioned *Natural Law and Natural Rights*. Its intended audience appears to have been legal academics like Hart who find the idea of moral absolutes problematic.[20] It aspires to be written in the style of analytic philosophy. Since Finnis is a practising Catholic, however, the work was publicly *received* as a Catholic account of natural law, not as a merely neo-classical account for the modern educated atheist or agnostic disposed towards moral relativism.

Another early academic influence on both Finnis and Grisez was the epistemology of Bernard Lonergan, as found in his book *Insight*. It is not surprising, therefore, that the construction of the faith-reason relationship underpinning the New (Classical) Natural Law is closer to that of Transcendental Thomism than that of Augustinian or Neo-Classical Thomism (i.e. Thomism before the Patristic element has been abstracted to make it palatable to the modern mind).[21] It also evinces elements of the Neo-Thomistic approach to the faith-reason relationship.

Since Finnis held Chairs in legal philosophy at both the University of Notre Dame and at Oxford University, and since George was appointed the McCormick Professor of Jurisprudence at Princeton, they have succeeded in getting the study of natural law into the curricula of the world's elite universities. They have also followed in the trajectory of Maritain in attempting a reconciliation between the Catholic natural law and Liberal natural right traditions, and more broadly, between the Catholic faith and Liberalism in its political and economic manifestations. In his book *Aquinas*, Finnis endorsed the view of Lord Acton (1834–1902) that Aquinas was 'the first Whig'.

The New (Classical) Natural Law theory has, however, not received a favourable reception among Augustinian or Neo-Classical Thomists or Christian academics from the Reformed ecclesial communities. The reasons are several.[22] First, there is opposition to the principle of the incommensurability of the 'basic goods', especially the idea that religion is merely one good of human flourishing among others and does not occupy any kind of infrastructural status. The scholar who has offered the deepest analysis of this issue is Benedict M. Ashley OP (1915–2013), while Ernest Fortin's (1923–2002) commentary is the most colourful. On Fortin's reading of *Natural Law and Natural Rights*, 'the life of a great scholar, statesman or religious leader is not intrinsically superior to that of a music buff, a valetudinarian, or a ski bum'.[23] Second, there have been numerous criticisms of how one moves from the pre-moral (self-evident basic goods) level to the moral level of respecting each of the goods in human actions. Russell Hittinger has led the discussion here and argues that Grisez and Finnis offer no basis for getting from the pre-moral to the moral. Thirdly, when it comes to the nature-grace relationship, the New (Classical) Natural Law theorists follow the Neo-Thomist construction. This puts them off-side for many within the Catholic theological establishment, who follow either Transcendental Thomism or Augustinian-Thomism. Grisez, for example, explicitly rejects the classically Thomist idea that there is only one end to human nature. He follows in the tradition of Francisco Suárez (1548–1617) in holding to a two ends theory – one natural or mundane and one supernatural or eternal. Grisez states: 'My contention is that the human heart is not naturally oriented towards adoption as a child of God and the heavenly inheritance which goes with this status. It is naturally oriented towards human fulfilment, which is found in human goods in which one naturally can participate more and more'.[24] Scholars in *Communio* theology circles argue that this puts the Grisezian position at odds with the theological anthropology of Karol Wojtyła, who worked with an understanding of the grace-nature relationship influenced by Henri de Lubac, who famously went to academic war against this Suárezian 'mortal sin of Jesuit theology'.[25]

Similarly, the New (Classical) Natural Law theorists assume a very sharp division between faith and reason, which is consistent with the academic practices of the world's elite universities and with a Neo-Thomist reading of Vatican I's document *Dei Filius*.[26] The Neo-Thomist reading has, however, been subjected to extensive criticism for being too extrinsicist and not what the Fathers of Vatican I intended. The Neo-Thomist presuppositions suit a theory that seeks to offer a base or entry-level natural law to the world at large and a more advanced level to Christian theists. But just as Neo-Thomism gets ridiculed for having a 'cup-cake' theory of nature and grace and faith and reason, where grace and revelation are the mere icing on the cake, the analogous 'cup-cake' theory of natural law is criticised for its flawed anthropology. Furthermore, there is the issue of the love-reason relationship not addressed by the New (Classical) Natural Law theorists. In this context, in relation to all theories which have only one (viz. epistemological) focus, Livio Melina has argued that 'practical reason is not to be understood as a mere application of speculative knowledge, but as a specific mode of knowing the good, which arises from within the dynamism in which the subject is attracted to the good'.[27] This raises the issue of the place of love in a Catholic account of natural law.[28]

Finally, the public morality part of the project has been criticised for being too naïve about the Liberal tradition and the prospects for a reconciliation of the natural law and natural rights traditions. Alasdair MacIntyre is the leading Catholic theorist who argues that no such reconciliation is possible. Numerous scholars from the Anglican and Reformed ecclesial communities agree with MacIntyre's judgement that, however well-intentioned, the Catholic attempt to baptise Liberal natural right was a political 'own goal'. They also agree with Rommen's judgement that the Liberal tradition springs from regrettable intellectual moves made by mediaeval Franciscans, *not* by Thomas Aquinas. Instead of a project of *rapprochement*, they recommend a project of 're-weaving the tapestry', to remove the Franciscan elements. Stanley Hauerwas and John Milbank are the leading names in this context.[29]

NATURAL LAW IN MAGISTERIAL TEACHING

Amidst so much complexity, one of the safest entry-points into Catholic natural law ethics is the *Catechism of the Catholic Church*. It offers the following 'best practice' definition, drawing on the 1888 encyclical *Libertas Praestantissimum* of Leo XIII:

> Man participates in the wisdom and goodness of the Creator who gives him mastery over his acts and the ability to govern himself with a view to the true and the good. The natural law expresses the original moral sense which enables man to discern by reason the good and the evil, the truth and the lie: 'The natural law is written and engraved in the soul of each and every man, because it is human reason ordaining him to do good and forbidding him to sin ... But this command of human reason would not have the force of law if it were not the voice and interpreter of a higher reason to which our spirit and our freedom must be submitted'.[30]

The scriptural passage which is most often cited in support of the idea that the natural law is engraved on the human soul is St Paul (Romans 2:14–15):

> Indeed, when Gentiles, who do not have the law, do by nature things required by the law, they are a law for themselves, even though they do not have the law. They show that the requirements of the law are written on their hearts, their consciences also bearing witness, and their thoughts sometimes accusing them and at other times even defending them.

The *Catechism* goes on to state that the principal precepts of the natural law are expressed in the Decalogue of the Book of Exodus and it acknowledges that such precepts are not perceived by everyone clearly since 'sinful man needs grace and revelation so moral and religious truths may be known'. The *Catechism* also describes the Decalogue as a 'light offered to the conscience of every man' and it cites St Augustine's comment that 'God wrote on the tables of the Law what men did not read in their hearts'. With the transition from the Old to the New Testaments, from the Prophets to the Christian era, there arises the new element of the gifts of the Holy Spirit given to the faithful through the sacraments. What the Decalogue is to the Old Testament the Sermon on the Mount is to the New Testament. The *Catechism* expresses this principle in the following paragraph:

> The Lord's Sermon on the Mount, far from abolishing or devaluing the moral prescriptions of the Old Law, releases their hidden potential and has new demands arise from them: it reveals their entire divine and human truth. It does not add new external precepts, but proceeds to reform the heart, the root of human acts, where man chooses between the pure and the impure, where faith, hope and charity are formed and with them the other virtues.[31]

A more extensive treatment of these ideas can be found in *Morality: The Catholic View* by Servais-Théodore Pinckaers OP (1925–2008), who served on the drafting commissions of both the *Catechism* and St John Paul II's moral theology encyclical *Veritatis Splendor*. Pinckaers emphasises that Catholic ethics is never a mere baptism of Aristotle, since 'the advent of divine revelation has occasioned a profound transformation in the doctrine of virtue. The first source of moral excellence is no longer located in the human person, but in God through Christ'.[32] Pinckaers further argues that this transformation is 'evident in the doctrine of the "infused" moral virtues, which are not "acquired" by unaided human effort, but implanted in the human person by the Holy Spirit'.[33] Pinckaers defends a theological account of natural law by stating that 'if the demand for the autonomy of ethics leads us to restrict to reason alone the task of solving ethical problems, then in the final analysis the Church and faith itself will no longer have much role in the moral life, they will merely represent one opinion among others, and will, moreover, always be viewed with suspicion as being an authoritative imposition'.[34]

Russell Hittinger has described such attempts of providing a Catholic account of ethics, including natural law, without reference to revelation, as the construction of a 'doctrine for Cartesian minds somehow under Church discipline'.[35] In contrast, he argues that for both Aquinas (the founder of the Thomist tradition) and Hans Urs von Balthasar (one of the luminaries associated with *Communio* theology), practical reason is a participation in divine providence (to use Thomist language), or practical reason is a participation in a theo-drama (to use the Balthasarian idiom).[36] Fergus Kerr OP, a leading authority on the different versions of Thomism, concurs with this judgement. He states that 'St Thomas's concept of natural law is thoroughly theological, and his appeal is to Scripture (Romans 2:14, Psalm 4:6) not to philosophical authorities or considerations'.[37]

After the *Catechism*, the most significant magisterial treatment of natural law is to be found in the encyclical *Veritatis Splendor* of 1993. Paragraph 12 refers to Romans 2:15 and the Decalogue is described as a 'promise and sign of the *New Covenant*, in which the law would be written in a new and definitive way upon the human heart (cf. Jer 31:31–4), replacing the law of sin which had disfigured that heart (cf. Jer 17:1)'. Paragraph 36 then addresses the problem of a purely rationalist account of ethics:

> Some people, however, disregarding the dependence of human reason on Divine Wisdom and the need, given the present state of fallen nature, for Divine Revelation as an effective means for knowing moral truths, even those of the natural order, have actually posited a *complete sovereignty of reason* in the domain of moral norms regarding the right ordering of life in this world. Such norms would constitute the boundaries for a merely 'human' morality; they would be the expression of a law which man in an autonomous manner lays down for himself and which has its source exclusively in human

> reason. In no way could God be considered the Author of this law, except in the sense that human reason exercises its autonomy in setting down laws by virtue of a primordial and total mandate given to man by God. These trends of thought have led to a denial, in opposition to Sacred Scripture (cf. *Mt* 15:3–6) and the Church's constant teaching, of the fact that the natural moral law has God as its author, and that man, by the use of reason, participates in the eternal law, which it is not for him to establish.

Paragraph 40 goes on to refer to the 'rightful autonomy of man' and claims that this autonomy means that 'man possesses in himself his own law, received from the Creator'. But this does not mean that 'reason itself creates values and moral norms'. Pinckaers notes in this context that, although the encyclical affirms the notion of autonomy in a certain, non-Kantian sense, it also speaks of a 'participated theonomy' in paragraph 41 and this expression underscores the fact that the moral law has its original source in God.[38]

In paragraph 50, the concept of natural law is also distinguished from a mere respect for biology. Although natural law does relate to the ways that a human person chooses to use his or her body, it 'cannot be thought of as simply a set of norms on the biological level; rather it must be defined as the rational order whereby man is called by the Creator to direct and regulate his life and actions and in particular to make use of his own body'. This point was made to counter interpretations of *Humanae Vitae* that construed natural law as a reference to fertility cycles. Finally, in paragraph 59, we learn that whereas the natural law discloses the objective and universal demands of the moral good, conscience is the application of the law to particular cases.

JOSEPH RATZINGER'S TREATMENT OF NATURAL LAW

An emphasis on the theological foundations of natural law is also strong in the publications of Joseph Ratzinger (Pope Benedict XVI). In a paper written in 1962, entitled '*Gratia Praesupponit Naturam*', Ratzinger offered his own analysis of the word *physis* (nature) in the Pauline *Letters*. He concluded: 'if we try to summarise the Pauline data, we find that Paul no doubt attributes to nature a certain guiding character, but it by no means assumes the status of an unambiguous and absolute norm. Man receives true enlightenment about his being, not from "nature", but rather from his encounter with Christ in faith'.[39] Ratzinger goes on to assert that with the coming of Christianity, 'the biological concept of nature becomes a theological concept in a new sense: nature is understood, not in terms of biology or rational metaphysics, but rather in terms of the concrete history that has taken and is taking place between God and man'.[40] This is not to say that Ratzinger opposes what Hittinger calls the second possible focus: he regards the natural law as admitting an ontological explanation, but he believes also that human nature cannot be understood purely in secular terms. Aristotelian nature is not Christian nature, because Aristotelian nature does not incorporate the remedies of the Incarnation.

This is a central issue in Ratzinger's reading of the Vatican II document *Gaudium et Spes*. Like other commentators on this document, Ratzinger notes that there is a significant difference between an understanding of the human person that is in some sense made in the image of God (as in the account of creation in Genesis), and an understanding of the human person based on the Trinitarian anthropology of the New Testament. In the earlier sections of *Gaudium et Spes* the Old Testament vision predominates. For Ratzinger, the starting point of anthropology has to be the notion of Christ as the new Adam. A full theology of creation is intelligible only in eschatology. As he puts it: 'the Alpha is only truly to be understood in the light of the Omega'. In an article on the renewal of moral theology in the light of *Veritatis Splendor*, Ratzinger concludes that 'no ethics can be constructed without God'.[41] He argues that even the Decalogue is not to be interpreted first of all as law, but rather as gift. It begins with the words 'I am Yahweh, your Lord', and having noted this, Ratzinger argues that without the first tablet of the commandments and this preamble, the second tablet 'would not work'.[42] Somewhat emphatically, Ratzinger states that 'we cannot yield on this point: without God, all the rest would no longer have logical coherence'.[43]

Ratzinger/Benedict XVI has also referred to the natural law in various public speeches about the need for governments to recognise that they themselves are subject to a higher law. In these speeches, he commonly refers to the fact that this is not exclusively a Catholic idea, but one shared by all the 'wisdom traditions' of the world. These traditions accept the idea that there is an order in creation. However, Ratzinger acknowledges that this presupposition is not shared by contemporary post-modern intellectual elites. In discussions with post-modern scholars, Ratzinger has claimed that natural law discourse is a 'blunt instrument'.[44]

BIBLICAL NATURAL LAW

Consistent with Ratzinger's conclusions, Matthew Levering argues in his *Biblical Natural Law*:

> No matter how nuanced the schemes for exhibiting basic requirements of human flourishing or however much one attempts to provide an autonomous role for human practical reason apart from natural teleologies implanted by the Creator there are insuperable difficulties: the 'human flourishing' answers reduce to sophisticated pragmatism rather than real 'law'; the 'practical reason' answers appear to be a premature restriction of the possibilities of human freedom in ever evolving history.[45]

Accordingly, the focus of Levering's *Biblical Natural Law* is on exploring three questions: (1) whether there are biblical warrants for natural law doctrine, (2) what kind of natural law doctrine biblical texts support and (3) what happens when natural law doctrine is left out of constructive ethics arising from the Bible.

In his response to these questions, Levering proposes four constructive principles for understanding the relationship between Christian ethics, biblical revelation and natural law doctrine:

> First, Scripture presents certain goods as constitutive of true human flourishing and thus of moral order. *Genesis* 1–2 provides one place where such teleological ordering, rooted theo-centrically in God's creative providence, can be seen. Here we find in germ the human natural inclinations ... God creates human beings so that they are naturally ordered to preserve the good of their human existence. Without the inclination to preserve this good, God's warning about the tree of the knowledge of good and evil would not be intelligible ... God also inscribes within human beings an inclination toward the good of procreation and toward knowing the truth, ultimately the truth about the Creator.
>
> Second, Scripture does not countenance an absolute disjunction between divine positive law and natural law ... God in giving the Decalogue connects obedience to the Decalogue with a glorious new creation in justice – a renewed creation that reverses the Fall ... Jesus retains the Decalogue in the form given to Israel.
>
> Third, the Bible's understanding of law is theocentric. Law does not first pertain to 'nature' or to human 'reason' ... Law has its ground in

> God, not in human beings. Our participated wisdom cannot be understood without adverting to its divine source. We do not constitute wisdom, but rather we receive it by seeking to discern and participate in it.
>
> Fourth, the grace of the Holy Spirit does not negate, but rather fulfils the law's precepts.[46]

Levering's *Biblical Natural Law* is not only consistent with the general Trinitarian Christocentrism of *Veritatis Splendor*, it is also an account of natural law that addresses the sensitivities of members of the Reformed ecclesial communities about the need for Christian ethics to be both scriptural and Christocentric.

NATURAL LAW AND EMOTIONAL INTELLIGENCE

Once one introduces the role of the Holy Spirit, including the effect of the Gifts of the Spirit within the various faculties of the soul, one moves into the territory of linking affectivity with intellectual judgement, the will with the memory and intellect. Here it is significant that paragraph 54 of the International Theological Commission's 2009 document *The Search for a Universal Ethic: A New Look at the Natural Law* acknowledged the importance of the 'wisdom of experience', and paragraph 57 that of 'emotional intelligence' for the morality of human actions. Paragraph 55 noted also that 'the moral subject must be endowed with a certain number of interior dispositions that allow him to be open to the demands of the natural law'.[47] These insights were summarised in paragraph 59 with the statement: 'the subject needs to acquire the intellectual and affective dispositions that permit it to open itself to moral truth in such a way that its judgment may be adequate'. These various paragraphs are consistent with the desire, expressed in paragraph 10, to 'propose the traditional doctrine of the natural law in terms that better manifest the personal and existential dimension of the moral life'. Such an approach is consistent with Ratzinger/Benedict XVI's emphasis on the symbiotic relationship between love and reason – what he calls the 'twin pillars of all reality'.[48]

Contemporary natural law scholarship in no way denies the need for an intellect directed towards the truth, but it is also interested in the broader questions of how the various faculties of the soul interact with each other so that the natural law is both discerned and duly followed. With reference to the notion of the law being written on the hearts of the gentiles, Robert Sokolowski has argued that the word *kardia* in the passage from St Paul's *Letter to the Romans* (usually translated in the Vulgate as *cor*), does not connote the separation of heart and head that we take for granted in a world shaped by Descartes.[49] He concurs with Robert Spaemann's claim that, in the New Testament, the heart is taken to be a deeper recipient of truth than even the mind or intellect in Greek philosophy, since it deals with the person's willingness to accept the truth.[50] He describes his own work as an attempt to shed light on how natural law is 'promulgated' in human experience.

A number of these themes have been addressed by Pamela Hall in her *Narrative and Natural Law*, where she concludes:

> Thomas's conception of the Natural Law is fraught with an awareness of human life in its social and historical forms. On Thomas's own view, it is part of our inclinations that we live in community. The forms of community in which we participate, and in which we are educated, will then have serious consequences for the extent of our practical reasoning's excellence ... knowledge of natural law may be either nurtured or stifled through particular cultural forms and social practices.[51]

This conclusion highlights, in turn, the importance of the Catholic Church as a particular community through which knowledge of the natural law is mediated. Melina draws attention to this issue with reference to St Augustine's tract *De Moribus Ecclesiae Catholicae*:

> The Church is the 'mother' of the moral life of the faithful in a double manner: *praedicans* ('*exercens et docens*') and, above all, *ostendens exempla* of a holy life at her heart, fruit of the Spirit. The divine precepts are everywhere preserved ('*late et diffuse*') close to the Church, and morality is preached not as exterior obedience to a law, but as an assent of the heart to the Good.[52]

The Church exhorts, teaches and exemplifies so that, in Pinckaers' words, 'the Christian heritage forms a type of cultural memory upon which we all depend, even without our knowing it'.[53] In MacIntyre's parlance, human beings are not mere rational animals, but socially *dependent* rational animals.

CONCLUSION

At the beginning of the twenty-first century, natural law remains a foundation stone of Catholic ethical theory, but the direction of

Catholic magisterial teaching is moving away from the idea that natural law can be a key concept in a 'theologically neutral' public dialect, towards a more explicitly scriptural and Christological understanding. This is exemplified in the works of scholars such as Pinckaers, Levering and Melina, and such magisterial documents as the *Catechism of the Catholic Church* and *Veritatis Splendor*. There is also a trend away from explaining how the principles of the natural law are discerned by reference to the intellect alone. There is a growing interest in how the memory, will and intellect all play their part in the process of discernment, and how love works with or against reason. Today the Catholic natural law theories that have moved from Neo-Thomist foundations to more classically Thomist foundations are not so much a *lingua franca* for conversations with non-Christians, as the hallmark of the specific difference of Catholic ethical theory.

NOTES

1. For an overview of the faith-reason alternatives, see Sadler 2011. For the nature-grace alternatives, see Kerr 2002.
2. Hittinger 2007.
3. Schockenhoff 2003: 145–6.
4. St Isidore of Seville (c. 560–636): *Etymologies*, 5, 4, 1–2. For a recent translation, see Barney 2010.
5. For an account of the mediaeval reception of *synderesis*, see Crowe 1956: 151–64 and 228–45.
6. Chroust 1950: 285–315 at 298.
7. Three helpful sources on the intellectual history of this period are Crowe 1951: 194–204, Kilcullen 2011: 831–9 and Saccenti: 2016.
8. Cunningham 1967: 479–502 at 501.
9. Cunningham 1967: 502.
10. Crowe 1951: 293–305.
11. Maritain 1951: 87.
12. Maritain 1951: 90.
13. Maritain 1951: 90.
14. Rawls 1972: 553–4.
15. Schall 1998: 87–8.
16. For an appraisal of MacIntyre's contribution to Catholic natural law theory, see Cunningham 2009.
17. Simon 1965: 62.
18. Simon 1965: 63.

19. For an extensive account of new natural law theory, see Chapter 4 of this volume.
20. Legarre 2017: 82–98.
21. Lawrence 2012: 849–72; Lücke 2016: 193–249.
22. One of the most often cited of the critical articles is Long 2013.
23. Ashley 1994: 69–86 and Fortin 1982: 590–612.
24. Grisez 1983: 809–10.
25. For a defence of the argument that John Paul II's understanding of the nature-grace relationship is closest to that of de Lubac, see Kupczak 2000.
26. For an exposition of the different receptions of *Dei Filius* and criticism of the Neo-Thomist reading, see Kerr 2010.
27. Melina 2001a: 131.
28. The publications of Herbert McCabe O.P. (1926–2001) addressed this issue.
29. Hauerwas 2000; Milbank and Pabst 2016.
30. *Catechism of the Catholic Church* (1992) #1954.
31. *Catechism of the Catholic Church* (1992) #1968.
32. Pinckaers 2001: 71.
33. Pinckaers 2001: 71.
34. Pinckaers 2001: 49.
35. Hittinger 1999: 111.
36. Hittinger 1990: 406.
37. Kerr 2002: 106.
38. Pinckaers 1994: 43.
39. Ratzinger 2011: 153.
40. Ratzinger 2011: 156–8.
41. Ratzinger 2005: 367.
42. Ratzinger 2005: 367.
43. Ratzinger 2005: 367.
44. For the most comprehensive collection of Ratzinger speeches in this field, see Benedict XVI 2018. For an analysis of these speeches, see Hittinger 2014: 241–69.
45. Levering 2008: 17.
46. See Levering 2008: 58–65.
47. International Theological Commission 2009.
48. For a collection of articles reviewing the above ITC document, see Berkman and Mattison 2014, including my contribution, 'The Role of Natural Law and Natural Right in the Search for a Universal Ethics' at 156–67.
49. Sokolowski 2006: 230.
50. Sokolowski 2004: 507–29 at 525. Spaemann 1996: 29–30.
51. Hall 1994: 35.
52. Melina 2001b: 157.
53. Pinckaers 2001: 2.

8 Natural Law in Protestant Christianity

Jennifer Herdt

In the mid to late twentieth century, it was the norm for Protestant thinkers to reject natural law ethics. Karl Barth repudiated natural law as insufficiently Christocentric. Reinhold Niebuhr criticised natural law thinking for absolutising the relative. Stanley Hauerwas argued that 'natural law functions ideologically to justify the assumption that Christians have a responsibility to fulfil the demands of the state and institutions associated with it', thereby compromising loyalty to Christ.[1] Natural law was regarded as an essentially Catholic approach to Christian moral thinking. It seemed to constrain divine freedom, deny the radical character of the Fall, render scripture secondary and interfere with the intimacy of the divine–human relation. The Reformers, as the story had it, embraced divine command morality, not natural law. Even if there were a natural law embodying God's will for creation, the Fall rendered access to that law impossible. Morality was not to be grasped through nature and reason, but was rather divinely revealed in scripture, and scripture spoke to the individual situation of each Christian through the Spirit.

We are now in a position to see this conception of a deeply ingrained Protestant hostility to natural law ethics as a short-lived aberration, extending from the end of World War I to the end of the century.[2] In fact, the magisterial wing of the Protestant Reformation continued to employ the natural law tradition as a lingua franca for ethical reflection, even as that tradition was reinterpreted in light of new understandings of the Fall and of justification. The notion that the Reformers rejected natural law ethics stems largely from the influence of Karl Barth and Karl Holl, for whom natural law was bound up with the failures of liberal Protestantism, which was to be held responsible for the cultural captivity of Christianity and all the horrors that followed.[3] It was difficult for a historian like Holl to deny that so-called Protestant scholasticism had embraced the framework of natural law. But he argued that this was a betrayal of the first generation of Reformers.[4] In fact, in the early years of the movement, Protestant Reformers devoted relatively little attention to the natural law; their attention was focused elsewhere. Far from repudiating the natural law, however, they simply took it for granted.

What the Reformers inherited and furthered was an understanding of the natural law as a universally applicable morality, expressing God's intention for the proper ordering of human–divine and human–human relations. They regarded the Decalogue as a revealed restatement of the natural law. They tended to refer interchangeably to the natural law, moral law, law of God, law of the heart, conscience and light of nature. While they took for granted that fallen humankind could have only imperfect access to the natural law apart from revelation, they also believed that this incomplete access helped to account for the greatness of ancient pagan societies. There was nothing innovative in this general view. Catholic scholastics, too, had interpreted the natural law through scripture and vice versa, and had assumed that both access to the natural law and the ability to conform to its dictates were limited by the Fall.[5]

There were, of course, distinctive features of the Reformers' treatment of natural law. Particularly in the first generation of thinkers, the primary setting in which law was discussed was over against the Gospel; where the law convicts disobedience, the Gospel promises forgiveness. Law was relegated to the earthly kingdom, and attention focused instead on the heavenly kingdom of grace. Yet Lutheran and Reformed thinkers alike soon felt the need to speak of more positive uses of the law, particularly as they began to take responsibility for building Christian institutions independent of Roman Catholic control. Because magistrates were seen as possessing plenary lawmaking power, rather than sharing this with the church, and because canon law was at least partially discredited, there was a newly activist approach to lawmaking.[6] Lawmakers began sifting through all inherited law, including ancient Roman law as well as canon law, according to reason, conscience and scripture, especially the Decalogue. Initially, the shift away from multiple overlapping legal jurisdictions to the concentration of legal authority in the state led in Protestant territories to the consolidation of state power, upheld by church leaders.[7] Anxieties surrounding the Peasant Revolts and other antinomian movements encouraged an emphasis on passive submission to civil authorities as those responsible for interpreting and applying the law. This stance was soon recognised to be insufficient in the face of tyrants who flouted God's law, and Lutheran and Reformed thinkers alike recognised a duty and right of resistance.[8] Natural law played a significant role as a constraint on permissible positive law and a reference point for the critique of tyranny. Hence, the natural law contributed to the development of Reformed resistance theories. In addition, the doctrine of the natural law was employed by magisterial reformers as a resource for repudiating the Radical Reformation understanding of *sola scriptura*. While radical reformers regarded scripture as a comprehensive source for all law, magisterial reformers rejected bibliocracy, and argued that distinctions should be made between biblical laws that constituted restatements of the natural law, and therefore applied to Christians, and biblical laws that no longer applied. The distinctions made here, between natural/moral law, judicial law and ceremonial law, were traditional categories inherited from mediaeval scholasticism. Given changed social conditions and pressure from those who regarded the Bible as a comprehensive law book for Christians, there was increasing pressure to show that the natural law could be established by reason and thereby differentiated from biblical laws that no longer applied. Ironically, this theologically driven emphasis on reason, together with the separation of the earthly kingdom of law from the heavenly kingdom of grace, paved the way for the emergence of modern natural law doctrines that were, by the end of the seventeenth century, increasingly autonomous from theology. However, scripture continued to be regarded as offering the most perspicuous statement of the natural law, and in no case was the natural law understood in the way it came to be viewed in modernity – as a universally accessible source of determinate, action-guiding moral principles accessible to all persons without the assistance of divine revelation. That modern ambition was to evaporate, returning ethical reflection to the ongoing challenges of deliberation in the context of contested readings and arguable extrapolations.

That, in brief, is the story traced by this chapter, through attention to some of the key thinkers and texts in the Lutheran, Reformed and Anglican traditions of the sixteenth and seventeenth centuries. It is an account of a broadly shared, yet constantly evolving, tradition of moral reflection – one that Protestant and Catholic thinkers today are rediscovering as a shared resource for ethical reflection that is at once theologically disciplined and open to fruitful exchange with a pluralistic culture.

MARTIN LUTHER: FROM CHRISTIAN FREEDOM TO SUFFERING OBEDIENCE

While Luther's emphasis on Christian freedom is widely recognised, it is less common to regard his revolution as a rejection of the lawmaking authority of the Catholic Church. Yet it was precisely this. The Church, in his view, was properly a realm of grace, not of law; law belonged in the earthly kingdom, and hence in the hands of earthly, civil authorities.[9] Yet significant as Luther's doctrine of the Two Kingdoms was for Christian social thought, it did not involve a rejection of natural law.

Romans 2:14–15 had long been regarded as the *locus classicus* for a biblical account of the natural law. It provided unimpeachable scriptural authority for regarding 'the law' as something that did not need to be revealed to gentiles because it was written on their hearts, with the testimony of conscience bearing witness to that fact. Luther in his early lectures on Romans did not hesitate to identify 'the law' written on the heart, in Paul's Letter to the Romans, with the natural law, insisting, 'for naturally and indelibly the law of nature is imprinted on their minds, while their conscience bears witness to them, a good witness about the good works and an evil witness about the evil works'.[10] This basic affirmation remained a constant feature of Luther's theology.[11] God has inscribed the natural law on human hearts but also reached out mercifully to fallen humanity in order to inscribe it again on stone tablets; the Decalogue serves as the clearest expression of the natural law.[12] This natural law is permanent, in contrast to human laws.[13] It serves as the source and criterion of such laws.

In response to the antinomian surge released by his early proclamations of Gospel freedom from the law, Luther was quick to caution that the law written on the heart did not render superfluous the rule of civil magistrates. Quite to the contrary; were each individual simply to consult the law within, chaos would ensue. Some are made to rule, others to obey.[14] Having instilled natural knowledge of the moral law, God does not simply sit back to see how human beings will fare. Rulers, like their subjects, easily go astray without God's special assistance in specifying the principles of law and, even more importantly, in conforming their wills to God. Where good rulers are found, Luther was more prone to point to special divine aid than to natural moral knowledge.[15] Such special divine assistance explained how even heathen law (most notably Roman law) preserved considerable truth.[16] Luther did not hesitate to urge Christian magistrates to draw on the resources found in Roman jurists for wise management of physical and temporal goods.

Luther's openness to pagan moral and political thought can come as a surprise, given the vehemence with which he denounced 'the blind, heathen teacher Aristotle'.[17] Aristotle's 'book on ethics is the worst of all books', Luther insisted, since 'it flatly opposes divine grace and all

Christian virtues'.[18] In fact, however, Luther's target was really the scholastic theologians of the *via moderna*, who taught that salvation would be graciously bestowed by God if only Christians performed as best they could the actions required by God's law.[19] Luther recognised that Aristotle did not, after all, flatly oppose divine grace. Aristotle's ethics simply left grace out, knowing nothing of it. Luther was willing to grant that Aristotle offered a useful account of civic virtue. So long as we recognise that civic virtue is in no way salvific, there is nothing wrong with acknowledging its value; civic virtue contributes to the common good of political communities.[20] What is critical is differentiating properly between temporal affairs and a person's standing in the sight of God.

Luther's core insistence was that salvation was purely gratuitous, not in any sense a divine *quid pro quo*. Justification comes simply through faith, that is, through trust in God's mercy.[21] Luther thus proclaimed that Christians are free from the law: 'it is clear, then, that a Christian has all that he needs in faith and needs no works to justify him; and if he has no need of works, he has no need of the law; and if he has no need of the law, surely he is free from the law'.[22] The primary function of the law is to make patently evident the impossibility of its fulfilment.[23] Despairing of our own ability, we are induced to turn to God and to discover God's gracious promises.[24] Ironically, it is this trust in God that renders true obedience, in that it does not seek to displace God through the power of the sinner's own agency. Christians are not bound by the law, since they do not look to the law for salvation. However, they freely submit to the law. They do so because they recognise that the 'outer man' presents 'a contrary will in his own flesh which strives to serve the world and seeks its own advantage'.[25] This 'outer man' must be reduced to subjection, and obedience to the law serves this purpose. Moreover, subjection to the law is a way to serve the neighbour, and the freedom of a Christian is precisely freedom for this sort of service: 'faith is truly active through love, that is, it finds expression in works of the freest service, cheerfully and lovingly done, with which a man willingly serves another without hope of reward'.[26]

Luther had a tendency to speak interchangeably of 'works', 'ceremonies' and 'law', and to use the ceremonial laws revealed to the Jews as a way of speaking obliquely of practices prescribed by the Church, from fasting to indulgences. Where the scholastic tradition had differentiated quite sharply between the Decalogue as a revealed restatement of the natural law, and political and ceremonial laws given specifically to the Jews, to govern the particulars of their society, Luther often spoke quite generically of 'law' in order to underscore the contrast between law and the freedom of faith. The challenge was to defend justification by faith in no uncertain terms without thereby unleashing anti-nomianism. This Luther sought to do by underscoring free submission to the law: 'our faith in Christ does not free us from works but from false opinions concerning works, that is, from the foolish presumption that justification is acquired through works'.[27] Even prior to the Peasant Uprisings of 1524–5, Luther insisted that a Christian should be subject to the governing authorities and should patiently 'do the works of his profession and station'.[28] Luther was shocked by the ways in which his proclamation of Christian freedom was understood by the peasants, and insisted in response that it was the duty of Christians to suffer injustice. Not only did Christian freedom not mean anarchy, it meant that Christians should freely accept whatever injustices were perpetrated by the ruling authorities. With the split from Rome increasingly irreversible, Luther regarded civil authorities as key to securing the Reformation. Where Rome, and canon law, had failed, faithful Lutheran magistrates would step in, enacting laws that limned and further specified the Decalogue, curbing the wicked and assisting the faithful in living lives of Christian love and service to neighbour.[29] The earthly kingdom, albeit fallen, could continue as a realm of divinely ordained authority in which three orders operate to enforce the natural law: that of the household, the state and the Church.[30] Luther did not put forth his account of the three divinely ordained orders or estates as an alternative to the natural law but as an expression of it.

MELANCHTHON AND THE LUTHERAN RECOVERY OF ARISTOTLE

Luther's humanist colleague Philipp Melanchthon (1497–1560) is traditionally credited with systematising Lutheran theology and ushering in the era of Lutheran scholasticism. In terms of personality and intellectual style, the two men could hardly have been more different: Luther was brash, outspoken and attracted to paradox, while Melanchthon was mild and reconciliatory, seeking coherence and harmony. It was these sorts of differences that made it possible for Holl and Barth to construct a narrative according to which Luther staunchly rejected the natural law and Melanchthon fell away from the purity of Luther's Reformation insights.[31] It is significant, however, that Luther never wavered in his support and appreciation for Melanchthon. Indeed, despite Luther's outspoken critique of Aristotle's ethics, he never voiced criticism of the fact that Aristotle's ethics lay at the heart of Melanchthon's ethical and political thought.[32]

Melanchthon regarded moral philosophy as an important discipline, and Aristotle as its towering authority. From the late 1520s onward, he busied himself with editions, commentaries and lectures on Aristotle's ethics.[33] At the same time, while Melanchthon championed Aristotle's ethics, he consistently interpreted Aristotle, and pagan thought at large, through the Reformation categories of Law and Gospel, drawing sharp boundaries between philosophy and theology.[34] Philosophical ethics and politics are soteriologically irrelevant, however important to the right ordering of human social and political life. Without ever wavering on the principle of justification by grace through faith, Melanchthon devoted considerable energy to integrating moral philosophy with Lutheran theology. Moral philosophy, he argued, is part of God's law. The primary point of God's law is to direct humankind to honour and obey God.[35] Aristotle is not wrong to identify the human *telos* or end with virtuous activity, i.e. acting according to the highest human potency. But this is not our final end as such but a less final end; our ultimate end, fully grasped, is obeying and honouring God.[36]

There are, argues Melanchthon, moral principles that have been implanted in human nature, known through the light of reason.[37] He speaks of these as the law of God, the law of nature and divine law.[38] The light of reason has been darkened by sin, however.[39] It is because of this that (pagan) philosophers are able to grasp only virtue as our final end. Insofar as the highest virtue is the recognition and honouring of God, it is not false to say that virtue is our final end, but it is radically incomplete.[40] To honour God is to act according to human nature, in the way intended for human beings to act. Lacking an understanding of the Fall, Aristotle could not make sense of why we are not consistently inclined to act according to virtue, the true law of our nature.[41] Were human nature not fallen, obeying the law would be pleasurable. The church, therefore, can explain key features of human moral experience that remain a surd to moral philosophy.

While human nature is fallen and we are therefore disposed to resist the law, we retain epistemic access to that law. Melanchthon's insistence that human reason cannot prove the principles of the natural law has been seen as a 'deliberate departure from conventional medieval teachings that human reason can prove moral propositions that are consistent with divine revelation'.[42] In fact, Melanchthon's position here is continuous with the tradition, which insisted both on natural knowledge of the general principles of the natural law and on the disruption of that knowledge by the Fall; mediaeval scholastics did not seek a rational proof of natural law principles any more than Melanchthon. Here Melanchthon appeals both to Paul's notion of a law written on the heart, and to images of light; rays of divine light shine even in our fallen nature.[43] It is important to differentiate between unalterable principles that apply universally, and contingent principles that vary according to context. So the common ownership of goods was useful when human nature was in its pristine state, but is unsuitable after the Fall. Such contingent principles must be altered in order to sustain the higher, unalterable core principles of the natural law.[44]

One of the primary challenges facing Lutheran thinkers was that of offering an account of authority, and obedience to authority, which could make sense both of the fact that human lawmaking authority rested in the hands of the state, and of the fact that some civil authorities were clearly defying, rather than upholding, God's law. Melanchthon argued that political authorities are God-ordained to guard discipline and peace.[45] They are to punish the rebellious and protect the obedient. They are, he insisted, citing Aristotle, the guardians of the law. But this means that their authority is linked with the justice of their rule. Rulers must conform to the Decalogue, since it provides the clearest expression of the natural law and the unchangeable norm of human action, the very voice of God's own wisdom and justice.[46] They must also make laws, and these laws must serve as further determinations of the natural law in specific circumstances.[47] Both Roman law and canon law can offer useful prototypes for civil law, if carefully sifted.[48] The pope, meanwhile, is not a political ruler but a shepherd. He thus does not possess two swords, spiritual and temporal (as Pope Boniface had insisted at the end of the thirteenth century), but is charged with correcting with the word, not with bodily force.[49] Only civil magistrates have the authority to guard the law with force.

If Melanchthon initially echoed Luther in denying any right of resistance, by 1555 he had changed his tune; human laws are not binding if they contradict natural law, which, after all, is God's moral law. This teaching was in itself not new. But, as Harold Berman has pointed out, it had:

> radically different implications in a unitary Protestant state in which there were no longer concurrent ecclesiastical and secular

> jurisdictions to challenge each other's legislation on the ground of violation of natural law. It was now left to the people – acting either individually or else collectively through territorial and imperial diets – to resist officials who had strayed beyond the authority of their office and to disobey laws that had defied the precepts of natural law.[50]

Longstanding resources in the doctrine of natural law were thus deployed in ways that expanded both the lawmaking authority of civil rulers *and* the responsibilities of citizens.

Luther's distinction between Two Kingdoms was to become a defining feature of Protestantism. This is seen already in the Augsburg Confession of 1531, which Luther and Melanchthon developed at the behest of the Holy Roman Emperor, Charles V. In the Apology of the Augsburg Confession, which Melanchthon wrote later that year in response to the Pontifical Confutation, he wrote that 'All Scripture should be divided into these two main topics: the law and the promises. In some places it communicates the law. In other places it communicates the promise concerning Christ'.[51] By 1577, when key Lutheran leaders prepared the Formula of Concord (chief among them Jakob Andreä (1528–90) and Martin Chemnitz (1522–86)), 'Law and Gospel' had become a rallying cry; Article V of the Formula of Concord states that 'We believe, teach, and confess that the distinction between law and gospel is to be preserved with great diligence in the church'.[52] By that time, too, Luther's dramatic dialectical proclamation of Christian freedom from law, wedded with exhortations to tame the flesh and serve the neighbour, had (with Melanchthon's assistance) become systematised into Lutheran Orthodoxy's 'Three Uses of the Law'.[53] 'The Law', states the Formula of Concord, 'has been given to people for three reasons'. The first is to maintain 'external discipline' among sinners. The second is to lead sinners to awareness of their sins, thereby preparing the way for despair and a turn to grace. Thirdly, the law offers the regenerate 'a sure guide, according to which they can orient and conduct their entire life'.[54] The doctrine of the Three Uses of the Law allowed ample room for reflection on the natural law. Natural law gave lawmakers a way to distinguish in scripture between laws that were devised specifically for the Jewish people and those that continued to bind Christians because part of the natural law. It also offered a way to construe newly issued human laws as authoritative because mere specifications of the natural law.

If a law was authoritative when it conformed to the natural law, what of laws that failed so to conform? By and large, on this score Lutheran thinkers early on exhorted passive obedience to unjust and tyrannical rulers, following Romans 13 and the notion that the authority even of wicked rulers was ordained by God. At the same time, they did regard clergy and academic theologians as playing a critical role in advising magistrates on both theological questions and conformity to natural law. The Lutheran jurist Johann Oldendorp (1486–1567) did not hesitate to identify specific laws that he considered illegitimate due to their departure from the natural law, including 'human laws permitting bad-faith possession of property, allowing disinheritance of family members, causing undue delay in administering justice, rendering judgment in a case in which one has an interest, and instituting slavery and other strict forms of servitude'.[55] In order to exercise this advisory role effectively, it was important that theological and legal authorities be formally appointed to the civil authority or *Obrigkeit*. In the *Aktenversendung* process, 'court cases raising particularly difficult moral and theological issues were sent to both law faculties and theology faculties for resolution'.[56] In this way, the authority of magistrates was not allowed to go unchecked, and the subordination of civil authorities to the natural law was underscored.[57]

JOHN CALVIN AND THE GLORIFICATION OF GOD THROUGH LAW

When Calvin joined the movement for reform around 1530, he brought with him his training as a humanist lawyer, including considerable classical learning. Like Luther, however, Calvin believed the primary context for discussing law was in proclaiming justification by faith and hence the distinction between the law that commands obedience and the Gospel that promises forgiveness.[58] Calvin, too, proclaimed three uses of 'the law', inverting the first and second uses as enumerated in the Formula of Concord. The law exists (1) to convict and condemn sinners, (2) to restrain the wicked by fear of punishment and (3) to instruct believers in God's will, urging them on in goodness.[59] 'The law', Calvin wrote, 'is not now acting toward us as a rigorous enforcement officer who is not satisfied unless the requirements are met. But in this perfection to which it exhorts us, the law points out the goal toward which throughout life we are to strive'.[60] In this context, Calvin explicitly speaks of the natural law and identifies it closely with the

Decalogue. 'That inward law, which we have above described as written, even engraved, upon the hearts of all, in a sense asserts the very same things that are to be learned from the two Tables'.[61] We can discern the presence of this inward law through the activity of conscience.[62]

Calvin's 1559 *Institutes* is structured according to the doctrine of a two-fold knowledge of God (the *duplex cognitio Dei*): knowledge of God as Creator and knowledge of God as Redeemer. God can be known as Creator both from nature and from scripture, but extra-biblical knowledge of God does not reveal God as Redeemer and is not salvific.[63] Given the Fall, our grasp of the natural law is severely limited, in particular when it comes to the first table, that defining the proper human relation to God: 'man is so shrouded in the darkness of errors that he hardly begins to grasp through this natural law what worship is acceptable to God'. The revealed written law has been given to clarify what was obscure in the natural law and 'strike more vigorously our mind and memory'. Most fundamentally, what the law commands simply is obedience to God; conversely, 'the only lawful worship of him is the observance of righteousness, holiness, and purity'.[64] There is thus no separation of religion or worship and morality; living rightly glorifies God, and glorifying God requires following the natural law.

Knowledge of the natural law, while universal, is insufficient for obedience, however. Many errors are made in applying general principles to particular cases.[65] It is typical to interpret principles in ways that are self-serving. The primary purpose of the natural law is 'to render man inexcusable'; even fallen humanity is convicted by conscience.[66] The doctrine of the natural law made sense, for Calvin, of all the pagan wisdom he had encountered in his humanistic studies; commenting on Romans 2, he notes that 'there is nothing more common than for a man to be sufficiently instructed in a right standard of conduct by natural law (of which the apostle is here speaking)'.[67] Particularly when it came to matters concerning the direction of civil society, Calvin did not hesitate to draw on pagan learning, even if he cautioned that knowledge of the Second Table, too, was warped by fallen humankind's desire to throw off all governance.[68]

Given the Fall, the doctrine of the natural law is useful only for the regenerate. For Christians, it provides a tool for scriptural interpretation, for it makes it possible to distinguish amongst the laws given by God to the Hebrews the judicial laws intended to define their civil government, the ceremonial laws intended to define particular characteristics of their worship, and the 'perpetual duties and precepts of love'.[69] Not all law revealed by God to the Hebrew people remains binding on Christians, but only that part that restated the natural law. This is the Decalogue, summed up in Jesus' Two-fold Commandment to love God and neighbour.[70]

These distinctions among the various kinds of law, and the equation of the Decalogue with the Two-fold Commandment, were not new. They were scholastic commonplaces. What was new was the agenda of cutting through all the complex accretions of Roman law, canon law and civil law with the intention of designing, from the ground up, civil and church structures that glorified God by embodying the natural law while suiting local circumstances. 'Surely every nation is left free to make such laws as it foresees to be profitable for itself. Yet these must be in conformity to that perpetual rule of love, so that they indeed vary in form but have the same purpose'.[71] The responsibility of legislators is to take into account 'the condition of times, place, and nation', while honouring 'equity'.[72] In Geneva, Calvin had a laboratory for this experiment. The various councils composing Geneva's civil government were related intimately to the Consistory, an ecclesial body composed of pastors and elders, with elders being nominated and approved by the civil government and the Consistory referring cases to the city Council with recommendations for civil penalties.[73] Calvin regarded civil authority as responsible for enforcing both tables of the Decalogue.[74] If in theory, given that the Decalogue restates a natural law inscribed in the human heart, all civil authorities have this responsibility, in practice, only godly Christian rulers are capable of doing so well. Christians ought to be subject to rulers, whether good or bad, as God-ordained authorities. Yet Calvin did leave open a crack: lesser magistrates may be appointed precisely to restrain rulers and have a positive duty to resist tyrants.[75] This crack was to be widened by Reformed resistance theorists who drew on the doctrine of the natural law not just to shore up the power of civil government, but also at the same time to restrain it. Theodore Beza, Peter Martyr Vermigli and Johannes Althusius all made important contributions to forging Reformed resistance theories, even as they advanced the tradition of natural law.

NATURAL LAW AND THE RISE OF PROTESTANT RESISTANCE THEORY

If Calvin, while leaving room for recourse to the natural law for purposes of civil government, stressed that the primary purpose of the natural law was to render fallen humankind without excuse, other Reformed thinkers were more sanguine in their reading of that touchstone text in Romans 2. As David Steinmetz has argued, 'in the judgment of Calvin's contemporaries, Paul does not stress an acute noetic impairment because of sin or distinguish sharply between what is revealed in nature and what is perceived by fallen human reason ... The point that Paul makes is not how little the Gentiles knew, but, considering the circumstances, how much they did know and how little use they made of it'.[76] Theodore Beza (1519–1605), like Calvin a Frenchman and a humanist student of the law, arrived in Geneva in 1548, becoming Calvin's close associate and later successor, teaching at the Geneva Academy and advising both Genevan magistrates and Reformed leaders in France. Following the St Bartholomew's Day Massacre in 1572, he welcomed Reformed refugees into Geneva. Beza played a significant role in formulating Calvinist resistance theory.[77] In his 1574 *De Jure Magistratuum*, Beza argued that it is legitimate for a tyrannous magistrate to be opposed and even deposed by means of force by the people. Like Calvin, Beza affirmed the natural law, not simply as ground for holding fallen humanity responsible for evil deeds, but as ongoing touchstone for just human laws.[78] As an example, he noted that promises extorted by intimidation are known to be unlawful. This law of nature is at the same time the law of God; it comprises duties that 'men owe to their fellowmen both by the law of God and by the law of nature, for example children to their parents, a wife to her husband, the shepherd to his flock, and in fine one neighbour to another'.[79] If we are commanded to go against this law, we must disobey, since only in so doing can we obey God. No one may simply obey a superior blindly; commands must be assessed for their conformity with natural/divine law.[80] While private citizens may not resist a tyrant, subordinate magistrates may take up arms in order to protect the people against tyranny, and it is a special function of the orders or estates to offer such resistance.[81]

Like Melanchthon, the Italian-born Peter Martyr Vermigli (1499–1562) found Aristotle's ethics a natural conversation-partner for working out a systematic theological account of the natural law that, while rooted in Thomistic tradition, was firmly Reformed in doctrine.[82] Vermigli, whose career as a Reformer unfolded in Strasbourg, Oxford and Zürich, identified the natural law with the image of God. The image of God is a natural knowledge of God and God's purposes, implanted in the soul.[83] In the wake of the Fall, human beings retain knowledge of this law, but lack the impulse to act from a good will, referring their actions to the right end; their knowledge of God is 'frigid' rather than 'effectual'.[84] The proper *telos* of the commonwealth is contemplation of God. Grace-given virtues are necessary in order for political communities to reach this *telos*.[85] In the absence of grace, civic righteousness remains possible.[86] Vermigli espoused a resistance theory similar to that of Beza; while in general Christians are counselled to obey civil authorities, they should disobey if commanded to go against God's law, and lesser magistrates are permitted to resist tyrants.[87] Other Reformed thinkers, including Martin Bucer (1491–1551), Girolamo Zanchi (1560–90) and Johann Heinrich Alsted (1588–1638), espoused very similar accounts of the natural law and its significance for social and political life.

ALTHUSIUS AND THE DIALECTIC BETWEEN NATURAL LAW AND COMMON LAW

The German Calvinist jurist Johannes Althusius (1557–1638) is a key figure not simply for resistance theory but for the development of Reformed natural law as such, given his efforts to work out a fully comprehensive statement of the political significance of the natural law, drawing on Greek and Roman thinkers, mediaeval scholastics, canon law and Protestant jurists alike. A pioneer in the articulation of human rights theory, Althusius argued that there is a universal law, expressing the divine will for humankind, which is rooted in revealed divine commandments and in natural law alike.[88] This law comprises both First and Second Tables, that is, 'it pertains to the duties that are to be performed ... to the love of God and one's neighbour'.[89] This law directs humankind how to live well in society, but also how to live a 'pious' and 'holy' life.[90] Althusius did not hesitate to affirm that pagan thinkers had grasped the basic moral truths of both tables, mentioning Cicero in particular.[91] It is known also as the moral law (*lex moralis*) and as conscience. Conscience does not simply accuse those who violate the moral law; it also gives persons a 'secret inclination' to obey the law. In line with tradition, Althusius regarded both the Decalogue and Christ's two-fold love commandment as revealed restatements of the natural law.[92] He was particularly concerned to distinguish within scripture between the common law, applicable universally, and the proper law, which applied only to those to whom it had been revealed. Instead of appealing solely to the Decalogue as a touchstone for discerning what within Greek thought, Roman law, canon law etc. could be regarded as genuine natural law, Althusius regarded the hermeneutical dialectic as moving in multiple directions. The criterion of multiple attestation could be used to determine what within the Decalogue, and Mosaic law more broadly, was truly part of the universal natural law: 'the Decalogue has been prescribed for all people to the extent that it agrees with and explains the common law of nature for all peoples'.[93] Time set aside for worship was clearly prescribed by natural law; worship on the seventh day of the week was part of the proper law of the Jews.[94] Similarly, punishments prescribed in Mosaic law did not properly apply to Christians.[95]

While Althusius was confident that the natural law could be known by fallen humanity apart from revelation, he did not think that this natural knowledge was sufficient to secure a well-ordered society of pious and holy people. For one thing, while all have some knowledge of and inclination to obey the common law, there are 'different degrees of this knowledge and inclination'; it is 'not inscribed equally on the hearts of all', 'according to the will and judgement of God'.[96] The natural law is not after all 'so completely written on the hearts of men that it is sufficiently efficacious in restraining men from evil and impelling them to God. This is because it merely teaches, inclines, and accuses men'.[97] Furthermore, the fact that the natural law consists in highly general principles poses an additional challenge: not all have the capacity to draw particular conclusions from the general principles. Here Althusius cited Zanchi, but the point had been made by mediaeval scholastics as well.[98] He underscored these points in order to justify the need for a 'proper law'. Proper law supplements common law in two ways. First, it restrains evildoers by fear of punishment.[99] Hence, it helps to compensate for variations in knowledge of and inclination to the common law. Second, it draws particular conclusions from the general principles of the common law. Responsibility for this rests with the magistrate, who is to draw up proper law in conformity to the common law 'and according to the nature, utility, condition, and other special circumstances of his country'.[100] In doing so, the magistrate must use the natural law 'as a touchstone and a measure'.[101] Hence, the Decalogue is 'properly political', an essential reference point for rightly-ordered political life, the 'bond of human society and, as it were, the rudder and helm of the ship'.[102] Magistrates err severely, however, if they attempt to apply all of Mosaic law to contemporary society: 'if proper Jewish laws are established by a Christian magistrate, they destroy Christian freedom'.[103] 'Christian freedom' here is not Luther's freedom from works righteousness, but rather freedom from proper laws pertaining to other times and places. Since magistrates must be governed by the natural law, and the natural law requires care for the common good, tyrants violate the laws of God and nature and what is properly due to their people; they may rightly be resisted by lesser magistrates.[104]

The fact that Althusius offers such a robust account of the role of natural law in building a godly society does not mean that he lost sight of the core Reformation affirmation of justification by faith. Conformity to the Decalogue is not salvific and does not in and of itself please God; only obedience that issues from faith can be pleasing in God's sight.[105] Hence the works of the Decalogue, performed by an 'infidel' or 'heathen', are not able to please God, 'but in political life even an infidel may be called just, innocent, and upright because of them'.[106] Political life has its own integrity and significance, even if it is not salvific.

HOOKER AND THE LAW OF REASON

One major impetus for the development of increasingly autonomous doctrines of natural law came from the perceived need to correct the insistence, on the part of radical reformers, that scripture should comprehensively determine civil law and polity. In the English context, Richard Hooker (1554–1600), like magisterial reformers on the Continent, defended the traditional view against Puritans, who proclaimed the Bible as a divinely authorised guide to all aspects of life. This required distinguishing carefully between those parts of scripture that constituted restatements of the natural law, and which were therefore universally binding moral law, from parts of scripture that were particular to the Jews, whether ceremonial or legal. Hooker's *Laws of Ecclesiastical Polity* was intended in particular to refute Puritan arguments that scripture authorises a specific, unchanging form of church government, binding on Christians. In the course of arguing that civil and ecclesiastical polity are matters properly determined by positive human law, and thereby by the monarch as head and governor of the church as well as the state, Hooker developed a comprehensive account of the various forms of law, largely Thomistic and Aristotelian in character. Yet critics and defenders of the established Church of England both agreed on the major tenets of Reformed natural law. Where they parted ways was in more particular judgements, such as those concerning which specific parts of Mosaic law continued to bind Christian commonwealths.

In laying out the various kinds of law, ranging from the eternal law to human, divine and ecclesiastical law, Hooker differentiated between the law of nature and the law of reason. Aquinas had considered natural law to be the particular way in which rational creatures participate in the eternal law of God's government of all creation.[107] Non-rational creatures cannot properly be said to be subject to a law, since law properly speaking directs reason to the end, and so can provide a rule and measure only to rational creatures.[108] Hooker, by contrast, spoke of 'nature's law' as the part of God's eternal law that governs natural objects, differentiating this from the law of reason that constitutes God's eternal law for rational creatures.[109] Hooker's 'law of reason' was thus his preferred term for what the tradition had termed natural law.

Hooker affirms that the general principles of this law of reason can be known universally and without the assistance of revelation.[110] Hence, universal consent can be used to determine what precepts properly belong to the law of reason: 'The general and perpetual voice of men is as the sentence of God himself'.[111] Since humankind is able to decipher these precepts without the assistance of revelation, they may falsely regard themselves as having created these laws: 'they by natural discourse attaining the knowledge thereof, seem the makers of those laws which indeed are his, and they but only the finders of them out'.[112]

While this may appear to be a substantial shift in the direction of an autonomous, rationalistic natural law, Hooker's emphasis on reason and universal epistemological access to its law should not be overemphasised. In fact, Hooker espoused the traditional view that the fact that the general precepts of the natural law are in principle knowable by all does not mean that they are in fact known by all. Knowledge of the natural law requires 'labour' and 'travail', and in the wake of the Fall, whole nations have fallen into darkness.[113] Hooker and the Puritans agreed that scripture restates and illuminates the natural law of equity, even as reason assists us in interpreting scripture. Where Hooker's understanding of the natural law parted ways with his opponents was primarily in terms of whether the judicial law of Moses continues to bind Christians, or whether all Mosaic law beyond the moral or natural law has expired.[114] Puritans such as Thomas Cartwright argued that the judicial law of scripture perfectly expressed natural equity by leaving as little undetermined as possible; given its perfection, it remained binding.[115] Hooker, by contrast, emphasised the diversity and mutability of human communities and thus the need for human law to render concrete the general principles of the natural law in ways suitable to particular circumstances.[116] Despite the distinction between the civil and spiritual kingdoms, civil authorities are responsible for the spiritual and not merely the bodily welfare of citizens, and can properly determine the shape of public worship in ways that vary over time and place. Indeed, this responsibility for spiritual welfare is a principle of natural law.[117] Hooker's Puritan opponents argued, by contrast, that scripture laid out the proper shape of ecclesiastical polity and that it was an impermissible arrogation of merely human authority to deviate from these divine mandates.

PURITAN COVENANTS AND THE NATURAL LAW

In New England, the Puritans had the opportunity to move beyond criticism of the established Church and to put into practice their vision of proper Christian polity, and the appropriate division of responsibilities between church and state. One of the ways in which they did so was through developing the traditional doctrine of Two Kingdoms into an account of multiple Covenants. The Puritans, like other Reformed thinkers, held that God had subjected all persons to the natural law at the Creation. This natural law, which prescribes duties to God, neighbour and self, instructs persons to join together in social covenant and form particular societies.[118] While distinct from the salvific Covenant of Grace, this Covenant of Works remains binding. John Cotton (1584–1652), for instance, regarded civil government as ordained to bodily welfare and things of this life, while the church is ordained to the spiritual welfare of souls, even as both are ruled by Christ and ordered finally to the glory of God.[119] Much like Hooker, Cotton argued that civil magistrates should foster true religion, and that this duty is known not just from scripture but from natural law and the consent of nations.[120] At the same time, Cotton argued that Christian commonwealths ought properly to adopt biblical law.[121] It is not the case that all judicial laws of Moses continue to bind; those peculiar to Israel do not.[122] There is appropriate scope for human law: 'God Almighty has left it to the natural Reason of Mankind, in every Nation and Country, to set up that Form, which, upon a thorow Consideration of the Nature, Temper, Inclinations, Customs, Manners, Business, and other Circumstances of a People, may be thought best for them'.[123] However, Cotton regarded large swaths of Mosaic juridical law as embodying moral equity, i.e. as restating the natural law, and therefore as continuing to bind Christian societies: 'Cotton seemed intent on finding the judicial law primarily of universal application and its expired aspects the exception'.[124] In this way, Puritans could echo standard Reformed affirmations of the natural law even while drawing divergent conclusions concerning ecclesiastical polity and the proper relation of church and state.

FROM MODERN NATURAL LAW TO THE PRESENT

Much could be said about the so-called modern natural law tradition of Grotius, Pufendorf, Hobbes and Locke in relation to the story I have told thus far of Protestant natural law. The crucial point to be made in this context is simply that we should call into question the tendency to retroject a premature secularisation into modern natural law, even as we attend to subtle shifts that did take place, paving the way for modern assumptions that the natural law was an autonomous rationalist enterprise of deducing moral norms from human nature. Much has been made, for instance, of Grotius' insistence that the natural law would bind even if God did not exist (a premise he denies immediately as impious). But this famous *etiamsi daremus* was no novelty introduced on behalf of an autonomous natural law; it was a scholastic commonplace intended to mark the fact that natural law flows immediately from the natural order, albeit ultimately from God, Creator of natural order and of all natures.[125] In fact, Jean Barbeyrac takes Grotius to task for too *great* a reliance on the scholastics in supposing 'that one would be under an obligation to do or to omit certain things even when there is no one to whom he must answer for his conduct'.[126] John Cotton's immediate contemporary, the Dutch Arminian jurist Hugo Grotius (1583–1645) inhabited a very different world. His extensive theological writings, dedicated to the pursuit of Christian unity, give the lie to any notion that Grotius was a secular thinker. What is the case is that he proceeded, in developing his massively influential theory of international law, under the assumption that God's intentions for humankind could be reliably discerned through the empirical analysis of salient features of human nature. This made it possible to sidestep interminable wranglings over the proper interpretation of scripture, a very appealing prospect in the midst of the Thirty Years' War (1618–48). Thomas Hobbes (1588–1679), meanwhile, whatever his own theological beliefs (intense speculation continues on that front), devoted major portions of his *Leviathan* to showing how scripture supported his own argument that supreme power to interpret and apply the natural law be placed in the hands of the civil sovereign. Even as he innovated, therefore, Hobbes continued the tradition of using scripture to shore up claims concerning the natural law. Samuel Pufendorf (1632–94), holder of the very first university chair in the law of nature and of nations, was concerned to develop an explicitly theological account of natural law, authenticated by scripture.[127] John Locke, too, understood his reflections on the natural law to be investigations of humans' moral responsibilities, given their creation as free creatures answerable to their creator.[128] Modern natural law continued to be an enterprise carried out within the framework of Christian theological assumptions. A comprehensive account of Protestant natural law, then, would need to include modern natural law within its scope.

The expanding differentiation of academic disciplines and social professions meant that reflection on natural law, under the name of international law, was increasingly regarded as a free-standing enterprise that could take place without constant reference to theology. In some sense, the foundation for a separation had been laid much earlier, with Two Kingdoms theology (and even earlier than that, with the distinction between natural and supernatural ends). The distinction between earthly and heavenly kingdoms supported a division of labour – although not a separation – between moral philosophy and moral theology, the former focused on the proximate end of this-worldly human flourishing. The final end of human friendship with God could drop out of sight, particularly when responsibility for addressing its relationship to proximate ends lay with other academic disciplines and professions. In the early decades of the twenty-first century, however, even as natural law discourse has little cultural authority and is primarily associated with certain strands of Catholic philosophy, an energetic Protestant retrieval of natural law thinking is under way.[129] In many respects, this movement, which claims theological justification for hope in the possibility of a common morality, has a greater claim to continuity with the longstanding tradition of Christian natural law reflection than do either the natural law of neo-scholasticism or the rationalist 'New Natural Law' of Grisez, Finnis and Boyle.[130]

NOTES

1. Barth 1946; Niebuhr 1940; Hauerwas 1975: 3.
2. Grabill 2006: 21–53; Van Drunen 2010: 316–47.
3. Holl 1959: 49–51.
4. Frank 2008: xxi.

5 Porter 1999: 121–86.
6 Berman 2003: 4, 97; Witte 2002: 76.
7. Berman 2003: 82.
8. Berman 2003: 85.
9. Berman 2003: 6.
10. Luther 1957 vol. 25: 19–20; Luther 1883 vol. 56: 23–4.
11. McNeill 1946: 168.
12. Luther 1883 vol. 39: 1, 374 (*Die Erste Disputation gegen die Antinomer*, 1537).
13. Luther 1957 vol. 13: 369–71; Luther 1883 vol. 31.1: 409–11.
14. Luther 1957 vol. 13: 161, *Commentary on Psalm 101* (1534); Luther 1883 vol. 51: 242.
15. Luther 1957 vol. 13: 167–8; Luther 1883 vol. 51: 216–18.
16. Luther 1957 vol. 13: 198–9; Luther 1883 vol. 51: 242.
17. Luther 1957 vol. 44: 200, *To the Christian Nobility of the German Nation* (1520); Luther 1883 vol. 6: 457.
18. Luther 1957 vol. 44: 201; Luther 1883 vol. 6: 458.
19. Luther 1957 vol. 32: 153–4; Luther 1883 vol. 8: 54, 104–5.
20. Luther 1957 vol. 26: 256, 262; Luther 1883 40.1: 402, 410–11.
21. Luther 1957 vol. 31: 346; *Freedom of A Christian*; Luther 1883 vol. 7: 23.
22. Luther 1957 vol. 31: 349; Luther 1883 vol. 7: 24–5.
23. Luther 1957 vol. 31: 348; Luther 1883 vol. 7: 23.
24. Luther 1957 vol. 31: 350; Luther 1883 vol. 7: 25.
25. Luther 1957 vol. 31: 359; Luther 1883 vol. 7: 30.
26. Luther 1957 vol. 31: 365; Luther 1883 vol. 7: 35.
27. Luther 1957 vol. 31: 373.
28. Luther 1957 vol. 31: 369.
29. Berman 2003: 76.
30. Witte 2002: 92–4.
31. Holl 1959: 51; Holl 1979: 103–8, 147.
32. Frank 2008: xxiii.
33. Frank 2008: xxx.
34. Frank 2008: xlii.
35. Frank 2008: xxxvii.
36. Melanchthon 2008: 16.
37. Berman 2003: 79.
38. Frank 2008: xxxix.
39. Melanchthon 2008: 16.
40. Melanchthon 2008: 18.
41. Melanchthon 2008: 20.
42. Berman 2003: 79; Witte 2002: 124.

43. Melanchthon 2008: 167.
44. Melanchthon 2008: 167.
45. Melanchthon 2008: 189.
46. Melanchthon 2008: 191.
47. Witte 2002: 76.
48. Witte 2002: 77.
49. Melanchthon 2008: 193.
50. Berman 2003: 85–6.
51. Kolb and Wengert 2000: 121.
52. Kolb and Wengert 2000: 500.
53. Witte 2002: 127–9.
54. Kolb and Wengert 2000: 502.
55. Witte 2002: 162.
56. Witte 2002: 133.
57. Berman 2003: 97.
58. Calvin 2006: II.VII, 348–66.
59. Calvin 2006: II.VII.6–12, 354–60.
60. Calvin 2006: II.VII.13, 362.
61. Calvin 2006: II.VIII.1, 367–8.
62. Herdt 2014; Grabill 2006: 90, 92.
63. Grabill 2006: 76–7.
64. Calvin 2006: II.VIII.1, 369.
65. Calvin 2006: II.II.23, 282.
66. Calvin 2006: II.II.22, 281.
67. Calvin 2006: II.II.22, 281.
68. Calvin 2006: II.II.24, 284.
69. Calvin 2006: IV.XX.15, 1503.
70. Calvin 2006: IV.XX.15, 1503.
71. Calvin 2006: IV.XX.15, 1503.
72. Calvin 2006: IV.XX.16, 1505.
73. Witte 2005: 69–71.
74. Calvin 2006: IV.XX.9, 1495.
75. Calvin 2006: IV.XX.31, 1519.
76. Steinmetz 1995: 30.
77. Witte 2007: 88.
78. Beza 1956: 65.
79. Beza 1956: 28.
80. Beza 1956: 28.
81. Beza 1956: 38, 43, 44.
82. Grabill 2006: 102.

83. Vermigli 1583: 1.26, 124.
84. Grabill 2006: 114–15, 119.
85. Jenkins 2013: 88.
86. Vermigli 1583: 2.2.3, 254; Grabill 2006: 117.
87. Kingdon 1980: xiv–xvii.
88. Althusius 1964: 134; Witte 2007: 151.
89. Althusius 1964: 134.
90. Althusius 1964: 134.
91. Althusius 1964: 134–5.
92. Grabill 2006: 131–2; Carney 1995, although Carney does not recognise this as a traditional position.
93. Althusius 1964: 139; Witte 2007: 160.
94. Althusius 1964: 141.
95. Althusius 1964: 142.
96. Althusius 1964: 135.
97. Althusius 1964: 140.
98. Grabill 2006: 145.
99. Althusius 1964: 140.
100. Althusius 1964: 139.
101. Althusius 1964: 134.
102. Althusius 1964: 142.
103. Althusius 1964: 143.
104. Witte 2007: 154.
105. Althusius 1964: 142.
106. Althusius 1964: 143.
107. Aquinas 1947: I-II.91.2.
108. Aquinas 1947: I-II.90.1.
109. Hooker 2013: I.8, 60–68.
110. Hooker 2013: 1.8, 66.
111. Hooker 2013: I.8, 62.
112. Hooker 2013: I.8, 62.
113. Hooker 2013: I.8.9, 69; Littlejohn 2017: 212–15.
114. Littlejohn 2017: 112–13.
115. O'Donovan 1991: 122–3.
116. Hooker 2013: I.10.9, 70–80.
117. Hooker 2013: VIII.1.4; Littlejohn 2017: 229.
118. Witte 2006: 151–3.
119. Cotton 1663: 7; Van Drunen 2010: 219–20.
120. Cotton 1663: 23–4; Cotton 1647: 59.
121. Cotton 1647: 97.

122. Witte 2006: 158.
123. Barnard 1734: 273, quoted by Witte 2006: 163.
124. Van Drunen 2010: 231.
125. St Leger 1962: 144–5.
126. St Leger 1962: 48.
127. Moore and Silverthorne 1995: 178.
128. Waldron 2002.
129. E.g. Grabill 2006; Van Drunen 2010; Helm 2004.
130. Finnis 1980; Finnis et al. 1987b. I would like to express my thanks to Justin Hawkins for research assistance and helpful conversation on the subject of this chapter, and also to James Dunn for sharing with me the fruits of his own current research on Luther and Melanchthon.

9 Natural Law in Islam

Anver Emon*

This chapter will introduce the basic, theoretical architecture of competing Islamic natural law theories from the pre-modern period (ninth to fourteenth centuries). Specifically, it will outline juristic debates in the *usul al-fiqh* genre on reason as a source of law, where revelation is silent. Thereafter it will reflect on a range of doctrinal debates in which many of those same pre-modern jurists came to a legal determination without reference to scriptural (or any other) texts. Drawing on a curious heuristic they labelled *huquq Allah* and *huquq al-'ibad* (the claims of God and the claims of individuals), I will show that despite not invoking (expressly or otherwise) any natural law account of Islamic law, jurists nonetheless developed law based on a mode of rationality that could be called anything from 'rational' to 'common-sense' to 'pragmatic'. Whether or not the *huquq Allah/huquq al-'ibad* heuristic is proof positive of natural law in Islam is less important than recognising the scope of questions that have yet to be examined. But as I will suggest in the third and concluding part, there are political reasons (some of which enjoy disciplinary cover) that help explain why some questions are not asked, and why some answers are deemed naïve, if not impolitic.

DISCIPLINARY CALIBRATIONS

Drawing on the work of Pierre Bourdieu, any analysis of Islamic natural law theories must locate the substantive argument within some or all of the following: (1) the discursive space of natural law across different traditions, (2) the disciplinary approaches to the study of Islam, (3) the different genres within the Islamic literary tradition and (4) the larger institutional and funding apparatuses that structure the production of research in the academy (Bourdieu 1987, 1988). This multistage negotiation is not straightforward. It is fraught with a range of political questions in the guise of disciplinary questions of method and competence.

For instance, if the study of natural law is framed in theological terms, the entire inquiry will be cast in light of the academic study of Islamic theological history, with implications for which genre within the Islamic literary tradition is best suited to such an analysis. But a theological orientation to the natural law question also happens to coincide with the institutional organisation of Islamic studies in the European university context. As Suzanne Marchand recounts in detail, the German university study of Islam was often framed in theological terms, in large part because of the support this field of inquiry provided to biblical historicism (Marchand 2009). Moreover, a theological frame of reference coincides with the imperative to cast the study of religion in Christian – if not distinctively Protestant – terms, with the focus being on a narrow conception of theology that often excludes the legal as somehow outside the realm of religion. In the shadow of the Gelasian Doctrine and Investiture Controversy – which evinced a symbolic contest between the sacerdotal and princely authority – and the Wars of Religion and Treaty of Westphalia – which have since posited the secular state as solution – it is unsurprising that this theological orientation renders law and legality (including natural law) outside the purview of religion.

For example, for Frank Griffel, a German-trained scholar of Islamic theology and philosophy,[1] any Islamic approach to natural law is theological in disciplinary orientation, and thereby requires a focus on theological writings from the Islamic literary tradition. For him, theologically inflected writings on *fitra* reflect the relevant genre for early Islamic thought on natural law. Noting the distinctive lexicon of natural law in Islam, Griffel writes: 'The terminology used by *Muslim theologians* when discussing these issues is, however, quite different. In the West the language comes from Greek philosophy and Roman law, but in Islam the issue of natural law is discussed in notions that stem from the Qur'an' (emphasis added).[2] Addressing the Qur'an's use of terms such as *fitra* (natural dispositions) and *hanif* (faithful monotheist), Griffel again locates debates on natural law within a theologically orientated frame of reference: 'Although the Qur'an is not explicit about what exactly the original constitution of humans is, *Muslim theologians* understood ... that being a *hanif* is the original religion of humans and that polytheists, as well as Jews and Christians, have distorted this natural religion' (emphasis added).[3] Where he writes about the more theoretical debates that informed the jurisprudence of natural law (as elaborated below), he never ventures far from the narrow theological frame of reference, giving special attention to the voluntarist ideals that have assumed the mantle of Sunni orthodoxy.[4] Indeed, he goes so far as to question the possibility of natural law from the unproblematised vantage-point of an assumed Sunni theological orthodoxy, stating that 'most Sunni theologians and jurists denied the existence of natural law'.[5]

A theological approach to natural law also tacitly supports a confessional conservativism informed by what passes as orthodoxy in Sunni Islam. As will be shown below, pre-modern debates on natural law (among Sunni jurists at least) began from competing first principles of theology, namely about the justice of God (*ʿadl Allah*). For the Ashʿarites, who are often presumed to represent Sunni orthodoxy, God's justice is a function of the divine will. Following a voluntarist logic, Ashʿarites argued (and still do) that whatever God wills is by definition just. Others, who were cast as heterodox, argued in ethical rationalist fashion that God wills only what is just; in a sense, God's will is constrained by the demands of justice.

Arguably, to frame natural law inquiry by reference to this theological disagreement presumes a content-laden notion of 'orthodoxy' that gives primacy to a *disjunction* between reason and authority. A natural law approach to Islamic law, on the other hand, gestures to a *conjunction* of reason and authority, and thereby raises new and important questions about the relationship between knowledge and coercion, the indices of authority, the nature of reason and the relationship between ethics, morality and law. Intriguingly, the natural law theories described below circumvented the theological divisions between orthodoxy and heterodoxy, between inclusion and exclusion. In other words, merely suggesting that orthodox and heterodox theological camps came to a shared approach to the authority of reason undermines the very premise upon which claims to Sunni Islamic orthodoxy are based. If the exclusionary force of theological heresy can be dulled by recourse to jurisprudence, the claim to orthodox belief loses its political force and effect. Indeed, we cannot but appreciate that inherent to the study of Islamic natural law theories is a politics of constructing orthodoxy in Sunni Islam.

A more philological approach to natural law might focus on the Arabic equivalent of the term 'nature', which for many is *tabiʿa*. Tracking this term across the Islamic literary tradition brings us to the field of Islamic natural philosophy, and thereby to the academic discipline of philosophy (see Emon 2014a). Substantively, we must appreciate that the field of natural philosophy (*al-tabiʿiyyat*) is not the same as legal philosophy. The debates between Ibn Sina (d. 1037), al-Ghazali (d. 1111) and Ibn Rushd (d. 1198) in philosophy (*falsafa*) reflected different questions from those that animate legal theory about natural law. Indeed, when al-Ghazali, for instance, addressed natural philosophy, he focused his interventions on topics such as causation and miracles, and their implications for notions of truth and veracity, rather than reason and its authority for legal determinations. To claim that natural law in Islam is best explored through the concept of *tabiʿa,* therefore, is to make a positive argument for the priority of philology, and thereby natural philosophy, in the study of Islam (cf. Emon 2014a).

Since the nineteenth century, the academic study of Islam generally, and Islamic law specifically, has been done in fields characterised by the discipline/method of philology. Philology is variously defined, and in some quarters even out of fashion (see Emon 2018). At a minimum, it centres textuality and diction in a way that is more linguistic and historical than legal and jurisprudential. To move away from philology toward a jurisprudential discussion of natural law in Islam, therefore requires we pay close attention to (and show disciplinary humility concerning) the intellectual standpoint we occupy as scholars.

The academic study of Islamic philosophy cannot fully be appreciated, moreover, without also accounting for Leo Strauss' catalysing influence on the renaissance of mediaeval philosophy generally, and mediaeval political philosophy in particular (cf. Gutas 2002). But in recognising Strauss' catalysing support for the academic study of mediaeval philosophy, we cannot ignore his doubt about the possibility of natural law. His *Natural Right and History* poses the question of whether natural law can overcome the unrepentant moral relativism that he bemoaned in the human sciences. But Strauss offered only critique as a mode of engaging the natural law question (Strauss 1965; Batnitzky 2016). Correlatively, one cannot ignore the influence of Strauss in the construction of Islamic philosophy as a sub-speciality within the academy. We can in fact thank Strauss' students, such as Charles Butterworth, Muhsin Mahdi and Ralph Lerner for their translations of important Arabic texts within the Islamic philosophical tradition. At the same time, and perhaps unsurprisingly, these Straussian scholars of Islamic philosophy channel some of Strauss' dubiousness about the possibility of natural law amidst the constant presence of the political (Gutas 2002: 22). For instance, in the Introduction to his translation of Ibn Rushd's *Fasl al-maqal,* a treatise on the harmony of law and philosophy, Charles Butterworth emphasises that philosophy and law share the same intention towards governance or politics:

> both seek to provide for the well-being of all to the extent possible . . . The agreement between the two depends in no way upon determining to what extent individual philosophers privately assent to the Law, nor in probing the sincerity of their various efforts to buttress its claims. The reasoning leading to this interpretation looks, rather, to what is required for sound political life.[6]

Following Strauss' *Natural Right and History,* Butterworth ends his Introduction by reference to Ibn Rushd's political intention, despite other texts by Ibn Rushd (such as his *Bidyat al-Mujtahid wa Nihayat al-Muqtasid*) that one might 'plumb [for] the content of that intention', beyond the merely political.

FRAMING THE QUESTION, SELECTING THE GENRE: ISLAMIC NATURAL LAW BETWEEN THEOLOGY AND LAW

A study of Islamic natural law, as understood within the broader disciplinary field of jurisprudence, will require moving between the fields of theology and law. Bridging both fields is a curious genre of legal literature called *usul al-fiqh.* This genre has been variously translated as 'legal theory' or 'jurisprudence'; in short, it is a genre of Islamic legal literature in which mediaeval scholars trained in both theology and law debated ontological first principles and developed an epistemological framework that moved from those first principles to derivations of law. While some consider this genre committed to delineating a 'legal method' of deducing the law, I suggest instead that this genre was designed to discipline the jurist to 'think like a lawyer', while also providing sufficient space for 'play' at the boundaries of orthodoxy. It disciplined the subject-jurist into a compliant participant in the field of law, trained as he (and exceptionally, she) was in a legal grammar used to articulate conclusions of law. Importantly, that genre created a wide-enough space in which jurists could explore, contemplate and elaborate ideas that might be too dangerous to consider in the genre of theology (cf. Ahmed 2012). Indeed, to the extent that theology was a policed site of compliant belief, *usul al-fiqh* offered a space for intellectual play without the dangers that might come from such play in the field of theology.[7] In this space of play, jurists articulated competing theories of natural law that, despite distinct theological first principles, shared key jurisprudential positions on the relation between reason, nature and legal judgement.

Notably, jurists did not illustrate how their theoretical approach might result in specific legal outcomes. For that kind of analysis, one needs to look to different genres of legal literature, the *fiqh* (legal doctrine) and *khilaf* (legal disputes), genres which posit *possible* examples where natural legal reasoning took place. Ranging from single-volume handbooks to multi-volume encyclopaedias, *fiqh* sources detail the doctrine of one legal school of thought (*madhhab*) or another, while the *khilaf* genre examines the differences between the schools and why they exist. I say 'possible' because jurists did not mechanically insert the lexicon of natural law jurisprudence into their more particularised doctrinal debates. This admission precludes, of course, any definitive determination of natural law operating in the interstices of Islamic doctrinal analysis. Rather, as a thought experiment, this chapter gestures to the *possible* existence of natural law reasoning in doctrinal debates by reference to the legal heuristic of *huquq Allah* (claims of God) and *huquq al-ʿibad* (claims of individuals). Jurists utilised this heuristic to determine legal doctrines in circumstances where there was no express, divine will. While this turn to *fiqh* debates as a site of natural law reasoning is speculative and exploratory, it nonetheless extends this analysis of Islamic natural law by inquiring into the possibilities of reasoning about the law in Islamic legal history. To debate or disagree on matters of legal doctrine – whether concerning ritual, worship or wrongful death and liability rules – was not to engage in theological disputes, despite the subject matter of the legal doctrine. It was to engage, rather, in the art of legal reasoning, even in those cases (indeed, especially in those cases) where no source text was definitive – if one existed at all.

THEOLOGICAL FIRST PRINCIPLES OF ISLAMIC NATURAL LAW

Pre-modern debates on Islamic natural law began with a fundamental theological question about God, in particular God's justice (*ʿadl Allah*). While all agreed that God is just, the theological debate centred on how best to characterise God's justice. Ashʿarites, who were committed to theological voluntarism, argued that something is just when God says it is. In other words, if God commands us to do X, then X is necessarily just; if God prohibits us from doing Y, then Y is necessarily unjust. Whether we can appreciate why X and Y are just or unjust is irrelevant.

In contrast to the voluntarist Ashʿarites were the ethically rationalist Muʿtazilites (Makdisi 1985; Hourani 1985). Muʿtazilites argued that God commands X only because X is already understood as just; God prohibits Y because Y is already understood as unjust. The evaluation of justice and injustice, they argued, is something that humans can reason about and presume of God. Voluntarist Ash'arites, as one might expect, found the Mu'tazilite view outrageous; it violated the omnipotence of God by imposing human standards of justice upon His divinity.

A natural law account that would be framed in these theological terms would become a site of considerable policing. Theology was the discursive space within which orthodoxy, heterodoxy and heresy were determined. Theology, in other words, was not a safe or playful space to reflect on the possibilities of reason. The material stakes of falling on one side of that line or the other could be substantial, if not dire. The history of Islamic theology is fraught with the political implications of adopting one position or the other (Nagel 2010; Watt 1998).

TO THE REALM OF JURISPRUDENCE

Muslim jurists were not only theologians. The scale and scope of their intellectual corpus spanned a range of fields that they considered distinct and different. Indeed, as George Makdisi and others have shown, the mediaeval disciplinary boundaries between law and theology were policed through a curriculum that offered many 'off-ramps' based on the particular talents or competencies of the mediaeval student (Makdisi 1981). Moreover, not all these off-ramps were as consequential as the realm of theology. For Muslim jurists, disputes about law did not occur under a similar shadow of policing theological orthodoxy. Whereas differences in theology could put someone outside the ambit of orthodoxy, differences in law were to be expected. This is an important disciplinary distinction for purposes of our inquiry into natural law in Islam. Vis-à-vis the Latin West, we all too often take for granted what the Gelasian doctrine propounded as compromise: a jurisdictional division between the world of the sacred and the profane. This jurisdictional division allowed two legal worlds to flourish, the ecclesiastical or canonical on the one hand, and what we might call the 'secular' (for purposes of governance) on the other. Moreover, this division between the religious and the secular helped create the conditions for a secularism that both animates how we understand the political project of the state, and still structures debates about the extent to which the state's legal arm can and should reach into our private or intimate lives.

Islamic law does not operate in the shadow of such a Gelasian contrast. The scope of Islamic legal reasoning operates at a scale that we consider outside the competence of the modern state and its legal system. For instance, Islamic legal debates include matters of ritual worship, formation of contract and admissible evidence in trial, all addressed in *fiqh* texts. Theology and *fiqh* constitute different subject matters along a spectrum of intellectual history that is reflected tangibly in the literary genres they helped inspire. In neither subject area do we find the jurisprudential debate on natural law: neither on the battlefield of theology (*kalam*) nor in the doctrinal technicality of *fiqh*. The genre of *usul al-fiqh* (legal theory) is where we find jurists thinking theoretically about reason and its contribution to the law. Specifically, we find a curious debate that bears the hallmarks of natural law thinking, allowing us to identify two versions of natural law among pre-modern Muslim jurists, which we will call Hard Natural Law and Soft Natural Law.

Hard Natural Law

Hard Natural Law was mostly, though not exclusively, proffered by Muʿtazilite jurists such as al-Qadi ʿAbd al-Jabbar (d. 1025) and Abu al-Husayn al-Basri (d. 1044). It is important to emphasise that not all Hard Natural Law jurists were necessarily Muʿtazilite. Sources are unclear or ambiguous on the theological affiliation of the Ḥanafī al-Jassas, for instance. Whereas al-Jassas offered a Hard Natural Law account, it would be historically inaccurate to call him a Muʿtazilite, despite his playing with Muʿtazilite first principles in his *usul al-fiqh*. Hard Natural Law advocates rooted their natural law jurisprudence in a particular understanding of God, or a theology of first principles. They began by asking whether humans can know the good and the bad (*husn, qubh*), and whether they can *subjunctively* attribute that knowledge of good and bad to God, *as if* God made it clear to humanity. They argued that when God created the world, He did so to create a benefit. Indeed, the world could not have been created to cause harm, as that would have been either futile or unjust of God, which for them was contrary to their understanding of God's justice (*ʿadl*). For them, since God is already perfect and moreover just, He must have created the world to benefit humanity and not Himself. These first principles about God were the bases on which Hard Natural Law jurists imagined the world to provide a foundation for the normative implications of their reasoned deliberation about the world. If the world is for the benefit of humanity, they argued, then one can reason about the world and human experience to reflect on norms for ordering human welfare. God's creative act both creates the physical reality of the world, and gives positive *normative* content to that reality. Put differently, God's creative act made nature a scriptural-text-analogue, subject to reasoned analysis and deliberation. In this manner, Hard Natural Law jurists fused fact and value in the natural order, enabling them to reason from an 'is' to an 'ought'.

Many modern philosophers will accuse this form of reasoning as indulging the 'naturalistic fallacy'. The 'is' is not always something that is good or right; sometimes what exists may be bad, if not evil. Moreover, sometimes what we might think is good or right is contradicted by revelatory texts. For a Hard Natural Law jurist such as Abu al-Husayn al-Basri, though, Hard Natural Law offered a method of analysis that created a rebuttable presumption. That presumption could be rebutted by findings from revelation or elsewhere. The point for him was that as a presumption, it is sufficiently justified theoretically to inform the law, unless sufficient countervailing evidence or considerations existed.

Soft Natural Law

Soft Natural Law theory was proffered by Ash'ari theologians, such as Abu Hamid al-Ghazali (d. 1111), al-Tufi (d. 1316), al-Shatibi (d. 1388) and others. They did not believe that God created the world for human benefit. On the contrary, to assert such a position would be theologically unacceptable, as it would limit God's omnipotence by reference to human presuppositions about justice (*'adl*). But neither was the world created to humans' detriment. To maintain their orthodox theological position, they simply insisted that God creates the world as He sees fit. They also argued, however, that out of God's grace (*rahma, tafaddul*), it just so happened that God created the world to benefit humanity. In other words, rather than rendering the natural order into a scriptural-text-analogue by reference to God's justice (*'adl*), which was a fraught theological issue, they rendered it a scriptural-text-analogue by reference to God's *rahma* and *fadl*.

This turn to grace is vital because it allowed Soft Natural Law jurists to fuse fact and value in nature without giving up their theological voluntarism. Because their theory of grace implied God can change His mind, it allowed Soft Natural Law jurists to retain their commitment to God's omnipotence. From this theological position, Soft Natural Law jurists could get to the same *jurisprudential* position as the Hard Natural

Law theorists, while preserving their commitment to a voluntarist theology. They sustained their natural theory by arguing, at the interstices of theology and jurisprudence, that since there is no evidence that God has changed His mind, the natural world must be for the benefit of humanity. Consequently, Soft Natural Law jurists claimed they too could reason from the natural world to a normative conclusion, or, in other words, reason from an 'is' to an 'ought'. Their shared teleological approach with the Hard Natural Law theorists reflects the historical Islamic contribution to debates on natural law.

Maqasid al-Shariʿa: *Controlling for the Slippery Slope*

As much as their jurisprudential position technically circumvented the confines of voluntarist theological orthodoxy, Soft Natural Law jurists were anxious that their natural law jurisprudence did not do enough to avoid theological heterodoxy. Though the genre of *usul al-fiqh* is located between the disciplines of theology and legal doctrine (*fiqh*), its in-between-ness led Soft Natural Law jurists to anticipate and control for mistaken perceptions from the more theologically inclined. They worried that merely distinguishing their position on grounds of God's grace was not robust enough to distinguish their theory from the theologically suspect Hard Natural Law approach. Out of an abundance of theological caution, Soft Natural Law jurists articulated a method of legal reasoning that maximally preserved their theologically voluntarist first principles.

Soft Natural Law jurists such as al-Ghazali articulated a circumscribed mode of legal reasoning that revolved around two terms of art, namely *maqasid* and *maṣlaḥa*. He expressly designed his method of reasoning to limit the scope of reason's authority in law, out of deference to his voluntarist theology. *Maqasid* is the Arabic term for aim, object or purpose; *maṣlaḥa* is often defined as welfare or public interest. According to al-Ghazali's model, a *maslaha* was a local, specific and particular issue that invoked a core aim or purpose of the law, and for which a *maqasid*-based analysis was appropriate. Al-Ghazali argued that there are five basic purposes of the law, namely the preservation of life (*nafs*), lineage (*nasl*), mind (*ʿaql*), property (*mal*) and religion (*din*). In the absence of scriptural authority, al-Ghazali argued that particularised public interests (*maslaha*) may very well uphold those aims. In some cases, the *maslaha* upholds an aim that is deemed a necessity (*darura*), whereas in other cases the interest is merely a 'need' (*haja*) or purely edificatory (*tahsin*). For al-Ghazali, any *maslaha* that is (1) not addressed by scripture (i.e. is based on reason), (2) upholds the *maqasid* and (3) identifies a necessary interest *(maslaha darura)*, has the authority of law. Framed in subjunctive fashion, the proposed judgement or rule derived from a necessary *maṣlaḥa* is treated *as if* God had legislated it. Anything less than a necessary *maslaha* falls short of offering the necessary foundation for law; indeed, to impute such a *maṣlaḥa*-based rule to God would so empower reason as to vitiate the primacy of voluntarist first principles concerning God's divinity. By hierarchising *maslaha* for legal purposes, al-Ghazali restricted the scope of reason's authority, out of deference to theologically voluntarist first principles.

TO THE REALM OF LEGAL DOCTRINE

Recalibrating our disciplinary starting point from theology or philosophy or philology to jurisprudence, the scope of plausible inquiry shifts and opens up new possibilities. This recalibration offers different standpoints from which to appreciate what might be otherwise taken for granted as merely ordinary, mundane, even uninteresting modes of legal discourse. Specifically, a jurisprudential approach to Islamic natural law theory offers a new appreciation of the rationality inherent in particular sites of doctrinal debate (*fiqh*). While there is no direct, express or deductively reassuring application of *usul al-fiqh* theory on specific *fiqh* doctrines, there are various modes of reasoning in *fiqh* debates that are worth examining, from the standpoint of natural law jurisprudence.

One example is the pre-modern legal heuristic of *huquq Allah* and *huquq al-ʿibad* (respectively, claims of God and claims of individuals). It is important to specify that by claims of God, we are not suggesting some legal theology in which God appears as claimant or litigant. The tendency to read *huquq Allah* in theological terms reflects the tendency to characterise Islamic law too quickly as 'religious'. Likewise, the tendency to read *huquq al-ʿibad* (or *huquq al-nas*) as human rights assumes too readily the context of the post-seventeenth-century European state and the Enlightenment liberal rights tradition. In the context of the historical *fiqh* tradition, *huquq Allah* serves metaphorically to refer to the well-being of society and public policy interests. The phrase *huquq al-ʿibad* refers to the kinds of claims and interests and expectations we have as individuals living in a society with others, e.g. property, privacy, contract and so on (cf. Hohfeld 1913). In the aggregate, the two terms of this heuristic highlight the fact that any given wrong will have both a public and a private dimension. Importantly for the purpose of this chapter, it was up to jurists to determine in many cases what those dimensions were, the values at stake, how best to resolve possible conflicts or contradictions, and whether scriptural sources were on point or not (see Emon 2006).

Most readers will be familiar, for instance, with the Qur'anic injunction against theft, namely amputation of the hand. In the event A steals B's property, A may be subject to the punishment of hand amputation, so the argument goes. But even if A loses his hand, that does not make B whole. B suffers an ongoing loss that the corporal punishment does not redress. Does this seem fair, right or good? A natural law theorist might ask, 'Is it just?' These kinds of questions animated juristic debate about legal doctrine; the vehicle by which jurists posed these questions was the legal heuristic of *huquq Allah* and *huquq al-ʿibad*.

For jurists of the Ḥanafī legal tradition, the answer to the question of compensatory liability for theft came in the form of a source text, specifically a prophetic tradition or *ḥadīth*. In this textual tradition, a victim of theft was allowed to choose compensatory damages in lieu of the corporal punishment for theft. Whereas the ruling regime would impose the corporal sanction to serve the public interest, the victim could prevail against that public interest, demanding to be made whole once again. For the Ḥanafīs, the victim enjoyed a superior claim against the public interest, the latter being served by the deterrent function of corporal sanctions. On the one hand, the Ḥanafī position was justified by recourse to a text, thus taking it outside the scope of natural law reasoning. On the other hand, the position can be explained (rather than justified) by reference to comparative loss-spreading competencies: whereas society could distribute the loss occasioned by the theft (e.g. social costs concerning reliable possession), the individual was not always in a position to distribute his loss. The Ḥanafīs relied on a textual tradition to introduce a degree of choice in the outcome of theft, based on the victim's capacity to sustain the loss or not.

Other Sunni schools of law considered the Ḥanafīs' source text inauthentic, however, and of no legal consequence. These other jurists had to resolve the issue without reference to a source text. For them, the question remained: must B suffer his loss in silence, or can B somehow claim compensatory damages when the thief/defendant also suffers the corporal sanction? These other jurists turned to the *huquq Allah–huquq al-ʿibad* heuristic to reason to their preferred legal outcome. They held that the Qurʾanic injunction on amputation upheld a *haqq Allah,* or claim of God, which served as a proxy for the public interest in securing private property possession. Indeed, they fully recognised that without such security of possession, one could not have a reliable market for trade and exchange (Al-Ayni 2000: 216–17). But security of possession was not merely a public matter that scaled outward in macro-economic terms. At the micro-, individual level, theft meant that the victim suffered a direct and specific harm, which was not easily distributed to others. This harm, which was both real and sustained, could not go unaddressed by the law.

According to the Shafiʿis and Hanbalis, to redress one sort of harm (e.g. the public harm via amputation) did not mean the other went away or could simply be ignored (e.g. the private harm of lost property). Both the private and public harms existed at the same time; resolving one did not render the other irrelevant or resolved. Consequently – and *without reference to scriptural sources* – Shafiʿi and Hanbali jurists argued that the victim in theft has a claim against the thief for compensatory liability, even though the thief may also be subjected to the corporal Qurʾanic sanction.

Malikis recognised that both claims coexist, but they also introduced a third claim, namely that of the defendant. Malikis worried that to impose on a defendant both forms of liability (i.e. punitive and compensatory) might appear as a double punishment for the single underlying offence. Certainly, the victim of theft has a claim against the defendant. But the Malikis worried that if the defendant-thief lost his hand through amputation, and must financially compensate the victim of his theft, the defendant-thief may end up in a form of involuntary servitude, having to pay off a debt that he could not reasonably afford. To impose this dual form of liability may transform an impoverished defendant-thief into a ward of the regime, posing an extra cost to the public weal. Given these countervailing concerns, Maliki jurists came up with a compromise position. Whether the defendant was liable to pay compensation – in addition to suffering the corporal sanction – depended on his financial capacity between the moment he stole and the judgement of guilt. If he was sufficiently wealthy to compensate the victim without suffering unduly, he had to compensate the victim. If he was too poor to compensate the victim, then no compensatory liability was imposed.

How did jurists develop these rules? Their *fiqh* texts suggest that they simply reasoned to a range of values about property, possession, the public weal and the interests of both victim and defendant. Without invoking the *usul al-fiqh* or theology discussed above, jurists nonetheless reasoned towards the good, the right and the just using the *huquq Allah* and *huquq al-ʿibad* heuristic. Whether we agree with their assessments is beside the point. Rather, these doctrinal debates illustrate that reason operated in the absence of source-texts to determine specific legal outcomes. Indeed, these doctrinal debates implicitly posit the de facto use of reason to do so.

THE POLITICS OF ISLAMIC NATURAL LAW THEORY

The significance of reason resonates differently depending on the disciplinary field within which it is examined. If we view the question about reason and authority only through the lens of theology or philosophy, we miss something important about the plurality embedded within Islamic law, and within Islamic intellectual history more broadly. Our challenge in the academy, whether in research universities or seminary contexts, is to scale our disciplinary approaches so as not to mistake a part for the whole. Nevertheless, the politics of naming, let alone proffering, a jurisprudence of 'natural law' in Islamic legal studies has been and will remain subject to varying political critiques and forms of instrumentalisation, ranging from contests over discipline, the polemics around Orientalism, and even the rhetoric of security and anti-terrorism.

For instance, some argue that natural law embodies the inappropriate application of a phrase with origins in the Latin West, making it inapposite to the Islamic intellectual tradition. The thrust of this critique stems from the seminal work of Edward Said's *Orientalism*, and the extensive subaltern tradition of post-colonial analysis that followed in *Orientalism*'s wake (Said 1979). For Said and his intellectual descendants, the study of the East generally, and Islam and Muslims specifically, is structured around Europe as both centre and norm, rendering the 'Islamic' as a foil for re-instantiating the legacy of Europe (culturally, politically and so on) as a measure against which to evaluate non-Europe, or in this case, the 'Islamic' (Chakrabarty 2000). On this understanding, any study of 'Islamic natural law theories' must take the Latin Christian study of natural law as standard and norm, against which the success or failure of the 'Islamic' is measured. This post-colonial critique is not without merit. However, it also runs the risk of so insisting on the uniqueness and particularity of the 'Islamic' as to take the study of Islam outside a globally connected history. Paradoxically, it runs the risk of rendering the 'Islamic' no less exceptional than the Orientalist scholars once did (and still do).

Admittedly, post-colonial critics of Islamic natural law theories are correct that Muslim jurists did not have a specific or express term to denote 'natural law'. But the absence of such a term does not mean that the fundamental questions underlying a broad range of natural law theories (e.g. questions of reason and authority) were unknown to Muslim jurists or irrelevant to them. Nor does this lexical absence suggest they did not think or reflect on creation and its implications for how they might reason to norms and law to govern the infinite variations of human experience and conflict. As scholars have shown extensively, these questions were at the forefront of their inquiries in legal theory manuals (*usul al-fiqh*). Whether one could or should put these questions under the rubric of 'natural law' depends in part on the institutional stakes involved in producing different kinds of Islamic research. The more one is located within departments narrowly focused on Islamic law or religious studies (e.g. area studies programmes or religious studies programmes), the more likely it is one will adopt an approach to Islam that emphasises its uniqueness and particularity. The force of those disciplines, the incentives to produce, the professional associations within which one works will all contribute to this narrowing of the inquiry.

Nonetheless, post-colonial critics are right to be cautious. Around the world, the study of Islam stands alongside national security projects of combatting Muslim extremism. This politics of, on, and around Islam and Muslims are no less relevant to the study of Islamic natural law theory. Indeed, for some, if there were a natural law in Islam, it might offer a recipe for a more harmonious global order.

For example, in 2009, the Vatican's International Theological Commission (ITC) issued a report on natural law, implicitly suggesting that religious and value-based traditions the world over could locate functional equivalents in their own tradition (International Theological Commission 2009). The ITC cast the natural law tradition in Islam in terms of the theological debates between the voluntarist and ethical rationalists of Islam (i.e. the Ashʿarites and Muʿtazilites), suggesting that Muslims would do well to adopt a more rationalist, Muʿtazilite orientation. In the report, the Commission distinguished the voluntarist theology of the Ash'arites from the rationalist one of the Mu'tazilites, creating an intellectual dichotomy that reduced the 'Islamic' to terms that were familiar to the Commission (i.e. theological terms), but ones not particularly enlightening about the complex Islamic tradition. By representing Islamic natural law in Islamic theological terms, the Commission did not fully appreciate the disciplinary logics, not to mention the material implications, that distinguish between Islamic theology, jurisprudence and law (Emon 2014b). Such material implications include, for instance, the apostasy-related trials of the Egyptian intellectual Nasr Hamid Abu Zayd (Johansen 2003; O'Sullivan 2004). Moreover, their endorsement of one side over the other is exactly what post-colonial critics identify as the entitling of Europe and the bearers of its legacy to define the 'Islamic' for Muslims themselves.

In an entirely different vein, Sunni Muslims committed both to a voluntarist theological orthodoxy and to modernist legal reform may find the restrictive casting of the historical *maqasid* model unacceptable. Some modern liberal or progressive Islamists look to *maqasid* and *maslaha* as ways to reform Islamic law and allow for greater reasoned deliberation (Auda 2016). The irony, though, is that the *maqasid-maslaha* model was designed to limit the scope of reason's authority in the law. This is not to suggest that modern reformers cannot draw upon the *maqasid* tradition. Rather, the inefficacy of *maqasid*-based reform efforts to date is due to the inability or unwillingness of reformers to reflect on the original design of *maqasid* as a narrowing, limiting device on reason's scope and sway (Nassery et al. 2018).

CONCLUSION

The debate on Islamic natural law in the academy and among Sunni theologians reflects a broader conundrum that lies at the heart of natural law's very promise. The promise of natural law lies in the ideal of universal common ground or values, whereby such values presumably transcend human difference, despite differences in tradition and value systems. There is a paradox involved in locating the universal in particular traditions. Universals tend by their very nature to be ahistorical, yet the traditions from which these universals are sought are nothing if not historical, rooted in time, space and the practices of communities. In some sense, universals are not unlike the claim of something to be 'common sense', which itself has a history (see Kuhn 1996; Schabas 2007; Rosenfeld 2014). The seemingly interminable, hope-laden inquiry into natural law across traditions is meant to create a new cultural product – one that people of all traditions can contribute to and participate in. While this remains a highly laudable goal, it might better be understood in terms of an eternal, yet agonistic *struggle*, rather than a formal process of *discovery*.

We can see this agonistic tendency in the history of human rights in the latter half of the twentieth century and into the twenty-first. The Universal Declaration of Human Rights, and the various subsequent instruments thereafter, articulate in the aggregate a universal set of values for all of humanity. But as scholars have already illustrated, these instruments do not promise the same freedom for everybody. The European Court of Human Rights has shown repeatedly in its religious freedom cases (e.g. *Sahin v Turkey, Dahlab v Switzerland, Lautsi v Italy*) that it cannot help but articulate the scope of freedom by reference to the particular, historically situated demands of the European state (Bhuta 2012; Shany 2005; Spielmann 2014).

If there is a universal at all, it is the agonistic character of debates about universals. Rather than trying to identify the content of a universal (which is little more than a claim of truth), the challenge is to create maximal space for claims about what the universal might be. But to do so will require, in addition, a humility that has thus far evaded conversations about value, since no one can meaningfully claim, in this imagined, expansive dialogical space, to have an exhaustive grasp of the truth.

NOTES

* An earlier version of this chapter was presented in April 2018 at the Pontifical Athenaeum Regina Apostolorum (Rome), at the conference 'Natural Law in Mediaeval Philosophy', organised by Dominic Farrell LC. Many thanks to Professor Farrell and those in attendance for their helpful comments and feedback. Likewise, the author wishes to thank Rumee Ahmed, who reviewed a slightly earlier draft, offering important comments and editorial suggestions that helped clarify its interlocking arguments. Needless to say, the author assumes responsibility for the chapter's limits and errors.

1. See e.g. Griffel's academic website listing his training in Germany: https://religiousstudies.yale.edu/people/frank-griffel.
2. Griffel 2007: 42.
3. Griffel 2007: 43.
4. Griffel 2007: 44–5.
5. Griffel 2007: 45.

6. Butterworth 2001: xxxviii. Butterworth completed his PhD in political science at the University of Chicago in 1966, three years before Strauss left the political science department.
7. This curious function of *usul al-fiqh* would arguably require Straussian advocates to recognise the limits of Strauss' argument about exoteric and esoteric readings of mediaeval texts.

PART IV Applied Natural Law Ethics

10 Bioethics and Natural Law

Jacqueline Laing

By acknowledging the place of reason in bioethics, natural law theory promises an ethics of life and death which, whilst acknowledging the social significance of consensus, consequences, cultural practices and competing religious precepts, offers a school of thought not reducible to these shifting, arbitrary and contradictory criteria. Advances in technology suggest that natural law theory can assist in the conduct of bioethics, if only because the natural law tradition entertains the possibility of universality, reason, objectivity and right answers in the realm of bioethics.

There are schools of thought that regard the death penalty a sound punishment for a change of religion or causing religious offence. In thirteen countries such legislation is recognised as binding and enforceable. These mandates are also seen by millions, both clerics and faith communities alike, as enforceable outside the jurisdictions that enact them. Again, the targeting of the innocent is often seen as a legitimate means of conducting war, striking bargains, achieving the release of prisoners, expanding territory or winning funds. Whether in the context of lone wolf global terrorism or technologically advanced warfare, like the infamous reprisals on Hiroshima and Nagasaki, questions of justice arise. In medical research and organ transplant too, it is often thought permissible to harvest the vital organs and body parts of live, non-consenting patients to increase the supply of tissue and organs. Here again, we are greeted with the demand for rationality and objectivity. Contradiction abounds where consensus rules. It is reason – or more specifically, practical reason – that drives us to seek the truth about such matters.

LIBERALISM: ARTIFICIAL REPRODUCTION AND HUMAN CLONING

Although freedom and personal autonomy are central to practical reason as understood by the natural law tradition, modern liberalism both sees itself, and is, at odds with the natural law tradition. Liberalism is not a meta-ethical theory so much as an ethical and political methodology. Unlike libertarianism, a political theory that advocates minimal intervention by the state in community and state affairs, liberalism focuses its attention on specific freedoms, often in the realm of marriage and the family. It calls for the rejection of prohibitions on personal freedom such as monogamy, marriage itself and male-female, sperm-egg strictures within marriage. Indeed, the very classification of men and women precisely as men and women is challenged by contemporary Western liberalism as overly precise and unjustifiably rigid in a world in which sexuality is regarded as fluctuating and subject to changing individual desire over time.

In this respect, contemporary Western society (though not Chinese, Russian, African or Middle Eastern society), exemplifies the liberal ideal of fluctuating sexuality, in which no assumptions may be made about how a man or woman chooses to define himself or herself. Equally, monogamy is regarded as a Christian relic of a bygone age, while polygamy, the cultural preference of many, is hailed as a liberating possibility for men and women and those in between. In the realm of artificial reproduction too, for example, the biological facts about children, the identity of their biological mother and father, brothers and sisters, grandparents, aunts and uncles, the name and location of their birth-mother, the whereabouts of the fertility technicians creating them, information about race and medical inheritance and so on, are regarded as tangential matters that ought neither concern the people created by the industry nor the lawmakers that profess to safeguard their interests.

The result of this is that where sex and reproduction are concerned, for the modern liberal, there are few conceptual limits. A man wishing to create a child with another man may seek the services of a surrogate mother and egg donor (who might have 'transitioned' to become a man, and is therefore classified as a man). He may, in turn, donate thousands of sperm and father hundreds of children with willing, anonymised women prepared to gestate children for contracting parties. This man may also transition to womanhood and insist that he not be called the biological father of the child, even though he is the sperm donor and therefore undoubtedly the biological father to his children. Offspring may also be created for homosexual monogamous or polygamous partners using paid surrogate and legally irrelevant biological mothers. This instrumentalisation of men and women and the systemic, deliberate separation that attends the conception and birth of the children created is then classified as unproblematic for the children artificially reproduced. Any efforts to challenge these commercial assumptions are standardly repudiated as morally irrelevant, both to offspring and society alike. Sex and marriage, it is thought, have nothing to do with sperm or eggs or birthing (involving, as they do, unnecessarily rigid male and female roles). These, it is thought, can be manufactured in the name of equality. The people so created must see themselves as having no serious interest in their own identity, origins, race, medical inheritance or kin. Whether their parents are alive or dead, their siblings numbered in the thousands, or their origins the result of human cloning or animal-human hybridisation, artificially reproduced offspring are routinely regarded as having few legal, emotional or financial rights against those who created them. The separation, confusion and injustice involved are clear, but for a lucrative industry in child creation, predicated on the idea that sex, gender, sperm and eggs are infinitely malleable concepts having nothing to do with the interests of future generations, these realities are irrelevant.

For those writing in the natural law tradition, autonomy and freedom must be understood in their rational sense, subject to demands of intergenerational justice, public interest, cultural and civilisational sustainability, the needs of children and the common good. A consensus, however shrill and overwhelming, need not supply the right moral answers. On the contrary, this plethora of ethical questions will naturally consult reliable evidence on the needs of offspring in healthy, sustainable societies, able to reproduce themselves over time with transparency, compassion and truth.

Into the moral gap created by liberalism, minimal-state libertarianism and even statist (e.g. communist) philosophies, emerge institutions more than willing to exploit the potential for productivity or shareholder profit, whatever the costs in human rights abuse and the exploitation of the vulnerable. Such is the openness to exploitation by corporate and state powers, that liberalism and its conceptual bedfellows constitute the easy-going facade for unjust discrimination and human rights abuse. The natural law tradition, by contrast, cognisant of the human propensity for vice, supplies the theoretical apparatus for protecting rational autonomy, the public interest, the common good and intergenerational justice.

NATURAL LAW PRECEPTS

Natural law theory supplies an account of nature that locates binding moral law in human reason. The law of nature is objective and universal. It exists independently of human consensus, human convention and human construction. For Cicero, 'law in the proper sense is right reason in harmony with nature'.[1] There is then a part of the law that is not in permanent flux and yet binds the human conscience. For Cicero, 'there will not be one such law in Rome and another in Athens, one now and another in the future, but (where the natural law is concerned) all peoples at all times will be embraced by a single and eternal unchangeable law'.[2] Although principally a metaphysical theory, finding its instantiation in thinkers as diverse as Socrates, Plato, Aristotle, Augustine, Aquinas, Maimonides,[3] Averroes,[4] Avicenna[5] and others in the Eastern tradition, it has implications for ethics, politics, jurisprudence, administration and a variety of human activities.[6] It marks out the limits of positive law, given cultural, religious, linguistic and legal differences between states, communities and individuals. How then does natural law theory differ from the metaphysical, ethical, political and jurisprudential alternatives? What does it offer the globalised world of competing cultures and contradictory societal norms?

TELEOLOGY, POTENTIALITY, CAPABILITY AND FORMATION

Among the metaphysical ideas that make up the foundations of natural law theory is the concept of teleology. This concept, based as it is on Aristotelian conceptions of function and purpose, allows physical, biological, anthropological and social investigations into the idea of types of things achieving their true end. In the realm of ethics, it holds that '[i]n all he does man seeks some good as end or means'. So, for example, Aristotle at the beginning of his *Nicomachean Ethics* begins by observing that:

> Every art and every inquiry, and similarly every action and pursuit, is thought to aim at some good; and for this reason the good has rightly been declared to be that at which all things aim. But a certain difference is found among ends; some are activities, others are products apart from the activities that produce them. Where there are ends apart from the actions, it is the nature of the products to be better than the activities.[7]

The *Nicomachean Ethics* investigates the nature of the good life for human beings. These first paragraphs posit an ultimate good towards which all human actions ultimately aim or tend. The ultimate good is complete, final, self-sufficient and continuous, and the good towards which all human actions tend is happiness or, in Greek, *eudaimonia*, sometimes translated as blessedness, flourishing or living well – an activity rather than a state of affairs.[8]

To understand human happiness, the function and potentiality of a human being must be comprehended, for a person's happiness will consist in fulfilling the natural function towards which his being is directed. Natural functions are specific to human beings and essential to human nature. Whilst humans are undoubtedly animal, they are specifically animals endowed with human reason. To say so is not to make the universal claim that each and every human being exercises reason, for there may be exceptions. Mentally incapacitated people may not exercise reason, but they remain human beings, and thus rational animals, in virtue of being members of the species 'human being'. Equally, babies, the sleeping, comatose and intellectually disabled[9] retain their status as rational animals even though they may not be exercising those capacities at any given moment.[10] 'Rational animal', then, is a species characteristic that assists in the determination of how best to understand happiness. While desire and will are significant characteristics of the human being, reason or what Aristotle classifies as the rational part of the soul, is properly understood as the essence of humanity. Desire and the will do not describe that which is essentially human. The highest part of humanity is for him the function of reason. Human happiness, then, is precisely an activity of the soul in accordance with reason. And when humans direct their actions according to reason, they are, Aristotle maintains, engaged in virtue.

INNOCENCE AND JUSTICE

A dichotomy is often drawn between natural law, i.e. virtue-based ethics, and deontological or Kantian ethics.[11] This dichotomy is based on a misunderstanding. Central to the natural law tradition is the concept of justice, both as a human virtue and as a philosophical concept. Accordingly, it is perfectly compatible with deontological ethics and also the concept of rights. To illustrate this dovetailing between natural law, virtue and deontology, let us take Aquinas' analysis of the ethics of self-defence.

Aquinas is famous for articulating the principle of double effect in his discussion of the permissibility of self-defence in the *Summa Theologiae*.[12] Intention is central to the concept of legitimate self-defence. Whereas Augustine argued 'private self-defence can only proceed from some degree of inordinate self-love', Aquinas, by contrast, observes that 'Nothing hinders one act from having two effects, only one of which is intended, while the other is beside the intention … Accordingly, the act of self-defence may have two effects: one, the saving of one's life; the other, the slaying of the aggressor'. Aquinas holds that the intention to save one's life need not be the same as the intention to kill, though that be a foreseen side-effect: 'Therefore, this act, since one's intention is to save one's own life, is not unlawful, seeing that it is natural to everything to keep itself in being as far as possible'. Self-defence, then, is not an evil in itself, and indeed is an affirmation of justice.

Aquinas nevertheless regards the permissibility of self-defence as conditional: 'And yet, though proceeding from a good intention, an act may be rendered unlawful if it be out of proportion to the end. Wherefore, if a man in self-defence uses more than necessary violence, it will be unlawful, whereas, if he repel force with moderation, his defence will be lawful'. This introduction of proportionality introduces further distinctions between proportionality in relation to the nature of the act (e.g. killing a child for stealing a flower is disproportionate), using unreasonable force, mistake as to the nature of the wrongful act being performed, and so on. But the principle of proportionality is introduced only after consideration of the nature of the end in question, the nature of the means used and the nature of the side effects involved. Needless to say, subjective mistakes as to the nature of the act being undertaken by an aggressor (the legal defences available to him, the voluntariness of the act etc.) bear on the subjective culpability of the person undertaking an act of defence (whether on behalf of a threatened third party or himself).

Accordingly, Aquinas' analysis of self-defence may be interpreted as formulating a principle of justice that allows one to defend oneself from unjust aggression. Extrapolating from this, there are duties and permissions to intervene, all things being equal, to defend third parties from unjust aggression. For to stand by and watch while aggressors attack the innocent when intervention is legitimate, feasible and likely to succeed, is itself a type of complicity, by omission, in the act of unjust aggression. So the principle outlined by Aquinas emphasises the paramountcy of justice over transient realities.[13] Accordingly, intervening to defend an innocent third party subject to unjust attack is permissible precisely as a matter of justice. Defending the innocent and even the self from unjust attack is, then, a rational good. It is closely related to the virtues of courage and justice, so long as it is prudently and proportionately conducted.

Related to this formulation is the popular idea that 'the end does not justify the means'. This idea flies in the face of much utilitarian thinking, by insisting that better consequences do not necessarily justify the means used to achieve them. The double effect doctrine, for its part, highlights the need to consider the intention behind an action. It recognises that there are, more often than not, side effects to what we do, and insists that – so long as our further intentions are not intrinsically evil, are not a means to our end and are proportionate to our intrinsically good intention – those side effects may be permissible.

Reaffirming the compatibility of Kantian deontology[14] with natural law theory, modern formulations of the doctrine of double effect highlight the role of justice in ethics, the significance of the nature of means-end reasoning and the insistence that morality is not exhausted by maximising good outcomes. The Thomistic formulation supplies four conditions for the doctrine's application:

The act itself must be morally good or at least morally neutral;
The agent must not intend the bad side-effect, but may foresee it as a side-effect of a morally good intention;
The bad side-effect must not be a means to the good end;
The bad side-effect must be proportionate to the intended good end.[15]

The principle that the end does not justify the means has its critics, to be sure. The fundamental idea behind it, however, is that one must not do evil that good may come. Maximising happiness is not always the test of rightness. Maximising body parts, for example, by killing an innocent man might yield better consequences all round. But that fact in itself – that more people will be made happy by the death of the one innocent for use as body parts – is no justification for killing the one innocent. Parameters may be built into the example to ensure that the innocent is homeless and therefore unlikely to be missed, or that there are many more people likely to benefit from his body parts. Indeed, a trafficker in illegal body parts might well maximise his own happiness and prosperity by so lucrative a haul, so that this happiness would outweigh the homeless man's loss of life. But the point of this example is not to plead the case for killing the homeless man. On the contrary, the example is designed to demonstrate the tenuousness of the link between happiness-maximisation and morality, properly understood.[16] In this, it exists in tandem with Kantian deontology, which holds that rational human beings should be treated as 'ends in themselves', and not merely as means: a loose injunction, perhaps, but one that captures the concerns about instrumentalising intrinsic goods in nefarious ways.

Elizabeth Anscombe, in her famous challenge to the award of an honorary doctorate to President Truman for authorising either excessive defence in war, or straightforwardly intentional assaults on cities of innocents, constitutes a reminder of the continuing power of the doctrine of double effect in ethical reasoning.[17] In addition, Philippa Foot's trolley problem[18] – a thought experiment in which a runaway train may be diverted from its destination, where it will kill five people as distinct from one, given the intervention of an ethical decision-maker – continues to supply generations of thinkers with important conceptual alternatives to utilitarianism.

COMMON GOOD

Among the ideas that animate the natural law tradition, then, are concepts such as virtue and vice, innocence and justice, public interest and the common good. The natural moral law is neither a sceptical one, except perhaps where 'grey areas' are identified, nor is it a consequentialist one. It regards ethics as intrinsically concerned with will, intention and action, and is therefore neither reducible to a calculus nor determinable by reference to maximands or minimands. The human will is central to the moral act. No effort to reduce the nature of morality to a calculation of consequences is any substitute for a proper investigation of the moral deed's action-theoretic foundations. Likewise, understanding the concept of the common good naturally involves one in a study of innocence, justice and the rational autonomy that underpins public-interest questions over time. If a constitutionally unsustainable arrangement is elevated as a successful strategy (of, say, human reproduction over time), that very strategy is likely to reveal itself as a self-defeating one, affecting deleteriously not merely the young, innocent and vulnerable members of society, but even society itself, seen intergenerationally as a coherent whole over time.

BIOETHICAL EXAMPLES

Unjust Law and Punitive Excess

We started by considering punitive excess. Death for a change of religion, capital punishment for altered commitments, death or other serious penalties for giving religious offence or as an excessive response (e.g.

public stoning or hanging) to private vice. Here lie public responses that invite mob rule, public lynching, homicidal spectacles, community whisperers and petty but lethal informants. This is the very epitome of totalitarian thinking. States that enforce such excess hound out critics, bloggers and thinkers, promote thought police, elevate informants and annihilate dissent. These regimes are nothing if not oppressive. They invite dictators, i.e. strongmen able to quell the mob. Each person must compete with the next to prove his or her compliance. A residential street becomes of hotbed of treachery. Philosophers must hide their desire for truth, careful at all times instead to affirm their allegiance to the tenets of political correctness.

Once a state has conditioned men, women and children to excessive official response, torture and silent opposition, it is destined to spiral into despotism. Institutions persecute critique, encumber the weak, trample on enterprise and feast on terror. Recklessness and moral indifference become inevitable, supported as they are by institutions, autocrats, bureaucrats and oligarchs. Indeed, thirteen countries punish apostasy (the renunciation of one particular religion) and alleged blasphemy with death.[19] Proponents of the death-for-apostasy law object that silent apostasy is not so punishable; only the public defence of intellectual opposition to the state religion attracts death. This nuance merely underscores, however, the irrationality of the laws in question. Indeed, it emphasises the terror that surrounds membership in such societies.

Attacks on the Innocent

Widespread and systemic attacks on the innocent, whether by terrorism, genocide or certain kinds of advanced technological warfare, are a high sign of injustice. Widespread and systemic vice, in turn, frustrates individual virtues and thwarts human potentiality. Individual attacks on the innocent also imply individual wrongdoing. Elizabeth Anscombe's concerns about Mr Truman's degree emphasise the centrality of the will, intention and means-end reasoning to questions of innocence and justice. Philippa Foot's trolley problem and its variants expand on the Thomistic doctrine of double effect, and continue to apply in new technological environments. The use of reason assists in the understanding of the defence of the innocent where, for example, surveillance allows greater prediction of aggression and the concomitant possibility of pre-emptive prevention. Far from being at odds with the natural law tradition, these possibilities introduce greater clarity, applying coherent precepts and thought experiments to new technological contexts. In this, the natural law tradition, with its commitment to reason and objectivity, is well-placed to found a universal bioethics and to bolster the hope for wisdom, prudence and justice.

Abortion

Within the realm of ordinary medicine, the notion of 'human rights from conception until natural death' is traditionally taken as a foundational precept of natural law bioethics, a logical inference from the principle of the right to life. Attacks on the innocent, whether by way of infanticide, abortion or medical homicide on the non-consenting incapacitated, are regarded as an attack on the good of life. Intentional attacks on the innocent are not only seen as ipso facto illegitimate, they are also regarded as contributing to a culture of death, one that is likely to have serious consequences for societies that practise them. Just as propositions like 'nuclear pollution undermines the well-being of future generations' can be true, propositions like 'non-replacement birth rates undermine culture, law and intergenerational survival', may also be true in a similar way. To combat intergenerational decay, and promote a culture of life, it is necessary to affirm certain truths and promote strategies that affirm them.

It is often said that abortion is bad for the mother, bad for society and catastrophic for the unborn child. These are empirical propositions that should be testable and open to demonstration. Certainly the catastrophe to the child involved cannot be doubted. The child's life is terminated, whether chemically or surgically. In order for the tests of detriment to mother and society to be rational, however, they must be neutral. Where lobby groups exist, their assumptions should be challenged. Whether there are injury- and trauma-related consequences to abortion remains a question that continues to receive empirical attention. A sizeable bibliography addressing the physical and mental sequelae of abortion, whether related to attachment, sexuality, trauma, mental health, fertility, substance abuse, cancer or physical injury is freely available online.[20] The debate excites opposition. In the context of these intellectual controversies, the foundational precepts of opposing lobbies need attention. Is it true, for example, that populations are fully replaceable by foreign populations without social, cultural, and legal consequence? Certainly this assumption is fundamental to the liberal ideal. Both liberalism and its financial benefactor, the population control lobby, have long proposed population replacement as a solution to the birth dearth that characterises the immediate future of Europe. Accordingly, in 2000 the UN issued the document entitled *Replacement Migration: Is It a Solution to Declining and Ageing Populations?* This was taken as the blueprint for the decline and replacement of the population of Europe. At no point was the population decline questioned by this international organisation tasked with the business of assuring international security and justice. Indeed, population decline was promoted as a sign of social progress. Nowhere was the nature and quality of the replacement analysed.[21] Yet these assumptions are central to the question of whether an abortion culture, a culture of death, can sustain civilisations and future generations.

Whether or not abortion is 'bad for society' is an empirical question that is likely to generate greater interest in years to come, especially given the alarm observable across Europe at the prospect of cultural change. Clearly, the empirical question is likely to be less marked in large populations. A society of over a billion people is not likely to elicit the same kinds of intergenerational survival anxieties as a small society already sustained by replacement migration. These are, without doubt, among the empirical questions that need discussion in the context of debates over abortion.

Euthanasia

Euthanasia is now represented as a progressive initiative in the West. At a time when palliative care, anaesthesia and analgesia has never been better, the Western world now chooses medicalised killing as a solution to an alleged problem of pain nowhere recognised in the developing world. Marketed as autonomy-enhancing, pain-minimising and subject to watertight 'safeguards', euthanasia (and its variants) appear to offer a solution to an ageing and ailing population.

Not only have Western hospices, hospitals and care homes been found to be practising sedation-dehydration strategies as a means of bringing patients' lives to an end, Western populations are now being softened up for active euthanasia using advance directives, with removal of tissue and organs in advance. While it is true that voluntary euthanasia is not conceptually the same as involuntary euthanasia (or outright homicide), the conceptual subject matter depends upon an understanding of the danger and gravity of murder.

Just as it is necessary to comprehend why murder attracts a more serious penalty than parking offences, it is necessary to understand the dangers of attracting an industry in homicide given the financial, medical, political and research interests that there are in bringing about people's deaths. Medical homicide licenses healthcare workers to become killers. The moral significance of this, together with the political implications of attracting homicide for a population no longer desirous of continued existence should not be underestimated. Politically directed, the strategy might well be nothing short of genocidal.

One central concern about efforts to institutionalise homicide or suicide, as we have seen, is that it erodes respect for human life. Recognition of the intrinsic and equal dignity of human life underlies any plain reading of the Universal Declaration of Human Rights and the European Convention on Human Rights. Both international instruments emerged after a period in history that saw the enactment of laws and regulations once thought progressive, but which merely institutionalised gross human rights abuse. The World Medical Association ('Resolution on Euthanasia', adopted by the UN General Assembly, 2002) condemns euthanasia whether by lethal injection or by medically assisted suicide, and urges all domestic medical associations to refrain from complicity in such practice, even if domestic law professes to legalise it. The Hippocratic Oath denounces it. Numerous sacred traditions reject it.

Euthanasia raises the very real prospect of homicidal discrimination against at-risk groups like the disabled and susceptible races. Fears of murderous discrimination are far from irrational. Efforts to institutionalise euthanasia are predicated invariably on the idea that certain subjects (but not others) are appropriate for termination, while others are of sufficient quality to be worth preserving. Discrimination against the vulnerable bedevils the practice of euthanasia. The sick, the terminally ill, the disabled, the non-productive and the unemployed are invariably the first to be regarded as proper subjects for medically assisted suicide. The logic of active euthanasia endangers the vulnerable by inviting one of the gravest of crimes in law. In this way, the practice undermines the dignity of those susceptible to unjust discrimination.

Once it is made legal, the practice invariably involves a move towards the termination of those who have not asked to be killed, those who are unwanted, those who are lonely and low-income,[22] and those whose deaths offer some advantage to third parties controlling the process. It does so because medical homicide, socially acceptable killing, involves a radically altered mindset. The Dutch experience suggests that the in-itself logically questionable, but empirically reasonable, slippery slope argument is far from irrational. In the Netherlands, voluntary euthanasia has given way to non-voluntary euthanasia, false reporting and under-reporting. In this euthanasia-driven medical environment, failures of transparency, i.e. lies and deception, are both pragmatic and inevitable. Belgium is now well known for its failures of transparency, with only 52.8 per cent of euthanasia cases reported to the authorities in Flanders. Furthermore, the practice has undermined the goals of medicine by effectively destroying palliative care.

Proponents of euthanasia seriously underestimate the human capacity for error and vice. Because, in this context, they beget an act as grave as unlawful homicide, as in other areas of law where individual autonomy is limited for reasons of public interest (e.g. helmets, seatbelts, drug possession, tax, parking offences), there is every reason to limit the invitation to medical homicide. In short, it is contrary to the public interest to invite medical homicide. If individual autonomy is limited for reasons of parking and traffic management, how much more interest should there be in preventing, rather than inviting systematised homicide.

By dismissing the catalogue of corporate, financial, medical and political interests there are in controlling death, euthanasia's corrosive effects on public and professional attitudes, and the discrimination implicit in its implementation, the easy-going liberal defence of euthanasia with its strategic foot-in-the-door approach to medical homicide, invites, institutionalises and incentivises murder.

Organ Harvesting and Non-Therapeutic Research on Non-Consenting Patients

It is now regarded as progressive and licit to harvest the body parts of non-consenting patients to increase the supply of tissue and organs. The practice of non-consensual, non-voluntary organ harvesting is defended in the name of pain and cost minimisation. The practice of presumed-consent organ harvesting is now recognised by twenty-four European countries and many others in South America. England recently legalised 'opt-out organ donation'. What this means is that the vital organs of non-consenting patients may be harvested (upon alleged death) if a patient has not specified his opposition to it. This invites all manner of abuse, as witnessed in war zones around the world, where organ harvesting is lucrative business, and in totalitarian regimes, where prisoners and dissenters are routinely killed for their body parts. Little attention has been paid in the West to the impossibility of demonstrating that a patient has not been murdered for his body parts.

Moves to harvest organs from non-consenting patients exist, despite the Nuremberg Code[23] and the First Declaration of Helsinki.[24] The latter placed the responsibility to protect patients on medical professionals. It also placed the interests of the patient above the 'interests of science and society', and drew heavily on traditional medical ethics, as summarised in documents such as the World Medical Association's Declaration of Geneva.[25] This required that the physician have the 'utmost respect for human life' in accordance with 'the laws of humanity'.

By 2013, however, the Declaration of Helsinki had omitted all mention of the interests of the patient taking precedence over the 'interests of science and society'. The patient was seen as an appropriate subject of medical experimentation and tissue harvesting, consensual or non-consensual, in the 'service of humanity'. The Declaration of Geneva, too, had altered the pledge of 'the utmost respect for human life from the time of conception; even under threat, [never to use] medical knowledge contrary to the laws of humanity'. By 2017, this had been altered, so that the doctor pledged himself only to the 'autonomy of the patient', meaning consent, however obtained, was paramount. All mention of the unborn had been omitted.

Preying on the autonomy of the incapacitated, the helpless, the weak and the ignorant, Western medicine now promises, in the name of commerce, medical progress and social advancement, what amounts to a twenty-first-century genocide. An understanding of human vice, totalitarianism and the impracticality of policing alleged 'safeguards' is thus central to a sound understanding of the question of 'presumed-consent' organ harvesting. We will learn soon enough whether or not these warnings of widespread torture and homicide, deriving as they do from foundational principles of the natural law tradition, are evidentially sustainable.

CONCLUSION

As we enter into a globalised era, in which execution for either a public change of religious commitment or perceived religious insult is regarded as binding and enforceable law in thirteen countries, the use of reason becomes ever more necessary a part of the common language of humanity. For millions, the targeting of innocents and excessive punitive response are thought a doctrinally mandatory means of achieving political, religious and deterrent ends. Likewise, the harvesting of human body parts and non-therapeutic research on non-consenting patients is increasingly accepted as a licit way of maximising experimental research, human tissue, human life and profits. This life-threatening strategy, coming as it does after the lessons of the twentieth century, raises the prospect of moral atrocity. The gravity of the offence and the systemic slaughter it invites, threatens innocence with the beguiling promise of socially useful ends. The problem is not so much with the long-term trust it erodes (though that may be an outcome too), but with the wrong to the innocent that it countenances. It is unjust behaviour in itself. And with widespread acceptance, it institutionalises oppression, invites despotism, undermines the common good and normalises violence, pathology and vice. The industrialisation of non-consensual organ harvesting presents a danger whose reality will take decades to expose, by which time the violations will have taken place in huge numbers. When combined with euthanasia and the abolition of the dead donor rule, systemic slaughter can be expected for commercial, political and research ends. Forensic evidence of torture and homicide will become almost impossible once dead bodies, from whom body parts have been extracted, become standard.

Metaphysical realism underpins the natural law tradition. Among the concepts that animate it are potentiality and function, virtue and vice, innocence and justice, public interest and the common good. The natural moral law is neither sceptical nor consequentialist, and is intrinsically concerned with the will, intention, action and practical reasoning. It is neither reducible to a calculus nor determinable by reference to maximands or minimands. It expands the moral field beyond fluctuating and contradictory consensus, beyond feeling, belief and opinion to enduring realities. Amidst the contradiction and incoherence of human consensus and human convention, the natural law tradition recognises virtues and vices in agents, steering clear of totalitarian solutions to moral questions and identifying right answers where such answers are available.

NOTES

1. Cicero 1998: 3.32.
2. Cicero 1998: 3.33.

3. Maimonides 1912.
4. Averröes 1921.
5. Avicenna 1945.
6. See Laing and Wilcox 2013.
7. Aristotle 1984: Book 1, chapter 1.
8. Aristotle 1984: Book 1, chapter 4 (1095a15–22).
9. Laing 2013: 336–40.
10. In recent times, Martha Nussbaum and Amartya Sen have adopted a distinctive 'capabilities approach', which affirms the ethical significance of the concept of potentiality. See Nussbaum 2000 and Sen 2004: 30–53.
11. See e.g. Kant 1785.
12. Aquinas 1920: II-II, Q. 64, Art. 7
13. The Hebrew concept of *rodef* or aggressor also imports the concept of self-defence and places certain proportionality limitations on it, e.g. killing an aggressor who may have been prevented by less severe means constitutes murder. See *Babylonian Talmud*, Tractate Sanhedrin: 73–4.
14. Natural law is also compatible with the concept of rights: see Grotius 1814; Finnis 1980; George 1999; Oderberg 2000.
15. Aquinas 1920: II-II, Q. 64, Art. 7.
16. Laing 1997.
17. Anscombe 1981a: 62–71.
18. Foot 1978. Cf. Thomson 1985.
19. Laws Criminalising Apostasy (Library of Congress): see www.loc.gov/law/help/apostasy/index.php.
20. https://aaplog.org/complete-bibliography-on-abortion-and-mental-health.
21. Yet the reasoning behind the policy was indeed challenged, if only by a tiny minority. Instead of welcoming discussion, the dialogue was, more often than not, suppressed. See Laing 2004.
22. KNMG Dutch Physicians Guidelines, Position Paper, 23 June 2011.
23. Nuremberg Code 1947.
24. Declaration of Helsinki 1964, 1975, 1983, 1989, 1996, 2002, 2004, 2008, 2013.
25. Declaration of Geneva 1948, 1968, 1983, 1994, 2005, 2006, 2017.

11 Economics and Natural Law

Samuel Gregg

Of all post-Enlightenment social sciences, economics might be easily classified as having the least in common with natural law theory. To the extent, for example, that economics is concerned with matters such as utility maximisation, cost–benefit analysis or identifying unintended consequences of particular decisions, its goals differ from natural law theory's central focus on individuals and communities (including the state) knowing and choosing the good through right reason. Typically, what is called 'positive economics' – famously defined by the British economist Lionel Robbins as 'the science which studies human behaviour as a relationship between ends and scarce means which have alternative uses' (Robbins 1952: 16) – brackets off the type of normative questions with which natural law theory is concerned.

Those engaged in natural law reflection have, however, always brought their methods of reasoning to bear upon questions with significant economic components. In considering questions such as what constitutes a just distribution of wealth, natural law analysis has long taken into account certain human motivations to which post-Enlightenment economics gives considerable attention.

The arguments marshalled by Aristotle and Thomas Aquinas in favour of private property being preferable, in most instances, to common ownership, are examples of this. Long before Adam Smith focused on the effects of people's tendency to pursue what they perceive to be in their self-interest, natural law theorists pointed out that common ownership did not incentivise people to act responsibly or creatively with material goods. Repeating Aristotle, Aquinas stated that people tend to take better care of what is theirs than of what is common to everyone, since individuals tend to shirk a responsibility which is nobody's in particular (Aquinas 1963: II-II, q.66, a.2).

Likewise, while economics seeks to function in many ways as a value-free social science, some of the reasons that economists engage in this work are normative. To employ an analogy from the realm of medicine: the medical researcher enquires into the nature of particular diseases and potential cures because they want greater understanding of the nature of diseases; i.e. they want to know truth for the sake of the good. The same research and subsequent knowledge helps individuals and communities to make free choices that improve their own and other people's health.

Likewise, economists 'do economics' partly because they think it is good *per se* to distinguish truth from falsehood, and are thus involved in the search for truth as a good in itself. Economists also 'do economics' because they believe better understanding of the economy can furnish individuals, groups and public authorities with specific types of information which may lead to better decisions being made in areas ranging from private investment decisions to the development of public policy. That, in turn, leads to improvements in the material conditions that form part of the common good of a given society.

Considered in these terms, there is less of a gap between the activity of economists and natural law theorists than might initially be supposed. The purpose of this chapter is to clarify the relationship between economics and natural law theory by explaining (1) how economic analysis emerged out of a context of natural law reflection; (2) the nature of the economic technique; and (3) the place of modern economics in a natural law approach to the making of free choices by persons and communities.

THE BEGINNINGS OF ECONOMICS

Prior to the publication of Adam Smith's *The Wealth of Nations* in 1776, the type of questions which modern economics seeks to address were explored as part of moral theology and/or moral philosophy and jurisprudence. Subjects of an economic nature were not treated through the lens of a stand-alone social science (Schumpeter 1954: 83). Particular topics such as the legitimacy of charging interest received specific and often lengthy treatments. Yet even these were examined primarily with regard to questions of justice, and from the perspective of three forms of justice to which natural law theory is especially attentive.

The first (and overarching) instance of these is legal (or general) justice. Properly understood, this involves one's general willingness to promote the 'common good' of the communities to which one belongs. The 'common good' here should be understood as the conditions that promote the all-round integral flourishing of individuals and communities within a given political society (such as a sovereign state).

The second mode of justice, which flows from legal justice, is distributive justice. This involves the ordering of the relationship between individuals and communities regarding the just distribution of common resources according to criteria such as merit, desert, function and need. The third form of justice, which also flows from legal justice, is commutative justice. This is concerned with justice in the relations between individuals and groups engaged in particular exchanges. An example are those exchanges mediated through the legal device of contracts.

All three expressions of justice touch upon issues surrounding the use and possession of material goods. In identifying the demands of justice vis-à-vis such questions, natural law thinkers have recognised that particular institutional arrangements, such as the aforementioned private property, have proved better than others at facilitating more peaceful and lasting distributions and exchanges of material goods. Following Aristotle, one of Aquinas' three reasons for private property being preferable to common ownership is that dividing things up generally produces a more peaceful state of affairs, whilst sharing common things often results in tension (Aquinas 1963: II-II, q.66, a.2).

Natural law thinkers also made observations of an empirical nature when answering certain questions with a high degree of economic content. Aquinas, for instance, determined (contra Adam Smith and Karl Marx) that the economic value of a good or service is not determined by how much labour has been invested in it. The economic value of a good or service, he argued, is reflected in its price, and price is determined by what people are willing to pay for a good or service in the setting of a free and open market (Aquinas 1963: II-II, q.61, a.4c; q.77 a.1, a.4c and ad.2). That is not the end of the question of what constitutes a just price. But natural law theorists considered it important to pay attention to this type of information when contemplating how to determine, for instance, a just price.

Scholastic and neo-scholastic theologians in the Middle Ages and early modern period incorporated these and other insights into their analyses. They also engaged in extensive inquires into the nature of different forms of commercial activity, in order to better understand the area to which they wanted to apply principles of justice.

The Jesuit scholastic Luis de Molina (1535–1600) wrote widely, for instance, on financial subjects, ranging from coinage to taxation, bank-deposits and money-exchanges more generally. Molina also went out of his way to consult people actually engaged in these practices. He did so because he believed such people would have insights likely to escape a theologian's attention. 'The practice', Molina stated, 'of the merchants makes a better estimation of goods than the scholastic doctors, and the merchants' judgment is rather to be abided by about the value of the goods, especially when they are used in the business they do with one another' (1759 [1593]: Disputation 407, ¶ 7).

Over time, this type of inquiry contributed to the development of many insights into economic life. In his monumental *History of Economic Analysis*, Joseph Schumpeter explored scholastic commentaries on economic topics at length. His conclusion was that 'the economics of the doctors absorbed all the phenomena of nascent capitalism and ... served ... as a basis for the analytic work of their successors, not excluding A. Smith' (Schumpeter 1954: 94). Looking at natural law philosophers of the early modern period such as Samuel von Pufendorf, Schumpeter emphasised their attention to important distinctions that would become standard reference points in modern economics. In Pufendorf's case, Schumpeter states:

> Distinguishing value from use and value in exchange ... he lets the latter be determined by the relative scarcity or abundance of goods and money. Market price then gravitates toward the costs that must normally be incurred in production ... He goes on to discuss various problems of public policy, such as the repression of luxury by sumptuary laws, the regulation of monopolies, craft guilds, inheritance, entails, population ... The welfare aspect is always kept in view. Again, we behold an embryonic *Wealth of Nations*.
> (1954: 122)

That said, we should note that these natural law scholars – mediaeval or modern, Catholic or Protestant – did not think of themselves as 'doing economics' or as 'economists'. They approached these subjects primarily as theologians, philosophers or lawyers. Hence their focus remained upon, for instance, applying the requirements of distributive and commutative justice to forms of interest-charging, or exploring the implications of commutative justice for contracts, or assessing whether legal justice required the state to establish a monopoly over a particular trade route or product. Strictly speaking, this is not economic inquiry.

Schumpeter's point was that these individuals helped to clarify and consolidate the meaning of economic concepts such as utility, price-formation, the functions of money, opportunity-cost, the nature of capital, the economic role played by interest, the idea of comparative advantage, the impact of monopolies, the notion of scarcity, the government welfare function etc. Paying attention to this type of information is not, however, the same as engaging in economic analysis or 'thinking economically' in a systematic manner about the world.

That particular development did not occur until the late eighteenth century. Nonetheless, economic analysis continued to be taught as part of a battery of topics grouped together under the title 'moral philosophy'. This included natural theology, natural law (or ethics), jurisprudence and public finance (Schumpeter 1954: 141). This remained largely the case until the middle of the nineteenth century. It was with Adam Smith that the domain of economics began to emerge out of, and separate itself from, this natural law framework.

THE RISE OF THE ECONOMIC TECHNIQUE

Studying and teaching at the University of Glasgow, Smith wrote and taught widely, beyond the realm of what would come to be called economic science. Like all other professors of his time, Smith knew natural law philosophy well. This is amply demonstrated by his *Lectures on Jurisprudence*. Recorded in 1762, 1763 and 1766, these discourses reflect the influence of modern Protestant natural law scholars such as Pufendorf and Hugo Grotius.

In the first of these lectures, Smith states that law and government 'cannot be supported without some expense'. He immediately adds that the furnishing of this expense relies on the 'industrious part of the people' (1982 [1762–3, 1766]: (A), i. 4–5). Later in the *Lectures*, Smith comments that, through 'the division of labour' which maximises the productivity of work through specialisation, more efficient use of time and the subsequent invention of machines (1982 [1762–3, 1766]: (A), vi. 52), it becomes possible to increase 'the opulence of a nation' (1982 [1762–3, 1766]: (A), vi. 50).

All these and other observations of an economic nature are integrated by Smith into reflections whose focus are topics ranging from public jurisprudence, to domestic law, private law and the police power. Smith describes the last of these as 'the second general division of jurisprudence' (1982 [1762–3, 1766]: (B), 203). It contains by far the majority of Smith's pre–*The Wealth of Nations* observations on subjects such as money, price, the division of labour and the balance of trade.

By contrast, Smith's *The Wealth of Nations* does not approach its subject matter within a jurisprudential or moral philosophical framework. Questions of law and the role of the political authorities are subsumed *into* Smith's economic analysis rather than the other way around.

The Wealth of Nations is thus very much a work of political economy, understood as an inquiry into the economic, social and political arrangements which affect what is called 'wealth'. By wealth, we mean more than just capital. Wealth is properly understood as including (1) *all* aspects of material well-being, such as health, employment, education etc. and (2) the capacity of an individual or community to meet its needs and wants.

Certainly, Smith's analysis of the causes of wealth was stimulated by some normative impulses. These include Smith's conviction that the prevailing mercantilist practices of his time undermined human freedom and tended to foster corruption, as well as his conclusion that the new society coming into being as a result of the spread of trade and commerce was, on balance, more conducive to the advance of liberty and overall societal well-being than previous social and economic arrangements.

But while such normative concerns underlie Smith's project, they are not the *substance* of Smith's analysis. For it is with Smith's *The Wealth of Nations* that the various pieces of information – 'from', as Lionel Robbins put it, 'investigations of the Balance of Trade ... [and] discussions of the legitimacy of the taking of interest' – start to 'become sufficiently unified' (Robbins 1952: 3). The relationships between these hitherto relatively isolated data-points start to be clarified, and the implications of these relationships for other questions of an economic nature are explored.

At the same time, as John Finnis observes, one of Smith's crucial contributions to the development of economic analysis is his willingness to 'systematically call attention to the side effects of individual choices and action and behaviour' (Finnis 1990: 338). By 'side effect', we mean an effect that is not intended; i.e. not chosen as a means or end. One insight of natural law theory into human action is that all choices have more than one effect. Many of these effects are not intended.

This point is core to grasping the import of Smith's famous line that 'It is not from the benevolence of the butcher, the brewer or the baker that we expect our dinner, but from their regard to their own interest' (1981 [1776]: I. 1. 2). The baker does not make and sell bread to others because he loves his customers and wants nothing but their praise in return. Rather, the baker primarily bakes bread and sells it to others in order to pursue goals that he regards as being in his self-interest. This self-interest isn't necessarily confined to goals such as material gain. It may also include a desire to provide for *himself* and *his* family and/or to fulfil *his* laudable desire to be a good baker for the sake of being a good baker. Others are subsequently provided with bread and these exchanges create a web of mutual collaboration and benefits. These networks of exchange and the provision of baked goods to specific and known individuals are not, however, the objects of the baker's choice as he pursues his self-interest. They are side effects, some of which may be foreseeable by the baker, but they are not chosen by the baker.

We first see Smith elaborate on this important distinction and its importance for thinking economically in his earlier work, *The Theory of Moral Sentiments*. Here Smith writes:

> The rich ... are led by an invisible hand to make nearly the same distribution of the necessaries of life which would have been made had the earth been divided into equal portions among its inhabitants; and thus, *without intending it, without knowing it*, advance the interest of society. (1982 [1759]: IV. 1. 10)[1]

This emphasis on the difference between what is chosen intentionally and the side effects of that same choice reappears in *The Wealth of Nations* when Smith states that the person who pursues wealth '*intends* only his own gain' yet is nonetheless 'led by an invisible hand to promote an end which was not part of his *intention*' (1981 [1776]: IV. 2).[2] That unintended end is the overall economic well-being and increases in the sum total of wealth in society.

Henry Ford, for example, pursues his new idea of the car because he is interested in creating something new, highly useful, and in acquiring wealth. Some side effects of that choice were long-term employment for many, a period of unemployment for others (such as those in the horse-and-buggy business), growth in the United States' overall wealth, and a major spur for the development of the oil industry over time. Perhaps Ford foresaw some of these side effects. Perhaps not. Whatever the case, they were not the object of his choice.

We thus began to see that economics involves close study of the side effects of choices (or what might be called the 'invisible hand' writ large) that lead to the creation and maintenance of ways of meeting people's material needs and wants. For part of the economist's work is to examine the relationship between the effects of the choices of individuals and communities which go beyond what is immediately being chosen.

In the case of Smith, the steps of his analysis are as follows: (1) the division of labour allows an increase in production; (2) an increase in production leads to greater availability of goods and services and thus a decrease in price; (3) greater availability and decreasing prices enable more people to purchase and enjoy the good or service; (4) as this process is repeated across different industries, increasing numbers of people can enjoy increasing numbers of goods and services; and thus (5) the increasing division of labour leads to greater general prosperity for more and more people (Otteson 2011: 89).

Note that none of the moves from step 1 to step 5 is intended to lead to the other. They are *all* side effects. People don't decide to specialise in a particular skill because they intend to create greater material prosperity for all. They have other reasons for doing so, and these need not be all self-regarding. But the side effect of their choice to specialise helps to set in motion and maintain the process by which greater wealth for more people is created.

THE NATURE OF THE ECONOMIC TECHNIQUE

Exploring the ways in which these choices and their known and unknown effects relate to one another is core to economic inquiry. Economics is especially attentive to what the German economist Wilhelm Röpke called 'the logic of relationships' (1963: 118). For economists, it is second nature to know, for instance, that employment levels and wage levels are reciprocally related. The logic of relationships is nevertheless not just one of dualities. To use the same example, economics stresses that the interdependency of wages and employment affects the supply and demand of given goods, and vice versa.

Consistent study over time of these relationships and the achievement of a high degree of predictability about how these interdependencies affect one another is central to economic analysis. By identifying these relationships and sometimes even quantifying them, economics assumes the analytical characteristics of a positive science, one that often focuses on understanding the reasons for discernible changes in economic activity, especially those that represent responses to alterations in economic variables and policy. What, for example, are the likely effects of tax-cuts or tax-increases on wealth creation and distribution among certain income-segments of the population?

This does not mean that the study of these relationships acquires the same degree of certainty that we find in some of the natural sciences. Alongside known side effects (or known consequences) there are also unknown side effects (or unknown consequences). Knowledge of all these known or unknown side effects of choices is not possible for one economist or group of economists. No one can know all the different side effects of the choices of millions of people and the way they affect each other. It is therefore reasonable to be sceptical of the capacity of economics to make the type of predictions characteristic of the natural sciences.

In that sense, positive economics is less about the precise prediction of future events or developments in the economy, and more concerned with the reduction of uncertainty through the accumulation of greater theoretical and empirical knowledge of the effects of people's actions. It may involve, for instance, economists' highlighting certain consistencies across time in the logic of relationships: that wage levels, for example, do have an impact on the labour market, or that certain approaches to monetary policy may boost employment, albeit at the expense of increasing inflation.

One particular contribution of economic analysis is that it provides information about the full costs of alternative uses of the same resources. 'Costs' means the renunciation of alternative utilities, i.e. opportunity costs.

This may be understood using the analogy of the decision to build a bridge. An economist compares, for instance, the cost of building the bridge with the costs of alternative means of routing traffic, with the cost of raising the taxes needed to pay for the bridge, and with the cost of requiring taxpayers to renounce part of their wealth. The economist then offers a view of whether the bridge should be built from the standpoint of whether it represents the most efficient use expressed in measurable and quantifiable terms of the available scarce means in the context of a given economy. As an economist, however, he does not argue that it is morally right or just to build the bridge. For that would be to move from positive analysis to offering normative judgements (Gregg and Harper 1999: 12).

In engaging in this type of positive analysis, economists pay particular attention to two propositions. The first is *scarcity*: we do not have unlimited supplies of everything that we desire. Because goods and services and the objects we use to produce these goods and services are limited in supply, choices must be made. Everyone must choose to give up certain things so they might enjoy the benefits of other things. The very act of choosing option A means rejecting options B, C, and D (Gregg and Harper 1999: 11).

A second proposition considered by economists is that people generally prefer more to less. Note that this is a statement of fact and *not* of values. Economics does not insist that it is morally good for people to prefer more to less. It simply states that they do. Economists notice that when faced with several alternatives, people generally choose the one that gives them more personal satisfaction or what economics often denotes as 'utility' (Gregg and Harper 1999: 11).

Economics thus helps us to understand how to generate maximum material wealth from a limited supply of resources. This in turn leads economists to analyse the question of *efficiency*; i.e. how to best allocate scarce resources of capital, labour and enterprise amongst an unlimited number of competing alternative uses in a given community such as a business, town or even country. An 'efficient' allocation is one that generates maximum satisfaction of material needs and material wants for those who are members of that community.

This does not mean that the economist presents his proposed way of satisfying a particular group's material needs and wants as a *normative* end (though economists who are philosophical materialists or who understand morality in Epicurean terms – neither of which are compatible with natural law – may indeed view their research's normative purpose in such terms). Nor does it imply that the insights of positive economics should be the decisive element in determining the choices of individuals and communities. It simply means that economics can furnish us with specific information that helps in the formulation of better decision-making – including, as we will see, the making of free choices on the premises of natural law reasoning. Economics consequently does not involve making moral judgements about these decisions.

Economics does not, for example, attempt to determine whether a business' profits were made justly. Rather, it seeks to tell us *how* profit has been or could be realised. To this extent, as Ludwig von Mises pointed out, economics

> is a theoretical science . . . It is not its task to tell people what ends they should aim at. It is a science of the means to be applied for the attainment of ends chosen, not, to be sure, a science of the choosing of the ends . . . Science never tells a man how he should act; it merely shows how a man must act if he wants to attain definite ends. (1966: 10)

Thus while economics can provide us with valuable information about how wealth is created and how, once created, it has been distributed, economics cannot tell us how wealth *should* be distributed from the standpoint of *justice*. Economists may indeed have normative commitments, such as greater equity in wealth-distribution or a growth in negative liberty. It is also true that economists may use their status as social scientists to confer legitimacy upon particular normative judgements. In these cases, however, the economist has crossed over into the realm of offering normative-laden policy-advice, and should acknowledge that they are acting with a concern for particular normative or political goals rather than, strictly speaking, as an economist (Gregg and Harper 1999: 13–16).

ASSESSING ECONOMICS FROM A NATURAL LAW STANDPOINT

If this is an accurate depiction of the nature and ends of economics, how might it be assessed from the standpoint of natural law?

One way to answer this question is to consider the methodology of economics. Economic analysis focuses on assessing the relative costs and benefits of a given proposal. It is not concerned with determining the morality of the proposed action. Instead, it seeks to identify and compare those side effects which lie outside the immediate intention of those who initiate an action but which are nonetheless caused by that same act.

In short, economics involves discerning and comparing known *consequences*. Its methodology therefore closely tracks a way of ethical reasoning first described by the English philosopher Elizabeth Anscombe as 'consequentialism'.

There are many variants of consequentialism. They range from act or rule utilitarianism to what is known as proportionalism. A common characteristic of consequentialist ethics is, as one of its primary critics Germain Grisez stresses, that it proposes 'efficiency in promoting measurable good results – and/or in preventing measurable bad results – as the methodological key'. Consequentialist moral judgement, Grisez adds, involves looking at 'the results it can be expected to bring about'. The consequentialist subsequently 'tries to predict with reasonable probability the measurable good and bad results … The right act is the one which is expected to yield the greater good – that is, the greatest net good or, in case there is no desirable prospect, the least net evil' (Grisez 1978: 24).

Grisez emphasises the heavy use of the language of quantity by consequentialists – measurable, probability, greater, greatest, least net etc. – for a reason. For natural law thinkers like Grisez take it that herein lies the weakness of consequentialist ethical reasoning. Consequentialist ethical reasoning assumes, at some level, that humans can measure moral goods and moral evils and weigh them against one another. But the difficulty for consequentialism is that such commensuration is impossible.

Humans can certainly weigh those outcomes which *are* quantifiable. But, as spelt out by Pope John Paul II in his encyclical *Veritatis Splendor* (1993), whether it calls itself proportionalist, utilitarian or consequentialist, any such method of ethical reasoning proposes that we can compare things evaluatively which are, in many ways, unmeasurable and unquantifiable.

Precisely how might you determine, for instance, that three evils potentially realised in an act outweigh, say, two goods potentially realised by the same act? Can we really know all the possible side effects of any one of your choices in the short, medium and long term? How do you measure the effects of an evil like stealing against the impact of pursuing a good like knowledge of truth? From what perspective can any human being propose to engage in such weighing in a way that is reasonable?

In other words, consequentialists propose a commensuration of things which are *incommensurable*. They literally seek to measure the non-measurable. Thus John Paul II highlighted 'the difficulty, or rather the impossibility, of evaluating all the good and evil consequences and effects ... of one's own acts'. Such 'an exhaustive rational calculation', the encyclical added, 'is not possible. How then can one go about establishing proportions which depend on a measuring, the criteria of which remain obscure?' (1993: ¶ 77).

It follows that if you embrace proportionalism or consequentialism, then, at some point, you are bound to become arbitrary in the way you make moral judgements. And to be arbitrary in one's moral reasoning is to be irrational. Indeed, the only being who could possibly know all the foreseen (let alone the unforeseen!) good and evil effects of any given free choice would be an all-knowing, all-seeing Deity.

Prominent twentieth-century utilitarian and consequentialist thinkers have conceded that these are major flaws in their position. The English-Australian utilitarian philosopher, J. J. C. Smart, noted that it was precisely these types of methodological difficulties which meant that 'the utilitarian is reduced to an intuitive weighing of various consequences and their probabilities. It is impossible to justify such intuitions rationally, and we have here a serious weakness of utilitarianism' (Smart 1967: 210).

But for our purposes, the question is: does consequentialism's essential irrationality and incoherence mean that the economic *method* and therefore modern economics are fundamentally irrational? By no means.

In his critique of consequentialism, Grisez specifies that 'measuring, counting, and weighing do have a place in practical reasoning ... "Greater good", "proportionate means", and like expressions can be used meaningfully' (Grisez 1978: 49). One context in which this can occur is what he calls those instances in which 'a practical but non-moral judgment is made'. Grisez does not mean by this that the calculation or cost–benefit analysis is about trying (but failing) to determine what is morally good or just. Rather, he means that such analysis aims at 'what is better in some non-moral sense' (Grisez 1978: 49).

Notions of 'greater good', Grisez writes, 'have a legitimate place in *technical* judgement. *If* one has a well-defined objective and knows the costs of various ways of achieving it, one can rate a certain means best. "Best" here means "most efficient"' (Grisez 1978: 52). This is core to the enterprise of economics. In that sense, economics, Finnis points out, 'constantly reminds us that to spend on one thing is to use up what might have been spent (time and labour, money, other resources) on other purposes' (Finnis 1992: 242–3). Thus while economics can say little, for example, about what constitutes a just distribution of wealth, it can provide a good deal of information about the measurable and quantifiable costs and benefits associated with different means of achieving particular wealth distributions.

A problem arises when the economic technique is elevated to the status of an all-embracing way of making reasonable free choices. First, it encounters all the methodological problems listed above with any form of consequentialist moral analysis. Second, it involves identifying good and evil in terms of something like desire-satisfaction or pleasure-maximisation/pain-minimisation. But since one person's pleasure can be another's pain, the 'good' in such a schema becomes highly subjective and thus non-measurable. How does one measure the satisfaction or pleasure of being a great athlete against the satisfaction or pleasure of being a good farmer?

John Stuart Mill tried to circumvent this problem by arguing that, when it came to weighing pleasure and pain, people should consider the quality of a pleasure rather than simply its quantity. Thus we ought to ascribe more weight to, for example, the refined pleasure of watching opera as opposed to the raw thrill of watching a boxing match. But Mill himself conceded that 'it must be admitted that when utilitarian writers have said that mental pleasures are better than bodily ones they have mainly based this on mental pleasures being more permanent, safer, less costly and so on – i.e. from their circumstantial advantages rather than from their intrinsic nature' (Mill 1998 [1863]: 6). It follows that the 'quality' of a pleasure, higher or lower, is highly subjective and variable, thus making meaningful measurement even more elusive.

It is also the case that any number of non-material goods, like freedom of religion or rule of law, are unquantifiable and thus cannot be compared in a cost–benefit manner. Is one instance of rule of law, for example, worth more or less than three instances of freedom of religion? In this way, we see the correctness of Grisez's observation that 'at the level of basic commitments, the economic model is useless' (Grisez 1978: 38). Notions of greater good may work when speaking of instrumental goods like wealth. But they don't work when discussing *unquantifiable* goods like life, religion and practical reason.

These difficulties with turning economics into a moral theory do not mean that economics can be safely ignored. On the contrary, it merely echoes the argument of James Buchanan and Geoffrey Brennan that 'The fact that the whole set of "non-economic" motivations are more difficult to model than the "economic" should not lead us to deny their existence' (Buchanan and Brennan 1987: 55). This is surely important if economics is not to be pushed into the realm of the absurd. Writing in the late 1980s, another economist, Murray Rothbard, complained that:

> In recent years, economists have invaded other intellectual disciplines and, in the dubious name of science, have employed staggeringly oversimplified assumptions in order to make sweeping and provocative conclusions about fields they know little about. This is a modern form of 'economic imperialism' in the realm of the intellect. Almost always, the bias of this economic imperialism has been quantitative and implicitly Benthamite, in which poetry and pushpin are reduced to a single-level, and which amply justifies the gibe of Oscar Wilde about cynics, that they (economists) know the price of everything and the value of nothing. (1989: 45)

THE PLACE OF ECONOMICS IN NATURAL LAW

Given the nature and limits of economic analysis, is it possible to integrate the economic technique into a natural law approach to moral reasoning?

In the nineteenth and twentieth centuries, natural law reflection was brought to bear upon economic topics, primarily by different schools of Christian social thought, especially official Catholic social teaching. Here we find acknowledgement that post-Enlightenment social sciences like economics provide new insights into social and political problems. This is not the same as considering how economics qua economics might fit into natural law approaches to any number of ethical and political questions.

One way forward is to reflect on this question through the lens of 'new natural law theory' (NNLT) or 'new classical natural law theory'. This is associated with Germain Grisez, John Finnis and Joseph Boyle, among others.[3] Their account of the nature of human flourishing and how one makes free choices allows economic analysis to be incorporated into the process of practical reasoning in a way that respects economics' specific competence and its contributions to knowledge, while also preventing economics from becoming an all-encompassing explanation of reality.

According to NNLT, practical reason recognises as self-evidently desirable what are called 'basic goods'. These goods are the essence of authentic human flourishing and thus give basic reasons for action to human beings. Among these goods are the goods of knowledge and beauty; skilled work and play; friendship; life and health; marriage; practical reason itself; and religion, understood as harmony with the truth about the transcendent (see Tollefsen 2012).

NNLT maintains that these goods are incommensurable with one another. Hence, one cannot say that any one of these goods contains all the good of another, plus more. Religion is not life, life is not work and work is not marriage. Instead, each good is beneficial to human beings and thus desirable, each in its unique way. Morality in NNLT arises when people begin to deliberate and choose *which* of the basic goods, or which particular realisation of these goods, to pursue when we are faced with desirable options for choice. To help determine whether a decision is practically reasonable and thus worthy of choice, NNLT maintains that we can derive from practical reason itself what are called 'modes of responsibility' or 'moral norms'. These principles are very attentive to how feelings and emotions can divert us from, or distort our participation in, the basic goods (Tollefsen 2012). They also seek to ensure that we don't confuse the basic goods with what NNLT calls 'instrumental goods' – goods such as money, wealth, employment etc. – whose final purpose is found in helping us to participate in the basic goods, but which themselves are not basic. Through the creation and acquisition of wealth, for instance, we can create conditions that allow us to promote and protect health, life, beauty, work etc.

In his book *Natural Law and Natural Rights* (1980), Finnis lists nine moral norms to guide upright free choices for the basic goods.[4] Among these 'modes' are certain moral absolutes (such as those expressed in the second tablet of the Decalogue) which specify certain actions (lying, killing, stealing etc.) as never to be done, because such actions always and in every case are intended to damage or destroy particular basic goods. Another moral norm is a coherent plan of life, in the sense of 'a harmonious set of purposes or orientations' (Finnis 1980: 103). If a person is committed, for instance, to becoming a scholar (for the sake of the good of truth), then he won't make choices that commit him to pursuing a different profession. Yet another mode concerns not acting in a way that reflects arbitrary preferences amongst persons: in other words, the Golden Rule – do unto others as you would have others do unto you (Finnis 1980: 107–9).

These and the other modes of responsibility acknowledge that any one choice for a basic good means that you do not choose the other goods. And this because – as we have seen economics acknowledge – 'the context of choice is that of incompatible options for action' (Tollefsen 2012). NNLT also recognises that the nature of moral causation is such that one free choice for a good also has consequences or side effects. While these may be good or bad, and even foreseen in some instances, they fall outside the intended object freely willed by the acting person.

This NNLT emphasis on the implications of the distinction between intentionality and side effects allows economics to enter the picture. As noted, this distinction was crucial to Smith's development of the economic technique. Moreover, in its articulation of the modes of responsibility, NNLT has focused considerable attention on how consequences fit into the process of practical reasoning as people pursue 'integral human flourishing'.

Some may be surprised by this, given that NNLT is firmly anti-consequentialist as an ethical theory. Many NNLT theorists have also devoted much time to refuting consequentialist approaches to ethics, whether in the realms of moral philosophy or moral theology. In detailing the modes of responsibility, however, Finnis specifies as one moral norm

> the requirement that one bring about good in the world (in one's own life and the lives of others) by actions that are efficient for their reasonable purpose(s). One must not waste one's opportunities by using inefficient methods. One's actions should be judged by their effectiveness, by their fitness for their purpose, by their utility, by their consequences. (1980/2011: 111)

Efficiency, utility, effectiveness, consequences – this is the language of economics. Is the use of similar terminology all that is at work here?

Finnis maintains that there are many contexts in which we can and should 'calculate, measure, compare, weigh, and assess the consequences of alternative decisions' (Finnis 1980: 111). If we have to choose between saving human life (a basic good) and saving property (an instrumental good), we choose the former.

Another context in which we can legitimately weigh and measure as part of the process of making moral choices is what Finnis calls 'the technical domain' or what falls within the realm of 'cost–benefit analysis' (Finnis 1997: 237–8). There are four criteria which allow us to identify whether something properly falls within this realm:

1 The goal is well-defined.
2 We can compare the costs and benefits of realising the goal via reference to a fixed unit of value. Money permits, for instance, a comparison of economic value.
3 It is possible to quantify the alternative benefits and costs associated with different ways of realising the goal in a manner that makes them measurable against each other. I can, for instance, compare and contrast the different amounts of capital which I need to invest in different enterprises if I want to achieve a certain rate of return.
4 The difference among the means – apart from measurable benefits and costs and other characteristics of their efficiency as means – are not important. The means by which I can increase the capital at my disposal might include investment in shares in publicly traded companies, investment in a family business, investment in managed funds, some combination of these approaches etc. The differences between these means are not important from the standpoint of

morality. That would change if one of the means was investment in the slave trade or a brothel.

The most obvious place in which these types of commensuration can be made is the market. 'Where one is considering objects or activities in which there is reasonably a market', Finnis writes, 'the market provides a common denominator (currency) and enables a comparison to be made of prices, costs, and profits. Where there are alternative techniques or facilities for achieving definitive objectives, cost–benefit analysis will make possible a certain range of reasonable comparisons between techniques or facilities' (Finnis 1980: 111–12).

Someone who possesses a particular sum of money, and who needs to make choices about how much to spend on purchasing food, paying rent, buying petrol for his car etc., over a set period of time, can engage in the type of cost–benefit analysis which permits him to compare the respective costs and benefits associated with different ways of meeting these needs. The same person can also calculate how much it costs in financial terms to realise particular goals over different time-periods. Through such cost–benefit analysis, he can estimate how long he needs to work and at what hourly rate or at what annual salary if he is to save enough to become a major investor in a small business.

These are applications of the economic technique on a micro-scale, which help people make approximate comparisons of comparable options as they seek to pursue and participate in the basic goods in an efficient way. Likewise, the economic technique, insofar as it permits us to identify the side effects of particular economic policy choices, can also provide important information to governments as they seek to establish economic conditions that assist people in a given political community to realise their particular ways of participating in the basic goods.

A government may decide, for instance, to rid a society's economy of rampant inflation, because it undermines the ability of millions of people to engage in the type of cost–benefit analysis which helps them to participate in the basic goods in an efficient way. Thinking economically yields the information that radical anti-inflationary measures will gradually realise the type of monetary stability that allows people to make more accurate comparisons of the costs and benefits associated with different economic options. The same technique, however, also tells us that a likely side effect of this policy will be a rise in unemployment for a period of time. This is likely to damage some people's ability to find work. That will increase demand for welfare, which in turn may necessitate more taxes. This will reduce the capital available for private investment, and so forth. These are foreseeable consequences which are useful for individuals, groups and government authorities to know as they decide what to choose in a context of incompatible choices.

NNLT also highlights the limits of the types of contribution that economics can make to people's efforts to make practically reasonable choices. In the first place, the economic technique and the cost–benefit analysis is one expression of only one of nine modes of responsibility. To make it the *only* mode through which practical reason is expressed is to ignore the considerations which arise from applying all the other moral norms derived from practical reason.

The economic technique may determine that it is more cost-effective to use slaves rather than paid employees to build up a business. It might also suggest that we could substantially reduce a nation's annual welfare bill by euthanising anyone over the age of eighty. Yet in both instances, the efficiency can be realised only by unreasonable means. Both examples involve intentionally damaging the good of human life and violating the Golden Rule, inasmuch as some people are intentionally reduced to being mere means to realising other people's ends.

Second, to adopt the economic technique as the only or primary way of determining the morality of an individual or community choice – to embrace what might be called 'economism' – is effectively to embrace a consequentialist ethics. But, as illustrated, consequentialism as a moral theory is irrational.

Third, the elevation of the economic technique to the only or primary mode of responsibility amounts to claiming that there are no basic goods, or no self-evident reasons for action beyond utility – utility understood as whatever gives pleasure or satisfies preferences. These, however, tell us nothing about morality. For one thing, we know that some people derive pleasure from acts that are self-evidently evil (e.g. torture).

Certainly no one wishes to experience dullness and melancholy. Yet pleasurable sensations cannot reasonably be equated with fulfilment. Such equations take into account only one aspect of human existence. This may be illustrated by the example of a person who derives much pleasure from consuming poisoned food, and dies as a consequence. However enjoyable that person's state of consciousness while eating may have been, one can hardly conclude that the experience was fulfilling for the person (Grisez and Shaw 1988: 36).

No less than Adam Smith underscored in his *The Theory of Moral Sentiments* how concern for utility, the pursuit of pleasure and a focus on technical achievement can seriously misdirect people's choices, leading them away from all-round human flourishing and even producing considerable degradation. In Smith's words, 'How many people *ruin* themselves by laying out money on trinkets of frivolous *utility*? What pleases these *lovers of toys*, is not so much the utility as the aptness of the machines which are fitted to promote it' (Smith 1982 [1759]: IV, I; cf. Finnis 1990: 338).[5]

These unflattering sentences illustrate how Smith understood the difference between genuinely morally fulfilling choices, and those that confuse human flourishing with questions of usefulness and pleasure. But they also lead Smith to bring to light a general paradox, further clarified by subsequent economic reflection: that it is precisely the powerful desire for acquisition of these instrumental goods and utility that 'arouses and keeps in continual motion the industry of mankind' (Smith 1982 [1759]: IV, I, 10), and that creates, in turn, the immense wealth that meets the needs and wants of the rich (and also, very gradually, those of the less wealthy).

Does this mean that thinking economically, rigorous application of the economic technique and any material benefits accrued are bound to blur understanding of the content of the all-round human flourishing to which right reason directs us? Without doubt, it can have that effect, as Smith seems to have understood. That, however, is all the more reason to ensure that the economic technique, inasmuch as it helps to frame moral choices, is integrated into the kind of account of how individuals and communities make free choices which is offered by natural law.

NOTES

1. My emphasis.
2. My emphasis.
3. For an extensive account of NNLT, see Chapter 4 of this volume.
4. The nine norms, according to Finnis (1980: 100–133), are (1) practical reasonableness; (2) a coherent plan of life; (3) no arbitrary preferences among values; (4) no arbitrary preferences among persons; (5) detachment and commitment; (6) the limited relevance of consequences – i.e. efficiency, within reason; (7) respect for every basic good in every act – adherence to the moral absolutes; (8) the requirements of the common good; and (9) following one's conscience.
5. My emphasis.

12 Political Theory and Natural Law

Christopher Wolfe

Natural law is part of an ethical theory, guiding our moral actions. The question I would like to discuss in this chapter is the implications of natural law theory for the political order. If someone were to take natural law ethics as a starting point, what principles of political life would flow from it?

This chapter will begin with a description of the fundamental principles of natural law ethics (in its classic form, in Thomas Aquinas), noting the importance of its integral connection with a virtue ethics and a philosophical anthropology. From there, I will try to unfold the moral principles that guide political and social life, drawing the connections between them and general natural law principles.

A brief preliminary point: the classical exposition of natural law in Aquinas' *Summa Theologiae* occurs in a theological context, and philosophical and theological arguments overlap a good deal. I will be focusing especially on those elements that are philosophical (based on reason) rather than theological ones (based on revelation). It is important to recognise, at the same time, that Aquinas considered the existence of God and Providence (a 'natural theology') very much philosophical, as well as theological, truths.

NATURAL LAW ETHICS

The Context of Aquinas' Natural Law Teaching

Aquinas' account of natural law comes at the end of the first part of the second part of the *Summa* (especially in II-I, Q. 90–97 and Q. 100). Part I of the *Summa* is on God and His creation, which includes angels, corporeal creatures, the bodily spiritual creature man and divine governance. Part II turns again to man, beginning with man's last end (happiness) and then to acts proper to man and those proper to man and animals (including the passions), the intrinsic principles of human acts (habits in general and habits in particular, both good and bad, virtues and vices), and finally the extrinsic principles of human acts, namely law and grace. The second part of Part Two deals primarily with the theological virtues (faith, hope, charity) and the cardinal virtues (prudence, justice, fortitude and temperance).[1] So one might say that the natural law teaching is 'sandwiched' between a general and a more particular discussion of virtues.[2]

Within the 'Treatise on Law' (II-I, Q. 90–108), Aquinas begins with the definition of law (an ordinance of reason for the common good made by one who is in charge of the community and promulgated), and then identifies and describes four different kinds of law (eternal, natural, human and divine), and he discusses the force (or power) of law and whether it changes. The latter part of the treatise (Q. 98–108) concerns the Old Law and the New Law, with some significant discussion of natural law in the sections on the moral precepts of the Old Law.

Natural Law Ethics

A brief summary of Aquinas' natural law ethics might go something like this:

1 The first principle of practical reason, which is self-evident to human beings (paralleling the principle of non-contradiction for speculative reason), is that the good ought to be done and pursued and evil to be avoided. All the other precepts of natural law are founded on this principle, so that what practical reason naturally apprehends as goods are to be pursued and the contrary evils to be avoided.[3]

2 How do we know what is good for human beings? The ordering of the precepts of the natural law corresponds to the ordering of human inclinations, and Aquinas identifies three categories of inclination towards good in human beings: (1) goods he shares with other substances, such as self-preservation; (2) goods he shares with other animals, such as the union of male and female and the education of offspring; and (3) goods proper to man, a rational creature, including knowing the truth about God and living in society.[4] (Note that rational creatures should pursue the first two categories according to reason as well.) Our natural inclinations towards such human goods means that, even in a pluralistic society, which is notable for its disagreements on many fundamental questions, we ordinarily and generally can agree in recognising some basic human goods, e.g. life, health, knowledge, living in family and community.[5]

3 The general or common precepts of natural law, which (like the first precept), Aquinas argues, are self-evident and known to all, include

that man should act according to reason, and therefore should act virtuously. (It is acting according to virtue in general that is part of the natural law; the virtues in their proper species do not all belong to the natural law, strictly speaking, since it is by rational inquiry that men discover that many aspects of them are advantageous to living well.)[6] In his discussion of the moral precepts of the Old Law, Aquinas includes love of God and of neighbour among these common precepts.[7]

4 There is a tremendous richness, diversity and variety in human goods and in ways of pursuing them well, and we are not commanded to pursue them all, which would not be possible. Our recognition of what is good for us means, rather, that, in all we do, we should always respect these goods – i.e. respect (honour, value) God, for example, our parents, human life, our sexual faculty, property and truth-telling – and not act in ways that attack or undermine them. That 'in all we do' means the things about which we must make choices about how to act in the specific circumstances of our lives. There is ordinarily a multiplicity of positive ways to respect (or honour or value) these goods, no one of which is necessary by nature. The negative commands or precepts of the natural law, however, set necessary boundaries within which we can pursue the multiplicity of goods: e.g. don't blaspheme, dishonour parents, murder, steal, commit adultery or lie.[8]

5 The general principles of the Ten Commandments, though they occur in a religious document, can be understood as broad natural law precepts, essentially telling us to act reasonably with respect to various important areas of human life (various human goods): our Creator, parents, human life and bodily integrity, property, the sexual faculty (the basis of the family) and truth. Aquinas maintains that the principles of the Decalogue are universally known and indispensable, but in a response to an objection, he tempers this somewhat by indicating they are immutable with respect to the character of justice they embody, but the specification of the precepts as to singular acts (whether this or that act is or is not homicide or theft or adultery) may change, and knowledge of them may be obscured through the perversion of reason by passion or bad habits or a bad natural condition.[9] (Aquinas gives the example of the Germans, who, according to Caesar, did not consider theft bad.)[10]

6 All human actions are aimed at some human good, but some goods are only apparent. Actions can be evil in various ways. The object of the

act may be evil, as in the case of stealing (taking what belongs to another), and good intentions (e.g. stealing to give to the poor) don't cure that evil. Alternatively, the motive or intention or end of an act whose object is good in itself can make the act evil, as when a person makes a fine baseball bat, but with the intention of using it to harm someone. Or an act that is intrinsically good can be evil because it is done in the wrong circumstances, as marital lovemaking would be if performed at high noon in a downtown public park.[11]

7 As we elaborate moral principles in more detail and consider their application to concrete circumstances – as we reach 'secondary precepts' of natural law – they are more difficult to know (they, or at least some of them, are still self-evident, but their self-evidence may, in some cases, be known only to the wise, who understand the terms of the proposition that is self-evident). Moreover, the rectitude of the principles as directives for action are also less likely to be universal – more particular conclusions of practical reason hold for most cases, but not for all. For example, in general, borrowed goods should be returned to their owners, but not a borrowed gun to an owner with murderous intentions. And the further one descends into particulars, the more likely the possibility that the general rule fails.[12] Nonetheless, there are still some exceptionless moral norms, e.g. do not directly kill innocent human beings, do not torture, do not commit adultery.[13] The specification of moral norms – what exactly murder is, for example – may require prudence, however: not all killing is murder. Likewise, the specification of what is stealing or lying and many other acts may require knowledge that not all possess.[14]

8 Moral life is especially about developing a ready ability to see and to choose the practical good and to avoid what is evil. The habits of readily choosing the good are virtues and the habits of readily pursuing evil are vices. Prudence is the master virtue of the practical life, enabling us – with our wills firmly 'locked onto' the good – to discern how the general moral principles we naturally know direct us to act in concrete circumstances. Our actions that bear upon others are governed by the principle of giving to each his due (justice). Our pursuit of good is buttressed by habits that enable us to resist distorting effects of pleasures (temperance) and of pain (courage). In the multitude of choices that we make throughout life, we carve out our character, 'incarnating' the moral good in our lives, to a greater or lesser

extent. This is the way in which rational creatures participate in the eternal law, not merely being subject to it (as inanimate, vegetable and animal life is), but sharing in God's Providence by the use of our free will.[15]

Aquinas: Philosophical Anthropology

Aquinas' natural law teaching also involves a notion of nature and of human nature – a philosophical anthropology. This does not mean that natural law norms are somehow 'deduced' from a complex and articulate theory of human nature. But it does mean that the natural law precepts orientated towards human goods require some knowledge (if only implicit) of the kind of being that flourishes due to these goods. Following Aristotle, Aquinas holds that various beings have 'natures', which are internal sources of change and rest in those beings (*Physics* 192b14). The change and rest for which a thing's nature is responsible are directed towards an end or ends. 'The tendency to achieve its end which is imparted to a thing in virtue of its having a nature is what Aquinas refers to as a natural "inclinatio"'.[16] So human inclinations are ordered to what is good for the human being.

Human beings are distinctive, because they do not participate passively in the eternal law (the Creator's providential ordering of reality), as do other sorts of beings, but actively, using their free will to pursue what they recognise by reason is good for them. Those capacities are integrally related to the fact that human beings are not merely matter, but matter and spirit. Their capacity to know the truth and to freely choose the good – shared, in principle, by all human beings, irrespective of their present actualisation of such capacities – is the source of their special dignity among creatures. Accordingly, the good or well-being of every human being is valuable and worth pursuing, and should not be acted against.

NATURAL LAW AND POLITICS

The notions of nature, and of human nature, and what is good for man, provide a transition to the discussion of natural law politics. Aquinas' description of the human good, insofar as man is a rational animal, involves living in society, and therefore 'things that are related to this sort of inclination belong to the natural law, e.g. . . . that he not offend the others with whom he has to live in community, and other such things related to this inclination'.[17]

Human beings live in society because they cannot generally survive and develop themselves and fulfil a wide range of human goods without doing so. They are naturally born into the most elementary society, the family, which exists to provide for everyday needs, and groups of families form villages, which can supply a wider range of needs. (There never was a 'state of nature' in which human beings were completely isolated individuals.) As Aristotle says, communities begin by providing for mere life – survival – and they develop by providing for more goods, until they reach the self-sufficient community (the *polis*), which, in principle, makes possible a full range of human goods (*Politics* 1252b27). Individuals are limited in what they can do. It is not possible for one person to develop fully a comprehensive multiplicity of human goods. And even communities require sufficient resources so that citizens can afford to indulge in activities that go beyond what is needed simply for survival (such as the systematic study of reality in the intellectual life, or an extensive development of the various arts).[18]

The Common Good

The 'self-sufficient community' that makes possible the fulfilment of a full range of human goods has for its end the common good. (The more determinate content of the common good is discussed further below.)

The common good is not simply the collection of mutual advantages accruing to private individuals through their coordinated activity ('the greatest good of the greatest number'). Yves Simon says that the common good is distinguished by 'collective causality, communion in immanent actions, and communion-causing communications'.[19]

Collective causality means that 'some transitive actions are traceable not to any particular individual but to [for example] the team or to the army', whereas 'in mere partnership each action is traceable to some partner ... and none is traceable to the partnership itself'. Examples in public life include 'security against enemies, both foreign and domestic; binding commitments with foreign societies; over-all status of expansion, both within existing boundaries and toward new boundaries; over-all status of ownership, of education, of temporal life in its relation to the spiritual'.[20]

Sharing in 'immanent actions of knowledge and desire in which members commune' prepares and intrinsically conditions the transitive actions of the community. The members of a community know and desire a common objective, and know that the other members of the community know and desire the same objective and want it to be effected by the action of the community (none of which is required by, for example, a contractual relationship). Examples are the feelings of 'patriotism, loyalty, and allegiance to one's country, especially as expressed in ceremonies whose purpose is to give the individual comfort and the community more abundant life', such as 'inaugurations, national funerals, and daily raising of the flag in schoolyards'.[21]

The communion in immanent actions is brought about by certain communications. Various words and signs 'are calculated to produce communions and to entertain them', having the purpose 'to cause in souls certain cognitions and certain emotions and awareness that the objects of these cognitions and emotions of mine are also objects for the cognition and emotions of' others in the community (such as companions, superiors and subordinates on a team or in an army). The previously mentioned public ceremonies are examples of such communion-causing communications, as is the teaching of civics in school.[22]

The common good, in a given order, is higher and nobler than private goods of that order, as Aristotle attests: 'Even if the good is the same for a single man and for a state, that of the state seems at all events something greater and more complete whether to attain or to preserve; though it is worthwhile to attain the end merely for one man, it is finer and more godlike to attain it for a nation or for city-states' (*Nicomachean Ethics* 1094b7). The common good (in a given order) is broader, fuller, more complete. This does not mean, however, that individuals are mere parts of a whole, in the way that an arm is part of the body, because each person (unlike an arm of an individual) is a subsistent being in his own right.

It is important to note that the common good exists *in* men, not in some separate, reified state apart from individual human beings.[23] And the common good, of its nature, must be distributed among men, shared.[24] Accordingly, the notion that there must be 'equal concern and respect'[25] for the well-being of every person in the community is not an invention of modern liberalism, but an integral element of the common good in natural law theory.

Political Authority

The necessary individual and common actions of members of a political community to secure the common good do not happen spontaneously, but require coordination. In some cases, authority is required because of human limitations or deficiencies. Since various human limitations and deficiencies are a permanent part of human nature, political authority will always be required, in order to bring the actions of members of the community in line with the common good, whether through means backed by the force of law (e.g. the criminal and civil law) or through positive cultivation (e.g. various forms of education and public honours).

But classical natural law theorists argue that authority is necessary for more essential reasons, even apart from human defects. First, it plays an important role when the common good cannot be achieved only by one particular means. In such a case, it is necessary to effect unity of action in the implementation of a particular means. For example, parents determine whether the family will vacation at the beach or in the mountains – either of which would be good (a way of attaining the rest that is part of the family's common good), but neither of which is strictly necessary. Likewise, in politics, while there is sometimes only one way to achieve the common good, more often there is a great multiplicity of ways to pursue the many different aspects of the common good – all of them good, but not compatible with each other – and it is necessary in those cases for a particular authority to specify, for that community, a given way of achieving it.[26]

Moreover, political authority is also necessary to guarantee the willing of the common good materially considered. This is necessary because the members of a community are also members of smaller communities that demand their commitment, and yet the good of the overall community may be compromised by pursuing the good of the smaller community. Simon gives the example of a wife who would, and should, as part of her commitment to the family's common good, oppose the execution of her husband for a capital crime. This commitment to the private good of the family is a very important part of the common good, which requires such intense commitments. Such a wife wills the common good formally, but not materially. But it is necessary that, in addition to these commitments to private goods, which are so important, there be a public authority that, focused on the whole, wills the common good materially.[27]

That political authority is natural and essential for the common good is the foundation for political and legal obligation. The necessity of authority to secure the common good – the coordination of individual and common actions to attain it – taken together with the obligation of men to pursue the good, including and especially the common good, requires that members of the community obey the directives issuing from legitimate authority.[28]

Forms of Government

Natural law does not dictate a single form of government as the proper one. The right form of government for a particular people will reflect the particular circumstances of that people, which can and do vary widely.[29]

At the same time, it can be said that natural law theory points in the direction of certain principles guiding the choice of government. Historically, some earlier natural law thinkers (including Aquinas himself, in some parts of his writing) supported monarchy.[30] However, it should be remembered that the social circumstances of earlier centuries included widespread (almost universal) illiteracy and therefore a lack of the most elementary knowledge of political and social circumstances among the general populace. Yet, even then, a more characteristic position on forms of government among natural law thinkers was some form of mixed government. This appears in Aquinas' discussion of the government of Israel, in his *Treatise on Law*:

> Hence, the best manner of constituting the ruling offices occurs in a city or region in which (a) there is a single person who is placed in authority of the basis of virtue [*secundum virtutem*] and presides over everyone, and in which (b) under him there are certain others who govern in accord with virtue, and yet in which (c) this political arrangement involves everyone [*ad omnes pertinet*], both because the rulers can be chosen *from among* everyone and also because they are chosen *by* everyone. This is the best political arrangement, with a good mixture of (a) *monarchy*, insofar as there is a single preeminent ruler, and (b) *aristocracy*, insofar as many govern in accord with virtue, and (c) democracy, i.e., rule by the people, insofar as the rulers can be chosen from among the people and the choice of rulers falls to the people [*ad populum pertinet electio principium*].[31]

Natural law theory today confronts a different situation, in which large majorities of the population in most countries are literate, for example. And in line with what will be said below about subsidiarity, participation of all people in self-government is, in principle, desirable, because the participation of people in government encourages the growth of citizens (an essential part of the common good) in various ways.[32] At the same time, participation can take many forms (that vary in both kind and degree, according to the circumstances of the community), none of which is morally necessary. So natural law theory continues, prudently, to recognise the legitimacy of a wide range of forms of government.

Natural Law and Human Law

What is the relationship between natural law and human law? Law is a dictate of practical reason, and both practical and speculative reason proceed from given, naturally known indemonstrable principles to given conclusions discovered by the activity of reason. And so, 'from the precepts of natural law, which are, as it were, common and indemonstrable principles, human reason must proceed to determine certain matters in a more particular way. And these particular determinations, devised by human reason, are called human laws'. But Aquinas also notes that 'practical reason is concerned with actions (*operabilia*), which are singular and contingent, and not with necessary things like those which speculative reason is concerned with. And so human laws cannot have the sort of infallibility that the demonstrated conclusions of the sciences do. Nor is it necessary that every measure should be in every way infallible and fixed; rather, it should be as fixed as is possible within its own genus'.[33]

According to Aquinas, human laws are derived from the natural law, but this can happen in two ways. First, human laws can be conclusions derived from natural law. So '*One should not kill* can be derived as a conclusion from *One should not do evil to anyone*'. But second, human laws may be specifications (*determinationes*) of what is general, so those who do evil should be punished, according to natural law, but 'that an evildoer be punished by *this specific* punishment' is a specification of the law of nature.[34] Or, similarly, that people should drive safely, so as not to endanger others, is a natural law principle, but a particular speed limit is a specification of that principle.

How broad is the scope of human law? Aquinas asks whether the human law commands the acts of all virtues, and he responds negatively. The objects of various virtues 'can be traced back to the private good of an individual or the common good of a multitude'. For example, one might be courageous in order to defend the community or to defend a friend's rights. But law is ordered to the common good, so, although there is no virtue whose acts cannot be commanded, human law does not issue commands concerning all the acts of all the virtues. It 'commands only those acts which can be ordered toward the common good', in one of two ways: 'either (a) *immediately*, as when certain acts are done directly because of the common good, or (b) mediately, as when the lawmaker commands certain acts pertaining to good discipline through which citizens are formed in such a way that they might conserve the good of justice and peace'.[35]

Likewise, in dealing with the question of whether human law should suppress all vices, Aquinas says 'no'. Laws should be 'imposed on men according to their condition' – and, quoting Isidore, he says that the 'law must be possible both according to nature and also according to the customs of the country'. But 'human law is made for the multitude of men, and the greater part of this multitude consists of men who are not perfected in virtue', and so the law prohibits only the more serious vices that the greater part of the multitude can abstain from, 'especially those vices which are harmful to others and without the prohibition of which human society could not be conserved', such as murder and theft. In one of the responses to an objection, he points out that, if human law attempts to impose on the multitude of men what the virtuous can do, then 'those who are imperfect, unable to bear the precepts of the sort in question, would erupt into worse evils'.[36] An example of this is given later in the *Summa*, where Aquinas cites Augustine to the effect that prostitution should not be prohibited, because '[i]f you do away with harlots, the world will be convulsed with lust'.[37]

So the scope of political authority and law are limited in important ways in natural law theory. Moreover, perhaps the simplest, but most important, limit is that government must obey the moral law, just as individuals do.[38]

Relationships among Human Communities

Since human beings are members of various communities, the question of the relation of individuals to those communities, and of the communities to each other, is an important one. As has been noted, for Aquinas, as for Aristotle, the political community is preceded by, and grows out of, the natural community of the family and elementary communities composed of various families. Moreover, within a given community there are many different associations of human beings for various purposes (voluntary associations). There may also be arrangements in which a given political community is subdivided into subordinate political communities for various purposes (as in communities that are federal in structure). Beyond individual political communities or nations, there are relations between a given political community and other such communities, both bilateral and multilateral (between two or more nations) and collective (groups of nations). There are also, in principle, relationships between political communities and communities that claim a transcendent status, such as universalistic religions. The question naturally arises, then, about the relationships among these various communities.

As already noted, the political community is the self-sufficient community that has a special responsibility and authority with respect to the common good. Those who exercise authority in the political community have to exercise a general supervisory power over the entire political community, coordinating the activities of its members in order to ensure, as well as possible, the common good. This concern for the common good, the well-being of the entire community, must extend into the lives of its members. Both rulers and ruled are required to participate in the ideal of 'civic friendship'.[39] While the well-being and interests of parts of the community – including our personal self-interest – are legitimate considerations, they can never be the exclusive reasons for political action, but must be subordinated to the common good, which includes the good of all the citizens.

At the same time, the great responsibility of those who exercise political authority is also limited in important ways. First, the various lower communities have their own special responsibilities and ways of contributing to the common good, which have to be respected. So, for example, the family is a natural community in its own right, and ordinarily parents, who exercise authority in the family, have the duty and the right to make decisions regarding the common good of the family. Only in very serious cases of parents failing to exercise their responsibilities ought the political community to step in and substitute for parental authority.

Second, those who exercise political authority in the political community ought to recognise that the common good is best achieved when they act according to the principle of subsidiarity.[40] This principle states that various functions relative to the common good should be performed by the lowest level of community that can perform those functions adequately. The basis for this principle is that human beings, to the extent possible, should take care of matters relative to the well-being of themselves and of those for whom they are responsible, rather than being taken care of by others, because in so doing they will develop their own virtues and capacities, which is itself a very important part of the common good. And, for the same reason, to the extent possible, even when the capacities of lower communities are inadequate, higher authorities ought to intervene in ways that assist those lower communities rather than simply displace them or take over their functions completely.

The importance of preserving and assisting lower levels of community that subsidiarity requires should, however, not obscure the requirement it contains that functions need to be performed adequately.

Church and State in Natural Law Theory

A particularly important question for natural law theory is the relationship between political communities and religious communities that make claims to transcend politics. Historically, the assertion by classical natural law theorists like Aquinas that the temporal rulers can, and sometimes should, punish heresy at the behest of the spiritual authority of the Church has been viewed as part of natural law theory and is sometimes a ground for rejecting it.[41]

But twentieth-century Neo-Thomists argued that mediaeval church-state relations adopted by classical natural law theorists like Aquinas are not a necessary or inherent part of natural law theory. Jacques Maritain[42] and Charles Journet[43] argued, for example, that earlier church-state understandings reflected a society that had not differentiated spiritual and temporal powers with sufficient clarity.

In terms more familiar to modern Americans, natural law has very strong conceptions of 'free exercise' rights, while being open, in appropriate cases, to 'establishments of religion'.[44] Man has a duty to worship the Creator, according to natural law, but that duty can be fulfilled only according to each person's conscience, for compelled 'worship' is no true worship at all. And even efforts that are not intended to impose religious belief on people, but simply to prevent them from leading astray other people, undermine the likelihood of winning people over to true belief.[45] Accordingly, the free exercise of religion, including the opportunity to act according to that belief (in ways compatible with public order) and to spread it, are essential parts of the common good.

Under certain conditions, however – especially a broad consensus in a society about religious truth – positive efforts by the political community to promote or facilitate true religious belief, without impinging on the freedom of conscience of those who do not share that belief, can be part of the common good. The 'thickness' or 'thinness' of that belief will vary from country to country. For much of American history, for example (through the mid twentieth century), at a national level, there was a consensus on a basic natural theology that was captured in the Declaration of Independence (all men are *created* equal and endowed by their *Creator* with unalienable rights) and exemplified by Thanksgiving Day proclamations and the inscription of 'In God We Trust' on coins. On a state level, especially earlier in that history (until 1833), there were sometimes thicker religious beliefs, such as the generally Protestant Christian beliefs that received support from state government in various ways (through required religious instruction, if available conveniently in a form compatible with a person's conscience, or financial support for the building of religious buildings).[46] A significantly thicker religious consensus exists even today in some cases (unusual in the West), such as Poland, where the Catholic faith is dominant in the nation (with a generally strong tradition of religious toleration, despite certain historical exceptions), and where Catholicism is part of national life (e.g. various religious feast days are celebrated as national legal holidays).[47]

Natural law does not see political communities as having power over transcendent religious communities, to direct them – for to say that they are 'transcendent' is to say that they far exceed the capacity of the state to govern. Yet, where circumstances make it appropriate, it is possible to work out harmonious arrangements whereby political communities can, in limited ways, foster or assist those transcendent communities, even in their trans-political ends (as well as for the benefits to society derived from religious belief, which contributes indirectly to the well-being of the political community).[48]

Elements of the Common Good

There are many different elements of the common good, as there are many aspects of the good of human beings in general. Some of these elements are:

- the protection of life and the security of person and property, access to the necessities of life (food, clothing, shelter, medical care, rest), and a safe and healthy environment in which to live;
- a stable and healthy family life, which is among the most important of human goods, since the family is so foundational for many other goods; the possibility of stable family life is conditioned to a great

extent by the social ecology of the community, including its mores and laws; monogamy, unity, lifelong duration, sexual complementarity and exclusivity, the rights and duties of parenthood, and fecundity are all important features of healthy family life;

- the opportunity to engage in productive work, in decent conditions, at a just wage, both to support oneself and to make a contribution to the larger community, and done well, according to the intrinsic requirements (both technical and moral) of the job; this provides the opportunity to own private property, which should be properly administered in light of its social responsibilities (i.e. in light of the fact that property provides the necessary resources for all human beings to achieve their self-development);
- support to grow in knowledge of the truth and the freedom to live in accord with it (i.e. to grow in intellectual and moral virtue); this includes, pre-eminently, religious liberty for individuals and groups to worship God according to their consciences and to act according to their beliefs, within the bounds of public order; it also includes opportunities for growth through a continual, wide-ranging and comprehensive education (of which there are many kinds, formal and informal), according to people's capacities, interests and circumstances; such opportunities for growth in the knowledge of truth, and freedom to act in accord with it, are highly dependent on a healthy broader culture – viz. a social and moral ecology that supports those pursuits;
- the recognition and support of opportunities to associate with others and to participate in a wide range of communities, through a multitude of voluntary civil associations for many different purposes, in accordance with the principle of subsidiarity;
- participation in political communities, as citizens, according to their capacities; such capacities require, in turn, opportunities to acquire information about matters of the common good and to learn necessary skills of communication; citizens also have the duty to respect legitimate political authority and laws, to pay taxes and to serve in the military when necessary (and just); and citizens have important rights to due process and to fair, impartial treatment, according to the rule of law;

In addition to the common good, strictly defined, it is also proper to recognise what might be called a rather inchoate 'universal common good' of all mankind, which carries with it various requirements of justice among nations, including the recognition of the legitimate self-determination of peoples/nations (within moral limits), the duty to pursue peace, employing force (when it is necessary) according to just war requirements, and to act justly in economic and cultural relations with other nations.

CONCLUSION

The various components of the common good can be described (as they are here) at a high level of generality, but the right way to pursue the common good in the specific circumstances of a particular people or nation requires knowledge of a daunting range of facts. As Aquinas indicates in his general discussion of natural law precepts, the general precepts are universally known and they hold consistently, but the greater the level of detail into which one descends, the more often the knowledge is not recognised by all and the more likely that the secondary principles will not hold. In efforts to achieve the concrete common good, the virtue of prudence will therefore be the supreme political virtue.

Political communities have their own histories and circumstances, of extraordinary variety, and so the specific ways of pursuing the common good will vary greatly. Each nation has its own 'public philosophy' – that complex web of assumptions, beliefs and convictions that make up an understanding of how a people should act in history, in a given time and place. Public philosophies should be formed and shaped in light of the fundamental principles of natural law, which – because they reflect the ordering principles embedded in reality – provide the broad moral horizon or framework in light of which political life should be lived.[49]

NOTES

1. Part III focuses on deeply theological issues like the Incarnation and sacraments.
2. On the importance of virtues in Aquinas' political theory, see Keys 2008: Part III.
3. Freddoso 2009: 40.
4. Freddoso 2009: 40–41.
5. For more on Aquinas' understanding of the natural inclinations, see Chapter 2 of this volume. See also Pakaluk 2018.
6. Freddoso 2009: 42.

7. Freddoso 2009: 109. But note that he says these precepts are known to human reason, 'either by nature or by faith'.
8. McInerny 1997: 47–8.
9. Freddoso 2009: 44–5.
10. On this passage, see Budziszewski 2018: 56–7.
11. *Summa Theologiae*, I-II, Q. 18, a. 4. See also McInerny 1997: chapter 5.
12. Freddoso 2009: 43–5. See also McInerny 1997: 56–8 and Sigmund 1993: 225.
13. For an argument for exceptionless moral norms in both Aquinas and Aristotle, see Kaczor 1997.
14. Freddoso 2009: 130–31. In this section, Aquinas differentiates three levels of moral precepts: (1) absolutely certain and evident principles; (2) other more specific moral principles that even an ordinary man can grasp the reason of easily and immediately, but regarding which human judgement can be perverted in a fewer number of cases; and (3) other moral precepts that are not so easy to grasp and which are evident only to the wise. The second category includes the precepts of the decalogue, which are common precepts known to all, but the application of which to specific circumstances may not always be clear to all.
15. McInerny 1997: 99–102.
16. Pakaluk 2018: xx.
17. Freddoso 2009: 41.
18. For a discussion of the importance for Aquinas of Aristotle's account of the naturalness of political and social life, and ways in which he developed it, see Keys 2008: chapter 3.
19. Simon 1951: 64.
20. Simon 1951: 64, 66.
21. Simon 1951: 66.
22. Simon 1951: 65. A striking example of communion-causing communications that bring about communion in immanent actions can be found in Voegelin 1952, another of the Walgreen Lectures of which Simon's book was a part. In chapter II, s. 7, Voegelin uses Aeschylus' *The Suppliants* as an instance of Greek tragedy serving as a state cult through which the people of Athens enter into a shared reflection on and experience of what justice requires Robert George, in an insightful discussion of natural law grounds for free speech, notes the importance of communication for coordinated action for the common good. See George 1993: 192–208.
23. In this respect, Simon argues that the common good is not a work of art, something external to man. Simon 1965: 92.
24. Simon 1965: 98. 'Because society does not exist except in individuals (connected by definite relations), the good of society demands, by nature and not by accident, a constant distribution to individuals'.

25. Dworkin 1977: 180.
26. Simon 1951: 19–35.
27. Simon 1951: 36–47.
28. NB Finnis 1998: 269: 'Morally speaking, talk of authority is tightly correlative with talk of obligation: to say that some person or body has authority to make laws is to say that, presumptively and defeasibly, laws made by that person or body will be morally binding on their subjects. This correlativity is based not on some linguistic "given", but rather on the judgement that the same common good which calls for lawmakers with authority calls also, and to essentially the same extent, for the compliance of the law's subjects with their legal obligations'.
29. Bigongiari 1957: xxvi.
30. For a nuanced discussion of Aquinas on monarchy, see Finnis 1998: 259–63.
31. Freddoso 2009: 224. For an analysis of mixed government in Aquinas, see Stoner 2007. Sigmund 1993: 219–21 emphasises the constitutional element of Aquinas' political thought.
32. Tocqueville 1972 vol. 1, chapter 14: 'It is incontestable that the people frequently conduct public business very badly; but it is impossible that the lower orders should take a part in public business without extending the circle of their ideas and quitting the ordinary routine of their thoughts. The humblest individual who cooperates in the government of society acquires a certain degree of self-respect; and as he possesses authority, he can command the services of minds more enlightened than his own. He is canvassed by a multitude of applicants, and in seeking to deceive him in a thousand ways, they really enlighten him. He takes part in political undertakings which he did not originate, but which give him a taste for undertakings of the kind. New improvements are daily pointed out to him in the common property, and this gives him the desire of improving that property which is his own'.
33. Freddoso 2009: 12–13.
34. Freddoso 2009: 52.
35. Freddoso 2009: 62.
36. Freddoso 2009: 60–61.
37. *Summa Theologiae* II-II, q. 10, a. 11.
38. For an extensive discussion of natural law and limited government, see Finnis 1998: 258–66 and Finnis 1996. However, for a critique of his contention that the common good is only an instrumental good, see Pakaluk 2001.
39. Schwarzenbach 1996: 97–128.
40. Finnis 1980: 146. For an essay that shows how subsidiarity is not just one isolated factor but a principle that pervades the whole of natural law theory, see Pakaluk 2002.

41. D'Entrèves 1948: xxii–iii.
42. Maritain 1951: chapter VI. It is worth noting that an important factor in the union of spiritual and temporal power in the early mediaeval period was the collapse of civil society at the end of the Roman Empire, creating a vacuum that the churches and monasteries felt compelled to fill.
43. Journet 1955: chapter VI.
44. For a more common, and different view, see Murray 1960, which argues for a principled rejection of establishments as well as any denial of free exercise rights.
45. Wolfe 2006: chapter 10.
46. See the Massachusetts Constitution of 1780, in Munoz 2013: section II.C.
47. Of course, there are various Muslim states that make religion even more central to their political communities, but these 'establishments' generally curtail free exercise of other religions as well, e.g. by prohibition of public non-Muslim religious ceremonies or prohibitions of blasphemy.
48. Tocqueville 1972 vol. I, chapter 17 (especially the section on 'Indirect Influence of Religious Opinions Upon Political Society in the United States').
49. Wolfe 2006: chapter 11.

PART V Natural Law Ethics

Challenges and Prospects

13 Challenges Facing Natural Law Ethics

Sophie Grace Chappell*

1

Not every creature has reason to live so as to fulfil its purpose in life. Just ask a battery hen. Her purpose in life is to produce as many eggs at as little cost as possible, then be turned into a raw material of the fast-food industry. The resultant misery and distress to the hen is just a corollary of her living according to her purpose, her *telos* – as a frank egg-farmer might admit. From the battery hen's own point of view, there is no reason at all for her to live this way. As she would see it (if she had a chance to consider the question), she would be better off doing almost anything other than fulfilling her *telos*. Her *telos* and her flourishing are not the same thing. Almost all of the time, they do not even coincide. A flourishing battery hen is of course imaginable – but it is one that has escaped from the battery.

'But a battery hen is not living the natural life of a *hen*. If we want to think about the *purpose* of a hen's life, we need to look not at battery hens, but at hens in natural conditions'.

Really? The complaint has a certain irony about it, because you might have thought that one thing we humans do know for certain about battery hens is their purpose in life. We know that for certain, because we *set* the battery hens' purpose in life. By contrast, there is something decidedly obscure about the idea that animals living in natural conditions, free from human interference, have *any* purpose in life. Unless perhaps one assumes a background of very specifically providential theism. But even then the problems are not negligible, as we'll see.

Supposing we overlook this irony, the next question is: what are 'natural conditions'? Hens have been so extensively domesticated for so long now that your average barnyard hen bears little or no relation to her ancestors in the wild. For a Bantam or a Rhode Island Red, there is arguably no such thing as 'natural conditions'. Sure, there's an intuitive sense in which a free-range hen, strutting round a barnyard with other hens pecking at stones and seeds (and other hens), is flourishing more than a battery hen. But that is not about a barnyard hen being in *natural* conditions. It's about her being in *favourable* conditions, conditions where she gets to get up to more of what she wants to get up to.[1]

For a case where we do know what natural conditions are, and can also see that they are not at all the same thing as favourable conditions or an animal's freedom to do her own thing, take rabbits. What is a wild rabbit's *telos*? Apparently, it is to provide predator species like foxes, stoats and eagles with abundant prey. But then again it is obvious that the rabbit's flourishing (what it is for a rabbit to live well) is not the same thing as the rabbit's *telos* (what a rabbit 'is for', the point of a rabbit's life, if any). Contrast wild rabbits and (well-kept) house-rabbits. A house-rabbit's life-expectancy at birth is ten years; a wild rabbit's is ten months. A typical house-rabbit lives its ten comfortable, warm, dry, well-fed, predator-, parasite-, and mostly disease-free years, then dies painlessly in a vet's clinic; a typical wild rabbit lives its ten months in almost constant terror, hunger, cold, wet and illness, then is eaten alive by an eagle or a stoat or a fox. The house-rabbit's life is almost completely 'unnatural', but that is hardly a reason to think that it is, from a rabbit's point of view, less attractive. Give any individual rabbit the choice between the withered heath and your living room, suitably predator-proofed, and I can tell you from experience that she will vote, with her paws, for the living room.

One difference between *telos* and *eudaimonia* that emerges from these cases is that while we can to some extent isolate the flourishing of any individual animal from its ecological background, it is much harder to do this with an animal's *telos*. If we can talk about individual species' *telē* at all, we need to see them in their environment, maybe to the extent that the *telos* we are really talking about is the *telos* of the entire ecosystem, which overall *telos* acts as a limit both on the *telê* and on the *eudaimonia* of particular species within it.

Of course, to push the talk of purpose up to the level of the entire ecosystem in this way is to postpone, not to resolve, the conceptual problem of the very idea of purpose-talk in zoology. But leaving that aside, my point is that in normal zoological discourse, the *eudaimonia*, the flourishing, of individual species is much more easily isolable from their ecological background than their *telê*, their purposes, are. Here is an illustration:

> [In] the 1930s, when the wolf was killed off in Yellowstone ... the absence of wolves took a huge amount of predatory pressure off the elk. As a result, elk populations did very well – perhaps too well. Two things happened: the elk pushed the limits of Yellowstone's carrying capacity, and they didn't move around much in the winter – browsing heavily on young willow, aspen and cottonwood plants. That was tough for beaver, who need willows to survive in winter.
>
> This created a counterintuitive situation. Back in 1968, when the elk population was about a third what it is today, the willow stands along streams were in bad shape. Today, with three times as many elk, willow stands are robust. Why? Because the predatory pressure from wolves keeps elk on the move, so they don't have time to browse the willow intensely ... With elk on the move during the winter, willow stands recovered from intense browsing, and beaver rediscovered an abundant food source that hadn't been there earlier. As the beavers spread and built new dams and ponds, the cascade effect continued ... Beaver dams have multiple effects on stream hydrology. They even out the seasonal pulses of runoff; store water for recharging the water table; and provide cold, shaded water for fish, while the now robust willow stands provide habitat for songbirds.
>
> In Yellowstone, biologists have the rare, almost unique, opportunity to document what happens when an ecosystem becomes whole again, what happens when a key species is added back into the ecosystem equation.[2]

If we want to talk about the flourishing of e.g. elk, we can do that by talking about elk pretty much in isolation, elk set against pretty well any background context; for what it is for elk to flourish follows intuitively from an understanding of elk, just in themselves. Whereas if we want to talk about the *telos* of e.g. elk, it's not possible to do so except by placing them within the background context of a wider environment with many other species in it – if even then.

II

From these brief and simple reflections on natural history I draw five provisional morals:

First, under natural conditions – under most conditions, irrespective of their link or lack of it with nature – a creature's *telos* is typically not at all the same thing as its *eudaimonia*. There is a difference in logical structure: as I put it above, to specify a creature's *eudaimonia* in ecological isolation is much more nearly possible than to specify its *telos* in ecological isolation. And there is a difference in content: insofar as a creature *has* a purpose or function aside from any that humans or other external agents might set for it, fulfilling that function need not take the creature in anything like the same direction as movement towards a state of flourishing would take it in.

Secondly, then, it should seem a remarkable fact about humans if, for them, their *telos* and their *eudaimonia* do coincide or come to the same thing. If that is how it is for humans, then humans are very much the exception in nature, not the rule. (They are also exceedingly lucky.)

Thirdly, without a guarantee that our *telos* and our *eudaimonia* point in the same direction, we humans evidently have reason to pursue our *eudaimonia* (or so you might think – though I will raise some doubts about this in sections IV–V); but we have no reason to pursue our *telos*.

Fourthly, historically the most important way to (attempt to) guarantee that our *telos* and our *eudaimonia* do point us humans in the same direction is providential theism. This guarantee is not always on clear display in typical modern expositions of natural law ethics – far from it. Even in Aquinas, whose philosophy is a paradigm of the kind of divinely backed natural law ethics that I mean, 'divine law' is one thing and 'natural law' another. Yet the two run in parallel. The close association, to this day, between natural law ethics and influential versions of providential theism such as Catholicism is no accident. If your aim is to argue that it is both good and right for humans to live according to their natural purpose, and that so living is what flourishing is for them, then it is not only useful but perhaps also essential to the theory to have God as the ultimate guarantor of this large-scale cosmic harmony.

We do not need Darwin to show us that there is a deep problem about reconciling concepts of well-being and purpose in nature; just open minds and observant eyes. But more than ever post-Darwin, our optimistic confidence that the human *telos* (if any) and human *eudaimonia* go together has to be shaken, and it takes something substantial like a faith in providential theism to keep that optimism anything like intact. This is why it is something of a surprise to see a modern exposition of natural law ethics from a professing atheist, such as Philippa Foot.[3] Indeed, an atheist who endorses natural law ethics might surprise us as much today as Nietzsche was surprised, in 1888, by George Eliot (1819–80):

> They are rid of the Christian God and now believe all the more firmly that they must cling to Christian morality. That is an English consistency ... In England one must rehabilitate oneself after every little emancipation from theology by showing in a veritably awe-inspiring manner what a moral fanatic one is. That is the penance they pay there.
>
> We others hold otherwise. When one gives up the Christian faith, one pulls the right to Christian morality out from under one's feet ... Christianity is a system, a whole view of things thought out together. By breaking one main concept out of it, the faith in God, one breaks the whole. (*Twilight of the Idols* (Nietzsche 1998), 'Expeditions of an Untimely Man', paragraph 5)

Mind you, there is another guarantor of the requisite cosmic harmony to whom an atheist natural law ethicist might look, namely Aristotle. (Ignore for the moment, as atheists usually do, the point that Aristotle himself was clearly a theist, and in a sense a providential theist too: his god does not intervene in the world, but he does make everything for the best, and nothing in vain.) So, then, my fifth and final moral: Aristotle was not merely setting up some terminology when he said that the human *telos* is *eudaimonia* (*Nicomachean Ethics* [NE] 1097b20), and went on to specify that *eudaimonia*, the fulfilment of the human *ergon* or function (NE 1098a8–10), is a particular kind of 'realisation of the soul in line with virtue' (NE 1098a17–19). These are not mere stage-setting preliminaries. In these few words, Aristotle makes some huge, and hugely optimistic, assumptions.

III

Those were *provisional* morals, for I now encounter an important objection. It starts from my fourth moral, my assertion that the coincidence of *telos* and *eudaimonia* needs underwriting by some kind of cosmic optimism: most likely, historically speaking, the kind of cosmic optimism that is provided by the providential theism different forms of which were accepted by most of the great natural law theorists, such as Aristotle, Cicero, Augustine and Aquinas. This assertion can be denied, if we take a different notion of *telos* from the arguably polemical and unfair notion that I have deployed so far. A *telos*, it can be objected, needn't be thought of as an externally imposed purpose, like the egg- and meat-producing role of the battery hen or the feeding of the wild rabbit's predators.

Instead, we can take the *telos* of any animal to be, not top-down-imposed in this kind of way, but *emergent from its flourishing.* A species' – any species' – *telos*, we will say on this view, is just its unimpeded flourishing. If you visualise that unimpeded flourishing – which, you might also note, is what individuals of the species typically strive for anyway – then you are already visualising the *telos* of that species; and it should already be evident to you, too, in what sense that creature's *telos* is the good for it, and is something that it does indeed have reason to pursue.

What you will then have hold of is what Michael Thompson calls a 'representation of life'. And Thompson is emphatic that to have hold of this is not to have hold of an externally imposed purpose, but a conception of what it is like when a creature like that gets on well, which derives, ultimately, from the creature's own 'inner causal structure':

> We are . . . as far as can possibly be imagined from the category of intention or psychical teleology – a fact that is also shown in this, that if the [following] complex thought about . . . blossoms is true, then the judgments joined in it are also true: ['They have blossoms of such and such type in order that such and such insects should be attracted and thereafter spread the pollen about'.] Here . . . 'P in order that Q' straightforwardly entails both P and Q. In making out this sort of connection one links a plain fact, not with a possibly unrealized end, but with another plain fact. Natural teleological judgments may thus be said to organize the elements of a natural history; they articulate the relations of dependence among the various elements and aspects and phases of a given kind of life . . . And so, I think, even if the Divine Mind were to bring a certain lifeform into being 'with a view to' securing an abundance of pink fur along the shores of the Monongahela, this 'purpose' would have no effect on the inner natural teleological description of that form of life, for this is its inner causal structure, taken generally. The intimation of the divine that some found in these particular propositions was, I think, always a matter of grammatical illusion. (Thompson 1995: 78–9)

In Thompson's picture, we have three things. First, a statement of 'plain fact' about (some part of) what it is for the species to flourish, e.g. that this plant has its pollen spread about; label this Q. Secondly, a statement of 'plain fact' about a mechanism that achieves this instance of flourishing, e.g. that the plant has blossoms of this or that sort; label this P. Thirdly, we have a particular connection between the P and the Q:

P *in order that* Q. It is this third element that so to speak carries the teleology: *in order that* is an explanatory connective, a connective which says that one thing is as it is *so that* something else may be as it is. And this, not the external imposition of some transcendent agent's intention, is the core of what Thompson means – and thinks we all should mean – by teleology.

Now certainly we *can* see the teleology of nature in this 'immanent' way, as emergent bottom-up from the creature's pursuit of its own *eudaimonia*, and therefore not even potentially in conflict with that *eudaimonia* in the way that a 'transcendent', top-down imposed teleology might be – and not only in battery hen cases. Perhaps Thompson's is even the best way to see teleology: certainly Foot seems to see teleology, and the notion of *eudaimonia*, in the same sort of immanent and individualistic way, as when she tells us (2001: 33) that 'The way an individual *should be* is determined by what is needed for development, self-maintenance and reproduction'. But supposing we do take this immanent-individualistic view of teleology, notice what follows. Briefly, what follows is that the closer *telos* gets to *eudaimonia*, the further it gets from normativity.

First consider nature, and specifically, the notion of ecological balance. Suppose the *telos* of a rabbit or a hen or an elk or a wolf is what Thompson's argument suggests it is: not *its function within the overall ecology* but, roughly – as with the blossoming plant – *what it does instinctively to survive and reproduce and what it is inclined to do and will do if unimpeded.* If so, then not just the *telos* of any individual animal, but not even the *telos* of any individual species, taken on its own, will be enough to give us any clear normative guidance at all about what we should promote or preserve or prevent in our interactions with the natural world. Hens peck seeds. Elks graze saplings. Rabbits breed (like rabbits). Wolves eat all of them. In Thompson's sense of *telos*, we can't read an environmental policy off *any* one species' *telos*. As I said in section I, what we need is a conception of the *telos* of the whole ecology. But the whole point of Thompson's immanent notion of *telos* is that that is precisely what it isn't. Of course, his description of the blossoms refers to pollen, and that implies a reference to pollinators (bees or the like). That aside, each and every time he presents a 'representation of life', he is talking about the *telos* of one species considered almost completely in ecological isolation. And he is followed in this by Foot and Hursthouse and other proponents of this sort of zoological or biological naturalism (as I have called it elsewhere; see Chappell 2009: chapter 8).

Moreover, whenever these writers consider the *telos* of some species, it is pretty well always a charismatic-megafauna species like the wolf or elk. Foot and Thompson do not often take mosquitoes or slime-moulds or bacteria or tapeworms as their examples of species-form, nor the beetles for which J. B. S. Haldane famously noted the Almighty's inordinate fondness. Their conceptions of animals can often seem frankly heraldic, more like a mediaeval bestiary than a modern zoology. Their lions, for instance, are noble and chivalrous beasts, the kings of the savannah, as brave and majestic as Aslan. But more on lions in a moment.

So if *telos* means what Thompson says it means, then humanity's *telos* can't on its own give us any definite guidance about where humans should fit in to the wider ecology. We know what humans are inclined to do, and what they do instinctively when unimpeded, and (at least roughly) what *eudaimonia* looks like for them. But when you consider the state of the world today, it's not altogether unnatural to wish that humans were *less* successful, not more, in pursuing their *telos* and their *eudaimonia*. If the human *telos* is seriously comparable with animal *telê*, in the way that zoological naturalists characteristically insist, then the normative force of considerations about human *eudaimonia* cannot be the foundation stone of a theory of normative ethics. On the contrary, that normative force, while it is (let me stress this) not *nothing*, is almost invariably nowhere near enough to be normatively decisive.

Consider, too, the notion of natural defect of which Foot, in particular, makes so much. A wolf that hunts alone, a bee that does not pollinate flowers, a mother lion that does not look after her own cubs: such creatures are, she confidently tells us, defective relative to their species-norms (see e.g. Foot 2001: 30). Now certainly there is a problem about how to make the transition from that zoological assessment to the moral assessment that a human who lacks the virtue of justice is also defective, and Foot spends a lot of time trying to deal with that problem (see Foot 2001: chapters 2 and 3). But the real problems have already begun *before* the transition.

For one thing, there are many, many regularities in species that we might well want to call species-norms given how endemic they are, and yet which do not look at all well-fitted to the normative role that Foot wants to give them, even when this is only a 'natural-normative' role as Foot calls it and not a morally normative one. One very obvious example is right under Foot's nose, though unfortunately she does not discuss it. As a rule, the main threat from which a lioness needs to protect her cubs is *adult male lions*, particularly non-alpha-males, who characteristically – and neither nobly nor chivalrously – kill lion cubs whenever they get the chance. There is a perfectly good explanation of this behaviour in evolutionary genetics, to do with freeing up the lioness to carry their genes rather than the alpha-male's. (And alas, there are clear analogues of such behaviour in our own species: adopted children are regularly under particularly serious threat from their adoptive fathers.) This behaviour is instinctive, hard-wired and species-wide; so, if you like, it's 'natural'. Still, unless we are rather drunk on Nietzsche, we might hesitate to say that the cub-killing lion's behaviour is the behaviour of a *flourishing* lion; or that such behaviour contributes to lion-flourishing in general; or that a lion who does not slaughter cubs is *defective*. Not even if, to underline it again, we mean defective not in the moral but in the natural-normative sense.

For another thing, species change over time, and one way that they change (alongside and usually in tandem with genetic mutation) is by changing their behaviour. For example, it is not a normal part of the behavioural repertoire of the New Caledonian Crow (*Corvus Moneduloides*) to shape a piece of paper into a token, and then slot it into a 'vending machine' token to 'buy' a piece of meat. But the crows can learn to do this, and when some do, other crows can learn to copy them:

> An experiment using a vending machine specifically designed for crows has revealed something about how intelligence evolves ... the idea was to create a task unlike anything crows would find in nature. 'They'd obviously never find paper or card in the wild', said Dr Jelbert, 'so we developed this vending machine that they could drop small pieces of paper into to release a treat – a little piece of meat'.
>
> First the birds have to be 'convinced' to operate this box-shaped machine. 'We place stones or bits of paper on top of the box with meat hidden underneath', Dr Jelbert explained. 'The birds will often nudge the stone or paper into the [slot, and] that triggers a reward from the vending machine'.
>
> Once the birds had learned how the machine worked, the team gave them a piece of paper too big to fit into the slot – to see if they would snip that into smaller pieces that would fit. 'About half of them did that spontaneously', said Dr Jelbert [and the others learned from them].[4]

Here we might say that the behavioural repertoire of *this population* of crows has changed, or if the learning spreads far enough, that the behavioural repertoire of *the entire species* has changed. (It is an important point about this kind of evolutionary change that its unit is the population, not the species. In fact, the notion of species as distinct from population has little if any genuine role in modern zoology, for good reasons, including the possibility of 'ring species'. Species also seems to do little work even in 'speciesist' ethics: it is a familiar thought that it could make no ethical difference if we were now to discover that humanity was in fact two quite distinct species. But I won't go on about this here.)[5] What we presumably won't want to say is that these crows are defective because their behaviour no longer fits their species-norm. It's true that it doesn't fit *the previous* species-norm. But changed behaviour produces *new* species-norms, and indeed new species. That is how evolution happens, or one way it happens. There was some first fish that flopped ashore and began to use its fins to propel itself along the Devonian beach. It may have been a defective fish, but it was also a non-defective proto-reptile. There was some first wolf that slunk into the firelight to sit with humans. If you like, it was a defective wolf, but it was also a proto-dog. And there was some first bird that laid its egg in 'the wrong nest' and thereby got some other bird to do the work of feeding and rearing its chick for it. Perhaps it was a defective bird of some other species, but it was also a perfectly good proto-cuckoo.

To say it again: species-norms and species' *telê* change over time, in response both to the emergence of new and more successful behaviour-patterns, and also to changes in the external environment that are decisive in settling which behaviour is or is not successful. What we might count as a defect relative to one supposed species-norm will work perfectly well relative to another. This is another reason why assessments of 'defect' are normatively indecisive, even before we leave the zoological level and try to make what Foot calls 'the transition to humans'. (*Which* humans, incidentally? Foot presumably means humans now, in Western society. But our society has been around for, at most, 1500 years; whereas the human species has been around for about two million years. It does not take much effort to scent parochialism here.)

It is worth bearing in mind also that teleological judgements of this form have, pace Thompson (and Jennifer Frey in this volume, Chapter 5), no special epistemic privilege. They are not 'common-sense' or 'intuitively obvious' or 'form-of-life' judgements, not at least if that means that they are somehow immune to refutation. Nor are they 'pre-scientific' judgements, even when, like Thompson's own case of the blossoms, they are cases of *very simple* science.

The best way to show this is to cite a case where we think we know something about teleology but in fact we don't, and it is new scientific research that proves that we don't. Here then is the chameleon, and some research from 2015:

> Chameleons don't . . . change colour for camouflage. They do change their colour – but for two lesser-known reasons.
>
> The first reason chameleons change their skin colour [is because] dark colours absorb light, and therefore heat, while light colours reflect it. Chameleons . . . use their skin colour like a thermostat to control their body temperature. When a chameleon is cold, he deepens his skin to a darker shade such as pine green. When a chameleon wants to cool off, he turns to lighter shades such as mint green.
>
> The second reason chameleons change colour [has to do with] their moods. They'll darken their colours when fearful and brighten their colours when excited. Males also change colour more often than females, who tend to use more subtle cues to communicate . . . Some pet owners can even read their chameleons' emotions just by looking at their colour.[6]

Our intuitive, common sense and traditional beliefs about teleology are not just normatively indecisive for the reasons outlined above. They are also normatively indecisive, or rather normatively provisional, because like most of the things we think we know, they are answerable to the tests of science. And when our traditional teleological beliefs fail those tests, as with the chameleon, it turns out that those beliefs are not just too normatively lightweight to settle anything. They have no normative weight at all, because they're false.

IV

The first wolf that deserted the pack and sought out the human firelight, the first bird that laid its egg in some other bird's nest, the first fish that flopped its way ungainly along the side of the much-resounding sea: we can imagine what such creatures might have to say about their ground-breaking choices, if they were in a position to speak to us. 'Yes, I went against the species-norm, but I created a new possibility'. A lone wolf, an unmotherly lioness or a bird that puts its eggs in, horror of horrors, somebody else's basket is 'defective' if you insist. But three other words for what it does are rebellion; invention; and *progress*.

I am talking about animals; but I am also talking about *human* animals. It can happen that we humans, or some of us, find *new* purposes; and when we do, they often look 'defective' relative to the old norms for our species. That may be because they *are* defective, as the cub-murdering lion perhaps is. But it may also be because there's something wrong with the norms; and perhaps not just with *these* norms, but with *any* idea of species-norms as settling, or at least as settling anything like completely, how we are to conduct ourselves in life.

It happens too – and it happens all too often – that we humans, or some of us, find many kinds of morally loaded disquisition on the human purpose little more enticing to – or inclusive of – ourselves than the battery hen might find what the egg-farmer has to say. Anyone who, like me, is bisexual and transgender, and has heard what the Vatican (for instance) tends to have to say about us, will know exactly what I mean. And perhaps we will have wondered why our kinds of alleged deviation from the Vatican's species-norm of 'family life' are so swiftly condemned as 'objectively disordered', while the ascetic's and the celibate's and the hermit's kinds of deviation from 'family life' are not condemned at all. What justifies the ascetic and the celibate, in traditional Catholic moral theology, is that they are a kind of moral pioneer or special agent, an exceptional case because they perform a special service to society at large. If that is true of them, is it so unimaginable that it might be true of other non-species-normal lifestyles as well? Not that no arguments can possibly be mustered in defence of the traditionalist answer to this question. But it is hard to see how, in the end, such arguments can avoid a kind of circularity. ('Those deviations are allowed because they're the *good* deviations – that is, er, the ones that are allowed'.)

Now it is hardly news that arguments based upon 'the norms of nature' can be deployed for all sorts of contradictory purposes. Aristotle's defence of slavery (*Politics* Book 1.4–7) is a notorious *locus classicus* for that theme. With certain Christianising modifications (to do with the role of human sin in setting up the conditions in which slavery is licit), what Aristotle has to say is endorsed both by Augustine (*City of God* 19.15) and by Aquinas (*Summa Theologiae* 2a2ae.57). If slavery is endorsed by *them*, great authorities as they are in ethics, then why not by modern zoological naturalists?

My question is designed to produce discomfort. But part of the answer to it, clearly, is that abolitionists too can and do appeal to the norms of nature. In his *De Indis* of 1539, the Salamancan Thomist Francisco de Vitoria OP (1492–1546) gives us – with admirable bravery, considering his political context – a comprehensive and careful scholastic argument against the enslavement of the native peoples of Latin America by the Spanish conquistadors. The nub of his argument is that humans, everywhere and just as such, have a natural right to 'dominion', i.e. to an unenslaved society of their own. In the case of any particular group of humans, such as the 'Indians', de Vitoria thinks that this natural right could be defeated on only four possible grounds: (1) that they are sinners; (2) that they are not Christians; (3) that they are mad; or (4) that they are 'insensate', i.e. feeble-minded and of low intelligence. But neither (1) nor (2), says de Vitoria, is a sufficient reason for enslaving anyone – there is no general right to enslave either sinners or unbelievers. As for (3) and (4), they simply do not apply to the 'Indians'. Pace writers like Aristotle, there is, as a matter of plain fact, nothing wrong at all with these 'barbarians'' rationality. (Not, at any rate, that is not also often wrong with the Spaniards'.) There is, therefore, de Vitoria concludes, an undefeated argument from nature against enslaving them.

The same sort of essentially Aristotelian appeal to nature is still there in debates about abolitionism in Protestant Northern European societies 250 years later. Despite empirical evidence like that appealed to by de Vitoria, apologists for slavery in America in 1780 are still insisting on the low intelligence of 'their' 'negroes' as the crucially relevant natural fact. (One wonders how bright these apologists would look – or their present-day analogues – if they were suddenly transplanted onto the bottom rung of a West African society, especially if they'd just spent two months in the hold of a slave-ship.) And abolitionist campaigners like Thomas Clarkson are still insisting, too, that it is 'the rights *of nature*' of which the African slaves in the US 'have been unjustly deprived'.[7] Here, as in sixteenth-century Spain, appeals to nature seem at least *prima facie* available to both sides of the debate – for quite contradictory purposes; here, too, arguments that depend on natural norms, whether species-norms or race-norms or both, seem thoroughly ambiguous and indecisive.

However, alongside the time-honoured appeal to 'nature', there is a new note in the writings of an eighteenth-century abolitionist like Clarkson. His anti-slavery essay began its career, remarkably enough, as a Latin dissertation, an undergraduate exercise in a prize-essay competition at Cambridge – which he won. Clarkson himself described the subsequent effect of his own arguments on his own mind like this:

> As it is usual to read these essays publicly in the senate-house soon after the prize is adjudged, I was called to Cambridge for this purpose. I went and performed my office. On returning however to London, the subject of it almost wholly engrossed my thoughts. I became at times very seriously affected while upon the road. I stopped my horse occasionally, and dismounted and walked. I frequently tried to persuade myself in these intervals that the contents of my essay could not be true. The more, however, I reflected upon them, or rather upon the authorities on which they were founded, the more I gave them credit. Coming in sight of Wades Mill, in Hertfordshire, I sat down disconsolate on the turf by the roadside and held my horse. Here a thought came into my mind, that if the contents of the essay were true, it was time some person should see these calamities to their end. Agitated in this manner, I reached home. This was in the summer of 1785.

What Clarkson describes is an agitation of his conscience. His mode of argument here is not the scholastic mode of appeals to zoological nature; it is the Protestant one of checking internally to see whether your own consciousness is 'uneasy' about something. We find both modes combined in the writings of other abolitionists, notably, for instance, in one of the greatest of all, the Quaker John Woolman:

> To consider mankind otherwise than brethren, to think favours are peculiar to one nation, and to exclude others, plainly supposes a darkness in the understanding: for as God's love is universal, so where the mind is sufficiently influenced by it, it begets a likeness of itself, and the heart is enlarged towards all men. Again, to conclude a people froward, perverse, and worse by nature than others, who ungratefully receive favours, and apply them to bad ends, will excite a behaviour toward them unbecoming the excellence of true religion. (Woolman, *Considerations on the Keeping of Negroes* (Philadelphia: The Tract Association of Friends, 1754))

Such a mode of argument about slavery seems very different from the arguments from biology or racial norms. On the other hand, we might say that it has this in common with the Aristotelian arguments: it too appeals to human nature, only to a different part of human nature. What might we mean by saying that?

One thing we might mean is to point out what seems an important weakness of zoological naturalism. This is the lack of space that it seems to make for the fact that human nature is, after all, not merely zoological. Human nature is not just biological but also, as Aristotle famously observed, *political*. And it is phenomenological too. Experiences of (something like) conscience such as Woolman's and Clarkson's – and come to that, for all the differences, Neoptolemus' in Sophocles' *Philoctetes* – such experiences are a key part of human nature, just as much as conscious experience itself is a key part of human nature. It is no accident that in some languages, for example French, 'consciousness' and 'conscience' are the very same word. If an 'ethics of human nature' concentrates solely on the zoological norms of the species, and has little or nothing directly to say about the kind of uneasiness that Woolman and Clarkson felt when they reflected on slavery, then we might reasonably wonder whether it is really an ethics of *human nature* at all. For it leaves out our phenomenology. And our phenomenology is just as essential to us as our biology; maybe more so.

Thus the battery hen's – or the gay or transgender person's – reasons for unhappiness with some zoological naturalists' talk about the purpose of life are not the only possible reasons. An essentially zoological account of the human *telos* might be purged of *that* kind of harshness and exclusivity, and still face a further objection, namely that it takes account only of the zoological, which for humans is certainly important, but often just a platform for many other things, and in particular their sociology and phenomenology. I here leave sociology aside, for reasons simply of space; but this much is surely clear about phenomenology: any adequate theory of the human good will have to talk about what our ethical life is like from the viewpoint of subjective consciousness, and give us an account of human flourishing that takes that viewpoint as central.

But even then, perhaps, it still won't be enough. One reason why not is the kind of normative indeterminacy that I explored in depth above: even when we have a plausible account of what the human species-norms are, and what human flourishing is, still the normative implications of that account are not at all clear. A second reason is that it is not obviously incoherent to reject the notion of flourishing *itself*, in *any* form. Someone might say that flourishing (of any kind) is simply not what matters to them. (Thomas Carlyle: 'What right dost thou have, O man, to be *happy*? What right dost thou have even *to exist*?'; Friedrich Nietzsche: 'Man does not *seek happiness*; only the Englishman does that'.) What matters is The Cause – to its idealists; or Authenticity – to existentialists from

Kierkegaard on; or the cultivation of a certain kind of dark but artistically fertile despondency, gloom and debility – to late-romantic poets in Paris in the 1890s, and to Emos in Washington, DC, in the 1990s. Maybe there is some good philosophical objection to the views of the idealists and the existentialists, the Baudelaires and the Emos. But that they reject the ideal of flourishing, in any and every form, is not an objection to their thesis. It *is* their thesis.

V

There are problems about philosophical appeals to the normativity of nature; but the problems do not include the traditional problem of 'the is–ought gap'.[8] It is not that there is *no* normativity in nature; it is rather that it is not clear what that normativity comes to, or where and how it is deliberatively decisive or even important.

Hence, then, my two main pointers for future work in the natural law tradition. First: for anything like a plausible 'ethics of natural law', our moral philosophy needs to be backed up by better science about what human nature, or other animals' nature, actually is. And secondly: the 'ethics of human nature' needs to be extended to say more about parts of human nature that in practice it currently neglects – such as sociology and, in particular, phenomenology, the viewpoint of our actual ethical experience.

When natural law is supplemented in these ways, I suspect it is likely to stop being straightforwardly an ethical *naturalism* altogether; it will become what I shall call a *not-just-naturalism*. For some things will become obvious, or obvious again, to its practitioners that I suspect their current *modus operandi* tends to obscure from them.

For one thing, they will see again how many of the most cogent ethical appeals to nature are not made in the positive mode, but in the negative: their form is not 'This is what humans naturally do and we need to aid and foster it', but rather 'This is what humans naturally do and we need to stamp it out'. (Think again of the lions that slaughter cubs, or of human stepfathers who abuse or kill their stepchildren.) A lot of the time, what matters about human nature is not what it is like when it goes right, but when it goes *wrong*. Our ethical story about human nature needs to be a story not just about its strengths, but also about its frailties and dangers. Here, too, the point is not that Neo-Aristotelians *cannot possibly* discuss this sort of issue; it is the modester point that, by and large, they don't.

Another thing that will become obvious given not-just-naturalism is this: we will see how much distance there actually is between the zoological and the political, and how impossible it is to give a plausible account of our life together without going deeply into the phenomenological, into what it is actually like, from the subjective point of view, for us to live together.

One philosopher from the natural law tradition who is well aware of the gap between his own tradition and phenomenological ethics, and who has done more than most to bridge that gap, or at least to point to its existence, is Alasdair MacIntyre. He points out the gap in a fine essay on Knud Løgstrup, Emmanuel Levinas and the gulf between them and the twentieth-century French Thomistic tradition. And he comments on that gulf as follows:

> Normativity without norms [which is what we get in both Løgstrup and Levinas] is intelligible only as the end result of a history during which the relevant set of norms had lost whatever it had once been that made those norms compelling. What remains is an awareness and a mode of response that can only be described through phenomenological techniques. About that phenomenologically apprehended and described awareness I have been advancing two theses and this so as to formulate a question.
>
> The first is that, rightly understood, Løgstrup's account of the ethical demand is complementary to rather than incompatible with a Thomist account of the precepts of the natural law ... My second thesis is that such phenomenological accounts of core experiences of the moral life, accounts which have found their way into the mainstream of moral philosophy only in the second half of the twentieth century, are reports of historical residues, reports of what remains when some larger scheme for understanding the moral life has, for whatever reason, lost its credibility. (MacIntyre 2010: 13)[9]

It is these two theses together that prompt MacIntyre's closing question:

> we need to understand a good deal better than we do how under certain circumstances the moral life can be fragmented, so that different aspects of it – on the one hand, schemes of reasoning about goods and virtues which enable us to be practically reflective, on the other, capacities of feeling and judgement that enable us to be immediately responsive to urgent need – take on a life of their own and by so doing perhaps become distorted. If we were to understand that

> fragmentation a good deal better than as yet we do, we might also begin to understand how to reintegrate those two fragments. How we might become able to do that is [my] question. (MacIntyre 2010: 14)

This question, about how the natural law tradition might begin to make adequate space for the phenomenological, is my question too. I add only this: that the best progress towards an answer to the question that I have yet seen is the careful, detailed and much more than zoologically naturalistic phenomenology of MacIntyre's own *Dependent Rational Animals* (MacIntyre 1999).

NOTES

* Thanks for comments to Tom Angier, Sarah Broadie and Alasdair MacIntyre.

1. For more on what a hen gets up to when she gets to get up to what she wants to get up to, see this from the *Jersey Evening Post*: https://jerseyeveningpost.com/news/2018/07/02/islanders-cry-fowl-over-marauding-feral-chickens/. We encountered these very birds ourselves, on a walk near L'Ecluse in St Mary, Jersey, in June 2018.
2. www.yellowstonepark.com/things-to-do/wolf-reintroduction-changes-ecosystem.
3. In Anglophone philosophy today, two of the most distinguished cases for a natural law approach are made by Foot 2001, a case which I will discuss at some length, and by MacIntyre 1999, to which I will turn very briefly at the end of this essay. Their books are almost exactly contemporaneous. Both Foot and MacIntyre walk closely in the footsteps of Anscombe and Geach: MacIntyre's subtitle echoes Geach's famous dictum (1977: 17) that 'Men need virtues as bees need stings', which Foot quotes not once but twice (Foot 2001: 35, 44). Both MacIntyre and Foot are professedly advocating, like Anscombe and Geach, not just a natural law approach but a Neo-Aristotelian and virtue-based form of the natural law approach. In the light of these commonalities, one big surprise about these two expositions of natural law is how little alike they are. Another surprise, perhaps an even bigger one, is that neither author even mentions the other. Foot is not in MacIntyre's index, and MacIntyre is not in Foot's. (But see MacIntyre 2002, which does discuss Foot's views, comparing them with Geach's.)
4. www.bbc.co.uk/news/science-environment-44654098.
5. 'The European herring gull (*L. argentatus argenteus*), which lives primarily in Great Britain and Ireland, can hybridize with the American herring gull (*L. smithsonianus*) (living in North America), which can also hybridize with the Vega or East Siberian herring gull (*L. vegae*), the western subspecies of which, Birula's gull (*L. vegae birulai*), can hybridize with Heuglin's gull (*L. heuglini*),

which in turn can hybridize with the Siberian lesser black-backed gull (*L. fuscus*). All four of these live across the north of Siberia. The last is the eastern representative of the lesser black-backed gulls back in north-western Europe, including Great Britain. The lesser black-backed gulls and herring gulls are sufficiently different that they do not normally hybridize; thus the group of gulls forms a continuum except where the two lineages meet in Europe"' (https://en.wikipedia.org/wiki/Ring_species). The notion of a ring species is controversial, but the controversies do not undermine my point, that it is populations of actual animals that count for zoology, not abstract species-essences. (For more on species from a different viewpoint, cf. Chapter 14 in this volume.)

6. www.thedodo.com/why-chameleons-change-color–1541739423.html. See further Jérémie Teyssier et al. 2015. My thanks to Róisín Chappell for the example.
7. Thomas Clarkson, *An Essay on the Slavery and Commerce of the Human Species, Particularly the African* (from the preface). See http://oll.libertyfund.org/titles/clarkson-an-essay-on-the-slavery-and-commerce-of-the-human-species.
8. For more on my doubts about the is–ought gap, see Chappell 2009: 6.2; 2013; 2017.
9. On such issues, see also MacIntyre 2006, 2009. (My thanks to MacIntyre himself for the first reference.)

14 Natural Law Ethics and the Revival of Aristotelian Metaphysics

Edward Feser

The natural law conception of ethics is more closely associated with Thomas Aquinas than with any other thinker, and Aquinas' position is famously grounded in a metaphysics of Aristotelian essentialism and teleology. It is often claimed that this metaphysics was decisively undermined by the scientific revolution. Hence it might appear that modern science has refuted what has been, historically, the main approach to understanding natural law.

Alternative versions of natural law may seem to sidestep this difficulty by looking for foundations in something other than an essentialist and teleological conception of nature. For example, Locke's theory of natural law is grounded in the thesis of divine ownership of human beings. Violating the rights to life, liberty and property that we have under natural law is, for Locke, essentially a matter of damaging God's property. The 'new natural law theory' of Germain Grisez and John Finnis holds that practical reason grasps certain basic goods as self-evidently desirable, and that this rather than a metaphysical account of human nature suffices to ground ethics.

Yet from the Thomistic natural law perspective, such theories really amount to a 'natural law without nature'.[1] They do not salvage the natural law tradition so much as replace it with something at most verbally, but not substantively, continuous with it.[2] They are also unnecessary, for in fact the Aristotelian metaphysical presuppositions of Thomistic natural law theory are as defensible today as they were in ancient and mediaeval times. More than that, they are actually being *defended* today, and by contemporary analytic philosophers who have no interest in their application within moral philosophy, and thus no natural law axe to grind.

In the next section, I will explain the Aristotelian metaphysical claims in question and how the Thomistic version of natural law theory presupposes them. In the section after that, I will examine the contention that science has refuted those claims and show that it does not withstand scrutiny. In subsequent sections, I will survey the Neo-Aristotelian developments in contemporary metaphysics and general philosophy of science as well as in philosophy of physics, philosophy of chemistry and philosophy of biology.

The developments in question are not always *labelled* 'neo-Aristotelian' – though sometimes they are – and even when they are, they represent a minority position. Naturally, then, I am not claiming that Aristotelianism has come remotely close to regaining its late mediaeval status as the orthodoxy within Western philosophy. The point is merely that the relevant Aristotelian metaphysical ideas are once again live options in mainstream academic philosophy. There is, accordingly, no basis in science or general metaphysics not to afford the Thomistic natural law approach to ethics the same status.

THE METAPHYSICAL FOUNDATIONS OF NATURAL LAW

The *felinity* of a particular cat is, for the Aristotelian, a nature or essence that it shares with all other cats. It is not something the human intellect invents, but something it discovers in mind-independent reality. This nature or essence grounds the *properties* of cats, in the technical Aristotelian sense of the attributes that are proper to them – being carnivorous, being four-legged, having distinctive grooming habits and so forth. The properties of a thing are said to *flow* or *follow from* its essence in a way that its merely contingent attributes do not. Being four-legged flows from the essence of a cat in the sense that any mature and normal instance of a cat will have four legs. Being grey, by contrast, is a merely contingent attribute of some particular cats, because a mature and normal instance of a cat could fail to be grey. But even a property or proper attribute might fail to manifest if a particular specimen of a kind of thing is not mature or is in some way damaged. The flow might be blocked, as it were. For example, a cat that has been injured or suffers from a genetic defect might have fewer than four legs.

That things are instances of universal essences that have an objective rather than conventional status, and that ground their distinctive properties, is the core of Aristotelian essentialism. Now, either a substance or an attribute might be said to have an essence. For example, the attribute *triangularity* has an essence, and geometry (a paradigmatically objective field of study) reveals this essence and the properties that flow from it. But attributes are ontologically less fundamental than the substances in which they inhere. *Felinity* is the essence of a kind of substance, namely cats. Every kind of substance has distinctive causal powers of both active and passive sorts, these being among the attributes that flow from its essence. For example, a cat has the active power to digest meat, and the passive power to be affected by impingements on its sense organs. Powers, on the Aristotelian analysis, entail teleology insofar as they are *aimed at* or *directed towards* their characteristic manifestations. For instance, a cat's digestive power aims at or is directed towards the end of digesting meat (among other things).

A substance might be either corporeal or incorporeal. An angel, understood as a creature of pure intellect and will, would be an incorporeal substance. A stone, a tree or a cat would be a corporeal substance. For the Aristotelian, a true corporeal substance possesses properties and causal powers that are irreducible to the sum of the properties and causal powers of its parts. For example, the properties and causal powers of water cannot be reduced to the sum of the properties and causal powers of hydrogen and oxygen. By contrast, the properties and causal powers of an aggregate such as a pile of stones can be reduced to the sum of the properties and causal powers of the stones that make up the pile. And the properties and causal powers of an artefact, such as a watch, can be reduced to the sum of the properties and causal powers of its parts, together with the intentions of the designers and users of the watch.

Scholastic Aristotelians like Aquinas express this difference by saying that to be an aggregate or an artefact is to possess a merely *accidental form*, whereas to be a true substance is to possess a *substantial form*. The true substances in the case of a pile of stones are the individual stones. *Being a pile* is merely an accidental form that these stones take on when they are arranged in the right way. By contrast, the true substance in the case of water is the water itself. *Being water* is a substantial form, not merely an accidental form that hydrogen and oxygen take on as an aggregate. Indeed, for the Aristotelian, strictly speaking, hydrogen and oxygen do not exist in water in the same way that the stones exist in a pile. The stones are all actually there in the pile, but hydrogen and oxygen are in water only *virtually*. That is why you can't burn the water, as you could if it contained actual hydrogen, and why the water does not boil at −183°C, as it would if it contained actual oxygen. Hydrogen and oxygen are present in water only in the sense that they can be produced from it, by electrolysis. The view of nature this implies is thoroughly anti-reductionist. The parts of a true substance, being in it only virtually rather than actually, are not more real or ontologically fundamental than the whole.

In Aristotelian philosophy, form (whether substantial or accidental) contrasts with matter, with form corresponding to actuality and matter corresponding to potentiality. For example, stones are only potentially a pile until the pile becomes actual by virtue of the presence of the relevant accidental form. *Prime matter* is matter without any form at all, the pure potentiality to take on form. *Secondary matter* is matter already possessing some form. An aggregate or artefact is a composite of secondary matter and accidental form. For example, a pile of stones is a composite of matter that already has the form of stone, together with the accidental form of being a pile. A true corporeal substance is a composite of prime matter and substantial form. Strictly speaking, what takes on the substantial form of water is not hydrogen and oxygen – again, they are there only virtually rather than actually – but prime matter.

Causation as contemporary philosophers think of it is, for the Aristotelian, essentially a matter of actualising a potential. To cause a pile of stones, for example, is to actualise the potential of the component stones to constitute such a pile. This brings us to the famous Aristotelian doctrine of the *four causes*. There is a thing's *material cause*, which is the matter (whether prime matter or secondary matter) out of which it is composed. There is the thing's *formal cause*, which is the form (whether substantial or accidental) that the matter has taken on. There is its *efficient cause*, which is whatever actualised the potential of its matter to take on the form in question. And there is its *final cause*, which is the end or set of ends towards which its causal powers point.

For example, in the case of a cat, the material cause would be prime matter; the formal cause would be the substantial form in virtue of which a thing has distinctively feline properties and causal powers; the efficient causes would be the cat's parents; and the final cause would be ends such as hunting prey, digesting food, making new cats and so on. In the case of a watch, the material cause would be the gears, mainspring, hour and minute hands and other physical parts; the formal cause would be the accidental form in virtue of which a collection of such parts exhibits the properties and causal powers characteristic of a watch; the efficient cause would be a watchmaker; and the final cause would be telling time. Notice that in the case of watches and other artefacts, the final cause is *extrinsic* or imposed from outside by the designers and users. The metal that makes up gears for example has no inherent or built-in tendency to function as a timepiece. By contrast, in a true substance, the final cause is *intrinsic* in the sense that it follows from its nature. Nothing has to impose on a cat ends such as seeking prey, digesting food, making new cats and so forth. That is just what cats tend to do, simply by virtue of being cats.

These additional concepts – actuality and potentiality, form and matter, efficient and final causality and so on – flesh out the Aristotelian essentialist analysis of corporeal substance. And they provide a foundation for the fundamental concepts of moral theory, beginning with the notion of *goodness*. Consider once again the example of a cat. A newly conceived cat has the potential to manifest properties such as having four legs, having two eyes, having a tail and so on. As it gestates these potentialities are gradually actualised. Once born, it has active and passive causal powers such as the power to hunt prey, to digest food, to see and hear and so forth. These potentialities and powers all have a teleological character, and the teleology is intrinsic to anything having the nature of a cat. To grow four legs, develop eyes, hunt prey, digest meat and so on is to realise various ends inherent in felinity.

Now, when a particular individual cat fails to realise these ends, we say it is deficient or defective. A cat which, due to genetic anomaly, injury or disease, has only three legs or lacks any predilection for hunting is a *bad* cat, in the sense of a bad specimen of its kind. A cat which does manifest these characteristic cat-like traits is to that extent a *good* cat, in the sense of a good specimen. This is an entirely objective standard of goodness and badness. To judge the one cat a bad specimen and the other a good specimen has nothing to do with any idiosyncratic personal tastes of the one who makes such judgements. These judgements simply follow from what it is to be a cat.

So far we are not talking about a moral standard of goodness or badness, but about a more general notion of which, for scholastic Aristotelians like Aquinas, the idea of moral goodness or badness is a special case. Moral goodness or badness enters the picture in rational beings, i.e. those with intellect and will. The intellect has as its natural end the attainment of truth, and the will has as its natural end the pursuit of what the intellect judges to be good. When a rational being's intellect correctly judges something to be good for that being and the will pursues it, we have moral goodness. When the intellect errs in such judgements or the will fails to pursue what is good, we have moral defect.

Natural law theory in the Aristotelian–Thomistic tradition is concerned to work out in systematic detail what the various goods for human beings are, how they are hierarchically ordered, the general moral principles they imply, how these principles get applied in different concrete circumstances, and so on. But the whole edifice rests on an account of the good metaphysically grounded in Aristotelian essentialism, with its commitment to intrinsic teleology and the other notions outlined above.[3]

THE OBJECTION FROM SCIENCE

The claim that this metaphysical foundation has been undermined by modern science derives from the association of the scientific revolution with the rise of what is sometimes called the 'mechanical world picture' or the 'mechanical philosophy'. The idea that the physical universe can be thought of as a vast machine or mechanism is part of this picture, of course. But it involves much more than the banal observation that physical things are made up of parts whose arrangement is in some ways reminiscent of the parts of a machine. No Aristotelian ever denied that much. What was distinctive about the mechanical world picture was rather its spelling out of the machine analogy in terms inspired by Aristotle's ancient rivals, the Greek atomists and the Pythagoreans. This entailed abandoning formal and final causes and redefining material and efficient causes.

On the ancient atomist picture, the closest thing to true substances in the Aristotelian sense of the term are the atoms, conceived of as microscopic unbreakable particles. Stones, water, trees, cats and all other everyday natural objects are really just aggregates of atoms. Whereas the Aristotelian affirms a sharp difference in kind between these natural objects, the mechanical philosophy insists that there are only differences in degree. Really these things are, at the deepest level, just the same kind of thing – atoms moving through empty space – just as a pile of stones arranged in the shape of a pyramid and a pile arranged in the shape of a cube are essentially the same kind of thing, with the difference in shape being superficial. Moreover, the properties and causal powers of everyday natural objects are, on this view, reducible to the aggregate of the properties and causal powers of the atoms that make them up. In short, there are no substantial forms in the world of everyday natural objects, any more than there are in the case of a pile of stones or a watch.

Nor is there any intrinsic teleology. Neither the atoms nor anything composed of them *aim at* or are *directed towards* any ends at all. For mechanical philosophers who happened to be theists or dualists, there was still *extrinsic* teleology insofar as God and/or the soul might impose certain ends on otherwise purposeless collections of particles, in much the same way as the designers and users of a watch impose a time-telling function on the metal parts that make it up. For these thinkers, natural objects are to be assimilated to artefacts, with God rather than human beings being the artificer in this case. But there is nothing about any material thing *in itself* that points towards any end. Theistic and dualistic mechanical philosophers, on the one hand, and atheistic and materialist mechanical philosophers, on the other, all agree that the natural world is devoid of any final causality at all. The difference is that the latter also think that there is nothing *beyond* the natural world that possesses teleology either.

The rejection of substantial form and intrinsic teleology entailed a transformation of the notions of material and efficient cause, and a revival of the Pythagoreans' 'mathematisation' of nature deeply influenced how this was done. Matter was no longer to be thought of as the potentiality to take on form. Rather, it was to be characterised in terms of the mathematical properties of particles in motion. Efficient causation was no longer thought of in terms of the operation of causal powers which aim or point beyond themselves towards their characteristic manifestations. Nor was it to be conceived of in terms of the actualisation of potential. Rather, what could be said about efficient causation was exhausted by mathematically expressed laws of nature governing particles and the larger objects composed of them. For example, Newton's law of universal gravitation describes the mathematical relationship between gravitational force, mass and distance, without addressing metaphysical questions about exactly *how* an object exerts gravitational force upon another.

There were disagreements among mechanical philosophers over the details. Some retained the ancient atomists' conception of fundamental particles as unbreakable in principle, others took the corpuscularian view that the fundamental particles were breakable in theory but unbroken in fact, and yet others denied that there is any fundamental or bottom level of particles. Some retained the atomist view that particles move through a void, others held that all space is occupied by matter. Moreover, some early aspects of the mechanical philosophy would eventually fall by the wayside, such as the tendency to think of efficient causation on a crude push-pull model. But the idea that everything in nature is reducible to the entities of particle physics, and that these entities ought to be conceived of in mathematical and non-teleological terms, has survived as the core of a mechanical conception of nature.

Now, the key thing to emphasise is that though this picture is commonly associated with modern science, and often even guides scientific research, it is not itself a *finding* of modern science. It is rather simply a methodology and a metaphysical model in terms of which the findings of science are commonly interpreted. One *could*, of course, argue that the mechanical-cum-mathematical world picture provides a correct and exhaustive description of nature. But one could also argue for an *instrumentalist* interpretation on which this picture of nature provides a useful tool for making predictions and developing technologies, but does not give us a strictly accurate description of the world as it really is. Or, alternatively, one could take an *epistemic structural realist* position, and argue that though the picture gives us a description of features that are really there, it does not give us an exhaustive description, but captures only those features susceptible of mathematical modelling. There is, on this view, more to nature than scientific method can reveal, even if what that method reveals is correct so far as it goes. Or one could take a partially instrumentalist and partially epistemic structural realist point of view. The point is that science by itself does not tell us which of these views to take. That requires extra-scientific philosophical argumentation.

In that case, though, it is open to the Aristotelian to argue that the absence of substantial form, intrinsic teleology and related concepts from the mechanistic-cum-mathematical *representation* of nature does not entail that they are absent from nature *itself*. The absence reflects only the limitations of a certain methodology, and not the reality studied by means of it. The argument from science against Aristotelian essentialism is not really a scientific argument at all. It is a philosophical position masquerading as a scientific one.[4]

DEVELOPMENTS IN GENERAL METAPHYSICS AND PHILOSOPHY OF SCIENCE

It is also a philosophical position that developments in contemporary analytic philosophy have shown to be highly problematic.[5] Let us begin with a consideration of *dispositional essentialism*, a view which, as

Stephen Mumford has noted, was initially developed largely independently within both recent analytic metaphysics and recent philosophy of science.[6] There are several versions of this view on offer and thinkers associated with it disagree about various details. But three key themes are relevant to our concerns. First, there is the thesis that dispositions or causal powers of a kind reminiscent of those posited by Aristotelians are, after all, real features of nature, at least at the microphysical level. Second, there is the idea that to identify these powers is to identify essences or natures of things of a kind reminiscent of those posited by Aristotelians. Third, there is the proposal that these powers or dispositions are *aimed* or *directed towards* their characteristic manifestations in a way reminiscent of the Aristotelian notion of intrinsic teleology.

In analytic metaphysics, the main motivation has been the imperative to find an alternative to the influential but problematic regularity and counterfactual theories of causation. A regularity theory holds that a particular event *A* causes a particular event *B* just in case, in general, events of the *A*-type happen as a matter of fact to be constantly conjoined with events of the *B*-type. A standard objection is that the regularity account captures only correlations, and correlation does not entail causation. The counterfactual theory is meant to remedy this defect. It holds that for *A* to cause *B*, more has to be true than merely that events of the first type are in fact regularly followed by events of the second type. It also has to be true that, in cases where an event of type *A* does not in fact occur, *if* such an event *had* occurred, then an event of type *B would have* occurred. And it has to be true that, in cases where an event of type *A* did occur, if such an event *had not* occurred, an event of type *B would not have* occurred either.

Against such theories, defenders of causal powers or dispositions have put forward a number of counterexamples. For instance, consider a live wire which, when it makes contact with a conductor, will cause electricity to flow into it.[7] The counterfactual analysis will say that we can capture this causal relation by saying that if the wire were live and touched by a conductor, then electrical current would flow from the wire to the conductor, and if the wire were not live and touched by the conductor, then electrical current would not have flowed from the wire to the conductor. However, consider a device (called an *electro-fink* in the literature) which renders a live wire dead when attached to a conductor, and a dead wire live when attached to it. Then the counterfactual analysis will be false. But it would still be true that live wires cause current to flow to conductors.

What such examples are said to indicate is that the right way to think of efficient causation is in terms of *powers* or *dispositions* that will either operate or not depending on circumstances. For example, the wire in the case at hand has a power to cause electricity to flow, but the actual exercise of this power can be blocked by the electro-fink. This has been taken to entail a distinction between a thing's *categorical* and *dispositional* properties, which essentially recapitulates the Aristotelian distinction between actualities and potentialities. The wire categorically or actually has a certain mass. But it is only disposed towards, or has a potentiality for, causing electrical current to flow. It is not always actually doing that, even when it has the potential or disposition to do so.[8]

Furthermore, for some powers theorists, powers or dispositions are *directed towards* or *point at* their characteristic manifestations.[9] The wire has a power that is directed towards the passing on of electrical current, the phosphorus in the head of a match has a power that is directed towards the generation of flame and heat, and so forth. Powers or dispositions are thus said to have *physical intentionality* or *natural intentionality*. It is a kind of intentionality insofar as involves directedness or pointing, analogous to the way a thought is directed towards or aims at its object. But it is called 'physical' or 'natural' intentionality because it is not associated with any thinking or mentality. Wires don't think about passing on electrical current and phosphorus doesn't think about generating flame and heat. Now this is more or less exactly what mediaeval Aristotelian philosophers had in mind in attributing teleology or final causality to natural phenomena. They meant, just as a contemporary analytic powers theorist does, that even a purely physical cause devoid of thought or mentality of any kind can point or aim towards the generation of certain characteristic effects, just by virtue of its nature or essence.[10]

Contemporary metaphysics has also seen a trend away from reductionism. As Crawford Elder has noted, even apparently obvious reductions are problematic on close inspection.[11] Consider, for example, the claim that a stone is really nothing but a collection of particles arranged 'stone-wise'. Exactly what is it about the specific group of particles in question that makes it true that it is those and only those – rather than some subset of particles, or particles additional to them – that are arranged stone-wise? If we identify them by reference to the stone itself, then the account is circular. Yet if we leave out any reference to the stone, we have no other way to pick out that particular collection of particles, and in particular no relation that holds between all and only the particles in question by means of which we might identify them. Nor will it do to suggest that the particles in question can be identified by their tendency to cause us to have an experience of a stone. For there are particles that play a role in the causal story which are not part of the stone (e.g. those in the air between us and the stone) and particles that are part of the stone that do not play a role in the causal story (e.g. those in the unobserved interior of the stone). So we need to consider the stone *as a whole* in order even to make sense of the parts.

As Elder also argues, we cannot make coherent sense of the idea that all of the essences of the ordinary entities of our experience are merely conventional or mind-dependent.[12] For if we pushed this idea through consistently, we'd have to say that the essence of the human mind itself is merely conventional or mind-dependent. But this is incoherent. For something to be merely conventional or mind-dependent is for it to be *caused by* the mind, and the mind cannot be its own cause any more than anything else can.

In philosophy of science, a number of thinkers have argued that a metaphysics of essences and powers is best able to make sense of the practice and results of scientific inquiry.[13] For example, Nancy Cartwright argues that laws of nature are strictly true only under artificial circumstances that rarely, if ever, obtain.[14] Coulomb's law of electrostatic attraction and repulsion describes objects with strict accuracy only when they are not being subjected to gravitational effects. Something similar could be said of Newton's law of inertia and Kepler's law of ellipses. But of course, in reality objects are always being subjected to gravitational attraction. What is really going on, in Cartwright's view, is that objects have various powers (or capacities, as she prefers to call them) which are such that, if the objects are arranged in just the right way (as in the artificial conditions of the laboratory), the interaction of their powers will give rise to a system whose behaviour approximates the laws.

Nor, Cartwright argues, do scientists typically seek to catalogue a large number of trials in order to discover law-like regularities. Rather, they draw general conclusions from a few highly specialised experiments conducted under artificial conditions. This is exactly what one would expect of the search for the hidden *nature* or *essence* of a thing. What one is inferring in such a case is how anything else with that same essence would behave under the same circumstances. 'The empiricists of the scientific revolution wanted to oust Aristotle entirely from the new learning', Cartwright says, but 'they did no such thing'.[15]

Powers, argues Brian Ellis, are the 'truthmakers' for laws of nature.[16] Scientists commonly describe the entities they posit in terms that presuppose powers. For example, negatively charged particles are characterised as having the power to attract positively charged ones, and electrostatic fields as having the power to modify spectral lines.[17] It is no good to retort that we can describe such phenomena instead in terms of laws of nature and eliminate reference to powers, because that merely raises the question of why the entities in question obey those laws rather than other laws or no laws at all. The dispositional essentialist has an answer, viz. that the laws reflect the powers a thing will manifest given its nature or essence. To appeal to laws in order to explain or eliminate powers is to put the cart before the horse.

As Ellis also points out, certain scientific classifications reveal exactly the sharp demarcation into distinct natural kinds that one would expect if essentialism were true. The periodic table of the elements is a vivid example.[18]

This only scratches the surface of the relevant literature, but the reader may wonder what connection these very abstract metaphysical concerns bear to natural law theory. The relevance is that the so-called scientific objection to Aristotelian–Thomistic natural law theory claims that Aristotelian metaphysics cannot be taken seriously in the context of ethics, because modern science has banished Aristotelian essences, powers, teleology and related notions from the natural world in general. As the developments I've been describing show, in fact science (to borrow Cartwright's words) 'did no such thing'. It is only a certain philosophical *interpretation* of science that has tried to do so, and that interpretation is not only challengeable but is in fact being challenged even outside the ranks of natural law theorists.

PHILOSOPHY OF PHYSICS AND PHILOSOPHY OF CHEMISTRY

To these considerations must be added new challenges to reductionism inspired by quantum mechanics and by findings in the special sciences.

There are several respects in which quantum mechanics sits poorly with reductionism.[19] First, microphysical phenomena such as the position and momentum of a particle are merely potential until actualised by interaction with macro-level entities such as observers. The micro and macro levels of physical reality are thus mutually interdependent in a way reminiscent of the relationship that Aristotelians say holds between a true substance and its parts. This is further illustrated by quantum entanglement phenomena. The properties of a system of entangled particles are irreducible to the properties of the particles considered individually or to their spatial relations and relative velocity. Again, the whole is more than the sum of its parts, as it is on the Aristotelian account of physical substances.

Quantum statistics treats elementary particles of the same kind as indiscernible and essentially *fused* within a larger system, thereby losing their individuality and 'merging into a kind of quantum goo or gunk', as Robert Koons observes.[20] As Dean Rickles puts it, in quantum mechanics, such particles are really 'excitations of one and the same basic underlying field' and best thought of 'as "dollars in a checking account" rather than "coins in a piggy bank": they can be *aggregated* but not counted and distinguished'.[21] Once again we have an echo of the Aristotelian position that parts exist in a substance virtually or potentially rather than actually.

Criticism of reductionism has been a common theme in the emerging sub-discipline of philosophy of chemistry. J. van Brakel notes that we can look for the chemical microstructure of a substance like water only because we already have an independent conception of it based on its macro-level characteristics.[22] Without reference to the macro-level, we have no way of identifying exactly which microstructural properties are essential to the substance and which are not. Hence there is more to the substance than can be described in purely microstructural terms, contrary to reductionism.

Furthermore, as noted already, water has properties and causal powers that hydrogen, oxygen and a mere aggregate of hydrogen and oxygen all lack. It also lacks properties and causal powers that hydrogen and oxygen have. This is exactly what we should expect if the hydrogen and oxygen are, as Aristotelians hold, in the water only virtually rather than actually. The Aristotelian view is similar to the 'fusion emergentism' of contemporary philosopher Paul Humphreys.[23] On Humphreys' account, emergent properties exist at a higher level within a system when lower-level properties are 'fused' in such a way that they cease to exist as separate entities and lose some of their causal powers, and where this fusion yields novel causal powers at the higher level. This is exactly what happens with hydrogen and oxygen when they combine to form water. As Humphreys emphasises, a failure to perceive that the emergence of higher-level properties involves such fusion bedevils much traditional debate over reductionism. Discussion about whether the higher-level properties supervene upon the lower-level ones, and whether, if so, the higher-level properties are causally superfluous, presupposes that the lower-level properties exist in the emergent system in just the same manner in which they exist apart from it, and that is exactly what fusion emergentists (and Aristotelians) deny. The higher-level properties neither supervene upon the lower-level ones nor causally compete with them, because the lower-level ones no longer exist *in the way* that the higher-level ones do.

A further well-known example of the failure of reductionist claims about modern chemistry concerns thermodynamics.[24] The thesis that temperature is molecular motion, like the claim that water is H_2O, is routinely cited in philosophical literature as an example of a successful chemical reduction. But as with water, the reality is more complicated. For one thing, molecular motion is not by itself sufficient for a system's having temperature; the system must also be in thermodynamic equilibrium. But equilibrium is a macro-level concept, so that for the reductionist to appeal to molecular motion together with equilibrium would not be to *reduce* the macro-level to the micro-level at all. Nor will it work to appeal to statistical mechanics in order to find some micro-level property to put in place of equilibrium, because the relevant processes from statistical mechanics cannot be characterised without reference to the very macro-level concept of temperature that the reductionist is trying to reduce.

These examples have to do with the question of reductionism *within* chemistry, where what is at issue is the relationship of macro-level chemical phenomena to micro-level chemical phenomena. But there is also the question of the reduction of chemistry itself to physics, and here too several philosophers of chemistry have expressed scepticism.[25] One problem is that the question whether chemistry has been reduced to physics is ambiguous. On the one hand, quantum mechanics has provided chemistry with computational methods of undeniable utility. In that sense, a reductionist methodology has proven fruitful. On the other hand, it is impossible to begin with quantum mechanics and predict from that alone the configuration of a particular atom or to deduce the periodic table. In particular, reductionist accounts face difficulty when time is factored in. For example, once we know the structure of a boron atom, it might appear obvious how its properties derive from those of its microstructure. But if we knew only the particles of which boron is composed, we could not have predicted the properties that would arise once they combine to form a boron atom. Robin Hendry also argues that there are cases of molecules which differ chemically (such as ethanol and dimethyl ether) even though their description at the level of quantum mechanics is the same.[26]

Such difficulties for reductionism in chemistry are now so widely acknowledged that in their survey article on the field, Michael Weisberg, Paul Needham and Robin Hendry speak of an 'anti-reductionist consensus in the philosophy of chemistry literature'.[27] In effect, Aristotle's critique of ancient atomism has largely been recapitulated in contemporary analytic philosophy.

PHILOSOPHY OF BIOLOGY

Once again, the reader might worry that the developments described are too remote from human life to be relevant to natural law theory, but here too such a conclusion would miss the point. The science-based objection to Aristotelian–Thomistic natural law theory derives its rhetorical force from the conceit that the relevant Aristotelian notions have been entirely banished from the vast expanse of the non-human world. It would be special pleading, the objection suggests, to think they might still have application within that small sliver of reality that is the human species. When this assumption is exposed as specious, the rhetorical force of the objection is undermined.

The point is reinforced by developments in the philosophy of the life sciences. Here three themes are especially relevant: the rise of an anti-reductionist near-consensus; the persistence of difficulties facing attempts to eliminate or reduce teleological notions such as the concept of function; and the revival of a fairly robust species essentialism.

One problem with reductionism in biology can be illustrated with the example of the gene. Two conceptions of the gene are sometimes distinguished. There is, first, the gene in the Mendelian sense of a hypothetical cause for a pattern of inheritance of traits (e.g. eye colour). Second, there is the gene in the biochemical sense of a sequence of nucleotides. It is often claimed that genes in the first sense have been reduced to genes in the second sense. But as John Dupré points out, that is not the case.[28] Typically, there are many genes in the biochemical sense involved in the production of any one trait, and any one gene is involved in the production of many different traits. Context determines how a gene will operate. Hence there simply is no smooth one-to-one mapping of genes in the Mendelian sense onto genes in the biochemical sense.

As Dupré also points out, the common assertion that the genome contains all the information required in order to build an organism is problematic.[29] The word 'information' is ambiguous. If the term is used in the ordinary semantic sense, then the claim in question is manifestly false. There is no 'information' in the genome in the sense in which there is information in a book or a lecture. If the term is used in the technical information-theoretic sense, then the idea is that there is a reliable causal link between a gene in the biochemical sense and a certain trait. But in that case the claim that genes carry information is trivial, because there are lots of other factors involved in the production of traits that carry 'information' in that sense. There is nothing special about genes in that case.

Dupré distinguishes between *what something does* and *how something does what it does*, where the former has to do with biological function and the latter with the mechanisms by which it performs that function.[30] What biochemistry reveals, Dupré points out, is the latter but not the former. Dupré's distinction essentially recapitulates the distinction between *formal-cum-final causes* on the one hand, and *material-cum-efficient causes* on the other. He and other anti-reductionists in the philosophy of biology, like anti-reductionists in philosophy of chemistry and philosophy of science in general, are essentially rediscovering the Aristotelian anti-atomist point that all four causes are needed for a complete description of natural phenomena.

This judgement is reinforced by consideration of the difficulties attending contemporary attempts to analyse the concept of biological function in terms of efficient causation.[31] Currently the most popular approach is to cash out the notion of function in Darwinian terms.[32] On this analysis, the function of a trait is to be understood in terms of the causal factors that led to its being favoured by natural selection. For example, the heart causes blood to be circulated throughout the body. It also causes a thumping sound, but the fact that it circulates the blood, rather than the fact that it makes a thumping sound, is the reason natural selection favoured it. Hence circulating blood, rather than making a thumping sound, is the function of the heart.

But there are several problems with this analysis. For one thing, it implies that you cannot know a thing's function without knowing its evolutionary history. But that is not plausible. We can know what hearts, eyes, ears, feet and the like are for, whether or not we know anything about evolution. For another thing, a trait's evolutionary history does not in fact determine a unique functional description of the trait. To cite a popular example, a frog will snap its tongue towards flies that flit by it, though also at pellets that are thrown its way. So should we say that the biological function of the underlying neural mechanism is *to catch flies* or *to catch small moving things*?[33]

It might seem that the reductionist could bite the bullet and respond that there simply is nothing more to function than whatever can be captured by such reductive analyses. The idea would be to eliminate the more robust common-sense notion of function and replace it with a deflationist theoretical conception. But there are two problems with this proposal. First, it faces the same objection that plagues other anti-realist moves in philosophy of science. The common-sense notion of function has enormous utility. It would be practically impossible to do biology without it. How could this be if it does not correspond to anything in objective reality? (This is an application of the well-known 'no miracles' argument for scientific realism.)

Second, this deflationist strategy cannot coherently be carried out in a consistent way. To follow it out consistently, we'd have to say that there is no objective fact of the matter about what human perceptual and cognitive faculties are for. If we say *that*, however, then we will also have to say that there is no objective fact of the matter about whether those faculties are malfunctioning in any particular case (in hallucinations, fallacious reasoning, mental illness etc.) Objectively speaking, there will be nothing to make any output of these faculties better or worse than any other. The distinction between genuine empirical evidence and illusion, and between good and bad reasoning, will collapse – taking all arguments, including arguments for reductionism, down with it.[34]

Then there is the recent trend towards a revival of a fairly robust notion of the essence of a biological species.[35] Biologists and philosophers of biology sometimes distinguish between *functional biology* and *evolutionary biology*.[36] Functional biology is concerned with the structure of an organism, the functions its parts serve, the developmental processes by which those parts form, their genetic basis and so forth, all considered in a more or less ahistorical manner. Evolutionary biology is concerned with the historical origins of organisms and their traits. These two forms of inquiry can be carried out more or less independently of one another.

As Michael Devitt has argued, an excessive focus on the historical or evolutionary approach can make it seem as if anything we might want to identify as the essence of a group of organisms captures only their relations to other organisms rather than any intrinsic essence.[37] But if instead we look at things from the approach of functional biology, the need to affirm an essence intrinsic to organisms of the same kind is clear. Simply as a prerequisite to carrying out such inquiry, biologists group organisms according to common traits and treat these *as if* they reflected some common intrinsic nature.[38] They do this whatever views they explicitly hold on the question of essentialism, and this approach is fruitful. We find that organisms within these groupings really do reliably tend to manifest certain common properties, to exhibit certain common characteristic behaviours, and so on. We need an explanation of why this is so, and the best explanation is that there *really is* an essence intrinsic to organisms of the same kind – that it is not just a useful fiction. Moreover, this metaphysical judgement seems to be confirmed empirically, by the results of genome research.

It is often claimed that evolution is incompatible with essentialism. One reason is that essentialism, it is argued, is inconsistent with the various notions of species that have become common in biology since Darwin. There is, for example, the 'biological concept', which takes a species to be an isolated and interbreeding population of organisms; and the 'phylogenetic-cladistic concept', which defines a species in terms of its evolutionary history. On these accounts, what species an organism belongs to is to be determined by reference to its relations to other organisms, rather than anything intrinsic to it. Yet a thing's essence, as Aristotelians understand it, is supposed to be something intrinsic to it.

But Devitt notes that we need to distinguish the question of what makes it the case that an organism belongs to a certain group from the question of what makes some group a species as opposed to a subspecies, a genus or whatever.[39] Essentialism is an answer to the first question, whereas the various species concepts in question are answers to the second. Hence, whatever one thinks of those concepts, they are not in competition with essentialism.

It is also sometimes claimed that there is no set of traits that is common to every member of any species and which could play the role that an essence is said to play. Yet as even one critic of essentialism concedes, 'there are important genetic similarities between members of a single species ... [and] species taxa are distinguished by clusters of covarying traits'.[40] Devitt suggests that such clusters are precisely what essences can be identified with, and that the objection in question has force only against a simplistic conception of essence.[41] Other essentialists argue that an organism's essence should be sought, not in either its genotype or phenotype *per se*, but in the 'developmental programme' that maps the one onto the other.[42]

Then there is the claim that essentialism requires sharp boundaries between species, whereas evolution requires that the boundaries be vague. But as some neo-essentialists emphasise, evolution simply doesn't require that at all. That a species *S1* and its descendant species *S2* will have certain traits in common doesn't entail that there is no sharp difference between their essences. Even if, among the intermediary groups of organisms in between *S1* and *S2*, it is hard to determine where one ends and the other begins, it doesn't follow that these intermediary groups lack sharp essences. The vagueness might be merely epistemic rather than ontological, and if we have independent reason to believe in essences (which we do), then we have good reason to conclude that that is all that is going on. Moreover, as Stephen Boulter argues, evolution if anything actually *presupposes* essentialism insofar as it holds that new species come into being and go extinct as a matter of objective fact, and not merely as a matter of changes in our classificatory practices. That entails that there must be objective facts that distinguish one species from another, which in turn requires essences.[43]

Now if, even in the context of contemporary philosophy of biology, one can defend the claim that organisms have essences and that their essences entail certain functions or teleological features, one can thereby defend the core metaphysical commitments of Aristotelian–Thomistic natural law theory. And since essences and teleology can be defended also at the level of chemistry and the level of fundamental particles, it cannot be maintained that such metaphysical commitments in biology and ethics do not sit well with what we know about the rest of nature.

Here I have attempted to provide only a survey of the relevant recent developments, and I have not attempted to rehearse objections to the arguments discussed or how Aristotelians would reply. It goes without saying that every one of the developments I've described is controversial. But that is precisely the point. Aristotelian metaphysics is *at worst* controversial – as opposed to dead. The same must be said of the natural law system of ethics that it grounds.

NOTES

1. I borrow the phrase from McInerny 1998.
2. For criticism of Locke's approach to natural law from an Aristotelian–Thomistic point of view, see Feser 2007: chapter 4. For criticism of the new natural law theory's abandonment of Aristotelian–Thomistic metaphysical foundations, see Oderberg 2010.

3. For book-length exposition and defence of general Aristotelian–Thomistic metaphysics, see Feser 2014b and Oderberg 2007. For a more detailed exposition and defence of the Aristotelian–Thomistic metaphysics of value in particular, see Feser 2014a.
4. I develop this line of argument in Feser 2014b and at book length in Feser 2019.
5. Anthologies of articles representative of the Neo-Aristotelian revival in contemporary analytic philosophy include Feser 2013; Groff and Greco 2013; Novak et al. 2012; Novotny and Novak 2014; Simpson et al. 2018; Tahko 2012.
6. Cf. Mumford 2009.
7. The example under discussion has famously been developed by C. B. Martin. See e.g. Martin 2008: chapter 2. Other counterexamples are discussed in Bird 2007: 27–9 and Molnar 2003: chapter 4.
8. See Feser 2014b: 53–63 and 79–87 for an overview of the debate in recent analytic metaphysics about these issues.
9. Cf. Molnar 2003: chapter 3; Heil 2003: 221–2; Place 1996. See Feser 2014b: 100–105 for an overview of the recent literature in analytic metaphysis on this topic.
10. Of course, the phosphorous in the match head will not generate flame and heat if submerged in water, just as the wire will not cause electricity to flow if blocked by the electro-fink. Context determines whether and how powers are manifested. As Molnar emphasises (2003: 194–8), an effect is typically 'polygenic' in the sense of being a combination of the manifestation of several powers operating in tandem, and powers are 'pleiotropic' in the sense of making contributions to different kinds of effect.
11. Cf. Elder 2004: 50–58; Elder 2011: 118–24. Other recent defenders of an anti-reductionist approach to physical substances include Thomasson 2007 and Koslicki 2008. For an overview of the relevant literature in recent analytic metaphysics, see Feser 2014b: 177–89.
12. Elder 2004: chapter 1. For an overview of the neo-essentialist literature in recent analytic metaphysics, see Feser 2014b: 211–16 and 237–41.
13. See Feser 2014b: 63–72 for an overview of the relevant literature.
14. Cf. Cartwright 1983, 1999: chapter 4.
15. Cartwright 1999: 103.
16. Ellis 2001: 112 and 222. Cf. Bhaskar 2008: 45–56; Chakravartty 2013.
17. Ellis 2001: 109–10
18. Ellis 2009: 59.
19. Cf. Koons 2018a, 2018b.
20. Koons 2018a: 163.
21. Rickles 2016: 161–3.
22. Van Brakel 2000: 73–82.

23. Cf. Humphreys 2008.
24. Cf. Sklar 1993; Van Brakel 2000: 123–8; Koons 2018a.
25. Cf. Scerri 1994; Van Brakel 2000: 128–50; Hendry 2006. Scerri has expressed some second thoughts in Scerri 2016, though his misgivings appear primarily to concern the significance of certain empirical considerations, and leave untouched the deeper conceptual problems with reductionism.
26. Cf. Hendry 2006, 2010, 2017.
27. Weisberg et al. 2011.
28. Cf. Dupré 1993: chapter 6; 2012: chapter 8.
29. Dupré 2012: 134–6.
30. Dupré 2012: 133.
31. See Buller 1999 for an anthology of key articles and Buller's introduction to the volume for an overview of the main theories and the main objections to them.
32. Cf. e.g. Millikan 1984.
33. The indeterminacy problem facing accounts of what natural selection selects *for* is a major theme of Fodor and Piattelli-Palmarini 2011.
34. Nagel 2012 flirts with the idea that acceptance of a Neo-Aristotelian teleology might be necessary in order to fit rational thought processes into nature.
35. Cf. Devitt 2008; Elder 2008; Dumsday 2012; Boulter 2013; Austin 2017.
36. Cf. Mayr 1961; Kitcher 1984.
37. Devitt 2008: 354.
38. Devitt 2008: 351–5. Cf. Thompson 1995.
39. Devitt 2008: 356–8.
40. Okasha 2002: 197.
41. Devitt 2008: 371.
42. Cf. Boulter 2013: 111–13; Austin 2017.
43. Boulter 2013: 108–9.

15 Prospects for Natural Law Ethics in the Twenty-First Century

Tom Angier

To examine the prospects for natural law ethics, we need first a working definition of it. But as the previous chapters suggest, any such definition is controversial. Thomas Aquinas defines law as 'an ordinance of reason directed towards the common good from him who has care of the community and promulgated'.[1] It follows that for a law to be natural, it must be not only grounded in human nature – something Aquinas affirms elsewhere – but also promulgated: the only available promulgator being God. Rosalind Hursthouse, by contrast, takes natural law ethics to be metaphysically less demanding. For her, its theistic underpinning is not salient, and appears even moot. What is salient is the provision of a naturistically grounded criterion of right or good action. Natural law ethics is thus distinct from ethical naturalism in general, which 'provides a criterion for a particular trait's being a virtue, *not* a criterion of right or good action, except indirectly'.[2] For John Finnis and other 'New Natural Law' theorists, natural law ethics is still less metaphysically demanding. It requires no theistic underpinning, nor need it provide a naturalistically grounded criterion of right action.[3] Instead, it specifies a range of self-evident 'basic goods', which are then chosen according to the canons of practical reason. (While new natural lawyers specify 'religion' as a basic good,[4] they hold that theism plays no role in the identification, or bindingness, of ethical norms as such.) In this way, although New Natural Law draws heavily on Aquinas, it is a suitor for the attention of theists and non-theists alike.

Which of these various conceptions of natural law ethics should we adopt? On the one hand, I see no reason, in principle, to exclude theologically inflected forms of natural law ethics. Work on natural law by traditional Thomists, for instance, is flourishing.[5] On the other hand, I think it is unreasonable to restrict natural law ethics within theistic bounds – and this for three reasons. First, the issue of whether natural ethical norms require theistic backing is very difficult to settle: even the form of backing itself is subject to dispute.[6] Secondly, some of the most promising work on natural normativity is now done – as I shall document – by philosophers whose theories incorporate no theistic commitments. It would hence be unduly narrow-minded and theoretically myopic to ignore their work. And thirdly, theologically non-committal natural law ethics can engage a wider audience than its theologically committed counterpart. Why so, in a world where most people are religious believers of some kind? Because there is, in short, an asymmetry between theistic and non-theistic natural law theories. Whereas the former lack import for the latter, the latter perforce have import for the former – and this because, in turn, nature is part of the theist's ontology, while God is absent from the non-theist's. On all three grounds, then, I will focus on types of natural law ethics that, though not in principle excluding theological content, are not crucially determined by it.[7]

Before turning to what are, I believe, the most promising forms of natural law ethics on offer in the first quarter of the twenty-first century, it is worth noting how auspicious a time this is for the idea that ethical norms are grounded in nature. The reasons for this are basically three-fold. First, the turn of the century has seen significant meta-ethical work challenging the supposed dichotomy between 'fact' and 'value'. Whereas, for much of the twentieth century, it was philosophically de rigueur to endorse G. E. Moore's view that goodness is logically and metaphysically independent of 'natural' facts,[8] this consensus has broken down. Work by Hilary Putnam and Judith Jarvis Thomson has argued for the pervasive entanglement of the 'descriptive' with the 'evaluative', something reinforced by work on 'thick' concepts like 'cruel' and 'sentimental', where this entanglement is made apparent at the linguistic level.[9] Granted, the existence of normative facts does not yet demonstrate that these are natural or grounded in nature: indeed, Putnam argues that they are not.[10] But such work opens up crucial meta-ethical space within which this argument can be made, and has been made, thanks notably to Thomson's contention that goodness is a functional concept.[11] As Sophie Grace Chappell puts matters, 'In human life as we actually experience it, there usually isn't an is–ought *gap* at all; there is an is–ought *continuum* ... we experience the world as value-laden, and value-laden from the bottom up; as *drenched* in value'.[12]

Secondly, the first decades of the new century have seen the resurrection of Aristotelian metaphysics. This has provided metaphysical heft to the largely conceptual and linguistic work above.[13] David Oderberg, for instance, has argued for what he calls 'real essentialism', the view that there are essences in nature which do not, pace the predominant analytic view, reduce to claims about possible worlds.[14] These natural essences embody species of objective finality or end-directedness that, in turn, undergird the kind of natural law ethics Oderberg espouses.[15] Such efforts at metaphysical retrieval have been complemented, moreover, by work in the philosophy of science, which argues that Aristotelian powers and forms of teleology are consistent with a post-Darwinian ontology.[16] Thirdly, the new millennium has seen the burgeoning of Neo-Aristotelian ethical naturalism.[17] This seeks to apply the general truths of Aristotelian teleological metaphysics to the particular case of human nature. Of paramount importance here is the work of Michael Thompson, which I will look at below, along with that of Philippa Foot.[18] Central to Thompson's work is the notion of an 'Aristotelian categorical', a form of judgement that captures those features of an organism – most saliently, those of the human organism – that make it a good, rather than defective, instance of its type. While, as I will argue, Thompson's project encounters difficulties, there is no doubt it has galvanised work on natural law ethics in the twenty-first century.

THE NATURALISM OF SECOND NATURE

Let us move on, then, to what I called the most promising forms of natural law ethics now on offer (leaving to one side those that are explicitly theistic). These can be divided usefully into four categories.[19] First, there is John McDowell's naturalism of second nature. In *Mind and World* (1994), McDowell argues that fitting norms into the world runs up against a systematic *impasse*, in the form of a false theoretical dichotomy. On the one hand, we find ourselves confronted with a 'bald naturalism', which construes nature as the 'realm of law', i.e. of deterministic regularities, which are inhospitable to normativity (or to what McDowell sometimes calls 'meaning').[20] But if nature is inhospitable to practical – as opposed to statistical – norms, it must also fail to be a 'space of reasons', for it is precisely such norms that supply us with reasons for action. And this recalcitrance to practical normativity and the rationality it subtends forces us to look elsewhere, beyond nature, for these vital sources of meaning. On the other hand, therefore, we are propelled towards a 'supernatural' realm,[21] the only realm, supposedly, which can accommodate the sui generis, non-naturalisable reasons that practical reasons have turned out to be. This purported repository of the normative is tantamount, however, to what

McDowell labels 'rampant platonism', since it involves 'picturing the space of reasons as an autonomous structure ... constituted independently of anything specifically human, since what is specifically human is surely natural'.[22] Rampant platonism is, in effect, an admission of defeat: it places normativity in a realm that is ineluctably alien to the human, both metaphysically and epistemically. It follows that we must revisit the theoretical dichotomy that gave rise to it.

In order to escape the dilemma between a wholly 'disenchanted', norm-free nature and an inaccessible 'platonic' realm, McDowell counsels that we return to Aristotle's conception of practical wisdom. This sober, eminently non-'occult' alternative denies the 'ideological' and anxiety-ridden premise that, in order to be secure, ethical reasoning must find 'external validation' in either the empirically verifiable or the metaphysically transcendent.[23] Instead, Aristotle provides access to the space of reasons through the common-or-garden method of moral habituation, or what McDowell calls a 'decent upbringing'.[24] It is this, he avers, that opens 'our eyes ... to the very existence of this tract of the space of reasons'.[25] Far from resting on an irrefragable foundation of natural facts, or of metaphysical axioms, a decent upbringing modestly imparts a 'second nature', by forming in us an array of emotional and intellectual dispositions that constitute our ethical character.[26] The content of that character is our participation in practical wisdom, and can thus change as the latter proceeds, piecemeal, or in 'Neurathian' fashion, to deliberate and critically reflect on its own deliverances.[27] True, the realm of 'first nature', i.e. the realm of law, is never irrelevant to second nature, since the latter 'could not float free of potentialities that belong to a normal human organism'.[28] But McDowell emphasises that we cannot 'reconstruct the idea of genuine ethical demands on us from materials that are naturalistic in that sense'.[29] Such demands are relatively autonomous or self-standing, not pointing outside the sphere of ethical thought and action itself.

McDowell labels this naturalism of second nature 'naturalised platonism' (McDowell 1994: 91–2). It is platonist because it affords the structure of the space of reasons a 'sort of autonomy' – those reasons are not visible, as it were, 'independently of having that structure in view' (McDowell 1994: 92) – but it is also naturalised, because what makes them visible is precisely something natural, viz. human upbringing. McDowell hopes, in this way, to avoid both the 'spookiness' of rampant platonism, and the supposedly delusive project of deriving norms from first nature. It is questionable, however, whether this *via media* can succeed as outlined. For when it is asked how, exactly, the space of reasons is constituted, or how, more pertinently, it is substantively (rather than merely nominally) 'natural', answers appear either unforthcoming or vague. On the issue of constitution, McDowell claims that any demand for an answer can legitimately be met with 'something like a shrug of the shoulders'.[30] Such demands presuppose, he implies, that the space of reasons is structured like empirical, first nature – i.e. it is simply open to view – or like a rampantly platonic realm. But, *ex hypothesi*, it is not. The trouble with this response, however, is that it does not sit well with McDowell's confident assertion that 'The ethical is a domain of rational requirements, which are there in any case, whether or not we are responsive to them'.[31] If this is genuinely so, are we not owed more by way of metaphysical texture and detail, in order to elucidate this domain? Instead, we are offered metaphors of 'space' and 'visibility', along with Wittgensteinian aspersions on the need for 'constructive philosophy'.[32] One might be forgiven for thinking this leaves naturalised or 'relaxed' platonism only marginally less 'spooky' than its rampantly platonic cousin.[33]

An immediate objection to this line of criticism is that naturalised platonism is robust in virtue of its naturalistic vehicle, viz. 'decent upbringing', which ensures that second nature is a thoroughly unmysterious phenomenon. It does not depend, after all, on anything supernatural. But while this may, *pro tanto*, be a strength, it is a relatively formal one, since it does nothing to unpack the authentically Aristotelian idea that second nature is a realisation or actualisation of first nature.[34] Indeed, McDowell would seem to have blocked this metaphysical route, from the start, by his assumption that first nature is merely the 'realm of law', as opposed to the locus of natural potentiality. As J. M. Bernstein puts things, McDowell effectively affirms the Kantian diremption between a deterministic nature and an abstract 'I', whose 'spontaneity' is confined to discerning and responding to an equally abstract 'space of reasons'.[35] But this is very far from the Aristotelian idea that such spontaneity is guided properly by norms which are inherent in nature. Bereft of this metaphysical framework, McDowell's first and second natures are fundamentally estranged, the latter being 'natural' in only a highly etiolated sense.[36] There thus appears nothing to prevent second nature from being the site of various different and conflicting upbringings, making any appeal to it an entry point for cultural relativism.[37] For once first nature ceases to be teleological in structure, there seem no *bona fide* limits on the content of second nature.[38]

THE NATURALISM OF EXTERNAL ENDS

The core lesson of the naturalism of second nature is, I suggest, that a genuine natural law ethics must supply both a convincing metaphysical account of the normativity of nature, and norms of nature that are both plausible and determinate. Rosalind Hursthouse claims to supply both in what I will call her 'naturalism of external ends'. For Hursthouse, all animals are ordered to four distinct ends, each species realising these ends in its own, characteristic way.[39] To the degree that an animal (human or non-human) realises them, to that degree it will not only count as a good specimen of its type, it will also flourish. The first end, Hursthouse maintains, is 'individual survival through the characteristic life span of [the species in question]'; the second is 'continuance of the species';[40] the third is 'characteristic freedom from pain and characteristic pleasure or enjoyment';[41] and the fourth is 'the good functioning of the social group'.[42] Many questions have been and could be raised about these four ends. Let me begin by canvassing a first, foundational issue they raise, then move on to what I think are less tractable problems.

Several philosophers have questioned why anyone should be motivated to attain the four ends Hursthouse outlines. Micah Lott, for instance, who labels this the 'authority-of-nature challenge', writes: 'if moral goodness is goodness as fixed by our nature, then morality's requirements seem to be normative only if our nature has authority over us ... The core idea behind the challenge is that rationality opens up a gap between whatever is naturally good, or normal, for humans as a species of living things, and whatever is normative for us, in the sense of having a claim upon our reason'.[43] This challenge has *prima facie* plausibility, since it is always possible, in the abstract, to step back from a proposed natural end and ask: 'but is this a worthwhile way for me to live?'[44] In practice, however, and in face of the ends Hursthouse actually proposes, such detachment looks little more than notional. After all, if someone were seriously to propose individual and species extinction, along with both pain and social dysfunction as rationally authoritative ends, we would have good reason to question their practical rationality. As Lott comments, while *some* natural ends may be candidates for rational rejection, 'ethical thinking – i.e., practical reasoning about what is good to do and to be – cannot proceed if we attempt to "step back" from everything that our human nature inclines us to recognize as good'.[45]

If we are fair to Hursthouse, then, we should grant that her four ends are neither implausible nor indeterminate, and therefore that they carry sufficient rational authority. The difficulties lie, I think, elsewhere. To begin with, how are Hursthouse's four ends to be weighed against each other, and are they always mutually consistent? In response to this, she concedes that 'The ends in relation to which [living things] are evaluated can conflict, and when they do, the truth or falsity of the overall summing-up judgement is not always clearly determined'.[46] But often, she adjures, there is a clear determination. As an example, she cites birds who fail to distract predators from their nests: while this safeguards their individual survival and ensures their freedom from pain, such birds are nonetheless defective specimens, since they fail to promote the continuance of their species. And this holistic judgement appears, I take it, adequate to the case. One wonders, nevertheless, how, exactly, Hursthouse's four ends can yield adequate guidance in the far more complex and contested realm of human action. As Scott Woodcock trenchantly remarks, 'the four ends specified ... set extremely broad limitations on the content of virtuous action. Yes, they will prohibit humans from extinguishing their own agency, extinguishing themselves as a species, and failing to promote pleasure, individual survival and group functioning in some way or another. But the range of ways in which these ends can be pursued is vast'.[47] If this criticism is well-founded, as it seems to be, it follows that – even if Hursthouse's four ends are cogent and sufficiently determinate *per se* – their implications for practical deliberation and judgement are markedly indeterminate.[48]

While such indeterminacy is a problem for Hursthouse, the more serious problem her theory faces is that of proposing the wrong *kind* of practical ends in the first place. For even if her four ends are, stated as such, plausibly natural and hence motivating, it does not follow that they are suited to enter into everyday contexts of practical deliberation. And this because, as Jennifer Frey puts it, they appear 'too external to human practical self-consciousness'.[49] How so? Their externality consists in the fact that only rarely do individual or species survival, pleasure or social functionality enter into practical deliberation directly and explicitly. Usually, and by Hursthouse's own lights, the ends we adopt fall under various virtue-descriptions ('courageous', 'just', 'generous' etc.), or at least under some good-making description ('deserved', 'answering a need', 'timely' etc.) But if so, it follows that the ends Hursthouse specifies will be external to the 'first personal, practical point of view' of the agent.[50] Indeed, the actual ends people set themselves will, if Hursthouse's schema is upheld, become essentially instrumental – instrumental, that is, to the four ends she posits. Acting justly, for instance, will become instrumental to preserving the human species, or to ensuring the well-functioning of a particular group. And there is something deeply counterintuitive about this form of motivation: such action, by instrumentalising justice, is no longer just. As Hacker-Wright contends, 'being just is not instrumental to achieving some good. Being just is a constitutive element of the human good'.[51]

So the challenge Hursthouse's theory faces is clear: her four-fold teleology of action threatens not only to instrumentalise virtue, but also to legitimise vice, since if injustice (say) could achieve individual or species survival, why not be unjust?[52] In response to this, Hursthouse has claimed that hers is not a foundational so much as a 'hermeneutical' project, in which we are 'not pretending to derive ethical evaluations of human beings from an ethically neutral human biology, but are already thinking about human beings in an ethically structured way'.[53] The trouble with this defence, however, is that not only are her four ends more than redolent of an 'ethically neutral biology',[54] they thereby leave the source of the 'ethical structure' she adverts to mysterious. At the very least, one is left wondering how the ethical norms she cites are norms of *nature* – rather than mere imports from an extant roster of the moral virtues. In the final analysis, by casting her four ends as a 'rational justification' of the virtues, Hursthouse has strayed too far from ordinary 'motivating reasons', and in so doing has embraced a natural teleology that is systematically external to our practical self-conception.[55] The task for any genuine natural law ethics will hence be to bring such reasons and such justification back together, and to show how both are thoroughly and discernibly grounded in nature.

THE NATURALISM OF LIFE FORMS

We have seen, then, that both the naturalism of second nature and the naturalism of external ends effect a fundamental dissociation: that between human nature on the one hand, and the ethical norms which govern it on the other. In McDowell's case, first nature is dissociated from second nature, while in Hursthouse's case, her four ends are dissociated from the virtues. True, the dissociation in either case is structurally different: in the former, it is metaphysical, since criteria for a decent upbringing do not flow clearly from the 'realm of law'; in the latter, it is moral psychological, since the four ends cannot guide the practical consciousness of the virtuous agent. But in both cases, we see dissociation where there should be deep continuity and intelligible interrelation. Does Michael Thompson's theory, which I shall call the 'naturalism of life forms', fare better?[56] This question is made difficult by the fact that his theory is complex, dense and finds expression in several publications. I will concentrate on his 2004 paper, 'Apprehending Human Form', which encapsulates the naturalism of life forms efficiently and elegantly, without undue sacrifice of detail.[57]

Thompson addresses two core questions: first, what is it to represent something as living?; and second, how do we assess living things as either good or defective instances of their kind? It is axiomatic for him that humans, as a sort of living thing, or particular 'life form', fall under the same logical and judgemental rubrics as other life forms. In order to unpack the representation of human life, Thompson distinguishes five types of judgement (labelled A to E), the most salient of which is type B. B-type judgements, which he refers to as 'natural historical judgements', take the following canonical form: 'S's are/have/do F', where S is a life form and F picks out a natural property or function.[58] For instance, 'sheep are timid', 'domestic cats have four legs' and 'yellow finches breed in spring' (respectively). Such judgements, Thompson contends, are logically unique. They are expressed atemporally, even though they often refer to activities or features that unfold over time, or take place at specific times. Although they look like Fregean universal generalisations, they are not falsified by counter-instances. For example, if a particular cat loses a leg, or a flock of yellow finches fail to breed one spring, the natural historical judgements that apply to them remain true. At the same time, the kind of generality such judgements embody is neither statistical nor *ceteris paribus* in form.[59] For even if whole populations of cats, for instance, failed to be quadrupedal, owing to an environmental disaster, the natural historical judgement above would still hold of them. And any *ceteris paribus* judgement about a species and its behaviour presupposes – rather than makes intelligible – the representation of life Thompson outlines.[60]

What is the purchase of all this? At the heart of Thompson's analysis is the natural historical judgement, and at the heart of this lies what he calls the 'Aristotelian categorical', viz. the kind of sentence that registers the kind of generality I have just adumbrated.[61] It is the Aristotelian categorical, in turn, which is pivotal to Thompson's normative critique. For once we know that (say) jellyfish have fifteen tentacles, we can infer that this particular jellyfish, which has only nine, is defective. Thompson calls such judgements ones of 'natural goodness and badness', which in their general form he calls judgements of type E, or judgements of 'natural standard': 'S's are defective/sound in a certain respect if they are/have/do G'.[62] Crucially, Thompson argues that type E judgements are not confined to plants and non-human animals, but apply also to humans – for they, too, partake of a life form that displays 'natural normativity' or 'natural goodness'.[63] The difference is that, in their case, such normativity reflects the peculiarities of their life form, which incorporates not merely biological, but also rational functioning. As Thompson puts matters, '[f]or a normative naturalist our fundamental practical evaluative knowledge is ... substantive knowledge of what makes for a good will and a good practical reason in a specifically *human being*'.[64] In illustration of this, he cites the practice of promise-keeping, which manifests the virtue of 'fidelity': these are paradigmatic, he claims, of a well-functioning practical reason, and therefore of human natural goodness.[65]

Perhaps the most common objection to the naturalism of life forms is that it ventures into natural scientific territory – viz. the proper functioning of different species – without heeding natural scientific method. According to Joseph Millum, for instance, there is no reason to think that natural goodness is tantamount to moral goodness, in the way Thompson's example of promise-keeping suggests.[66] For if one abides by the post-Darwinian, evolutionary conception of nature and 'proper function', there is no reason to think that humans are adapted to be virtuous. Quite the contrary: as Millum presses, 'insofar as we consider moral traits as adaptations, the optimally functioning human will be neither perfectly virtuous nor perfectly vicious, but lie somewhere along a continuum between the two'.[67] Alasdair MacIntyre reaches a similar conclusion, arguing that a society could tolerate, and even benefit from, a small class of promise-breaking free-riders, since 'their existence might have the important function of making other members of their society and species more vigilant in sustaining the practices necessary for the society's and the species' survival and functioning'.[68] And Woodcock argues, more boldly, that 'certain kinds of immoral behaviour are representative of the human life cycle'.[69] Any view to the contrary, he asserts, rests on an 'idealized conception of reason', which 'selectively puts forward the traits of our species that are normatively appealing'.[70] Indeed, the only way to avoid this conclusion, he maintains, is to endorse 'Kantianism, or some variant thereof, rather than a form of neo-Aristotelianism grounded in the natural facts of our species'.[71]

This critique, though confidently conveyed, is question-begging and essentially off-target. For it depends on what Lott calls the 'empirical science assumption',[72] namely the view that the natural and social sciences are the best guide to how life forms, and more particularly the human life form, function well. But this is precisely what is in contention. For the Aristotelian naturalist, as opposed to the scientific naturalist, proper function is not an historical notion, which explains the inclusive fitness and hence survival *tout court* of particular species. Rather, it is a comparatively synchronic notion, which appeals to patterns of behaviour and response that prescind from the evolutionary development that gave rise to them. As Peter Woodford maintains, Thompson's 'vital description of biological entities ... must antecede any question of origins ... because it tells us what it is that we are explaining in the first place ... In this way, teleological language is decoupled from evolutionary history'.[73] Far from being a statistical or inductive generalisation from individual observations,[74] therefore, Thompson's Aristotelian categorical is a relatively autonomous way of characterising how a life form flourishes. It is its sui generis character, indeed, which marks it out as distinct from the canons of both scientific naturalism on the one hand, and Kantian non-naturalism on the other.[75]

While this defence is robust, so far as it goes, a key vulnerability in the naturalism of life forms remains – viz. its positive method. For although Thompson castigates the sociobiologists' 'coarse empiricism',[76] it is one thing to find fault with their method, and another to arrive at an alternative that is both perspicuous and persuasive. On this score, I submit, the Thompsonian project has work to do. For not only does Thompson deny that his concept of life form satisfies the strictures of empiricism, he goes so far as to describe it as a 'logical or quasi-logical notion', indeed one that is a priori.[77] As he puts things, 'The concept *human* is a pure concept of the understanding devoid of even the least empirical accretion'.[78] But this strongly Kantian construal extrudes life forms from anything recognisable as naturalistic in an Aristotelian sense.[79] And given this, one wants to ask: how is the route from life forms to judgements of natural goodness or badness actually travelled? Thompsonians like Hacker-Wright appeal, at this juncture, to what they call 'internal observations' or 'reasoned self-constitution' as the source of such judgements.[80] But one wonders whether such terminology serves more to insulate Thompson's method from scrutiny than to unpack it. And this worry is exacerbated by the fact that his representations of non-human life forms are generally richer and more detailed than those of the human life form, where the only example of natural goodness he elaborates is promise-keeping. This paucity of 'results' may, admittedly, be explained by the relative youth of the Thompsonian research programme, rather than its methodological sterility. But even if more results are forthcoming, it is a real question whether they stem from a method that is genuinely and verifiably naturalistic.[81]

THE NATURALISM OF BASIC GOODS

I have argued, then, that notwithstanding the complexity and sophistication of the naturalism of life forms, it harbours a dissociation of its own, namely that between life forms on the one hand, and the normativity they display on the other. The dissociation in this case is epistemic, owing to the a prioricity of life forms. This serves as an instructive segue to the fourth and final contemporary form of natural law ethics, which I shall call the 'naturalism of basic goods'. Known generally as 'the new natural law theory', it is rare in being the joint product of several scholars from distinct disciplines.[82] It has received manifold elaboration over the years, and as a result has taken on slightly different forms.[83] I will focus on John Finnis' version of the theory, which by common consent is the standard or orthodox form of it.[84]

At the heart of the naturalism of basic goods is the idea that human welfare or well-being is conditioned by a set of seven 'pre-moral' goods: life; knowledge; play; aesthetic experience; sociability or friendship; religion; and practical reasonableness.[85] These are 'pre-moral' in the sense that they do not determine moral choice in and of themselves. Specifically moral choice is mediated by practically rational norms that prevent a merely emotional or otherwise disordered *bricolage* of goods. Practically rational norms include the principle that evil must not be done that good may come (the 'Pauline principle'); that there must be no intentional choice to destroy any of the basic goods; and that such goods should contribute to a coherent plan of life.[86] Practically rational choice further incorporates the recognition that the basic goods are incommensurable, there being no common scale or measure by which they can be summed or aggregated.[87] It does not follow, however, that the basic goods cannot be compared against each other at all. Such comparison is presupposed, indeed, by the practically rational requirement that such goods form part of a coherent plan of life, while both maintaining fairness towards others and upholding the common good. It is just that there is no antecedent or absolute decision-procedure that can determine what that common good amounts to.[88] Instead, practically rational choice is guided essentially by the life-plan of the particular agent concerned.[89]

Given this broad outline, how exactly are the goods it proposes *natural*? This question is of seminal importance for Finnis, since from his theory's inception he has been concerned to resist what he calls 'the illicit inference from facts to norms'.[90] For him, facts about human nature, including what Aquinas terms our natural 'inclinations', are properly 'speculative' or 'theoretical' truths, which do not entail any truths in the practical or moral order. To affirm otherwise would be, in effect, to commit the 'naturalistic fallacy'. So what is the alternative? The alternative, Finnis holds, is to appeal not to nature, but to the practical order *per se*, and hence to the basic goods which structure that order. For it is these that, on inspection, recommend themselves to our practical intelligence directly and non-inferentially. As Finnis contends, 'the first principles of natural law ... are *per se nota* (self-evident) and indemonstrable. They are not inferred from speculative principles. They are not inferred from facts ... They are not inferred or derived from anything'.[91] This strong claim is not only intended to save his theory from fallacy, it also has the warrant, Finnis alleges, of Aquinas: 'for Aquinas', he maintains, 'The *underived* first principles of practical reasonableness ... make no reference at all to human nature, but only to human good ... the "natural" is, from the point of view of his ethics, a speculative appendage added by way of metaphysical reflection, *not* a counter with which to advance either to or from the practical *prima principia per se nota*'.[92]

This meta-ethical *démarche* – to the effect that we know human nature from the basic goods, rather than vice versa[93] – has excited numerous responses, which among traditional Thomistic natural lawyers have been universally critical.[94] For our purposes, two objections stand out. First, the naturalism of basic goods is not true to Aquinas, since for Aquinas nature is teleological and thus inextricably normative or good-directed. Given this, no Humean wedge can be driven between fact and value, and the naturalistic fallacy cannot gain a foothold. Secondly, New Natural Law is only tenuously naturalistic. For by isolating the basic goods in the practical order, and hence severing them from any pertinent relation to the metaphysics of nature, Finnis licenses a doctrine of self-evidence or underivability which renders those goods inexplicable as the goods they are. Indeed, the doctrine of indemonstrable or *per se nota* basic goods entails an epistemic dissociation between the theoretical and practical orders so radical as to make that of the naturalism of life forms pale by comparison. We are left, in fine, with an a prioricity about value that is both intellectually unsatisfying (even arid) and practically deeply unresponsive to our moral psychological needs.[95] Far from being a species of naturalism, therefore, the 'naturalism of basic goods' is – despite its thinly textured Thomistic framework – closer to a species of Kantianism.[96]

I want to put the historical issue of truth to Aquinas on one side, along with the philosophical issue of whether Aquinas manages to dissolve the naturalistic fallacy. Instead, I want to focus on the criticism that Finnis' rejection of 'derivationism' for the basic goods leaves these without an adequate mooring in human nature.[97] The case here is more intricate than it seems. To begin with, the claim of self-evidence and indemonstrability does not entail that the basic goods admit of no support whatever. As Finnis puts things, citing Aquinas, there can be '"induction" of indemonstrable first principles of practical reason (i.e. of natural law) by insight working on felt inclinations and a knowledge of possibilities'.[98] This 'induction' does not amount to entailment, of course, but it constitutes a form of support nonetheless. Finnis further allows that 'anthropological and psychological studies' constitute 'an assemblage of reminders of the range of possibly worthwhile activities and orientations open to one'.[99] Indeed, if our nature were different, so would those activities and orientations be.[100] And this co-variance between norms and nature is suggested also elsewhere. Finnis holds, for instance, that one needs 'theoretical knowledge about one's own powers ... to know what one might choose to do';[101] the 'possibility of human fulfilment', he writes, 'presupposes ... the given reality of human nature – with its capacities and inclinations ... what still can be presupposes what already is; in particular, what one naturally is grounds all that one is to be'.[102]

It appears, then, that Finnis accepts what Mark Murphy calls a 'weak grounding' of human norms in human nature.[103] The former are not derived from the latter deductively, but the latter acts, nevertheless, as the background against which the former make sense.[104] And this assorts with Finnis' view that, although *epistemically* our grasp of what is good for us does not depend on knowledge of human nature – for such dependence would contravene his anti-derivationism – *ontologically* what is good for us does depend on our nature.[105] In this way, the naturalism of basic goods may yet be rescued as a genuine form of naturalism: if, that is, this 'weak' form of grounding is sufficient. At the same time, however, it should be admitted that not all new natural lawyers are open even to weak grounding. Christopher Tollefsen, for example, argues that 'the goods known in the third [practical or moral] order are fulfillments of human nature *in that order*, and not in the first [natural] order'.[106] And this on the grounds that 'our biological species life does not ... seem to possess any straightforward normativity for us'.[107] In other words, the basic goods cannot be fulfilments of human nature as such, because the latter is not intrinsically teleological; it is merely a concatenation of drives and morally disparate potentialities.[108] Now evidently, what is at stake here runs deep, and touches on the systematic disagreement between traditional and new natural lawyers on whether or not human nature is intrinsically teleological. But safe to say: if Tollefsen is right, and the basic goods are, at root, grounded not in the natural order, but only in a hypostasised moral order, then the door Finnis has opened to a *bona fide* naturalism of basic goods will be firmly shut.

CONCLUSION

In sum, I have argued that, as we approach the first quarter of the twenty-first century, the prospects for natural law ethics are encouraging – perhaps more so than at any time since the scientific revolution. This is due not only to developments congenial to Aristotelianism in both meta-ethics and metaphysics, but also to the various forms of Neo-Aristotelian ethical naturalism elaborated over recent decades. Among these, I have singled out the naturalism of second nature, the naturalism of external ends, the naturalism of life forms and the naturalism of basic goods. Each is a locus of fine-grained investigation into the conditions any theory must meet in order to count as a viable and robust natural law ethics.

At the same time, I have highlighted areas where work remains to be done. In particular, I have drawn attention to a systematic vulnerability in the ethical theories outlined above. That is, the dissociation they embody between nature on the one hand, and the norms it instantiates on the other: whether that dissociation is metaphysical, moral psychological or epistemic. Granted, none of these theories is irreparable, whether by internal adjustment, development or even combination with elements of another theory. But the field is open for new theories to do better.[109] This may be achieved by more explicit and ambitious engagement with the relevant meta-ethical and metaphysical literature, which, so far, has developed in relative isolation from positive normative theory. It may be achieved, alternatively, by re-engagement with older philosophical approaches, such as Thomism, this time in detailed and fruitful dialogue with twentieth- and twenty-first-century analytic (and other) sources.[110] However it occurs, the means are in place, and the prospects favourable – indeed, there is everything to play for.

NOTES

1. Aquinas, *Summa Theologiae* I-II 90.4.
2. Hursthouse 1999: 211.
3. See Chapter 5 of this volume.
4. See Finnis 2011a: 89–90. Finnis defines 'religion' very widely, as a relation to or harmony with the 'origins of cosmic order'. He seems open to the possibility that (contra traditional theism) these origins do not transcend that order.
5. See e.g. Goyette et al. 2004; Porter 2005; Brock 2005, 2011; Jensen 2015.
6. Jennifer Frey raises this issue in Section V of Chapter 5 of this volume. Jacques Maritain, for one, maintains that natural moral law cannot be 'secularised' (see Maritain 2001).
7. Indeed, I will treat only one natural law theory – viz. 'new natural law' – that has something to say about theology. But what it has to say is not foundational for the theory itself, and certainly never appeals to revelation. Though it might be thought that natural law ethics is necessarily wholly independent of revelation, this is not universally accepted. See, for instance, Matthew Levering's *Biblical Natural Law* (Levering 2008).
8. See Moore 1993.
9. See Putnam 2004a; Thomson 2008. Kirchin 2013 contains recent papers on thick concepts. See also Haldane 2009 and the wide-ranging collection *Facts and Values: The Ethics and Metaphysics of Normativity* (Marchetti and Marchetti 2017).
10. See Putnam 2004b.
11. For a useful summary of Thomson's argument, see Section III of Chapter 5 of this volume.
12. Chappell 2017: 714.
13. For a detailed account of this revolution in metaphysics, see Chapter 14 of this volume.
14. See Oderberg 2007.
15. For Oderberg on natural powers, finality and intentionality, see Oderberg 2017. For his application of Aristotelian metaphysics to natural law ethics, see Oderberg 2010. For his natural law ethics as such, see Oderberg 2004.

16 For a capacious collection, treating both philosophy of physics and of the life sciences, see Simpson et al. 2018.
17 See Chapter 5 of this volume.
18 See esp. Thompson 2008; Foot 2001.
19 There is, admittedly, some overlap between these. Rosalind Hursthouse, for instance, incorporates elements of McDowell's 'naturalism of second nature' and Thompson's 'naturalism of life forms' in her 'naturalism of external ends'. It remains the case, however, that her theory is distinguished by a commitment to what I call 'external ends'. So the overlap in question does not undermine the four (somewhat 'ideal') types I explore below.
20 See e.g. McDowell 1994: 77.
21 See e.g. McDowell 1994: 78.
22 McDowell 1994: 77.
23 McDowell denies that 'our capacity to respond to reasons look[s] like an occult power, something extra to our being the kind of animals we are' (McDowell 1994: 83). For the contrast between the space of reasons and the realm of law as 'ideological', see McDowell 1994: 78. McDowell refers to 'a kind of anxiety about the status of reasons' at McDowell 1994: 79, and he talks of 'the fantasy of an external validation' at McDowell 1994: 82.
24 See McDowell 1994: 82. Elsewhere, he uses the German term *Bildung*, i.e. moral-cum-cultural formation.
25 McDowell 1994: 82.
26 McDowell first uses the term 'second nature' at McDowell 1994: 84.
27 See McDowell 1994 81.
28 McDowell 1994: 84.
29 McDowell 1994: 81.
30 McDowell 1994: 178.
31 McDowell 1994: 82.
32 See McDowell 1994: 95.
33. For further criticism along the same lines, see Larmore 2002.
34. Cf. De Anna 2018: 316–17.
35. See Bernstein 2002: 229, 231.
36. As Bernstein remarks, 'If the space of reasons is as *sui generis* and autonomous as McDowell presents it, is calling it "second nature" any help in understanding it as *natural*? How are the facts of our animality meant to be present in our habitation of the space of reasons?' (Bernstein 2002: 223).
37. For this critique, see Toner 2008: esp. 227–8, 244, 248. McDowell denies that his conception of second nature means that the space of reasons is 'communitarian' or 'social pragmatist' in form (McDowell 1994: 92–3). But it is difficult to see how his positive account precludes this outcome.

38. For attempts to bridge the metaphysical gap between first and second nature, see Hacker-Wright 2009a; Liu 2017, 2018b.
39. See Hursthouse 1999: chapter 9, esp. 198–202.
40. Hursthouse 1999: 198.
41. Hursthouse 1999: 199.
42. Hursthouse 1999: 201.
43. Lott 2014: 762n4. Cf. McDowell 1998a; MacIntyre 2002: 624; Copp and Sobel 2004; Hacker-Wright 2012: § 4; De Anna 2018: 315–16, 320–21.
44. Fitzpatrick 2008: 172.
45. Lott 2017: § 4. The original passage is in German.
46. Hursthouse 1999: 204.
47. Woodcock 2015: 31.
48. This is so a fortiori if – contra Hursthouse's view that virtues always benefit their possessor (see Hursthouse 1999: chapter 8) – the four ends are *not* always thus beneficial. In that case, Hursthouse's teleology of action and her moral psychology come apart, rendering norms for practical deliberation and judgement even more opaque.
49. Frey 2018: 57.
50. Frey 2018: 57.
51. Hacker-Wright 2012: 18.
52. Cf. Lott 2012: esp. 410–18. Following Elijah Millgram, Lott calls this the 'Pollyanna Problem': why, that is, assume that natural ends of the kind Hursthouse stipulates are best achieved only by virtuous means?
53. Hursthouse 2012: 174.
54. NB 'the truth of . . . evaluations of living things does not depend in any way on my wants, interests, or values, nor indeed on "ours". They are, in the most straightforward sense of the term, "objective"; indeed, given that botany, zoology, ethology, etc. are sciences, they are scientific' (Hursthouse 1999: 202). For more on Hursthouse's four ends as unduly assimilating the natural to the natural scientific, see Lott 2012; De Anna 2018: 310–12; Frey 2018: 51–8; Liu 2018a: 269n2.
55. NB 'Secure within the outlook according to which the life I want to lead is the life lived in accordance with honesty, temperance, courage, charity, justice, etc., I am not in any need of motivating reasons, and when I explore the claims of ethical naturalism, such motivating reasons are not what I am looking for. I'm looking to see whether my beliefs about which character traits are the virtues can survive my reflective scrutiny and be given some rational justification' (Hursthouse 1999: 194; cf. 235).
56. A very similar theory is elaborated by Philippa Foot in Foot 2001. I will focus on Thompson's theory for two basic reasons. First, Foot admits her extensive debt to

Thompson at Foot 2001: 15n19, 27, 37, 46. Secondly, her version of the theory is confined to one short book, while Thompson's version has been developed in several papers (see esp. 1995, 2004), and subsequently in a very dense, sophisticated and substantial book (2008). Thompson's naturalism of life forms is, moreover, an ongoing project.

57. For more on Thompson's theory, see Section II of Chapter 5 of this volume.
58. See Thompson 2004: 49.
59. See Thompson 2004: 51.
60. See Thompson 2008: 70–71. For example, if I judge that, *ceteris paribus* (other things being equal), the red squirrel buries its nuts in summer, this presupposes knowledge of the life form 'red squirrel', rather than delivering such knowledge.
61. See Thompson 2008: 65.
62. See Thompson 2004: 55. To put things metaphorically, 'a life form is like a language that physical matter can speak' (Thompson 2004: 54): it follows that, if a particular instance of a particular life form is (as it were) partially mute or has a speech disorder, it is defective of its kind.
63. Thompson 2004: 58.
64. Thompson 2004: 60.
65. See Thompson 2008: part III, 'Practical Generality'. By parity of reasoning, promise-breaking is indicative of a defective practical reason and thus of human natural badness.
66. See Millum 2006: 199–200, 213.
67. Millum 2006: 210.
68. MacIntyre 2002: 627.
69. Woodcock 2015: 27.
70. Woodcock 2015: 27, 28.
71. Woodcock 2015: 29.
72. Lott 2012: 416.
73. Woodford 2016: 14.
74. Cf. Hacker-Wright 2009b: 319; Woodford 2016: 12.
75. Cf. Hacker-Wright: 'despite its distance from empirically-oriented ethical naturalism, ... neo-Aristotelian ethical naturalism ... does not merely fold into Kantian non-naturalism' (Hacker-Wright 2012: 23).
76. Thompson 2004: 63.
77. Thompson 2004: 63.
78. Thompson 2004: 69.
79. As Liu remarks, 'On the Aristotelian view ... the specific instantiations of life, or species, are matters of empirical, contingently determined fact ... Without the input of empirical content, it is unclear how an appeal to an a priori concept of

"human being" would ... ground [...] standards for human action and character' (Liu 2018a: 281).

80. Hacker-Wright 2009b: 320.
81. For P. M. S. Hacker, who claims to derive norms governing human nature from a purely conceptual or 'grammatical' investigation, this aspiration towards a naturalistic account does not arise. See Hacker 2010: esp. 8, 10, 30.
82. Germain Grisez was a theologian, John Finnis a jurisprudent and Joseph Boyle a philosopher. It has many adherents, especially among jurisprudents (NB the invaluable collection, *The Cambridge Companion to Natural Law Jurisprudence* (George and Duke 2017)). For more on new natural law theory, see Chapter 4 and the third section of Chapter 7 of this volume.
83. Mark Murphy and Alfonso Gómez-Lobo, for instance, specify basic goods that diverge from Finnis' list. See Murphy 2001: chapter 3 and Gómez-Lobo 2002: chapter 2, respectively.
84. Finnis' 1980 monograph, *Natural Law and Natural Rights*, retains its centrality as an exposition of new natural law theory (see Finnis 2011a). The theory is well summarised in a joint paper, 'Practical Principles, Moral Truth, and Ultimate Ends' (Finnis et al. 1987b). Given limitations of space, my treatment of the theory will have to abstract from many of its aspects.
85. See Finnis 2011a: chapter IV. Many new natural law theorists argued, from the 1990s onwards, that marriage is a distinct basic good. NB marriage is one of the basic goods Aquinas mentions at *Summa Theologiae* I-II 94.2.
86. For further examples and analysis, see Finnis 2011a: chapter V.
87. For criticism of Finnis' commitment to incommensurability between the basic goods, see e.g. Richardson 2004; O'Brien and Koons 2012.
88. From this it is clear that new natural law theory is deeply inimical to utilitarianism. See e.g. Grisez 1978.
89. Assuming this life plan is consistent with what the new natural lawyers call 'integral human fulfilment'. For criticism of this agent-centred approach to moral choice, see e.g. MacIntyre 2000.
90. Finnis 2011a: § II.4. See also § II.5 on Hume's argument that no 'ought' can be derived from an 'is'.
91. Finnis 2011a: 33–4.
92. Finnis 2011a: 36.
93. Tollefsen 2018b: 243–4, 255–6.
94. See esp. McInerny 1982; Hittinger 1987; Weinreb 1987; Lisska 1996; Feser 2009; Oderberg 2010.
95. For a more generous yet fundamentally similar critique, see Haldane 2013.
96. If accurate, this criticism would be isomorphic with Woodcock's criticism of the naturalism of life forms above.

97. The term 'derivationism' is Mark Murphy's. See Murphy 2001: chapter 1, § 1.
98. Finnis 2011a: 77. Cf. Finnis 1981: 268.
99. Finnis 2011a: 81.
100. NB 'Of course, Aquinas would agree that "were man's nature different, so would be his duties"' (Finnis 2011a: 34).
101. Finnis et al. 1987b: 111.
102. Finnis et al. 1987b: 116.
103. See Murphy 2001: 15.
104. Cf. Roger Teichmann's Wittgensteinian view of how human nature acts as the essential background for, and condition of, such 'making sense'. See Teichmann 2011.
105. See Finnis 1987; Finnis 1998: 90–94.
106. Tollefsen 2018b: 245.
107. Tollefsen 2018b: 253.
108. NB 'first order nature contains potentialities and actualities that are not and never will be realized by intelligible basic goods: potentialities clearly rooted in our animal nature to hurt, destroy, dominate, and the like … and potentialities that are simply neutral' (Tollefsen 2018b: 256).
109. MacIntyre gestures towards a naturalism of basic goods which is not encumbered by Finnis' worries over the naturalistic fallacy (see MacIntyre 2016: § 4.11). This could be developed in the directions I suggest below.
110. This is the route travelled and recommended by, for instance, Jensen 2015; Frey 2018; Hacker-Wright 2018.

References

PRIMARY

Albo, J. 1929. *Sefer ha-'Ikkarim (Book of Principles)*. 4 vols. Isaac Husik (ed. and trans.). Philadelphia: Jewish Publication Society.

Althusius, J. 1964. *The Politics of Johannes Althusius*. Frederick S. Carney (trans.). Boston: Beacon Press.

Aquinas, T. 1882. *Summa Theologiae*. Rome: Typographia Polyglotta.

Aquinas, T. 1918. *Summa contra Gentiles*. Rome: Typis Riccardi Garroni.

Aquinas, T. 1920. *Summa Theologica*. Fathers of the English Dominican Province (trans.). London: Burns Oates and Washbourne.

Aquinas, T. 1925. *Questiones Disputatae*. Paris: P. Lethielleux.

Aquinas, T. 1929. *Scriptum super Sententiis Magistri Petri Lombardi*. Paris: P. Lethielleux.

Aquinas, T. 1934. *In Decem Libros Ethicorum Aristotelis ad Nicomachum Expositio*. Turin, Italy: Marietti.

Aquinas, T. 1947. *Summa Theologica*. Fathers of the English Dominican Province (trans.). New York: Benziger Brothers.

Aquinas, T. 1948. *Summa Theologica*. Fathers of the English Dominican Province (trans.). Westminster, MD: Christian Classics.

Aquinas, T. 1962. *Summa Theologiae*. Madrid: Biblioteca de Autores Cristianos.

Aquinas, T. 1963. *Summa Theologiae*. T. Gilby (ed.). London: Blackfriars.

Aquinas, T. 1970. *Quaestiones Disputatae de Veritate*. Rome: Sanctae Sabinae.

Aquinas, T. 1982. *Quaestiones Disputatae de Malo*. Rome: Vrin.

Aquinas, T. 1996. *Quaestiones de Quolibet*. Rome: Éditions du Cerf.

Aquinas, T. 2009. *Treatise on Law*. A. Freddoso (ed.). South Bend, IN: St Augustine's Press.

Aristotle. 1897. *Nicomachean Ethics*. Ingram Bywater (ed.). Oxford: Clarendon Press.

Aristotle. 1941. *The Basic Works of Aristotle*. R. McKeon (ed.). New York: Random House.

Aristotle. 1983. *Politics*. C. Lord (trans.). Chicago: University of Chicago Press.

Aristotle. 1984. *The Complete Works of Aristotle*. Revised Oxford translation. Vol. 2. Jonathan Barnes (ed.), W. D. Ross and J. O. Urmson (trans.). Princeton: Princeton University Press.

Aristotle. 2000. *Nicomachean Ethics*. Roger Crisp (trans. and ed.). Cambridge: Cambridge University Press.

Augustine. 1993. *Confessions*. F. J. Sheed (trans.). Indianapolis, IN: Hackett.

Averröes. 1921. 'Ibn Rushd "On the Harmony of Religion and Philosophy"', in *The Philosophy and Theology of Averroes*, Mohammed Jamil-al-Rahman (trans.). Baroda, India: A. G. Widgery.

Avicenna. 1945. 'A Treatise on Love by Ibn Sina', Emil L. Fackenheim (trans.). *Mediaeval Studies* 7: 208–8.

Beza, T. 1956. *Concerning the Rights of Rulers over their Subjects and the Duties of Subjects toward Their Rulers*. Henri-Louis Gonin (trans.). Cape Town and Pretoria: H.A.U.M.

Calvin, J. 2006 [1960]. *Institutes of the Christian Religion*. John T. McNeill (ed.). Louisville, KY: Westminster John Knox Press.

Cicero, M. T. 1991. *On Duties*. M. T. Griffin and E. M. Atkins (eds.). Cambridge: Cambridge University Press.

Cicero, M. T. 1998. *The Republic and the Laws*. N. Rudd (trans.). Oxford: Oxford University Press.

Cicero, M. T. 1999. *'On the Commonwealth' and 'On the Laws'*. James E. G. Zetzel (ed.). Cambridge: Cambridge University Press.

Cicero, M. T. 2001. *On Moral Ends*. Julia Annas (ed.), Raphael Woolf (trans.). Cambridge: Cambridge University Press.

Cicero, M. T. 2008. *The Nature of the Gods*. P. G. Walsh (trans.). Oxford: Oxford University Press.

Cotton, J. 1647. *The Bloudy Tenent Washed and Made White in the Blood of the Lamb*. London: Matthew Symmons.

Cotton, J. 1663. *A Discourse about Civil Government in a New Plantation Whose Design Is Religion*. Cambridge, UK: Samuel Green and Marmaduke Johnson.

Cumberland, R. 2005 [1672]. *A Treatise of the Laws of Nature*. Jon Parkin (ed.). Indianapolis, IN: Liberty Fund.

Da Costa, U. 1967. *A Specimen of Human Life*. New York: Bergman.

Epictetus. 2014. *Discourses, Fragments, Handbook*. Robin Hard (trans.). Oxford: Oxford University Press.

Grotius, H. 1814. *On the Law of War and Peace*. London: A. C. Campbell.

Grotius, H. 1926 [1631]. *Introduction to the Jurisprudence of Holland*. R. W. Lee (ed.). Oxford: Clarendon Press.

Grotius, H. 2004 [1609]. *The Free Sea*. David Armitage (ed.). Indianapolis, IN: Liberty Fund.

Grotius, H. 2005 [1625]. *The Rights of War and Peace*. 3 vols. Richard Tuck (ed.). Indianapolis, IN: Liberty Fund.

Grotius, H. 2012 [1627]. *The Truth of the Christian Religion*. Maria Rosa Antognazza (ed.). Indianapolis, IN: Liberty Fund.

Hobbes, T. 1998 [1642/1647]. *On the Citizen*. Richard Tuck (ed.). Michael Silverthorne (trans.). Cambridge: Cambridge University Press.

Hobbes, T. 2012 [1651]. *Leviathan*. 3 vols. Noel Malcolm (ed.). Oxford: Clarendon Press.

Hooker, R. 2013. *Of the Laws of Ecclesiastical Polity*. 3 vols. Arthur S. McGrade (ed.). Oxford: Oxford University Press.

Inwood, B. and Gerson, L. P. 2008. *The Stoics Reader: Selected Writings and Testimonia*. Indianapolis, IN: Hackett.

Kant, I. 1785. *The Groundwork of the Metaphysics of Morals*. M. Gregor and C. Korsgaard (eds.). Cambridge: Cambridge University Press.

Leibniz, G. W. 1972 [1706]. 'Opinion on the Principles of Pufendorf', in *Leibniz: Political Writings*, Patrick Riley (ed.), pp. 64–75. Cambridge: Cambridge University Press.

Long, A. A. and Sedley, D. 1987. *The Hellenistic Philosophers*. 2 vols. Cambridge: Cambridge University Press.

Luther, M. 1883. *D. Martin Luthers Werke*. Kritische Gesamtausgabe. Weimar: Hermann Böhlau.
Luther, M. 1957. *Luther's Works*. Helmut Lehman (ed.). Philadelphia: Fortress Press.
Maimonides, M. 1912. *Eight Chapters of Maimonides on Ethics*. Samuel ibn Tibbon and Joseph Isaac Gorfinkle (trans.). New York: Columbia University Press.
Maimonides, M. 1963. *Guide of the Perplexed* [Arabic: *Dalâlat al-hâirîn*; Hebrew: *Moreh Nevukhim*]. 2 vols. Shlomo Pines (trans.). Chicago: University of Chicago Press. (Translated into Hebrew by Michael Schwartz. 2002. Ramat Aviv, Israel: Tel Aviv University Press.)
Maimonides, M. 1972. 'Kings and Wars', in *A Maimonides Reader*, Isadore Twersky (ed.), pp. 215–30. New York: Behrman House.
Melanchthon, P. 2008. *Ethicae Doctrinae Elementa et Enarratio Libri quinti Ethicorum*. Günter Frank (ed.). Stuttgart-Bad Cannstatt: Frommann-Holzboog.
Mendelssohn, M. 1983. *Jerusalem; or, On Religious Power and Judaism*. Allan Arkush (trans.). Hanover, NH: University Press of New England.
Mill, J. S. 1998 [1863]. *Utilitarianism*. Oxford: Oxford University Press.
Molina S. J. 1759 [1593]. *De Iustitia et Iure*. Vol. 2. Cuenca: Coloniae Allobrogum.
Moore, G. E. 1993 [1903]. *Principia Ethica*. Rev. edn. Cambridge: Cambridge University Press.
Moore, G. E. 2005. *Principia Ethica*. New York: Barnes and Noble Books.
Nietzsche, F. 1998 [1889]. *Twilight of the Idols*. Oxford: Oxford University Press.
Plato. 2004. *Republic*. C. D. C. Reeve (trans.). Indianapolis, IN: Hackett.
Pufendorf, S. 1729 [1672]. *Of the Law of Nature and Nations*. Basil Kennett (trans.). London: printed for J. Walthoe et al.
Pufendorf, S. 1991 [1673]. *On the Duty of Man and Citizen According to Natural Law*. James Tully (ed.). Michael Silverthorne (trans.). Cambridge: Cambridge University Press.
Pufendorf, S. 2002 [1695]. *The Divine Feudal Law: or, Covenants with Mankind, Represented*. Simone Zurbuchen (ed.). Indianapolis, IN: Liberty Fund.
Pufendorf, S. 2014. *The Pufendorf Lectures: Annotations from the Teaching of Samuel Pufendorf, 1672–74*. Bo Lindberg (ed.). Stockholm: KVHAA.
Saadiah ben Joseph al-Fayyumi Gaon. 1948. *The Book of Beliefs and Opinions*. Samuel Rosenblatt (trans.). New Haven, CT: Yale University Press.
Seneca, L. A. 2015. *Letters on Ethics to Lucilius*. Margaret Graver and A. A. Long (trans.). Chicago: University of Chicago Press.
Sidgwick, H. 2012 [1874]. *The Methods of Ethics*. Cambridge: Cambridge University Press.
Smith, A. 1981 [1776]. *The Glasgow Edition of the Works and Correspondence of Adam Smith, vol. II, An Inquiry into the Nature and Causes of the Wealth of Nations*. R. R. Campbell and A. S. Skinner (eds.). Indianapolis, IN: Liberty Fund.
Smith, A. 1982 [1759]. The Glasgow Edition of the Works and Correspondence of Adam Smith, *vol. I, The Theory of Moral Sentiments*. D. D. Raphael and A. L. Macfie (eds.). Indianapolis, IN: Liberty Fund.
Smith, A. 1982 [1762–3, 1766]. *The Glasgow Edition of the Works and Correspondence of Adam Smith, vol. V, Lectures on Jurisprudence*. R. L. Meel, D. D. Raphael and P. G. Stein (eds.). Indianapolis, IN: Liberty Fund.

Spinoza, B. 2001. *Theological-Political Treatise*. 2nd edn. Samuel Shirley (trans.). Indianapolis, IN: Hackett.

Spinoza, B. 2016 [1670]. 'Theological-Political Treatise', in *The Collected Works of Spinoza*, vol. II, Edwin Curley (ed.), pp. 65–356. Princeton, NJ: Princeton University Press.

Suárez, F. 2015. 'De Legibus, ac Deo Legislatore', in *Suárez: Selections from Three Works*, Thomas Pink (ed.), pp. 1–752. Indianapolis, IN: Liberty Fund.

Tocqueville, A., de 1972. *Democracy in America*. New York: Alfred A. Knopf.

SECONDARY

Ahmed, R. 2012. *Narratives of Islamic Legal Theory*. Oxford: Oxford University Press.

Al-Ayni, Badr al-Din. 2000. *Al-Binaya Sharh al-Hidaya*. Ayman Ṣāliḥ Sha'bān (ed.). Beirut: Dār al-Kutub al-'Ilmiyya.

Almotahari, M. and Hosein, A. 2015. 'Is Anything Just Plain Good?' *Philosophical Studies* 23: 1485–1508.

Annas, J. 2005. 'Virtue Ethics: What Kind of Naturalism?', in *Virtue Ethics, Old and New*, Stephen M. Gardiner (ed.), pp. 11–29. Ithaca, NY: Cornell University Press.

Anscombe, G. E. M. 1981a. 'Mr Truman's Degree', in *The Collected Philosophical Papers of G.E.M. Anscombe*, vol. III (Ethics, Religion and Politics), pp. 62–71. Oxford: Blackwell.

Anscombe, G. E. M. 1981b. 'The Justice of the Present War Examined', in *The Collected Philosophical Papers of G.E.M. Anscombe*, vol. III (Ethics, Religion and Politics), pp. 72–81. Oxford: Blackwell.

Anscombe, G. E. M. 1981c. 'On Promising and Its Justice, and Whether It Need Be Respected *in Foro Interno*', in *The Collected Philosophical Papers of G.E.M. Anscombe*, vol. III (Ethics, Religion and Politics), pp. 10–21. Oxford: Blackwell.

Anscombe, G. E. M. 2005a. 'Modern Moral Philosophy', in *Human Life, Action, and Ethics: Essays by G.E.M. Anscombe*, Mary Geach and Luke Gormally (eds.), pp. 169–94. Exeter: Imprint Academic.

Anscombe, G. E. M. 2005b. 'Good and Bad Human Action', in *Human Life, Action, and Ethics: Essays by G.E.M. Anscombe*, Mary Geach and Luke Gormally (eds.), pp. 195–206. Exeter: Imprint Academic.

Ashley, B. M. 1994. 'What Is the End of the Human Person? The Vision of God and Integral Human Fulfilment', in *Moral Truth and Moral Tradition: Essays in Honour of Peter Geach and Elizabeth Anscombe*, Luke Gormally (ed.), pp. 69–86. Blackrock: Four Courts Press.

Asmis, E. 2008. 'Cicero on Natural Law and the Laws of the State'. *Classical Antiquity* 27: 1–33.

Auda, J. 2016. *Maqasid al-Shari'ah as Philosophy of Islamic Law: A Systems Approach*. Herndon, VA: IIIT.

Austin, C. 2017. 'Aristotelian Essentialism: Essence in an Age of Evolution'. *Synthese* 194, no. 7: 2539–56.

Ayer, A. J. 2014. *Language, Truth and Logic*. New York: Dover.

Barbeyrac, J. 2003 [1718]. 'The Judgment of an Anonymous Writer', in *Pufendorf: The Whole Duty of Man, According to the Law of Nature*, Ian Hunter and David Saunders (eds.), pp. 266–305. Indianapolis, IN: Liberty Fund.

Barnard, J. 1938 [1734]. 'The Throne Established by Righteousness', in *The Puritans*, Perry Miller and Thomas Johnson (eds.), pp. 270–76. New York: American Book Company.

Barney, S. A. 2010. *The Etymologies of Isidore of Seville*. W. J. Lewis, J. A Beach and O. Berghof (trans.). Cambridge: Cambridge University Press.

Barth, K. 1941. *This Christian Cause: A Letter to Great Britain from Switzerland*. John A. Mackay (ed.). New York: Macmillan.

Barth, K. 1960. *Church Dogmatics*. G. W. Bromiley and T. F. Torrance (eds.). London: T&T Clark.

Barth, K. and Brunner, E. 1946. *Natural Theology*. Peter Fraenkel (trans.). London: Geoffrey Bles.

Batnitzky, L. 2016. 'Leo Strauss', in *The Stanford Encyclopedia of Philosophy*, Edward N. Zalta (ed.). https://plato.stanford.edu/archives/sum2016/entries/strauss-leo.

Benedict XVI. 2018. *Faith and Politics*. San Francisco: Ignatius Press.

Berkman, J. and Mattison, W. C., III. 2014. *Searching for a Universal Ethic*. Grand Rapids, MI: Eerdmans.

Berman, H. J. 2003. *Law and Revolution II: The Impact of the Protestant Reformations on the Western Legal Tradition*. Cambridge, MA: Harvard University Press.

Bernstein, J. M. 2002. 'Re-enchanting Nature', in *Reading McDowell: On Mind and World*, Nicholas H. Smith (ed.), chapter 12. London: Routledge.

Bhaskar, R. 2008. *A Realist Theory of Science*. London: Routledge.

Bhuta, N. 2012. 'Rethinking the Universality of Human Rights: A Comparative Historical Proposal for the Idea of "Common Ground" with Other Moral Traditions', in *Islamic Law and International Human Rights Law: Searching for Common Ground?*, Anver M. Emon, Mark Ellis and Benjamin Glahn (eds.), pp. 123–43. Oxford: Oxford University Press.

Bigongiari, D. 1957. *The Political Ideas of St. Thomas Aquinas*. New York: Hafner.

Bird, A. 2007. *Nature's Metaphysics: Laws and Properties*. Oxford: Clarendon Press.

Boulter, S. 2013. *Metaphysics from a Biological Point of View*. Basingstoke: Palgrave Macmillan.

Bourdieu, P. 1987. '"The Force of Law": Toward a Sociology of the Juridical Field', Richard Terdiman (trans.). *Hastings Law Journal* 38: 814–53.

Bourdieu, P. 1988. *Homo Academicus*. Peter Collier (trans.). Stanford, CA: Stanford University Press.

Boyle, J. 1998. 'The Place of Religion in the Practical Reasoning of Individuals and Groups'. *American Journal of Jurisprudence* 43: 1–24.

Boyle, J. 2002. 'Free Choice, Incomparably Valuable Options, and Incommensurable Categories of Good'. *American Journal of Jurisprudence* 47: 123–41.

Braine, D. 1992. *The Human Person: Animal and Spirit*. London: Duckworth.

Brennan, T. 2005. *The Stoic Life: Emotions, Duties, and Fate*. Oxford: Clarendon Press.

Brewer, T. 2009. *The Retrieval of Ethics*. Oxford: Oxford University Press.

Brock, S. 2005. 'Natural Inclination and the Intelligibility of the Good in Thomistic Natural Law'. *Vera Lex* 6, nos. 1–2: 57–78.

Brock, S. 2011. 'Natural Law, the Understanding of Principles, and Universal Good'. *Nova et Vetera* 9: 671–706.

Brooke, C. 2012. *Philosophic Pride: Stoicism and Political Thought from Lipsius to Rousseau*. Princeton, NJ: Princeton University Press.

Brouwer, R. 2014. *The Stoic Sage: The Early Stoics on Wisdom, Sagehood and Socrates*. Cambridge: Cambridge University Press.

Brugger, C. 2014. *Capital Punishment and Roman Catholic Tradition*. 2nd edn. South Bend, IN: University of Notre Dame Press.

Brüllmann, P. Forthcoming. 'Nature and Psychology in Cicero's *Republic*', in *State and Nature: Essays in Ancient Political Philosophy*, Peter Adamson and Christof Rapp (eds.). Berlin: De Gruyter.

Buchanan, J. and Brennan, G. 1987. 'The Normative Purpose of Economic "Science": Rediscovery of an Eighteenth Century Method', in *Economics: Between Predictive Science and Moral Philosophy*, James Buchanan (ed.), pp. 51–65. College Station: Texas A&M University Press.

Buckle, S. 1991. *Natural Law and the Theory of Property: Grotius to Hume*. Oxford: Clarendon Press.

Budziszewski, J. 2018. 'The Same as to Knowledge', in *Natural Law Today: The Present State of the Perennial Philosophy*, C. Wolfe and S. Brust (eds.), pp. 53–70. Lanham, MD: Lexington Press.

Buller, D. 1999. *Function, Selection, and Design*. Albany: State University of New York Press.

Butterworth, C. 2001. 'Translator's Introduction to the *Decisive Treatise*' in *Decisive Treatise and Epistle Dedicatory* (Averroes), Charles E. Butterworth (trans.), pp. xvii–xxxviii. Provo, UT: Brigham Young University.

Carney, F. S. 1967. 'Outline of a Natural Law Procedure for Christian Ethics'. *Journal of Religion* 47, no. 1: 26–38.

Carney, F. S. 1995. *Introduction to Johannes Althusius, Politica: An Abridged Translation of Politics Methodically Set Forth and Illustrated with Sacred and Profane Examples*. Frederick S. Carney (ed.). Indianapolis, IN: Liberty Fund.

Cartwright, N. 1983. *How the Laws of Physics Lie*. Oxford: Oxford University Press.

Cartwright, N. 1999. *The Dappled World: A Study of the Boundaries of Science*. Cambridge: Cambridge University Press.

Chakrabarty, D. 2000. *Provincializing Europe: Postcolonial Thought and Historical Difference*. Princeton, NJ: Princeton University Press.

Chakravartty, A. 2013. 'Dispositions for Scientific Realism', in *Powers and Capacities in Philosophy: The New Aristotelianism*, R. Groff and J. Greco (eds.), pp. 113–27. London: Routledge.

Chappell, T. 2009. *Ethics and Experience*. London: Acumen.

Chappell, T. 2013. 'There Are No Thin Concepts', in *Thick Concepts*, S. Kirchin (ed.), pp. 182–96. Oxford: Oxford University Press.

Chappell, S. G. 2017. 'The Objectivity of Ordinary Life'. *Ethical Theory and Moral Practice* 20, no. 4: 709–21.

Chroust, A.-H. 1950. 'St Augustine's Philosophical Theory of Law'. *Notre Dame Law Review* 25, no. 2: 285–315.

Copp, D. and Sobel, D. 2004. 'Morality and Virtue: An Assessment of Some Recent Work in Virtue Ethics'. *Ethics* 114: 514–54.

Crowe, M. B. 1951. 'The Natural Law before St Thomas'. *The Irish Ecclesiastical Record* 76: 194–204.

Crowe, M. B. 1956. 'The Term "Synderesis" and the Scholastics'. *Irish Theological Quarterly* 23, nos. 2/3: 151–64 and 228–45.

Crowe, M. B. 1977. *The Changing Profile of the Natural Law*. The Hague: Martinus Nijhoff.

Cunningham, L. S. 2009. *Intractable Disputes about the Natural Law: Alasdair MacIntyre and Critics*. South Bend, IN: University of Notre Dame Press.

Cunningham, S. B. 1967. 'Albertus Magnus on Natural Law'. *Journal of the History of Ideas* XXVIII: 479–502.

D'Entrèves, A. P. 1948. *Aquinas: Selected Political Writings*. Oxford: Basil Blackwell.

Darwall, S. 2012a. 'Grotius at the Creation of Modern Moral Philosophy'. *Archiv für Geschichte der Philosophie* 94, no. 3: 296–325.

Darwall, S. 2012b. 'Pufendorf on Morality, Sociability, and Moral Powers'. *Journal of the History of Philosophy* 50, no. 2: 213–38.

Daston, L. and Stolleis, M. 2008. *Natural Law and Laws of Nature in Early Modern Europe: Jurisprudence, Theology, Moral and Natural Philosophy*. Farnham, UK: Ashgate.

David, J. E. 2010. 'Maimonides, Nature and Natural Law'. *Journal of Law, Philosophy and Culture* 5, no. 1: 67–82.

De Anna, G. 2018. 'Potentiality, Natural Normativity and Practical Reason'. *The Journal of Value Inquiry* 52, no. 3: 307–26.

De Koninck, C. 1943. *De la Primauté du Bien Commun contre les Personnalistes*. Montréal: Fides.

Devitt, M. 2008. 'Resurrecting Biological Essentialism'. *Philosophy of Science* 75: 344–82.

Dewan, L. 1986. 'Jacques Maritain and the Philosophy of Cooperation', in *Altérité Vivre Ensemble Différents: Approches Pluridisciplinaires*, M. Gourges and G. Mailhiot (eds.), pp. 109–17. Montréal: Éditions Bellarmin.

Dewan, L. 2007. 'Natural Law in the First Act of Freedom: Maritain Revisited', in *Wisdom, Law, and Virtue: Essays in Thomistic Ethics*, pp. 221–41. Bronx, NY: Fordham University Press.

Dumsday, T. 2012. 'A New Argument for Intrinsic Biological Essentialism'. *The Philosophical Quarterly* 62: 486–504.

Dupré, J. 1993. *The Disorder of Things: Metaphysical Foundations of the Disunity of Science*. Cambridge, MA: Harvard University Press.

Dupré, J. 2012. *Processes of Life: Essays in the Philosophy of Biology*. Oxford: Oxford University Press.

Dworkin, R. 1977. *Taking Rights Seriously*. Cambridge, MA: Harvard University Press.

Efron, N. J. 2002. 'Nature, Human Nature, and Jewish Nature in Early Modern Europe'. *Science in Context* 15, no. 1: 29–49.

Elder, C. 2004. *Real Natures and Familiar Objects*. Cambridge, MA: MIT Press.

Elder, C. 2008. 'Biological Species Are Natural Kinds'. *Southern Journal of Philosophy* 46: 339–62.

Elder, C. 2011. *Familiar Objects and Their Shadows*. Cambridge: Cambridge University Press.

Ellis, B. 2001. *Scientific Essentialism*. Cambridge: Cambridge University Press.

Ellis, B. 2009. *The Metaphysics of Scientific Realism*. Montreal: McGill-Queen's University Press.

Emon, A. M. 2006. '*Ḥuqūq Allāh* and *Ḥuqūq al-'Ibād*: A Legal Heuristic for a Natural Rights Regime'. *Islamic Law and Society* 13, no. 3: 325–91.

Emon, A. M. 2010. *Islamic Natural Law Theories*. Oxford: Oxford University Press.

Emon, A. M. 2014a. 'Islamic Natural Law Theories', in *Natural Law: A Jewish, Christian and Islamic Trialogue*, Anver M. Emon, Matthew Levering and David Novak (eds.), pp. 144–87. Oxford: Oxford University Press.

Emon, A. M. 2014b. 'On Islam and Islamic Natural Law: A Response to the International Theological Commission's "Look at Natural Law"', in *Searching for a Universal Ethic: Multidisciplinary, Ecumenical, and Interfaith Responses to the Catholic Natural Law Tradition*, John Berkman and William C. Mattison (eds.), pp. 125–35. Grand Rapids, MI: Eerdmans.

Emon, A. M. 2018. 'On Reading Fiqh', in *The Oxford Handbook of Islamic Law*, Anver M. Emon and Rumee Ahmed (eds.), pp. 45–75. Oxford: Oxford University Press.

Feser, E. 2007. *Locke*. Oxford: Oneworld.

Feser, E. 2008. *The Last Superstition: A Refutation of the New Atheism*. South Bend, IN: St Augustine's Press.

Feser, E. 2009. *Aquinas: A Beginner's Guide*. Oxford: Oneworld.

Feser, E. 2013. *Aristotle on Method and Metaphysics*. Basingstoke, UK: Palgrave Macmillan.

Feser, E. 2014a. 'Being, the Good, and the Guise of the Good', in *Neo-Aristotelian Perspectives in Metaphysics*, D. Novotny and E. Novak (eds.), pp. 84–103. London: Routledge.

Feser, E. 2014b. *Scholastic Metaphysics: A Contemporary Introduction*. Heusenstamm: Editiones Scholasticae.

Feser, E. 2019. *Aristotle's Revenge: The Metaphysical Foundations of Physical and Biological Science*. Heusenstamm: Editiones Scholasticae.

Finnis, J. 1980. *Natural Law and Natural Rights*. Oxford: Clarendon Press.

Finnis, J. 1981. 'Natural Law and the "Is"-"Ought" Question: An Invitation to Professor Veatch'. *Catholic Lawyer* 26, no. 4 (Autumn): 266–77.

Finnis, J. 1983. *Fundamentals of Ethics*. Washington, DC: Georgetown University Press.

Finnis, J. 1987. 'Natural Inclinations and Natural Rights: Deriving "Ought" from "Is" according to Aquinas', in *Lex et Libertas: Freedom and Law according to St. Thomas Aquinas*, vol. 30, L. Elders et al. (eds.), pp. 43–55. Rome: Studi Tomistici.

Finnis, J. 1990. 'Allocating Risks and Suffering: Some Hidden Traps', in *The Collected Works of John Finnis, vol. IV, Philosophy of Law*, pp. 337–52. Oxford: Oxford University Press.

Finnis, J. 1992. 'Economics, Justice, and the Value of Life', in *The Collected Works of John Finnis, vol. III, Human Rights and Common Good*, pp. 242–50. Oxford: Oxford University Press.

Finnis, J. 1996. 'Is Natural Law Theory Compatible with Limited Government?', in *Natural Law, Liberalism, and Morality*, R. George (ed.), pp. 1–26. Oxford: Clarendon Press.

Finnis, J. 1997. 'Commensuration and Public Reason', in *Incommensurability, Incomparability, and Practical Reason*, R. Chang (ed.), pp. 215–33. Cambridge, MA: Harvard University Press.

Finnis, J. 1998. *Aquinas: Moral, Political, and Legal Theory*. Oxford: Oxford University Press.

Finnis, J. 2011a. *Natural Law and Natural Rights*. 2nd edn. Oxford: Oxford University Press.

Finnis, J. 2011b. 'Practical Reason's Foundations', in *Collected Essays of John Finnis: Reasons in Action*, pp. 19–40. Oxford: Oxford University Press.

Finnis, J., Grisez, G. and Boyle, J. 1987a. *Nuclear Deterrence, Morality, and Realism*. Oxford: Oxford University Press.

Finnis, J., Grisez, G. and Boyle, J. 1987b. 'Practical Principles, Moral Truth, and Ultimate Ends'. *The American Journal of Jurisprudence* 32, no. 1: 99–151.

Fitzpatrick, W. J. 2000. *Teleology and the Norms of Nature*. New York: Garland.

Fitzpatrick, W. J. 2008. 'Robust Ethical Realism, Non-Naturalism, and Normativity', in *Oxford Studies in Metaethics*, vol. 3, R. Shafer-Landau (ed.), pp. 159–205. Oxford: Oxford University Press.

Fodor, J. and Piattelli-Palmarini, M. 2011. *What Darwin Got Wrong*. Updated edn. New York: Picador.

Foot, P. 1978. 'The Problem of Abortion and the Doctrine of the Double Effect', in *Virtues and Vices*. Oxford: Basil Blackwell.

Foot, P. 2001. *Natural Goodness*. Oxford: Oxford University Press.

Foot, P. 2002. 'Rationality and Virtue', in *Moral Dilemmas*, pp. 159–74. Oxford: Oxford University Press.

Fortin, E. 1982. 'The New Rights Theory and Natural Law'. *The Review of Politics* 44, no. 4: 590–612.

Fox, M. 1990a. 'Maimonides and Aquinas on Natural Law', in *Interpreting Maimonides: Studies in Methodology, Metaphysics, and Moral Philosophy*, pp. 124–51. Chicago: University of Chicago Press.

Fox, M. 1990b. 'Maimonides' Views on the Relations of Law and Morality', in *Interpreting Maimonides: Studies in Methodology, Metaphysics, and Moral Philosophy*, pp. 199–226. Chicago: University of Chicago Press.

Frank, G. 2008. 'Die praktische Philosophie Philipp Melanchthons und die Tradition des frühneuzeitlichen Aristotelismus', in Philipp Melanchthon, *Ethicae Doctrinae Elementa et Enarratio Libri quinti Ethicorum*, Günter Frank (ed.), pp. xix–xlii. Stuttgart-Bad Cannstatt: Frommann-Holzboog.

Freddoso, A. J. (trans.). 2009. *Thomas Aquinas, Treatise on Law: The Complete Text, Summa Theologiae I-II, Questions 90–108*. South Bend, IN: St Augustine's Press.

Frey, C. and Frey, J. A. 2017. 'G.E.M. Anscombe on the Analogical Unity of Intention in Action and Perception'. *Analytic Philosophy* 58, no. 3: 202–47.

Frey, J. A. 2018. 'How to Be an Ethical Naturalist', in *Philippa Foot on Goodness and Virtue*, John Hacker-Wright (ed.), pp. 47–84. Basingstoke, UK: Palgrave Macmillan.

Gagnebet, M. 1948. 'L'Amour Naturel de Dieu chez Saint Thomas et ses Contemporains'. *Revue Thomiste* 48: 394–446.

Gallagher, D. 1999. 'Thomas Aquinas on Self-Love as the Basis for Love of Others'. *Acta Philosophica* 8: 23–44.

Geach, P. 1956. 'Good and Evil'. *Analysis* 17, no. 2: 33–42.

Geach, P. 1977. *The Virtues*. Cambridge: Cambridge University Press.

George, R. 1993. *Making Men Moral: Civil Liberties and Public Morality*. Oxford: Clarendon Press.

George, R. 1999. *In Defense of Natural Law*. Oxford: Oxford University Press.
George, R. P. and Duke, G. 2017. *The Cambridge Companion to Natural Law Jurisprudence*. Cambridge: Cambridge University Press.
Gill, C. 1988. 'Personhood and Personality: The Four-Personae Theory in Cicero, *De Officiis* I'. *Oxford Studies in Ancient Philosophy* 6: 169–99.
Goldish, M. 2010–11. 'Perspectives on Uriel da Costa's "Examination of a Life"'. *Studia Rosenthaliana* 42/43: 1–23.
Gómez-Lobo, A. 2002. *Morality and the Human Goods: An Introduction to Natural Law Ethics*. Washington, DC: Georgetown University Press.
Gottlieb, M. 2011. *Moses Mendelssohn: Writings on Judaism, Christianity and the Bible*. Waltham, MA: Brandeis University Press.
Goyette, J., Latkovic, M. S. and Myers, R. S. 2004. *St. Thomas Aquinas and the Natural Law Tradition: Contemporary Perspectives*. Washington, DC: Catholic University of America Press.
Grabill, S. J. 2006. *Rediscovering the Natural Law in Reformed Theological Ethics*. Grand Rapids, MI: Eerdmans.
Gregg, S. and Harper, I. R. 1999. *Economics and Ethics*. Sydney: CIS.
Griffel, F. 2007. 'The Harmony of Natural Law and Shari'a in Islamist Theology', in *Sharia: Islamic Law in the Contemporary Context*, Abbas Amanat and Frank Griffel (eds.), pp. 38–61. Stanford, CA: Stanford University Press.
Grisez, G. 1965. 'The First Principle of Practical Reason: A Commentary on the *Summa Theologiae*, 1–2, Question 94, Article 2'. *Natural Law Forum* 10: 168–201.
Grisez, G. 1978. 'Against Consequentialism'. *American Journal of Jurisprudence* 23, no. 1: 21–72.
Grisez, G. 1983. *The Way of the Lord Jesus, vol. 1, Christian Moral Principles*. Chicago: Franciscan Herald Press.
Grisez, G. 1987. 'Natural Law and Natural Inclinations: Some Comments and Clarifications'. New Scholasticism 61: 307–20.
Grisez, G. 1993. *The Way of the Lord Jesus, Vol. 2, Living a Christian Life*. Chicago: Franciscan Herald Press.
Grisez, G. 1999. 'Against Consequentialism', in *Proportionalism: For and Against*, Christopher Kaczor (ed.), pp. 239–94. Milwaukee, WI: Marquette University Press.
Grisez, G. 2013. 'Natural Law and the Transcendent Source of Human Fulfillment', in *Reason, Morality, and Law: The Philosophy of John Finnis*, J. Keown and R. George (eds.), pp. 443–58. Oxford: Oxford University Press.
Grisez, G. and Shaw, R. 1988. *Beyond the New Morality: The Responsibilities of Freedom*. South Bend, IN: University of Notre Dame Press
Groff, R. and Greco, J. 2013. *Powers and Capacities in Philosophy: The New Aristotelianism*. London: Routledge.
Gutas, D. 2002. 'The Study of Arabic Philosophy in the Twentieth Century An Essay on the Historiography of Arabic Philosophy'. *British Journal of Middle East Studies* 29, no. 1: 5–25.
Haakonssen, K. 1996. *Natural Law and Moral Philosophy: From Grotius to the Scottish Enlightenment*. Cambridge: Cambridge University Press.
Haakonssen, K. 2002. 'The Moral Conservatism of Natural Rights', in *Natural Law and Civil Sovereignty*, Ian Hunter and David Saunders (eds.), pp. 27–42. New York: Palgrave Macmillan.

Haakonssen, K. 2004. 'Protestant Natural Law Theory: A General Interpretation', in *New Essays on the History of Autonomy*, Natalie Brender and Larry Krasnoff (eds.), pp. 92–109. Cambridge: Cambridge University Press.

Haakonssen, K. and Seidler, M. J. 2016. 'Natural Law: Law, Rights and Duties', in *A Companion to Intellectual History*, Richard Whatmore and Brian Young (eds.), pp. 377–401. Oxford: Wiley-Blackwell.

Haara, H. 2016. 'Pufendorf on Passions and Sociability'. *Journal of the History of Ideas* 77, no. 3: 423–44.

Haara, H. 2018. *Pufendorf's Theory of Sociability: Passions, Habits and Social Order*. Dordrecht: Springer.

Hacker, P. M. S. 2010. *Human Nature: The Categorial Framework*. Oxford: Wiley-Blackwell.

Hacker-Wright, J. 2009a. 'Human Nature, Personhood, and Ethical Naturalism'. *Philosophy* 84, no. 329: 413–27.

Hacker-Wright, J. 2009b. 'What Is Natural about Foot's Ethical Naturalism?' *Ratio* (new series) XXII: 308–21.

Hacker-Wright, J. 2012. 'Ethical Naturalism and the Constitution of Agency'. *The Journal of Value Inquiry* 46, no. 1: 13–23.

Hacker-Wright, J. 2013. 'Human Nature, Virtue, and Rationality', in *Aristotelian Ethics in Contemporary Perspective*, Julia Peters (ed.), pp. 83–96. London: Routledge.

Hacker-Wright, J. 2018. 'Introduction: From Natural Goodness to Morality', in *Philippa Foot on Goodness and Virtue*, pp. 1–23. Basingstoke, UK: Palgrave Macmillan.

Haldane, J. 2009. *Practical Philosophy: Ethics, Society and Culture*. Exeter: Imprint Academic.

Haldane, J. 2013. 'Reasoning about the Human Good, and the Role of the Public Philosopher', in *Reason, Morality, and Law: The Philosophy of John Finnis*, J. Keown and R. P. George (eds.), chapter 3. Oxford: Oxford University Press.

Hall, P. 1994. *Narrative and Natural Law: An Interpretation of Thomist Ethics*. South Bend, IN: University of Notre Dame Press.

Hammer, D. 2014. *Roman Political Thought: From Cicero to Augustine*. Cambridge: Cambridge University Press.

Hare, R. M. 1957. 'Geach: Good and Evil'. *Analysis* 17, no. 5: 103–11.

Hare, R. M. 2013. *The Language of Morals*. New York: Oxford University Press.

Harris, E. 1983. 'Natural Law and Naturalism'. *International Philosophical Quarterly* 23: 115–24.

Hauerwas, S. 1975. 'Natural Law, Tragedy, and Theological Ethics'. *American Journal of Jurisprudence* 20: 1–19.

Hauerwas, S. 2000. *A Better Hope: Resources for a Church Confronting Capitalism, Democracy, and Postmodernity*. Grand Rapids, MI: Brazos Press.

Hauerwas, S. 2013. *Approaching the End: Eschatological Reflections on Church, Politics, and Life*. Grand Rapids, MI: Eerdmans.

Hayden, R. 1990. 'Natural Inclinations and Moral Absolutes: A Mediated Correspondence for Aquinas'. *Proceedings of the American Catholic Philosophical Association* 64: 130–50.

Hayes, C. 2015. *What's Divine about Divine Law? Early Perspectives*. Princeton, NJ: Princeton University Press.

Heil, J. 2003. *From an Ontological Point of View*. Oxford: Clarendon Press.
Helm, P. 2004. *John Calvin's Ideas*. Oxford: Oxford University Press.
Hendry, R. 2006. 'Is There Downwards Causation in Chemistry?', in *Philosophy of Chemistry: Synthesis of a New Discipline*, D. Baird, E. Scerri and L. McIntyre (eds.), pp. 173–89. Dordrecht: Springer.
Hendry, R. 2010. 'Ontological Reduction and Molecular Structure'. *Studies in History and Philosophy of Modern Physics* 41: 183–91.
Hendry, R. 2017. 'Prospects for Strong Emergence in Chemistry', in *Philosophical and Scientific Perspectives on Downward Causation*, M. Paoletti and F. Orilia (eds.), pp. 146–63. London: Routledge.
Herdt, J. 2014. 'Calvin's Legacy for Contemporary Reformed Natural Law'. *Scottish Journal of Theology* 67, no. 4: 414–35.
Hittinger, R. 1987. *A Critique of the New Natural Law Theory*. South Bend, IN: University of Notre Dame Press.
Hittinger, R. 1990. 'Theology and Natural Law'. *Communio: International Catholic Review* 17: 402–31.
Hittinger, R. 1999. 'Veritatis Splendor and the Theology of Natural Law', in *Veritatis Splendor and the Renewal of Moral Theology*, J. A. Di Noia and Romanus Cessario (eds.), pp. 97–128. Chicago: Scepter.
Hittinger, R. 2014. 'Natural Law and Public Discourse: The Legacies of Joseph Ratzinger'. *Loyola University Law Review* 60: 241–69.
Hohfeld, W. N. 1913. 'Some Fundamental Legal Conceptions as Applied in Legal Reasoning'. *Yale Law Journal* 23, no. 1: 16–59.
Holl, K. 1959. *The Cultural Significance of the Reformation*. New York: Meridian Books.
Holl, K. 1979. *The Reconstruction of Morality*. James Luther Adams and Walter F. Bense (eds.). Minneapolis, MN: Augsburg Press.
Holy See. 1992. *Catechism of the Catholic Church*. Vatican City: Libreria Editrice Vaticane.
Hont, I. 2005. *Jealousy of Trade: International Competition and the Nation-State in Historical Perspective*. Cambridge, MA: Harvard University Press.
Horn, C. 2017. 'Die Metaphysische Grundlegung des Rechts (*De Legibus* I)', in *Ciceros Staatsphilosophie: Ein Kooperativer Kommentar zu* De Re Publica *und* De Legibus, Otfried Höffe (ed.), pp. 149–66. Berlin: De Gruyter.
Hourani, G. F. 1985. 'Divine Justice and Human Reason in Mu'tazilite Ethical Theology', in *Ethics in Islam*, Richard G. Hovannisian (ed.), pp. 73–84. Malibu, CA: Undena.
Humphreys, P. 2008. 'How Properties Emerge', in *Emergence: Contemporary Readings in Philosophy and Science*, M. Bedau and P. Humphreys (eds.), pp. 111–26. Cambridge, MA: MIT Press.
Hursthouse, R. 1999. *On Virtue Ethics*. Oxford: Oxford University Press.
Hursthouse, R. 2012. 'Human Nature and Virtue Ethics'. *Royal Institute of Philosophy Supplement* 70: 169–88.
International Theological Commission. 2009. *The Search for a Universal Ethic: A New Look at the Natural Law*. Vatican City: Libreria Editrice Vaticana.
Inwood, B. 1999. 'Rules and Reasoning in Stoic Ethics', in *Topics in Stoic Philosophy*, Katerina Ierodiakonou (ed.), pp. 95–127. Oxford: Oxford University Press.

Inwood, B. and Donini, P. 1999. 'Stoic Ethics', in *The Cambridge History of Hellenistic Philosophy*, Keimpa Algra, Jonathan Barnes, Jaap Mansfeld and Malcolm Schofield (eds.), pp. 675–738. Cambridge: Cambridge University Press.

Irwin, T. 2008. *The Development of Ethics, vol. II, From Suarez to Rousseau*. Oxford: Oxford University Press.

Irwin, T. 2012. 'Obligation, Rightness, and Natural Law: Suárez and Some Critics', in *Interpreting Suárez: Critical Essays*, Daniel Schwartz (ed.), pp. 142–62. Cambridge: Cambridge University Press.

Jacobs, J. 2010. *Law, Reason, and Morality in Medieval Jewish Philosophy: Saadia Gaon, Bahya ibn Pakuda, and Moses Maimonides*. Oxford: Oxford University Press.

Jedan, C. 2009. *Stoic Virtues: Chrysippus and the Religious Character of Stoic Ethics*. London: Continuum.

Jenkins, G. 2013. 'Citizen Vermigli: The Political Animal in Vermigli's Commonwealth'. *Reformation & Renaissance Review* 15, no. 1: 84–98.

Jensen, S. 2015. *Knowing the Natural Law: From Precepts and Inclinations to Deriving Oughts*. Washington, DC: Catholic University of America Press.

Jewish Virtual Library. N.d. 'Babylonian Talmud'. www.jewishvirtuallibrary.org/babylonian-talmud-full-text.

Johansen, B. 2003. 'Apostasy as Objective and Depersonalized Fact: Two Recent Egyptian Court Judgments'. *Social Research* 70, no. 3: 687–710.

John Paul II. 1993. 'Encyclical Letter *Veritatis Splendor*'. http://w2.vatican.va/content/john-paul-ii/en/encyclicals/documents/hf_jp-ii_enc_06081993_veritatis-splendor.html.

Jospe, R. 2009. *Jewish Philosophy in the Middle Ages*. Boston: Academic Studies Press.

Journet, C. 1955. *The Church of the Word Incarnate*. London: Sheed and Ward.

Kaczor, C. 1997. 'Exceptionless Norms in Aristotle? Thomas Aquinas and Twentieth-Century Interpreters of the Nicomachean Ethics'. *The Thomist* 61: 33–62.

Kellner, M. 2006. *Maimonides' Confrontation with Mysticism*. Oxford: Littman Library of Jewish Civilization.

Kerr, F. 2002. *After Aquinas: Versions of Thomism*. London: Blackwell.

Kerr, F. 2010. 'Knowing God by Reason Alone: What Vatican I Never Said'. *The Dominican Council*, pp. 215–28.

Keys, M. 2008. *Aristotle, Aquinas, and the Promise of the Common Good*. Cambridge: Cambridge University Press.

Kidd, I. G. 1971. 'Stoic Intermediates and the End for Man', in *Problems in Stoicism*, A. A. Long (ed.), pp. 150–72. London: Athlone Press.

Kidd, I. G. 1978. 'Moral Actions and Rules in Stoicism', in *The Stoics*, John M. Rist (ed.), pp. 247–58. Berkeley: University of California Press.

Kilcullen, R. J. 2011. 'Philosophy between 500 and 1500', in *Encyclopedia of Medieval Philosophy*, H. Lagerland (ed.), pp. 831–9. New York: Springer.

Kingdon, R. M. 1980. *The Political Thought of Peter Martyr Vermigli: Selected Texts and Commentary*. Geneva: Droz.

Kirchin, S. 2013. *Thick Concepts*. Oxford: Oxford University Press.

Kitcher, P. 1984. 'Species'. *Philosophy of Science* 51: 308–33.

Klein, J. 2012. 'Stoic Eudaimonism and the Natural Law Tradition', in *Reason, Religion and Natural Law: Plato to Spinoza*, Jonathan Jacobs (ed.), pp. 57–80. Oxford: Oxford University Press.

Kolb, R. and Wengert, T. J. 2000. *The Book of Concord: The Confessions of the Evangelical Lutheran Church*. Minneapolis, MN: Fortress Press.

Koons, R. 2018a. 'Hylomorphic Escalation: An Aristotelian Interpretation of Quantum Thermodynamics and Chemistry'. *American Catholic Philosophical Quarterly* 92: 159–78.

Koons, R. 2018b. 'Knowing Nature: Aristotle, God, and the Quantum', in *Knowing Creation: Perspectives from Theology, Philosophy, and Science*, vol. 1, A. Torrance and T. McCall (eds.), pp. 215–36. Grand Rapids, MI: Zondervan.

Korsgaard, C. 2011. 'Natural Goodness, Rightness, and the Intersubjectivity of Reason: Reply to Arroyo, Cummiskey, Moland, and Bird-Pollan'. *Metaphilosophy* 42: 381–94.

Koslicki, K. 2007. *The Structure of Objects*. Oxford: Oxford University Press.

Kuhn, T. 1996. *The Structure of Scientific Revolutions*. 3rd edn. Chicago: Chicago University Press.

Kupczak, J. 2000. *The Human Person in the Philosophy of Karol Wojtyła/John Paul II: Destined for Liberty*. Washington, DC: Catholic University of America Press.

Laing, J. A. 1997. 'Innocence and Consequentialism', in *Human Lives: Critical Essays on Consequentialist Bioethics*, J. A. Laing and D. S. Oderberg (eds.), pp. 196–224. Basingstoke, UK: Palgrave Macmillan.

Laing, J. A. 2004. 'Law, Liberalism and the Common Good', in *Human Values: New Essays on Ethics and Natural Law*, D. S. Oderberg and T. D. J. Chappell (eds.), pp. 184–216. Basingstoke, UK: Palgrave Macmillan.

Laing, J. A. 2013. 'Infanticide: A Reply to Giubilini and Minerva'. *Journal of Medical Ethics* 154: 336–40.

Laing, J. A. and Wilcox, R. 2013. *The Natural Law Reader*. Oxford: Wiley Blackwell.

Larmore, C. 2002. 'Attending to Reasons', in *Reading McDowell: On* Mind and World, Nicholas H. Smith (ed.), chapter 10. London: Routledge.

Lawrence, F. G. 2012. 'Finnis on Lonergan: A Reflection'. *Villanova Law Review* 57: 849–72.

Lawrence, G. 2005. 'Snakes in Paradise: Problems in the Ideal Life'. *Southern Journal of Philosophy* 43: 126–65.

Lawrence, G. 2017. 'The Deep and the Shallow', in *Philippa Foot on Goodness and Virtue*, John Hacker-Wright (ed.), pp. 187–255. London: Palgrave Macmillan.

Lee, P. 1997. 'Is Thomas's Natural Law Theory Naturalist?'. *American Catholic Philosophical Quarterly* 71: 567–87.

Legarre, S. 2017. 'H.L.A. Hart and the Making of New Natural Law'. *Jurisprudence: An International Journal of Legal and Political Thought* 8: 82–98.

Levering, M. 2008. *Biblical Natural Law: A Theocentric and Teleological Approach*. Oxford: Oxford University Press.

Lewens, T. 2010. 'Footnote'. *Analysis* 70, no. 3: 468–78.

Library of Congress. 'Laws Criminalising Apostasy'. www.loc.gov/law/help/apostasy/index.php.

Lichtenstein, A. 1975. 'Does Jewish Tradition Recognize an Ethic Independent of Halakhah?', in *Modern Jewish Ethics: Theory and Practice*, Marvin Fox (ed.), pp. 62–88. Columbus: Ohio State University Press.

Lisska, A. J. 1996. *Aquinas's Theory of Natural Law: An Analytic Reconstruction*. Oxford: Clarendon Press.

Little, D. 1968. 'Calvin and the Prospects for a Christian Theory of Natural Law', in *Norm and Context in Christian Ethics*, Paul Ramsey and Gene Outka (eds.), pp. 175–97. New York: Scribners.

Littlejohn, W. B. 2017.*The Peril and Promise of Christian Liberty: Richard Hooker, the Puritans, and Protestant Political Theology*. Grand Rapids, MI: Eerdmans.

Liu, I. 2017. 'Elevating Human Being: Towards a New Sort of Naturalism'. *Philosophy* 92, no. 4: 597–622.

Liu, I. 2018a. 'The Limits of Aristotelian Naturalism'. *The Journal of Value Inquiry* 52, no. 3: 269–86.

Liu, I. 2018b. 'Ethical Pluralism and the Appeal to Human Nature'. *European Journal of Philosophy* 26, no. 3: 1103–19.

Lombardo, N. E. 2011. *The Logic of Desire: Aquinas on Emotion*. Washington, DC: Catholic University of America Press.

Long, A. A. (ed.). 1971. *Problems in Stoicism*. London: Athlone Press.

Long, S. A. 2004. 'Natural Law or Autonomous Practical Reason, Problems of the New Natural Law Theory', in *St. Thomas and the Natural Law Tradition: Contemporary Perspectives*, J. Goyette, M. Latkovic and R. Myers (eds.), pp. 165–93. Washington, DC: Catholic University of America Press.

Long, S. A. 2013. 'Fundamental Errors of the New Natural Law Theory'. *The National Catholic Bioethics Quarterly* 13, no. 1: 105–32.

Lott, M. 2012. 'Moral Virtue as Knowledge of Human Form'. *Social Theory and Practice* 38, no. 3: 407–31.

Lott, M. 2014. 'Why Be a Good Human Being? Natural Goodness, Reason, and the Authority of Human Nature'. *Philosophy* 42: 761–77.

Lott, M. 2015. 'Justice, Function, and Human Form', in *Normativität des Lebens – Normativität der Vernunft?*, M. Rothhaar and M. Hähnel (eds.), pp. 75–91. Berlin: Walter de Gruyter.

Lott, M. 2017. 'Aristotelischer Naturalismus und die Autonomie der Ethik' [Aristotelian Naturalism and the Autonomy of Ethics], in *Aristotelischer Naturalismus*, M. Hähnel (ed.), pp. 107–19. Stuttgart: J. B. Metzler.

Lücke, H. K. 2016. 'John Finnis at the University of Adelaide: The Christian Faith Half a Century Ago'. *University of Queensland Law Review* 35, no. 2: 193–249.

MacIntyre, A. 1984. *After Virtue: A Study in Moral Theory*. South Bend, IN: University of Notre Dame Press.

MacIntyre, A. 1999. *Dependent Rational Animals: Why Human Beings Need the Virtues*. London: Duckworth.

MacIntyre, A. 2000. 'Theories of Natural Law in the Cultures of Advanced Modernity', in *Common Truths: New Perspectives on Natural Law*, E. B. McLean (ed.), chapter 5. Wilmington, DE: ISI Books.

MacIntyre, A. 2002. 'Virtues in Foot and Geach'. *Philosophical Quarterly* 52, no. 209: 621–31.

MacIntyre, A. 2006. *Edith Stein: A Philosophical Prologue*. London: Continuum.

MacIntyre, A. 2009. 'Intractable Moral Disagreements', in *Intractable Disputes about the Natural Law*, Lawrence S. Cunningham (ed.), chapter 1. South Bend, IN: University of Notre Dame Press.

MacIntyre, A. 2010. 'Danish Ethical Demands and French Common Goods: Two Moral Philosophies'. *European Journal of Philosophy* 18, no. 1: 1–16.

MacIntyre, A. 2016. *Ethics in the Conflicts of Modernity: An Essay on Desire, Practical Reasoning, and Narrative*. Cambridge: Cambridge University Press.
Mackie, J. L. 1990. *Ethics: Inventing Right and Wrong*. Harmondsworth, UK: Penguin Books.
Makdisi, G. 1981. *The Rise of Colleges: Institutions of Learning in Islam and the West*. Edinburgh: Edinburgh University Press.
Makdisi G. 1985. 'Ethics in Islamic Traditionalist Doctrine', in *Ethics in Islam*, Richard G. Houvannisian (ed.), pp. 47–63. Malibu, CA: Undena.
Marchand, S. L. 2009. *German Orientalism in the Age of Empire: Religion, Race and Scholarship*. Cambridge: Cambridge University Press.
Marchetti, G. and Marchetti, S. 2017. *Facts and Values: The Ethics and Metaphysics of Normativity*. London: Routledge.
Maritain, J. 1951. *Man and the State*. Chicago: University of Chicago Press.
Maritain, J. 2001. *Natural Law: Reflections on Theory and Practice*. South Bend, IN: St Augustine's Press.
Martin, C. B. 2008. *The Mind in Nature*. Oxford: Clarendon Press.
Matava, R. 2011. '"Is", "Ought" and Moral Realism: The Roles of Nature and Experience in Practical Understanding'. *Studies in Christian Ethics* 24: 311–28.
Mautner, T. 1999 [1989]. 'Pufendorf and the Correlativity Theory of Rights', in *Grotius, Pufendorf and Modern Natural Law*, Knud Haakonssen (ed.), pp. 159–81. Dartmouth: Ashgate.
Mayr, E. 1961. 'Cause and Effect in Biology'. *Science* 134: 1501–6.
McDowell, J. 1998a. 'Two Sorts of Naturalism', in *Mind, Value, and Reality*, chapter 9. Cambridge, MA: Harvard University Press.
McDowell, J. 1998b. *Mind, Value, and Reality*. Cambridge, MA: Harvard University Press.
McDowell, J. 1994. *Mind and World*. Cambridge, MA: Harvard University Press.
McDowell, J. 1995. 'Two Sorts of Naturalism', in *Virtues and Reasons: Philippa Foot and Moral Theory*, R. Hursthouse, G. Lawrence and W. Quinn (eds.), pp. 149–80. Oxford: Clarendon Press.
McInerny, R. 1980. 'The Principle of Natural Law'. *American Journal of Jurisprudence* 1 1–20.
McInerny, R. 1982. *Ethica Thomistica: The Moral Philosophy of Thomas Aquinas*. Washington, DC: Catholic University of America Press.
McInerny, R. 1992. *Aquinas on Human Action: A Theory of Practice*. Washington, DC: Catholic University of America Press.
McInerny, R. 1997. *Ethica Thomistica: The Moral Philosophy of Thomas Aquinas*. Rev. edn. Washington, DC: Catholic University of America Press.
McInerny, R. 1998. 'Review of Aquinas's Theory of Natural Law by Anthony Lisska'. The Medieval Review, 10 January. https://scholarworks.iu edu/journals/index.php /tmr/article/view/14562.
McInerny, R. 2000. 'Grisez and Thomism', in *The Revival of Natural Law: Philosophical, Theological and Ethical Responses to the Finnis-Grisez School*, N. Biggar and R. Black (eds.), pp. 53–72. Farnham, UK: Ashgate.
McNeill, J. T. 1946. 'Natural Law in the Teaching of the Reformers'. *Journal of Religion* 26, no. 3: 168–82.

Melina, L. 2001a. 'Christ and the Dynamism of Action: Outlook and Overview of Christocentrism in Moral Theology'. *Communio: International Catholic Review*, Spring, 112–40.

Melina, L. 2001b. *Sharing in Christ's Virtues: For a Renewal of Moral Theology in Light of Veritatis Splendor*. Washington, DC: Catholic University of America Press.

Menn, S. 1995. 'Physics as a Virtue'. *Proceedings of the Boston Area Colloquium in Ancient Philosophy* 11: 1–34.

Milbank, J. and Pabst, A. 2016. *The Politics of Virtue: Post-Liberalism and the Human Future*. London: Rowman and Littlefield.

Millgram, E. 2009. 'Michael Thompson, Life and Action'. *Analysis* 69, no. 3: 557–64.

Millikan, R. G. 1984. *Language, Thought, and Other Biological Categories*. Cambridge, MA: MIT Press.

Millum, J. 2006. 'Natural Goodness and Natural Evil'. *Ratio* (new series) XIX: 199–213.

Mises, L., von. 1966. *Human Action: A Treatise on Economics*. Chicago: Henry Regnery.

Mitsis, P. 1993. 'Seneca on Reason, Rule, and Moral Development', in *Passions and Perceptions: Studies in Hellenistic Philosophy of Mind*, Jacques Brunschwig and Martha C. Nussbaum (eds.), pp. 285–313. Cambridge: Cambridge University Press.

Mitsis, P. 1994. 'Natural Law and Natural Rights in Post-Aristotelian Philosophy: The Stoics and Their Critics', in *Aufstieg und Niedergang der Römischen Welt*, Part II, Vols. 36–7, Wolfgang Haase (ed.), pp. 4812–50. Berlin: De Gruyter.

Molnar, G. 2003. *Powers: A Study in Metaphysics*. Oxford: Oxford University Press.

Moore, J. and Silverthorne, M. 1995. 'Protestant Theologies, Limited Sovereignties: Natural Law and Conditions of Union in the German Empire, the Netherlands and Great Britain', in *A Union for Empire: Political Thought and the British Union of 1707*, John Robertson (ed.), chapter 7. Cambridge: Cambridge University Press.

Moravcsik, J. M. 1994. 'Essences, Powers, and Generic Propositions', in *Unity, Identity, and Explanation in Aristotle's Metaphysics*, T. Scaltsas, D. Charles and M. L. Gill (eds.), pp. 229–44. Oxford: Oxford University Press.

Mumford, S. 2009. 'Causal Powers and Capacities', in *The Oxford Handbook of Causation*, H. Beebee, C. Hitchcock and P. Menzies (eds.), pp. 265–78. Oxford: Oxford University Press.

Munoz, P. 2013. *Religious Liberty and the American Supreme Court*. Lanham, MD: Rowman and Littlefield.

Murphy, M. C. 2001. *Natural Law and Practical Rationality*. Cambridge: Cambridge University Press.

Murphy, M. C. 2003. 'Philippa Foot, *Natural Goodness*'. *Ethics* 113, no. 2: 410–14.

Murphy, M. C. 2008 [2002]. 'The Natural Law Tradition in Ethics', in *Stanford Encyclopedia of Philosophy*, Edward N. Zalta (ed.). http://plato.stanford.edu/archives/fall2008/entries/natural-law-ethics.

Murray, J. C. 1960. *We Hold These Truths*. New York: Sheed and Ward.

Nadler, S. 2007. 'Baruch Spinoza and the Naturalization of Judaism', in *The Cambridge Companion to Modern Jewish Philosophy*, Michael L. Morgan and Peter Eli Gordon (eds.), pp. 14–34. Cambridge: Cambridge University Press.

Nagel, T. 2010. *The History of Islamic Theology: From Muhammad to the Present*. Princeton, NJ: Markus Weiner.

Nagel, T. 2012. *Mind and Cosmos: Why the Materialist Neo-Darwinian Conception of Nature Is Almost Certainly False*. Oxford: Oxford University Press.

Nassery, I., Ahmed, R. and Tatari, M. 2018. *The Objectives of Islamic Law: The Promises and Challenges of Maqasid al-Sharia*. Lanham, MD: Lexington Books.

Newman, L. E. 1998. *Past Imperatives: Studies in the History and Theory of Jewish Ethics*. Albany: SUNY Press.

Niebuhr, R. 1940. 'Christian Faith and Natural Law'. *Theology* 40: 86–94.

Nielsen, K. 1959. 'An Examination of the Thomistic Theory of Natural Moral Law'. *Natural Law Forum* 1: 44–71.

Novak, D. 1998. *Natural Law in Judaism*. Cambridge: Cambridge University Press.

Novak, L., Novotny, D., Sousedik, P. and Svoboda, D. 2012. *Metaphysics: Aristotelian, Scholastic, Analytic*. Frankfurt: Ontos.

Novotny, D. and Novak, L. 2014. *Neo-Aristotelian Perspectives in Metaphysics*. London: Routledge.

Nussbaum, M. C. 2000. *Women and Human Development: The Capabilities Approach*. Cambridge: Cambridge University Press.

O'Brien, M. B. and Koons, R. C. 2012. 'Objects of Intention: A Hylomorphic Critique of the New Natural Law Theory'. *American Catholic Philosophical Quarterly* 86, no. 4: 655–703.

Oderberg, D. S. 2000. *Moral Theory: A Non-Consequentialist Approach*. Oxford: Blackwell.

Oderberg, D. S. 2004. 'The Structure and Content of the Good', in *Human Values: New Essays on Ethics and Natural Law*, D. S. Oderberg and T. Chappell (eds.), chapter 6. Basingstoke, UK: Palgrave Macmillan.

Oderberg, D. S. 2007. *Real Essentialism*. London: Routledge.

Oderberg, D. S. 2010. 'The Metaphysical Foundations of Natural Law', in *Natural Moral Law in Contemporary Society*, H. Zaborowski (ed.), pp. 44–75. Washington, DC: Catholic University of America Press.

Oderberg, D. S. 2017. 'Finality Revived: Powers and Intentionality'. *Synthese* 194: 2387–425.

O'Donovan, J. L. 1991. *Theology of Law and Authority in the English Reformation*. Atlanta, GA: Scholars Press.

Okasha, S. 2002. 'Darwinian Metaphysics: Species and the Question of Essentialism'. *Synthese* 131: 191–213.

Olivecrona, K. 2010 [1977]. 'The Two Levels in Natural Law Thinking', Thomas Mautner (ed.). *Jurisprudence* 1, no. 2: 197–224.

Olsthoorn, J. 2018. 'Grotius and the Early Modern Tradition', in *The Cambridge Handbook of the Just War*, Larry May (ed.), pp. 33–56. Cambridge: Cambridge University Press.

Olsthoorn, J. 2019. 'Grotius on Natural Law and Supererogation'. *Journal of the History of Philosophy* 57, no. 3: 439–465.

Osborne, T. M. 2005. *Love of Self and Love of God in Thirteenth-Century Ethics*. South Bend, IN: University of Notre Dame Press.

O'Sullivan, D. 2004. 'Hisba Law and Freedom of Expression in Islam: Two Case Studies of Prosecution in Contemporary Egypt'. *Journal of Mediterranean Studies* 14, no. 1: 213–35.

Otteson, J. R. 2011. *Adam Smith*. London: Continuum Books.

Owen, G. E. L. 1960. 'Logic and Metaphysics in Some Earlier Works of Aristotle', in *Plato and Aristotle in the Mid-Fourth Century*, I. During and G. E. L. Owen (eds.), pp. 163–90. Stockholm: Almquist and Wiksell.

Pakaluk, M. 2001. 'Is the Common Good of Political Society Limited and Instrumental?' *Review of Metaphysics* 55, no. 1: 57–94.

Pakaluk, M. 2002. 'Natural Law and Civil Society', in *Alternative Conceptions of Civil Society*, S. Chambers and W. Kymlicka (eds.), pp. 131–50. Princeton, NJ: Princeton University Press.

Pakaluk, M. 2018. 'Natural Inclinations in Aquinas's Account of Natural Law', in *Natural Law Today: The Present State of the Perennial Philosophy*, C. Wolfe and S. Brust (eds.), pp. 19–32. Lanham, MD: Lexington Press.

Palladini, F. 2008. 'Pufendorf Disciple of Hobbes: The Nature of Man and the State of Nature: The Doctrine of *Socialitas*'. *History of European Ideas* 34, no. 1: 26–60.

Pinckaers, S.-T. 1994. 'An Encyclical of the Future: *Veritatis Splendor*', in *Veritatis Splendor and the Renewal of Moral Theology*, J. A. Di Noia and Romanus Cessario (eds.), pp. 11–72. Princeton, NJ: Scepter.

Pinckaers, S.-T. 2001. *Morality: The Catholic View*. South Bend, IN: St Augustine's Press.

Place, U. T. 1996. 'Dispositions as Intentional States', D. M. Armstrong, C. B. Martin and U. T. Place (eds.), in *Dispositions: A Debate*, T. Crane (ed.), pp. 19–32. London: Routledge.

Porter, J. 1999. *Natural and Divine Law: Reclaiming the Tradition for Christian Ethics*. Grand Rapids, MI: Eerdmans.

Porter, J. 2005. *Nature as Reason: A Thomistic Theory of the Natural Law*. Grand Rapids, MI: Eerdmans.

Putnam, H. 2004a. *The Collapse of the Fact/Value Dichotomy and Other Essays*. Cambridge, MA: Harvard University Press.

Putnam, H. 2004b. *Ethics without Ontology*. Cambridge, MA: Harvard University Press.

Quinn, W. 1994. *Morality and Action*. Cambridge: Cambridge University Press.

Ratzinger, J. 2005. 'The Renewal of Moral Theology: Vatican II and *Veritatis Splendor*'. *Communio: International Catholic Review* 32, no. 2: 357–68.

Ratzinger, J. 2011. *Dogma and Preaching: Applying Christian Doctrine to Daily Life*. San Francisco: Ignatius Press.

Rawls, J. 1972. *A Theory of Justice*. Oxford: Oxford University Press.

Rhonheimer, M. 2008. 'Practical Reason and the "Naturally Rational": On the Doctrine of the Natural Law as a Principle of Praxis in Thomas Aquinas', in *The Perspective of the Acting Person: Essays in the Renewal of Thomistic Moral Philosophy*, pp. 95–128. Washington, DC: Catholic University of America Press.

Richardson, H. S. 2004. 'Incommensurability and Basic Goods: A Tension in the New Natural Law Theory', in *Human Values: New Essays on Ethics and Natural Law*, D. S. Oderberg and T. Chappell (eds.), chapter 4. Basingstoke, UK: Palgrave Macmillan.

Rickles, D. 2016. *The Philosophy of Physics*. Cambridge: Polity Press.

Robbins, L. 1952. *An Essay on the Nature and Significance of Economic Science*. London: Macmillan.

Rödl, S. 2007. *Self-Consciousness*. Cambridge, MA: Harvard University Press.
Röpke, W. 1963. *Economics of the Free Society*. Chicago: Henry Regnery.
Rosenfeld, S. 2014. *Common Sense: A Political History*. Cambridge, MA: Harvard University Press.
Rothbard, M. 1989. 'The Hermeneutical Invasion of Philosophy and Economics'. *Review of Austrian Economics* 3: 45–9.
Rousselot, P. 1908. *Pour l'Histoire du Problème de l'Amour au Moyen Age*. Münster: Aschendorffsche.
Rudavsky, T. M. 2018. *Jewish Philosophy in the Middle Ages: Science, Rationalism and Religion*. Oxford: Oxford University Press.
Rutherford, D. 2010. 'Spinoza's Conception of Law: Metaphysics and Ethics', in *Spinoza's Theological Political Treatise: A Critical Guide*, Y. Melamed and Michael A. Rosenthal (eds.), pp. 143–67. Cambridge: Cambridge University Press.
Rynhold, D. 2009. *An Introduction to Medieval Jewish Philosophy*. London: I. B. Taurus.
Saastamoinen, K. 1995. *The Morality of Fallen Man: Samuel Pufendorf on Natural Law*. Helsinki: SHS.
Saastamoinen, K. 2006. 'Liberty and Natural Rights in Pufendorf's Natural Law Theory', in *Transformations in Medieval and Early-Modern Rights Discourse*, Virpi Mäkinen and Petter Korkman (eds.), pp. 225–56. Dordrecht: Springer.
Saccenti, R. 2016. *Debating Medieval Natural Law: A Survey*. South Bend, IN: University of Notre Dame Press.
Sadler, G. B. 2011. *Reason Fulfilled by Revelation: The 1930s Christian Philosophy Debates in France*. Washington, DC: Catholic University of America Press.
Said, E. 1979. *Orientalism*. New York: Vintage.
Saunders, D. 2002. 'Within the Orbit of This Life – Samuel Pufendorf and the Autonomy of Law'. *Cardozo Law Review* 23, no. 6: 2173–98.
Scerri, E. 1994. 'Has Chemistry Been at Least Approximately Reduced to Quantum Mechanics?'. *Philosophy of Science Association* 1: 160–70.
Scerri, E. 2016. 'The Changing Views of a Philosopher of Chemistry on the Question of Reduction', in *Essays in the Philosophy of Chemistry*, E. Scerri and G. Fisher (eds.), pp. 125–43. Oxford: Oxford University Press.
Schabas, M. 2007. *The Natural Origins of Economics*. Chicago: University of Chicago Press.
Schall, J. V. 1998. *Jacques Maritain: The Philosopher in Society*. Lanham, MD: Rowman and Littlefield.
Schneewind, J. B. 1987. 'Pufendorf's Place in the History of Ethics'. *Synthese* 72, no. 1: 123–55.
Schneewind, J. B. 1998. *The Invention of Autonomy: A History of Modern Moral Philosophy*. Cambridge: Cambridge University Press.
Schneewind, J. B. 2010. *Essays on the History of Moral Philosophy*. Oxford: Oxford University Press.
Schofield, M. 1999. *The Stoic Idea of the City*. Chicago: University of Chicago Press.
Schumpeter, J. 1954. *History of Economic Analysis*. Oxford: Oxford University Press.
Schwarzenbach, S. 1996. 'On Civic Friendship'. *Ethics* 107: 97–128.
Sedley, D. 2007. *Creationism and Its Critics in Antiquity*. Berkeley: University of California Press.

Sellars, W. 1962. 'Philosophy and the Scientific Image of Man', in *Frontiers of Science and Philosophy*, R. Colodny (ed.), pp. 35–78. Pittsburgh, PA: University of Pittsburgh Press.

Sen, A. 2004. 'Capability and Well-Being', in *The Quality of Life*, Martha Nussbaum and Amartya Sen (eds.), pp. 30–53. New York: Routledge.

Shany, Y. 2005. 'Toward a General Margin of Appreciation Doctrine in International Law?' *European Journal of International Law* 16, no. 5: 907–40.

Sigmund, P. 1993. 'Law and Politics', in *The Cambridge Companion to Aquinas*, N. Kretzmann and E. Stump (eds.), pp. XX–XX. Cambridge: Cambridge University Press.

Simmonds, N. E. 2002. 'Grotius and Pufendorf', in *A Companion to Early Modern Philosophy*, Steven Nadler (ed.), pp. 210–24. Oxford: Blackwell.

Simon, Y. 1951. *Philosophy of Democratic Government*. Chicago: University of Chicago Press.

Simon, Y. 1965. *The Tradition of Natural Law: A Philosopher's Reflections*. Vukan Kuic (ed.). New York: Fordham University Press.

Simpson, W., Koons, R. and Teh, N. 2018. *Neo-Aristotelian Perspectives on Contemporary Science*. London: Routledge.

Sklar, L. 1993. *Physics and Chance: Philosophical Issues in the Foundations of Statistical Mechanics*. Cambridge: Cambridge University Press.

Smart, J. J. C. 1956. 'Extreme and Restricted Utilitarianism'. *The Philosophical Quarterly* 6: 345–54.

Smart, J. J. C. 1967. 'Utilitarianism', in *Encyclopedia of Philosophy*, Paul Edwards (ed.). New York: Macmillan.

Smith, M. 2010. 'On Normativity'. *Analysis* 70, no. 4: 715–31.

Smith, R. 2011. 'What the Old Law Reveals about the Natural Law According to Thomas Aquinas'. *The Thomist* 75: 95–139.

Sokolowski, R. 2004. 'What Is Natural Law? Human Purposes and Natural Ends'. *The Thomist* 68: 507–29.

Sokolowski, R. 2006. *Christian Faith and Human Understanding*. Washington, DC: Catholic University of America Press.

Spaemann, R. 1996. *Personen: Versuche über den Unterschied zwischen 'Etwas' und 'Jemand'*. Stuttgart: Klett-Cotta. [English translation by Oliver O'Donovan (2006), published as *Persons: The Difference between 'Someone' and 'Something'*. Oxford: Oxford University Press.]

Spielmann, D. 2014. 'Whither the Margin of Appreciation?' *Current Legal Problems* 67, no. 1: 49–65.

Steinmetz, D. C. 1995. 'Calvin and the Natural Knowledge of God', in *Calvin in Context*, chapter 2. New York: Oxford University Press.

Stevens, G. 1953. 'The Disinterested Love of God According to Saint Thomas and Some of His Modern Interpreters'. *The Thomist* 16: 307–33, 497–541.

Stevenson, C. L. 1979. *Ethics and Language*. New York: AMS Press.

St Leger, J. 1962. *The 'Etiamsi Daremus' of Hugo Grotius: A Study in the Origins of International Law*. Rome: Pontificum Athenaeum Internationale 'Angelicum'.

Stoner, J., Jr. 2007. 'Was Thomas Aquinas a Republican?' Paper delivered at a panel on 'Religion and Politics' at the annual meeting of the Southern Political Science Association.

Straumann, B. 2015. *Roman Law in the State of Nature: The Classical Foundations of Hugo Grotius's Natural Law*. Cambridge: Cambridge University Press.

Strauss, L. 1965. *Natural Right and History*. Rev. edn. Chicago: University of Chicago Press.

Street, S. 2006. 'A Darwinian Dilemma for Realist Theories of Value'. *Philosophical Studies* 127, no. 1: 109–66.

Striker, G. 1987. 'Origins of the Concept of Natural Law', in Proceedings of the Boston Area Colloquium in Ancient Philosophy, vol. 2, pp. 79–94. [Reprinted 1996 in her *Essays on Hellenistic Epistemology and Ethics*, pp. 209–20. Cambridge: Cambridge University Press.]

Striker, G. 1991. 'Following Nature: A Study in Stoic Ethics'. *Oxford Studies in Ancient Philosophy* 9: 1–73. [Reprinted 1996 in her *Essays on Hellenistic Epistemology and Ethics*, pp. 221–80. Cambridge: Cambridge University Press.]

Sturm, D. 1965. 'Naturalism, Historicism, and Christian Ethics: Toward a Christian Doctrine of Natural Law', in *New Theology*, vol. 2, Martin Marty and Dean Peerman (eds.), pp. 77–96. New York: Macmillan.

Sullivan, E. 2014. 'Natural Self-Transcending Love According to Thomas Aquinas'. *Nova et Vetera* 12: 913–46.

Tahko, T. 2012. *Contemporary Aristotelian Metaphysics*. Cambridge: Cambridge University Press.

Teichmann, R. 2011. *Nature, Reason, and the Good Life: Ethics for Human Beings*. Oxford: Oxford University Press.

Teyssier, J., Saenko, S. V., van der Marel, D. and Milinkovitch, M. C. 2015. 'Photonic Crystals Cause Active Colour Change in Chameleons'. *Nature Communications* 6: 6368. www.nature.com/articles/ncomms7368.

Thom, J. C. 2005. Cleanthes' Hymn to Zeus: *Text, Translation and Commentary*. Tübingen: Mohr Siebeck.

Thomasson, A. 2007. *Ordinary Objects*. Oxford: Oxford University Press.

Thompson, M. 1995. 'The Representation of Life', in *Virtues and Reasons: Philippa Foot and Moral Theory – Essays in Honour of Philippa Foot*, R. Hursthouse, G. Lawrence and W. Quinn (eds.), chapter 10. Oxford: Clarendon Press.

Thompson, M. 2004. 'Apprehending Human Form', in *Modern Moral Philosophy*, Royal Institute of Philosophy Supplement 54, A. O'Hear (ed.), pp. 47–74. Cambridge: Cambridge University Press, pp. 47–74.

Thompson, M. 2008. *Life and Action: Elementary Structures of Practice and Practical Thought*. Cambridge, MA: Harvard University Press.

Thomson, J. J. 1985. 'The Trolley Problem'. *Yale Law Journal* 94: 1395–415.

Thomson, J. J. 2008. *Normativity*. Chicago: Open Court.

Tollefsen, C. 2008. 'The New Natural Law Theory'. *Lyceum* X, no. 1: 1–18.

Tollefsen, C. 2012. 'The New Natural Law Theory'. www.nlnrac.org/contemporary/new-natural-law-theory

Tollefsen, C. 2018a. 'A Philosophical Case against Capital Punishment'. www.thepublicdiscourse.com/2017/11/20393.

Tollefsen, C. 2018b. 'Aquinas's Four Orders, Normativity, and Human Nature'. *The Journal of Value Inquiry* 52, no. 3: 243–56.

Toner, C. 2008. 'Sorts of Naturalism: Requirements for a Successful Theory'. *Metaphilosophy* 39, no. 2: 220–50.

Tuck, R. 1987. 'The "Modern" Theory of Natural Law', in *The Languages of Political Theory in Early Modern Europe*, Anthony Pagden (ed.), pp. 99–120. Cambridge: Cambridge University Press.

Twersky, I. 1972. *A Maimonides Reader*. New York: Behrman House.

Van Brakel, J. 2000. *Philosophy of Chemistry*. Leuven: Leuven University Press.

Vander Waerdt, P. A. 1994. 'Zeno's *Republic* and the Origins of Natural Law', in *The Socratic Movement*, Paul A. Vander Waerdt (ed.), pp. 272–308. Ithaca, NY: Cornell University Press.

Van Drunen, D. 2010. *Natural Law and the Two Kingdoms: A Study in the Development of Reformed Social Thought*. Grand Rapids, MI: Eerdmans.

Van Zile, M. 2017. 'The Sons of Noah and the Sons of Abraham: The Origins of Noahide Law'. *Journal for the Study of Judaism* 48: 1–32.

Vatican Council II. 1988. *Vatican Council II: The Conciliar and Post Conciliar Documents*. Rev. edn. A. Flannery (ed.). Northport, NY: Costello.

Vermigli, Peter Martyr. 1583. *Common Places*. Anthonie Marten (trans.). London: Henry Denham and Henry Middleton.

Voegelin, E. 1952. *The New Science of Politics*. Chicago: University of Chicago Press.

Vogler, C. 2013. 'Natural Virtue and Proper Upbringing', in *Aristotelian Ethics in Contemporary Perspective*, J. Peters (ed.), pp. 145–57. London: Routledge.

Vogt, K. M. 2008. *Law, Reason, and the Cosmic City*. Oxford: Oxford University Press.

Waldron, J. 2002. *God, Locke, and Equality: Christian Foundations in Locke's Political Thought*. Cambridge: Cambridge University Press.

Watson, G. 1971. 'The Natural Law and Stoicism', in *Problems in Stoicism*, A. A. Long (ed.), pp. 216–38. London: Athlone Press.

Watt, W. M. 1998. *The Formative Period of Islamic Thought*. Rev. edn. Oxford: Oneworld.

Weinreb, L. L. 1987. *Natural Law and Justice*. Cambridge, MA: Harvard University Press.

Weisberg, M., Needham, P. and Hendry, R. 2011. 'Philosophy of Chemistry', in *Stanford Encyclopedia of Philosophy*, Edward N. Zalta (ed.). https://plato.stanford.edu/entries/chemistry.

Wiggins, D. 1997. *Needs, Values, Truth: Essays in the Philosophy of Value*. Oxford: Oxford University Press.

Wilson, C. 2008. 'From Limits to Laws: The Construction of the Nomological Image of Nature in Early Modern Philosophy', in *Natural Law and Laws of Nature in Early Modern Europe: Jurisprudence, Theology, Moral and Natural Philosophy*, Lorraine Daston and Michael Stolleis (eds.), pp. 13–28. Farnham, UK: Ashgate.

Witte, J. 2002. *Law and Protestantism: The Legal Teachings of the Lutheran Reformation*. Cambridge: Cambridge University Press.

Witte, J. 2006. *God's Joust, God's Justice: Law and Religion in the Western Tradition*. Grand Rapids, MI: Eerdmans.

Witte, J. 2007. *The Reformation of Rights: Law, Religion, and Human Rights in Early Modern Calvinism*. Cambridge: Cambridge University Press.

Witte, J. and Kingdon, R. M. 2005. *Sex, Marriage, and Family in John Calvin's Geneva, vol. 1, Courtship, Engagement, and Marriage*. Grand Rapids, MI: Eerdmans.

Wittgenstein, L. 1958. *Philosophical Investigations*. G. E. M. Anscombe (trans.). Oxford: Basil Blackwell.
Wolfe, C. 2006. *Natural Law Liberalism*. Cambridge: Cambridge University Press.
Woodcock, S. 2015. 'Neo-Aristotelian Naturalism and the Indeterminacy Objection'. *International Journal of Philosophical Studies* 23, no. 1: 23–41.
Woodford, P. 2016. 'Neo-Darwinists and Neo-Aristotelians: How to Talk about Natural Purpose'. *History and Philosophy of the Life Sciences* 38, no.4: 1–23.

Index

OTHER VOLUMES IN THE SERIES OF CAMBRIDGE COMPANIONS (continued from page ii)

FREGE *Edited by* TOM RICKETTS *and* MICHAEL POTTER
FREUD *Edited by* JEROME NEU
GADAMER *Edited by* ROBERT J. DOSTAL
GALEN *Edited by* R. J. HANKINSON
GALILEO *Edited by* PETER MACHAMER
GERMAN IDEALISM *2nd edition Edited by* KARL AMERIKS
GREEK AND ROMAN PHILOSOPHY *Edited by* DAVID SEDLEY
HABERMAS *Edited by* STEPHEN K. WHITE
HAYEK *Edited by* EDWARD FESER
HEGEL *Edited by* FREDERICK C. BEISER
HEGEL AND NINETEENTH-CENTURY PHILOSOPHY *Edited by* FREDERICK C. BEISER
HEIDEGGER *2nd Edition Edited by* CHARLES GUIGNON
HERMENEUTICS *Edited by* MICHAEL N. FORSTER *and* KRISTIN GJESDAL
HIPPOCRATES *Edited by* PETER E. PORMANN
HOBBES *Edited by* TOM SORELL
HOBBES'S 'LEVIATHAN' *Edited by* PATRICIA SPRINGBORG
HUME *2nd Edition Edited by* DAVID FATE NORTON *and* JACQUELINE TAYLOR
HUME'S 'TREATISE' *Edited by* DONALD C. AINSLIE *and* ANNEMARIE BUTLER
HUSSERL *Edited by* BARRY SMITH *and* DAVID WOODRUFF SMITH
WILLIAM JAMES *Edited by* RUTH ANNA PUTNAM
KANT *Edited by* PAUL GUYER
KANT AND MODERN PHILOSOPHY *Edited by* PAUL GUYER
KANT'S 'CRITIQUE OF PURE REASON' *Edited by* PAUL GUYER
KEYNES *Edited by* ROGER E. BACKHOUSE *and* BRADLEY W. BATEMAN
KIERKEGAARD *Edited by* ALASTAIR HANNAY *and* GORDON DANIEL MARINO
LEIBNIZ *Edited by* NICHOLAS JOLLEY
LEVINAS *Edited by* SIMON CRITCHLEY *and* ROBERT BERNASCONI
LIBERALISM *Edited by* STEVEN WALL
LIFE AND DEATH Edited by STEVEN LUPER
LOCKE *Edited by* VERE CHAPPELL
LOCKE'S 'ESSAY CONCERNING HUMAN UNDERSTANDING' *Edited by* LEX NEWMAN
LOGICAL EMPIRICISM *Edited by* ALAN RICHARDSON *and* THOMAS UEBEL
MAIMONIDES *Edited by* KENNETH SEESKIN
MALEBRANCHE *Edited by* STEVEN NADLER
MARX *Edited by* TERRELL CARVER

MEDIEVAL ETHICS *Edited by* THOMAS WILLIAMS
MEDIEVAL JEWISH PHILOSOPHY *Edited by* DANIEL H. FRANK *and* OLIVER LEAMAN
MEDIEVAL LOGIC *Edited by* CATARINA DUTILH NOVAES *and* STEPHEN READ
MEDIEVAL PHILOSOPHY *Edited by* A. S. MCGRADE
MERLEAU-PONTY *Edited by* TAYLOR CARMAN *and* MARK B. N. HANSEN
MILL *Edited by* JOHN SKORUPSKI
MONTAIGNE *Edited by* ULLRICH LANGER
NEWTON *2nd Edition Edited by* ROB ILIFFE *and* GEORGE E. SMITH
NIETZSCHE *Edited by* BERND MAGNUS *and* KATHLEEN HIGGINS
THE NEW CAMBRIDGE COMPANION TO NIETSZCHE Edited by TOM STERN
NOZICK'S 'ANARCHY, STATE AND UTOPIA' *Edited by* RALF BADER *and* JOHN MEADOWCROFT
OAKESHOTT *Edited by* EFRAIM PODOKSIK
OCKHAM *Edited by* PAUL VINCENT SPADE
THE 'ORIGIN OF SPECIES' *Edited by* MICHAEL RUSE *and* ROBERT J. RICHARDS
PASCAL *Edited by* NICHOLAS HAMMOND
PEIRCE *Edited by* CHERYL MISAK
PHILO *Edited by* ADAM KAMESAR
PHILOSOPHICAL METHODOLOGY *Edited by* GIUSEPPINA D'ORO *and* SØREN OVERGAARD
THE PHILOSOPHY OF BIOLOGY *Edited by* DAVID L. HULL *and* MICHAEL RUSE
PIAGET *Edited by* ULRICH MÜLLER, JEREMY I. M. CARPENDALE *and* LESLIE SMITH
PLATO *Edited by* RICHARD KRAUT
PLATO'S 'REPUBLIC' *Edited by* G. R. F. FERRARI
PLOTINUS *Edited by* LLOYD P. GERSON
POPPER *Edited by* JEREMY SHEARMUR *and* GEOFFREY STOKES
PRAGMATISM *Edited by* ALAN MALACHOWSKI
QUINE *Edited by* ROGER F. GIBSON JR.
RAWLS *Edited by* SAMUEL FREEMAN
RENAISSANCE PHILOSOPHY *Edited by* JAMES HANKINS
THOMAS REID *Edited by* TERENCE CUNEO *and* RENÉ VAN WOUDENBERG
ROUSSEAU *Edited by* PATRICK RILEY
BERTRAND RUSSELL *Edited by* NICHOLAS GRIFFIN
SARTRE *Edited by* CHRISTINA HOWELLS
SCHOPENHAUER *Edited by* CHRISTOPHER JANAWAY
THE SCOTTISH ENLIGHTENMENT *2nd Edition Edited by* ALEXANDER BROADIE *and* CRAIG SMITH
ADAM SMITH *Edited by* KNUD HAAKONSSEN
SOCRATES *Edited by* DONALD MORRISON
SPINOZA *Edited by* DON GARRETT

SPINOZA'S 'ETHICS' *Edited by* OLLI KOISTINEN
THE STOICS *Edited by* BRAD INWOOD
LEO STRAUSS *Edited by* STEVEN B. SMITH
TOCQUEVILLE *Edited by* CHERYL B. WELCH
UTILITARIANISM *Edited by* BEN EGGLESTON *and* DALE MILLER
VIRTUE ETHICS *Edited by* DANIEL C. RUSSELL
WITTGENSTEIN *2nd Edition Edited by* HANS SLUGA *and* DAVID STERN

Printed in the United Kingdom by TJ Clays Ltd.